Ogun's Children

Ogun's Children:
The Literature and Politics of Wole Soyinka Since The Nobel

Edited by
ONOOKOME OKOME

Africa World Press, Inc.

P.O. Box 1892
Trenton, NJ 08607

P.O. Box 48
Asmara, ERITREA

Africa World Press, Inc.

P.O. Box 1892
Trenton, NJ 08607

P.O. Box 48
Asmara, ERITREA

Cover Design: Ashraful Haque
Book Design: Roger Dormann

Library of Congress Cataloging-in-Publication data

Ogun's children : the literature and politics of Wole Soyinka since the Nobel Prize / edited by Onookome Okome.
     p. cm.
  Includes bibliographical references and index.
  ISBN 0-86543-666-5. -- ISBN 0-86543-667-3 (pbk.)
  1. Soyinka, Wole--Criticism and interpretation. 2. Politics and literature--Nigeria--History--20th century. 3. Soyinka, Wole--Political and social views. 4. Nigeria--In literature. I. Okome, Onookome.
PR9387.9.S6Z814 1999
822--dc21   99-22539

Contents

Dedication

for my friends who left too soon—
Sesan Ajayi and Frank Mowah

—real peace

Acknowledgment

This is essentially a labour of love and in the joy of doing this work, I was shown love too and formidable enthusiasm from many quarters. I wish to acknowledge these people here for I cannot pay back all they willingly gave to me.

I owe a lot to my long time friend and confidant, Frank Uche Mowah, who was at the beginning of this project but who, one late morning, passed on

I acknowledge with deep respect all those who lead my way into the rich world of the literature of Wole Soyinka: Adeyinka Adedeji, Biodun Jeyifo, Oyekan Owomoyela, Abiola Irele, Harry Garub, Kole Omotosho, Obi Maduako, Simon Obikpeko Umukoro, Kalu Uka, Femi Osofisan, Tanure Ojaide and Wole Soyinka himself who granted me two interviews, one in Ouagadougou and the other in Meiningen, Germany.

I am grateful to Uwem Onookome-Okome who often asked me during the course of *doing* this book: "so what about the Soyinka project".

I acknowledge the inspiration from the work of Bernth Lindfors. Nnimmo Bassy, poet and architect, gave generously of his time and financial help and I am indeed grateful for his confidence on the project.

Onookome Okome
Calabar, Nigeria.

1

Introduction

From Kongi To Kongi
The Drama of Soyinka Since The Nobel

ONOOKOME OKOME

I

Wole Soyinka, Africa's first Nobel Laureate for literature, will remain relevant in his homeland Nigeria. He will remain an important figure among conscientious writers and political analysts of the African continent for as long as the world of literature shapes our sense of things, of history and culture, politics and street life, gender and issues about women, hope and despondency, life and death. Like very few writers writing today, Soyinka will be remembered not simply for the personal sacrifices he has made to his nation and the African continent but also for the wealth of literary legacy he will has already bequeathed to mankind. Indeed, the evidence everywhere in the world shows that Wole Soyinka's literature and cultural theories have attracted enormous popularity, patronage and commentaries. This is not only gauged by the amount of his works we read or by the sheer number of academic dissertations that have been written on his books since his first published play was per-

1

formed. The wide popularity of his texts in the school system all over the world is a strong indication of his enormous place in contemporary African culture and letters.

But the man still lives. He still writes. He provides minute-to-minute account of where "the rain started beating" us to use the apt phrase by another famous Nigerian writer, Chinua Achebe. This is a source of joy and inspiration to those who consider his voice, his very presence, an alternative means of articulating life in a precariously balanced world. As long as he lives, it seems he will continue to produce more of the literature that chronicles our collective existence and the "recurrent circle of stupidities".

It was for this reason that a celebration was planned for Wole Soyinka in June 1994, at the National Theatre Complex in Lagos. The occasion was his birthday. Against his wishes, which he expressed in no uncertain manner, friends and well wishers made frantic, if not frenetic efforts, to celebrate this man of honour. Unlike one of his celebrated fictional characters, Elesin Oba, the vivacious, extremely boisterous Lord of his most lyrical play to date, *Death and The King's Horseman,* Soyinka truly declined this celebration and for good reason.

1994 was, as many would recall, the ferocious "year of the people's struggle". It was the year after the blatant denial of the voice of the people yearning for democracy after more than fourteen of brazen military politics during which Nigeria sank into political and economic chaos. This was also the year the inaugurated a deadly turning point for the vicious dictatorship that Nigeria may ever know—the reign of General Sanni Abacha.

So while the streets were burning, it was something of the abnormal for Soyinka to embrace the spirit of celebration. Soyinka cancelled all fanfares. He preferred instead to remain in the forested landscape of his country home in Abeokuta. It was for him the wise thing to do. It was the ultimate dictate of the time. Soyinka had reasons to believe that this season of "anomy" will pass, and that there will be plenty of time to celebrate.

His rejection of the fanfare associated with his 60th birthday was not to be. His younger compatriots thought that this was actually the right and auspicious time to celebrate him. It was a time to look back at this man's achievement, a writer who has consistently suffered

2

physical and mental torture for a country whose military leaders have shown little respect for good governance or even for the simplest principles of human rights. His younger compatriots thought that, against all odds, including the risk of invited foreign guests being hit by stray *molotov cocktails* in the burning streets of rioting protesters and pro-democracy activists; against the vicious immobility that the then famous petrol scarcity caused to movement of people and vehicles, a successful conference to celebrate Soyinka would indeed make the point that the literary opposition was not cowed in the least. This position, it was argued, would ultimately send a loud and clear signal to Abuja, the seat of the dictator, that all is not well. This book of essays is part of that botched celebration.

The reasons which the younger compatriots had for insisting on going on with the Soyinka celebration and for which I was invited from Calabar, my provincial University base, were as persuasive as those which Soyinka himself provided for not welcoming the celebration. But the odds were for overwhelming for the organisers from the beginning. Odia Ofeimun, then president of the Association of Nigerian Authors (ANA), was at the head of arrangements for this meeting in Lagos. While he insisted, and for good reasons that the meeting should go on in spite of the lack lustre opening, he did not contend with the fuel scarcity and the violence in the street. There was more to come. But the long and short of it was that right as he was about the need for this meeting, Odia Ofeimun did not take many things into consideration. He was shocked when the organization eventually went awry. Wole Soyinka and an entourage of friends did show up at the venue of the activities, the National Theatre Complex, Iganmu, Lagos, but it was simply a symbolic gesture.

After two days of loitering about, a very painful thing to guests, it became quite obvious to Ofeimun that indeed things had gone really bad. Although frantic efforts were made to provide some activities after Soyinka appeared briefly and left, nothing was really the same anymore. It was heart wrenching to see writers from all over the world that came to witness the celebration of an accomplished writer in his own turf loitering around and literally "hanging-out" on the impersonal balconies of the National Theatre from day to day. Although I did not stay long enough to speak with some of the writers and culture enthusiasts, I did manage to talk with Prof. Kofi Anyidoho who seemed to me to have taken the disappointment well. Since he said very little, I could not be absolutely clear how well he really took the monumental disappointment. He sat on those impersonal stairways of the National Theatre halls, listening to all who cared to talk with him. His way back home was indeed one of the briefest among the international guests.

On the second day, when it was obvious that nothing was going to happen, I returned to Calabar, but not before I had made up my own plans to contribute to the efforts of Odia Ofeimun and to the literary legacy of one of Africa's greatest writers. The personal decision was to summon a small body of scholars working on the literature of Soyinka and the politics of writing in Nigeria and to discuss what had gone wrong with the country in the light of recent happenings and to document the outcome between decent covers. Soyinka was to be at the core of this inquiry.

Part of the *grand* plan was to celebrate Soyinka in Calabar. After I left Lagos, I followed the literary news and reviews about the events and other matters on the respected literary pages of the *Nigerian Guardian*. I soon learned that some of the activities did in fact hold and that there was some successes recorded. This was heartening but the need to put together the intimate feelings about the literary figure that was the subject of this celebration was still something to be contemplated.

In the last days of the absolutism of the Babangida/Abacha regime, nothing short of muffled articulations of the role of Wole Soyinka in nation building could be made. Even in Calabar, a provincial town removed from the blaring glare of the chief of the SSS, (State Secret Service) at that time, there was the need to be on the right side of the dictatorship's *laws*, lest you are dubbed a *saboteur*, a word whose meaning was re-invented and abused by deadly and zealous officials of the regime. During those hazy days, it was wisdom to stay out of the actions of the *boys*. It was sheer foolhardiness to be taken into one of those massive buildings with inglorious underground tunnels that hosed the SSS (State Secret Services) offices. There was one located right across the airport in Calabar, not very far from the University of Calabar where I teach. It was (and still is) grey, ominous, towering over the plain, sleepy and poor neighbourhood.

At first, I thought the logic was simply not right and in some way "spooky." When I talked with some faculties in Calabar about the "Soyinka project" as it came to be known then, the answer was always "That is a great idea. We could do something like the "Eagle On Iroko stuff, you know. Honour this man properly as we did Chinua Achebe a couple of years back in Nsukka, but do you think the time is now?" I understood this sentiment. But I thought there was something missing. Close as the dark house was to the University, I did not see how the occupants of the house would know about our interest. The more I thought about this response, the more I tried to look beyond the provincial connotations of the remarks from faculty members I approached with the Soyinka project.

It was true that it was politically incorrect to discuss Soyinka after he fell out with the Babangida regime, which promised, as usual, to clean up the tepid mess that former dictators had laid upon the collective psyche of the nation. For this reason, it was inconceivable for anyone to gather a group of academics and scholars to discuss, in any meaningful way, the problems of the country at that time. Far from the troubles of finding the financial resources for doing this kind of cultural activity, there was also the looming presence of the grey home of the SSS. Everyone was carefully aware of this and nobody in particular was willing to get near it. Certainly the famous African hospitality was not practised there.

But there were more oblique reasons for the response I got when the suggestion was made that a small talk shop on the relevance of Soyinka's literature after the Nobel Prize be organised. I did not wait too long to know the main reason for this. The "political incorrectness" of the timing was simply a facade, a fine scholarly wool pulled over some confounded ethnic reasons. As events unfolded, the provincially ethnic sentiments soon opened up. Many of those with whom I talked about this matter would not put down a hair to support the cause of a man from the *other* part of a nation that has been effectively divided into three parts. The celebrant might be a good writer but for some people that is where it ended. The reading of his politics and that of his ethnic origin was judged as inextricably tied to a cultural root at variance with their needs and aspirations. It seemed

5

to me then that there was still a seething envy about where the first African award of the Nobel Prize for literature went. This feeling as I see it has not gone away.

However, a small group of enthusiasts in Calabar held some of the meetings in their homes, discussing Soyinka and the tepid political world in which we found ourselves. We talked about the new plays, indeed the new writings, which Soyinka had done since the Nobel was awarded him. I remember vividly one such meeting in my apartment sometime in 1994. I was becoming frustrated with progress on this project. This was because some naughty and hype-ridden people in Lagos had sent into the extremely malicious Lagos gossip mill the immense guilt that I should feel for devoting a whole edition of the journal of literature that I edited in Calabar, the *Calabar Journal of Nigerian Life and Literature,* to the relatively unknown and according to another source, a less important literary figure, Alhaji Abubakar Gimba. I had other problems and so I did not take this gossip to heart. I thought that the Soyinka project was worthwhile and quite significance to the current debates on our nation(s) and its nationalism(s). Somewhere in my mind, I also thought that by doing this project successfully, I will prove that the choice of whose works one chooses to deal with depends on personal convictions. Through this project I hoped to will prove to the malicious Thomas' (Okiemutes or Femis, if you prefer) that my intentions were not pedestrian in the least. The fact is that all literature edifices. All literature is relevant within certain cultural and social contexts. To keep this solemn oath of undertaking the Soyinka project became an important part of my scholarly pursuit and in some ways, my creative enterprise. The need to push on was forceful. But the conviction that no one writer is more important than the other has never left me. It will still over around my conception of writing in a postcolonial situation as in other context. A writer such as Ogali O. Ogali of the Onitsha market is important for reasons that Soyinka will not be. Soyinka is important to our literature and political life for the reason that Abubakar Gimba will not but Gimba also has a place in this literary tradition. He is important too. If we pay attention to Ogali O. Ogali, why shouldn't we do the same to and for Gimba who has written more than five novels? He has not done this to enhance his academic position. He is not from the University system. He has written these novels out of interest. He is a banker. He is not one of the "University people." A year later, I submitted the draft of the manuscript to Africa World Press (AWP), New Jersey. It was promptly assessed and accepted for publication.

II

The essays in this book are the narratives of the life of the Nigerian nation held in various forms of political captivity, the most brutal being that of General Sanni Abacha. The essays are about dictatorship and its consequences on the political and cultural life of the people as they are about the misadministration of different rulers who ran the country since 1986 when Wole Soyinka won the Nobel Prize for Literature. And because they attempt to discuss at some length what Wole Soyinka makes of the "nonsense" of this situation, it is no coincidence that they come back to what Soyinka has done with the social material of this period as he chronicles the life of rulers and subjects.

In Soyinka's new literature dealing with the social events of the years from the 1980s up until the death of the bloody General, he invents invented new characters to deal with the immediate situations, investing in each a new sense of place and a new social consciousness never before so banal. He puts these inventions in collision course with the nation and with the idea of governance. Ogunian in proportion, the characters of this new literature are not altogether new to the world of those familiar with Soyinka's literature. They go way back to Soyinka's *A Dance of the Forests, Before the Blackout* and *After The Blackout* sketches. What is noticeably different is that in the new plays (christened the postNobel plays here) a new sense of urgency is inscribed into the dramatic actions these characters are invested with. The many authorial interrogations injected in the texts become post of social debate that call up recent history and matters of cultural changes. Indeed, Soyinka seems to be saying through the characters of the postNobel literature that we have waited far too long and have tolerated despots and military sycophants for far too long. Now is the time to act. Surprisingly and contrary to all speculations, the postNobel literature, especially the drama, does not only question the national and the philosophical origins of despotism on the continent and in Nigeria in particular, it also discusses and reinforces the phenomenon of a class divide which despotic politics has made visible. This leads inevitably to a category of debate never before so forcefully presented in the older texts.

The aim of this project was clear from its conception: it was to examine the literature of Soyinka since he was awarded the Nobel Prize for literature in 1986, with a view of understanding his literary politics after the Nobel. This is a befitting celebration for Wole Soyinka. Of course, I was not unmindful that an army of radical critics, armed with the infallible Marxist Leninist philosophical argument, would prefer to add another phrase to this description—socially conservative radicalism—to describe the world of preNobel Soyinka. However, the obvious is that in his public and physical utterances, Soyinka has always put up a spirited fight when and where it mattered most in the literary and political history of his country. He was imprisoned for up to two years in solitary confinement during the Nigerian civil war for his opposition to the senseless bloodletting and just before he fled the country in 1993; his life was once more on the line for openly opposing the dictatorship of General Abacha. According to him, General Sanni Abacha would have had the singular honour of having to be the first African dictator to hang a Nobel Prize winner if he had not escaped when he did. (*Interview*, Meiningen, Germany, April 1999)

The central thesis of this project can be reposed in this question: Is postNobel Soyinka radically different from preNobel Soyinka? In other words, has Soyinka dispensed with the characters of his earlier works in whose quests we find the combined traits of Ogun and the other gods in the Yoruba pantheon? This project privileges the place of Ogun for obvious reasons. But the act of privileging is not made only because Ogun is the patron-god of Soyinka but also because the essence of Ogun, the god of iron and creative impulse, contains the seed that reactivates and directs the collective will of a people lost in the "bush of ghosts" and political vermins. Such was the situation that Nigerians found in the heady and hazy days of Abacha. Soyinka debated this in his usual eloquence in the W.E.B. Du Bois Lectures, which he gave in Accra, Ghana. Drafted into the service of theorising the intervention of the military in politics, Soyinka invents the theory of the "veil." This is the political mechanism, which according

Soyinka the military used to pull the "veil" over the face of the nation for over fifteen years. Long before this chaos wrought upon the Nigerian state by military *messiahs*, Ogun, whose hubris provided man with the source of light, had faithfully made the transition from the epic chaos of the original world to that of human beings. He brought the touch of knowledge to man in spite of the refusal of members of Yoruba pantheon for him to do so. That singular act of hubris is referred to as the *first sacrifice* that individuals ("the strong breeds") in the human communities must undertake from time to time on behalf of their communities and their humanity. It was Ogun who started it all. It was Ogun who showed the way for mankind to follow. It is no surprise therefore that Soyinka's strong-willed characters are cast in this frame; all them having a sense of communal existence that must be protected at all cost. Do we find a replication of the Ogunian traits in the postNobel literature of Soyinka? Yes.

No attempt is made here to discuss the entire content of the essays in the volume. They eloquently speak for themselves. However, an attempt is made to situate each within the broader context of the post-Nobel texts of Soyinka, which we proposed to investigate. The political context of the postNobel works is still the Nigeria of the postcolonial status and the literary and cultural paradigms are still found in the copious references of the Yoruba world. My preliminary and brief reading of the essays shows that all of them meet at some point with the *grand* idea, which propelled the subject of our inquiry: the significance of the Ogunian character in Soyinka's postNobel literature in contact with a modernity that is dubious. It is a modernity that predates on local means of generating meaning; a modernity that negates the "beingness" of the continent. It is also one that is being constantly absorbed in certain areas of popular and urban life. It is this dubious modernity that insists on the continuous veiling of meaning in the continent and its people that W. E.B. Dubois once described as the medium for the deception of the black man in the "white world of American slave and postslavery society"(Soyinka, 1993:1). African-Americans and Africans may have taken one step (or maybe two) from the excruciating servitude of slavery but were quickly re-integrated into what Soyinka describes as a "postslavery society". This society came about as the result of complex alliance of multinationals who rule the world, using local agents whose only desire is to be absorbed into modernity without having the faintest ideas about how it works. This is the society where military dictators feed their gluttonous appetite on the people in search for power and money. Soyinka's reaction to this society of pretentious and superficial modernity is *writ large* in the postNobel works. It is the metaphor of the perennial problems that confront the continent. The problems associated with this unholy alliance are not simple and cannot be squarely and truthfully located in the intervention from the outside alone. The greed of thieving, dominant class with dubious ties to the outside is also to be held accountable for some of the problems.

Frank Mowah's essay "The Logic of Disorder in Soyinka's Post-Nobelity" does not only reaffirm Soyinka's interest in the culture and politics of postcolonial African experience, it also emphasises a re-dedication on the part of this writer to continue his meticulous reading of the problems of Africa. The contention is that Soyinka lays the blame of the misfortune of the continent squarely where it ought to be—within and outside the shores of the continent. Mowah argues in this essay that Soyinka's preNobel literature is one and the same with the post-Nobel concerns, stressing that the triumph of the will of Nelson Mandela over the hateful notions of racial superiority upon which apartheid was built is a testimony of the power of hope and perseverance over the forces of darkness and greed. Working from the position that an understanding of culture, rather that an understanding of society strengthens mankind, Soyinka creates characters with the characteristics of Ogun, the god iron in Yoruba pantheon. Alone and against all odds, Ogun bridged the gulf between man and the other world. The Ogunian characters in postNobel Soyinka, according to Mowah, are used by Soyinka to investigate the meaning of the chaos that Africa has bequeathed to the world of violence, stressing that this chaos which we see on such global and devastating scale is nothing but the beginning of a new life, a new world. There may be *grand* human tragedies but the presence of redeeming figures such as Nelson Mandela will eventually moderate the carnage and redirect the path that the continent will go in the near future.

Mowah's essay does not emphasise the slight difference in the shift which postNobel Soyinka assumed from the late 1980s. This shift is more prominent in Soyinka's concern for the new urban culture of his country and the black world and the consequences that this cultural hybrid could possibly have on the political and cultural landscape of Africa in the 21st century. Mandela may be the incarnation of Shaka the Zulu, possessing the patience of Obatala, the Yoruba god of plasticity and inspiration and the tenacity of Ogun, the Yoruba god of the creative impulse, but he must also deal with the contingencies of a new world, which is different from the days of Shaka. He must deal with how the African continent and his country, Nigeria, interact with icons of this modernity. In other words, the need to constantly change strategy and to be constantly aware of changes in culture and society is a crucial factor of this strategy, so that the Mandela of *Mandela's Earth and Other Poems* is no longer the irreducible mythical figure. He must also step into the waywardness of contemporary African world. He must squarely face up to the invaders and their "philistinic" apparatus.

Mowah's second contribution situates the condition of the African predicament that the metaphor of Mandela symbolizes. It takes on the debate about the place of tradition (Ogunian or otherwise) and the modern in Soyinka's postNobel literature. Specifically, this essay theorizes the post-modern condition and contexts of literary production and consumption. The argument of this essay is hinged upon the fact that "What bestows legitimacy on social institutions in the face of technological onslaught for the postcolonial is not scientific knowledge but narrative authenticity". This argument connects the discourses of literary production and receptions to the world that Soyinka's pre- and postNobel literature captures so eloquently. Theorizing the significance of narrative knowledge, this essay sets out and sufficiently elaborates on one of the most often neglected aspects of literary discourse in Nigerian scholarship. Situated at the fringe of the so-called postmodern world, third world writers like Soyinka, try to make meaning, not from the images generated in postmodern media, but from the basic essence of mankind relating to his society: narrative power. By engaging and harnessing the power of man's primordial means of *telling*, Soyinka, like other third world writers, convert literature into what Mowah calls a "weapon of liberation". While third world writers do not completely neglect the use of the new media which make writing visible and accessible to a larger public, they often have to fall back to that form of pristine narrativisation of events in order to legitmize their existence. They do this by using "narratives like myths, legends, stories, songs, epic etc."

Harry Garuba's essay as well as that of Charles Bodunde presents a similar and incisive incursion into the world of Soyinka's *Isara*. They both provide the kind of reading, which Frank Mowah suggests in his second contribution, "Liberation Narrative and Post-modern Africa." Garuba's contribution, "Soyinka's *Isara* and The Myth of The Magic Box", is short and concise. It privileges the very core of Mowah's argument. Dealing with Soyinka's autobiographical account of a very crucial period of transition in Nigeria's cultural history and the role of a particular Yoruba community that make up this world, Garuba links the act of writing this liminal phase of national history yet again to the world of Soyinka's "compulsive mythologies" in which the pretext sets the narrative of events on a familiar terrain. He argues that Soyinka's "pattern of transforming lived experiences into myth or re-writing experiences into the structures and codes of mythology, runs through the whole book". Garuba's essay emphasises that Soyinka's is a mythmaker who often transforms events of everyday existence into a celestial plain where the hands of the gods and ancestors control the affairs of mankind. According to Garuba, "Ashtubala", the name of the small town where Essay (Soyinka's father) in *Isara* has his pen friend, is transformed into this mythical world where everything is a imaginable, especially good things. As Garuba eloquently argues, "Essay's imagination is so thoroughly marked with the register of myth that its association with the wonders of the North American continent is extended to all the wonders of Essay's fertile mind".

There is no concrete link to the world of the ancestors in *Isara*, at least not in the way that this is articulated in Soyinka's *Death and The King's Horseman* or *The Road* but the desire to reach a different realm of existence can be read as a reference to the mythical world that lurks in the background of the imagination of the characters. When Soyinka actually "opens the tin box belonging to his father" whose funeral he could not attend because of certain political contingencies, he is, in some sense, recreating the popular myth of the deprived child who has suddenly found a means to reach deep into the knowledge of which he was deprived." This is how Garuba describes the quintessential narrative technique of this book, one for which Soyinka has had to suffer critical barbs from those who object to the so-called frivolous mystification and mythication of known events. What Garuba's reading proves beyond reasonable doubt is Soyinka's ability to "raise social histories" to mythical dimension.

Charles Bodunde's contribution, "Beyond Biography: Characters and Journeys in Soyinka's *Isara*: A Voyage Around Essay" comes close to the reading in Garuba's paper. But Bodunde discusses the journey of the characters in this book and the liminal essence of a social transition in which they are inevitably implicated. Like Harry Garuba's essay, Bodunde argues that *Isara* is all about an important fragment of social history and that as a social *text*, *Isara* is indeed a document about a society in transition. This transition affects all the characters one way or the other. Like Garuba, Bodunde is of the opinion that "From myth figures to contemporary characters, Soyinka's adventurers [in *Isara*] link each other like a chain" and "Within this mythic dimension; Soyinka reinforces the idea of journey as a transition into new life and power." On this and more points, Bodunde and Harry's papers suggest that in Isara, Soyinka creates human equivalents of what he perceives the gods to be in the terrestrial world-view of Yoruba people. Both papers suggest, "that the world of *Isara* groping towards modernity" is still tied to traditional Africa, a mode of living and experiencing so "mystically tied to the land/ and the spirit of the ancestors" according to Tanure Ojaide (1997). In *Isara*, the ties the west is not an uncritical one. It is a journey of curiosity, a movement of another kind of search.

Kalu Uka's essay is like a praise song, an *oriki* of some sort, for Soyinka, a writer whose sense of history and of culture is shaped by the choice he has made. Kalu Uka, a contemporary and friend of Wole Soyinka, argues that Soyinka's chosen road has been recognized: it is the Yoruba matrix of his African vision has been enlarged into an African highway, the original path through the Frostian "yellow wood or as African anthropological detractors used to call it, the jungle pathways". According to Uka "it is not simply a matter of bringing together to a dazzling the victories of Soyinka in art, Samori

Marchel in death or Nelson Mandela's moving nearer to freedom for self, race and continent". The point is that as one of the "strong breeds" and like Machel and Mandela, Soyinka has contributed immensely to the definition of the African in his chosen field of endeavour. Soyinka has done so in spite or because of the deprivations and difficulties that he has had to face in this pursuit to see justice done to all. This *will* to overcome, to surmount all odds, belongs to Ogun, the patron god of artists. Soyinka appropriates and lives this *will*. It is this temperament that keeps Wole Soyinka going. Sixty odd years after, Kalu Uka tells us in this essay, Soyinka is still on that chosen path, defining and re-defining the African person. His *will* is still strong and the conditions in the world have not made his preoccupation any less important. Sixty years after the "path taken", Soyinka still finds the need to tackle old problems anew. He forges new methods to do this. This is in spite of some of the most vicious and reductionist criticism of Soyinka's chosen path during this period.

At sixty, critics of Soyinka's early myth plays cannot help but look back at the man's glorious road to intellectual and social, contentment. Not even 'Biodun Jeyifo, the most astute and keen observer of Soyinka's early writings, can convincingly deny the legacy which this man has left on the sands of time. As Kalu Uka rightly points out, none of these scholars have come near to disproving the depth and relevance of Soyinka's works such as *The Strong Breed* and *Death and The King's Horseman*. In fact, Femi Osofisan, one of the best-known and erudite scholars of Soyinka, and who is himself an accomplished writer, is unambiguous about his attachment to the works of this great writer and the influence he has derived from the literature and social activism of Wole Soyinka. (1979; 1994). Osofisan acknowledges that he "has been one of Soyinka's ardent critics, to whom he himself has replied with some of his most famous diatribe", but it is also true that "all quarrels with Soyinka are, in the end, nothing less than a tribute to his genius; that our disagreement with him represent, with all their fierceness, the kind of homage that admirers pay to masters" (1994:43).

So, if the indebtedness of this group of writers/critics is acknowledged, why were initial responses from members to Soyinka's works so vehement partisan against concieved feudalistic tendencies to paraphrase? The answer can be partly found in the intellectual spirit of that time and partly in the political choices that a particular generation of critics/writers in Nigeria took on at some period in Nigeria's literary history. Reactions to Soyinka's work by the two most visible groups of critics, scholars and writers- namely the Ibadan/Ife axis and the Nsukka school- have echoes of these political choices. Uka's essay mentions them in passing, but argues that it is the very reason for which Soyinka was mercilessly castigated in the 1970s and 1980s that he got the accolade and warm reception of the Nobel committee. Perhaps it was also for this reason that Soyinka is hunted continuously by all the dictators that have emerged so far on the Nigerian political platform. Soyinka simply refuses to die in the face of tyranny. He attacks the very base of tyranny.

A new intellectual frontier is opening up in the interpretation of the so-called mythopoeic plays, especially *Death and the King's Horseman* and *A Dance of the Forests*. For example, Simon Obikpeko Umukoro investigates the debate about the social contexts of these plays and their implications for contemporary society and culture in Nigeria. His analysis of *A Dance of the Forests* in *Drama and Politics in Nigeria* surely turns the focus from mythology and gods to practical issues connected with a living and dynamic society. While 'Biodun Jeyifo, the radical and insightful critic of Soyinka's work, can hold on to the notion that in *Death and the King's Horseman* the "the conflict of alien and indigenous African world view has suppressed the real, objective difference between conflicting groups and classes within the indigenous system", pursing the argument that this

> is illustrative of the gaps and dents of Soyinka's amour that he selected this particular metaphysical and philosophical African civilization and not the more egalitarian African cosmogony and metaphorical systems, the erosion of which ideological and political progress can, with greater reason, regret (*Truthful Lie* 35),

The point remains that an alternative reading which tells us that those onto whose hands society invests great trust must always live to fulfil their obligations is equally legitimate, if not sounder in judgement. Trust and obligation are crucial wheels upon which society builds its codes of existence and continuity. Elesin Oba abandons this trust. He tactfully tries to decline the obligation that his position as the King's Horseman demands of him. This reading is completely neglected by 'Biodun Jeyifo and those on the bandwagon of the "radical left". For now, this *brahala* seems to have died but the winner of this battle of wit is Wole Soyinka.

The Nobel Prize for Literature is a proof of the excellence of the work and life of Soyinka but the more meaningful and enduring proof is not the prize *per se*. It is not those angry rejoinders that Soyinka often sent to younger compatriots who dare challenge his position either. The meaningful and enduring proof is the fulfilled predictions that Soyinka's works make about our contemporary life. In every Nigerian dictator today, especially since General Babangida, there is an Elesin for whom the people matter less in the scheme of things. Personal and political aggrandizement have mattered more to these dictators. If this reading of contemporary Nigerian life poses any real problems to some, all we need to do is substitute it for one of Soyinka's more openly political texts. The example that would naturally come to mind is *Kongi's Harvest*. In this text, all doubts about the political concerns of Soyinka certainly dissolve. Although Soyinka does not provide a clear ideological option or a preferred political desire in *Kongi's Harvest* (see Okome 1997), once we recognize that this is a choice that a writer makes, we can then read our preferred meaning to the end of this bizarre situation of contemporary African political world as Josef Gugler (1997) does with his analysis of the play. He gives four suggestions as to how to end this drama of despot. He does not prescribe to the playwright how his plays should end. He simply provides his considered options.

Of course Soyinka has persistently rejected the critical position that critics of the "left" have put forward. But I think it is in Soyinka's texts themselves that the real basis for the rejection of this one tract critical analysis finds profundity. In his reply to the critics of the Nigerian *left*, Soyinka insists that concern with culture is important for mankind to understand itself and necessary for the engine of social progress. This is the point that he makes in *The Road, Strong Breed* and *Death and The King's Horseman*, the last two plays dealing with culture and myth in their most pristine expressions. Although the plays are not part of the postNobel oeuvre which this book seeks to elucidate, they form part some of the deeply thought-out exposition of the culture of the Yoruba world which Soyinka has continually mined for the meaning of life, of existence. His concern for culture is very evident in these and other plays. In these plays we can really reconstruct the concern with and of culture that Soyinka speaks of and writes about. Kalu Uka mentions these plays in his essay because he thinks them important. In them we find and actually feel the replicated existence of the Yoruba people, with each god properly represented. The qualities of Ogun, Soyinka's personal deity are adequately domesticated in the plays as well as in the personal lifestyle of Soyinka.

But the domestication of the Yoruba pantheon in his literature is only a metaphor. Soyinka uses this as leitmotif to examine the daily lives of the people of his country, Nigeria. This metaphor can be explained as a means of coming to terms with social realities in that physical existence, because it attempts to explain how the celestial world of Yoruba metaphysics managed to move away from that "primordial chaos", the "introit condition," into a balanced state of *being* and *beingness*. This metaphor is projected into the cultural and political situation on the African continent as well as Nigeria. It is in this regard that Eman, the Christ figure of Soyinka's *The Strong Breed*, becomes the scapegoat that could re-invent meaning in the society where he is found marooned as a "scapegoat". His sacrifice is an essential part of the social cohesion that the community seeks.

Daniel Grover's essay examines the need of society to sacrifice one or more of its own for its own collective good and continuity. According to Gover, we (re)turn to "the most instructive sets of contraries... of appetite and sacrifice". Gover argues that the "dualities that run through Wole Soyinka's writing, pursue the tensions of traditional Yoruba worldview." There are different kinds of sacrifices, the essay argues, each designed for a specific function in society. Instead of focusing on a specific number of texts, Gover's essay takes a wide range of Soyinka's dramatic texts. By choosing for special mention the early plays such as *Lion and The Jewel* and *Kongi's Harvest*, Gover demonstrates that "the theme of appetite and sacrifice play off against each other to create shifting balances of comedy and tragedy." This preoccupation comes from the abiding program of Soyinka's literary career, which has been carried over to the latter plays of the post Nobel era.

The significance of Gover's reading of Soyinka's dramatic texts, especially of the extended reading of *Death and The King's Horseman*, lies at the very heart of the project of this book. The fall of Elesin Oba, like the fall of other major characters in Soyinka's plays dealing with social attitudes and cultural systems, is ultimately the symptom of the collapse of a decadent world. It is the sign of the eroding of a system of social order that is essentially the bridge between the three con-necting realms of Yoruba worldview—the living, the dead and the unborn. It a sign of the decay of an old order. In Death *and the King's Horseman*, Elesin Oba who must destroy (his own life) in order to inaugurate a new (communal) life transgresses the very essence of his *being* in that social order. Having lived life to the fullest, with all the privileges of the King's Horseman, he must now go through the sacri-fices that must culminate in the ritual death that the office demands of him. But he breaks with that tradition when he refuses to undergo the ritual suicide demanded after the King's death. This break leads to a communal chaos. The consequence of his action goes beyond him, falling squarely on the darkening brow of this community of anxious souls. As Gover rightly concludes, "Elesin finally commits suicide as a modern man—out of the profound sense of loss and shame". Shame comes from an equally profound realization that he has set in motion the destruction of a world, which he was entrusted to keep together. Elesin's modernity (if we prefer to refer to his refusal to die and his declaration of an individual will in that manner) is only a brief flirta-tion with the immediate and direct European contacts: the Pilkings. Elesin Oba pays for it dearly, with his life.

Simon Obikpeko Umukoro's "The Organization of Symbols in Wole Soyinka's *From Zia With Love*", Tanimu Abubakar's "Anarchism and The Nigerian State in *From Zia With Love*", Onookome Okome's "The Political Conscious in The Cinema and Literature of Wole Soyinka" and Maurice Edde Iji's "*From Zia With Love*: Soyinka's Grafitti on The Nigerian Wall" deal essentially with the human chaos which has ravaged Nigeria as a result of the lack of faith in and absence of a true notion of sacrifice to that community. This is the result of personal greed and selfish aggrandisement by the self-seeking few put in positions of authority and governance. Tanimu Abubakar's essay points to the sources of this disturbing social situation, and compares it to the total lack of order, which he says is a result of "the assassination of conscience and morality in affairs of men throughout the world". Abukabar is less concerned with the presence of gods in his reading of a number of texts but he emphasizes the sociological character of the chaos and the need for a redemptive figure that will clean up the Aegean stable after. The restoration of the health of society, he concludes, is essential for human and social progress, bringing into focus the scapegoat paradigm that *The Strong Breed* adequately addresses. Army Generals who seize power in Nigeria are neither willing to neither take on this role nor give the opportunity for others who share this feature of human sacrifice on behalf of society. A new and damning ideal of the "politics of despotism" has taken over. The politics of the *Kongis* of this world can only breed naked violence. Tanimu Abubaka's reference to the *Kongis* of this world is important because it links his project (ours too) to the essence of Soyinka's literature before the Nobel Prize was awarded, signifying an essential and continuing link of themes and social meaning between the two periods. It is also important to our project because Kongi, the dictator in *Kongi's Harvest*, can really be seen and taken as the literary grandfather (or should we say ancestor) of the Generals we encounter in *A Play of Giants, From Zia With Love* and *Beatification of Area Boys*. In *Beatification*, the offsprings of Kongi of the third and fourth generations have indeed matured, and they are carrying on the havoc of their forbears on the hapless population of the continent of Africa.

The kind of anarchy which Tanimu Abukabar's paper addresses is more visible in the power plays. Soyinka's power plays deal more with the naked and vicious topic of political power and inordinate use of this power once the potential dictator has acquired it. In these plays, the "trickster motif" is no longer employed. Although Abubakar pays little attention to the mythic world in the affairs of the characters in *From Zia With Love*, he however hints at the mythical dimensions in the deadly game between the Wind Commander and Sebe:

> The Wind Commander is found dead on the road and some part of his body removed for ritual purposes. His body is recognized not by his uniform or official car, the symbol of his power, but by the wrapper and the black cap, the symbol of expiating Eshu.

Eshu is the trickster god, who is always ready and willing to goad wo/man deeper into the labyrinth of mischief with the ultimate purpose of leading humanity towards the recognition its stupidities, a prerequisite for reformation. Tanumu Abukabar argues that Soyinka rejects "the use of rituals and juju to settle scores" in this text. But it is interesting to note that Soyinka also captures the animist tendencies in the characters, showing how they interpret their actions as each of them compel reason and logic to the background in the actions of their everyday life. In the face of the obvious modernity, which the text privileges, the irony is not quite obvious. Tanimu Abukabar is aware of this and as he argues, this is just another "dimension of the anarchy," which is the result of the "spiritual vandalization" in *From Zia With Love*. Abukabar analysis leads us convincingly into the "hypocrisy of state power" and the telling result of this hypocrisy. Perhaps the real contribution of this essay is its spirited efforts to argue that Soyinka rejects the active role of the gods in the affairs of the characters in *From Zia With Love*. What this means is that Wind Commander and Sebe, to mention only two of the characters, are not Ogun's children. They are not instruments of change. In this way, Abubakar's reading is different from that of Simon Obikpeko Umukoro, yet we can say with certainty that the divergent critical positions give us insight into the equally diverse and rich textuality of this play. This much cannot be doubted.

Simon Obikpeko Umukoro's reading of *From Zia With Love* is tied to the interpretation of the mythic as espoused in the essays in *Myth Literature and The African World*. According to Umukoro, "the concern of the play is not so much to portray the interior life of individual characters, their personal and moral degeneration, as it is to illuminate the immoral character of the Nigerian society under Generals Buhari and Idiagbon". Umukoro argues that the author organizes the actions of the drama in symbols. Eshu, "that small potent god who throws a stone today and it kills a man next week" links all the atrocities of the characters as one continuous line of human ignorance. It is Eshu who is responsible for revealing all human stupidities, forever goading mankind into an awareness of its position. It is only through this process of self-knowledge that humanity reveals itself and is saved in the final point. Working closely with Ogun, Eshu is able to bring back our humanity's deplorable conditions to Ogun's creative and regenerative presence. In Ogun's forge, a new world is created. The idea which this essay puts forward is that the weakness of the characters in *From Zia With Love* and the chaos which this weakness causes can be redressed only after human agencies come to a full realization of their position in a full circle of life.

Maurice Edde Iji's contribution begins with the conclusion of Frank Mowah's first essay. Iji points out that "Soyinka's writing continues to echo his fervent concern for the dignity of man . . . even after the Nobel Prize" was awarded. He compares the works, especially the drama of the postNobel era, to what he describes as the *evil graffiti* on the Nigerian wall of social existence, stressing attempts by Soyinka to keep pricking the conscience of this nation and those of its leaders who have reduced life to the meanest regimes of barbarity. His contention is that *From Zia With Love* is one of the postNobel dramatic pieces that represent Soyinka's literary *graffiti* on the wall of contemporary Nigerian political history. Onookome Okome's essay deals with this decadent political history but in another narrative context-cinema. The essay gives a brief analysis of Soyinka's incursion into the media of cinema and music, explaining the urgency that propelled Soyinka into using these immediate and accessible means of popular communication. Okome concludes that this need has always been one of the overriding aims of Soyinka's social and political concerns. Although the essay also deals with the political nature of Soyinka's literature, it however stresses the social context of Soyinka's involvement in the making of *Blues for a Prodigal* and *Kongi's Harvest*. The essay also stresses another aspect of the creative potentials of Wole Soyinka—popular music. Although Soyinka does not consider his film experiment as successful as his work in the field of literature, it is important to stress, as this essay does, that the concern for and the need to expand the mediumistic horizon of protest against oppression has also been a significant part of Soyinka's creative and partisan strategy.

Chris Dunton's "The Value of Things: Soyinka's Cremation of a Wormy Caryatid" and Emevwo Biakolo's "*Mandela's Earth* in Soyinka's Poetic Corpus" deal with Soyinka's postNobel poetry. The essays celebrate the vision that Mandela symbolizes for Africa and Africans. Duntons' essay is concerned with the importance of the caryatid as a viable source of recovering a past about to disintegrate. In the dialectic between past and present, represented in Soyinka's handling of the life and death (by burning) of the caryatid, Dunton concludes that each moment of this exchange "invents itself, simply making do in an existential non-continuum."

Biakolo's study of *Mandela's Earth* is somewhat different from Chris Dunton's, at least on points of emphasis. Biakolo's takes us through what he prefers to describe as "heroes and the heroic quest" in this text, which according to him "is never too distant from Soyinka's creative consciousness". He argues that Ogun, the poet's patron god, resides at the centre of the mythical event in this long poem. Mandela is the human symbol of that event. In "Mandela's Earth", a poem which he describes as "a sojourn outside the usual hunt", Soyinka explains "the playful probe into the secrets of Mandela's . . . godlike strength of will".

It is no surprise then that Soyinka's speech at the Nobel ceremony is dedicated to Nelson Mandela. He praises Mandela's sense of purpose as well as his dedication to and concern for the entire African continent. For Soyinka, Mandela is the sum total of Ogun and Shaka, the warrior-King of the ancient kingdom of Southern Africa. Such figures do not come into life often. They are rare in human history. They have specific missions. Like Ogun, Mandela is part of the strong breed that society needs to clean its perennial and like Ogun's children, Eman in the *Strong Breed* and Olunde in *Death and The King's Horseman*, the Mandela figure takes on more than human attributes. He becomes a living legend and at other times assumes the exalted status of a god.

Chukwuma Okoye's essay deserves special mention for obvious reasons: it is the most direct and unencumbered reading of one of Soyinka's most prominent dramatic texts of the postNobel era dealing with social disorder. This essay concludes rather gloomily that the prison conditions, which the play depicts, are typical of Nigeria in the days of Generals Buhari and Idiagbon. Okoye's reading of the "familiarity with Soyinka's immersion in Yoruba mythology and his adoption of Ogun removes his essay from the "sociology of chaos into the mythology of meaning". The essay concludes: "one can liken the chaotic nature of the society of *From Zia With Love* to the primordial disquiet which Soyinka describes in *Myth, Literature and The African World*, the condition in the "cosmic order, which prompted Ogun's redemptive action". Emuke's eureka, "Na sign, I swear, na sign from heaven" (*From Zia With Love* 30) is one of the many examples that Okoye provides to show the hand of Ogun in the redemptive mission of the world of criminality in the prison. That the prisoners recognize the hand of Ogun in the actions and in their affairs is important because it shows the need and desperation for social change. It also shows awareness on the part of these criminals of the barbarity of their situation. On the other hand, Obododimma's contribution focuses on a stylistic device (face-threatening) that Soyinka employs as a strategy of satire in *From Zia With Love*.

Bernth Lindfors' contribution is one of the few essays that do not examine the role of Ogun or Ogun's children in the chaos of contemporary Nigerian (African) society, yet it is important to this project because it emphatically paints a picture of mythmaking at the University of Ife (now Obafemi Awolowo University, Ile Ife) in the 1970s. Two prominent Nigerian theatre directors/playwrights, Wole Soyinka and Ola Rotimi, are involved in this exercise of myth making as they interpret their roles and contributions to the Unife Theatre experiments. Bernth Lindfors' contribution is empirical. He draws a lot of evidence from an otherwise neglected source of scholarly debate—the daily newspaper—quoting profusely from newspaper writing rather than conjecturing what each participant said in the heat of the debate.

Okhakhu's project takes on a different interpretation from those of Tanimu Abukabar and Chukwuma Okoye by actively denying the active hands of the gods in the affairs men in *From Zia With Love*. According to Okhakhu, "Soyinka's philosophy tends to suggest that in spite of God's infinite goodness, if men were to rely solely on him, they might fail because men have not tried for solutions yet". But in this analysis, the God so denied a place in the affairs of men is not from the Yoruba pantheon. Okhakhu's concern is with the Christian God, spelt with the singular capital, GOD, instead of the plural description of gods with small letter in Yoruba pantheon. This is a different from say the contribution of Okoye. Yet we know that Soyinka's theories of African drama and society are less concerned with this "alien God". They are concerned with the gods the people that distinct cultural *godscape* which is Yoruba, the cultural backdrop of all Soyinka's plays.

Eshiet's essay, "From Metaphysical Profundity to Ferocious Topicality: The Paradigmatic Shifts in *Beatification of Area Boy*" is a political reading of a political play. It describes this play as propelling "a certain paradigmatic shift from the playwright's recurrent Ogunian metaphysical evocation to a more ferocious topicality often associated with Nigerian dramatists who cut their teeth long after the Nobel Laureate had carved his phenomenal niche in world dramaturgy". Lanre Bamidele's contribution also makes obvious reference to this aspect of Soyinka's play. The contribution of Eshiet's essay comes from the argument that *Beatification* . . . deals with the serious problems associated with bad military governance and that although the theme of governance is a serious one in this play, Soyinka still manages, at crucial points in the story of area boys, to make proper and effective use of what he refers to call the "dramaturgy of dark comedy". He argues that the playwright's genius in this regard is remarkable. One of the themes of *Beatification* is the attempt to understand why dictatorship operates the way it does. As a banal social testimony of the recurrent stupidities of Nigeria's recent past, Eshiet still finds it right to draw into his analysis Ogun's redemptive potentials for mankind. According to his summation, "Sanda is the Ogun." (or his human representative).

In the context of the whole project, Sanda, the enigmatic man of the street and leader of the "area boys." (street urchins and vagrants) becomes the chief-child of Ogun and it is possibly through him that societal change could occur. Eshiet is of the opinion that "Sanda acts as a buffer against the continued emancipation of the weak, the unprotected and the beleaguered". In this regard Sanda appropriates the qualities of Ogun, the protector of orphans and the unprotected. According to Eshiet, *Beatification* . . . is essentially a search for meaning in "a wasteland of lost souls".

Lanre Bamidele's essay, "Soyinka and The Interface of Dialogue: A Stylistic Analysis of *The Credo of Being and Nothingness*" turns the searchlight on an aspect of Soyinka's work that has been accorded little attention. It is about Soyinka's speeches, which are mostly responses to immediate social and cultural events. Bamidele studies one of such speeches, *The Credo of Being and Nothingness*, now published. *Credo...* deals with religious matters, a very touchy and volatile aspect of the history of the Nigerian peoples. Delivered in memory of the Rt. Rev. Olufosoye, the occasion was the first in the series of annual lectures to immortalize the memory of this reverend gentleman. It was organised by the Department of Religious Studies, University of Ibadan, Nigeria in the late 1980s. The presentation of speech took place at the Lakeside Chemistry Large Lecture Hall. I remember this lecture with fondness. The hall was packed full and a lot of people had come to see and hear Wole Soyinka talk about the burning issue of the day, which was prompted by statements credited to the highly respected Islamic cleric and scholar, Sheik Gumi. The Sheik was quoted at that time as having said, "Christianity means nothing," which infuriated the Christian community, who in turn, issued a number of responses, depending largely on their brands of Christianity. The Olufosoye Lecture was Soyinka's personal reaction to this statement. For Soyinka, the key word in the Sheik's utterance is "nothing," or "nothingness". The real turning point in Bamdele's analysis is his summation that Soyinka also uses speech-making opportunities to take a critical look at burning issues of the moment. This is an aspect of Soyinka's literary engagements that has not been given due recognition.

The motif of transition is the cardinal interest of Asodionye's Ejiofor's essay. He traces this concern in one of Soyinka's earlier plays, *The Road* and demonstrates how this play presages this concern in both the symbolic and literary senses in the later plays. This contribution suggests that both forms of transition are present in every society. In Soyinka's Yoruba worldview, the first (primordial) *transitor* is Ogun, his patron god, who is believed to have dared the other gods, and gave man light. The Ogun's example is very important to mankind. But transition itself is a very difficult process. This is what Professor tries to do in *The Road*. His attempt is a personal one; more of an intellectual exercise. It is esoteric. Ejiofor argues in this contribution that Soyinka has moved from a personal quest in *The Road* to a more urgent social call in *Beatification of Area Boy*. The link between the two plays is palpable but the perspective of the quest has changed from the philosophical in *The Road* to the mundane, almost banal social transition in *Beatification*.

Works Cited

Chinweizu, Onwuchekwa Jamie and Ihechukwu Madubuike. *Toward The Decolonisation of African Literature*. Enugu: Fourth Dimension, 1980.

Gugler, Josef. "Wole Soyinka's *Kongi's Harvest* From Stage To Screen: Four Endings To Tyranny." *Canadian Journal of African Studies*. 31/1, 1997: 32-45.

Jeyifo, 'Biodun. *The Truthful Lie: Essays in Sociology of African Drama*. London: New Beacon, 1985.

Ojaide, Tanure. *Poetic Imagination in Black Africa: Essays on African Poetry*. North Carolina: Carolina Academic Press, 1996.

Okome, Onookome. "Cinema and Social Change In Nigeria". *IRIS*. 18, 1995: 71-80.

Osofisan, Femi. "Tiger On Stage". *Theatre In Africa*. Ibadan: Ibadan University Press, 1979.

_____. "Wole Soyinka and A Living Dramatist: A Playwright's Encounter With Soyinka's Drama". *Wole Soyinka: An Appraisal* (ed.) Oxford: Heinemann Educational Books, 1994: 43-60.

Soyinka, Wole. *A Dance of the Forests*. London: Oxford, 1963.

_____. *The Road*. London: Oxford, 1965.

_____. *Kongi's Harvest*. London: Oxford, 1967.

_____. *A Shuttle In The Crypt*. London: Rex Collin/Metheun, 1972.

_____. *The Strong Breed*. In *Collected Plays* I. London: Oxford, 1975.

_____. *Ogun Abibiman*. London/Ibadan: Rex Collin/Metheun, 1976.

_____. *Myth, Literature and the African World*. London: Cambridge University Press, 1976.

_____. *Death and The King's Horseman*. London: Methuen, 1978.

_____. *A Play of Giants*. London: Methuen, 1984.

_____. *Isara: A Voyage Around Essay*. Ibadan: Fountain Publication, 1987

_____. *Mandela's Earth and Other Poems*.
Ibadan: Fountain Publication, 1989.

_____. *From Zia with Love*. Ibadan: Fountain Publication, 1992.

_____. *The Blackman and The Veil*. Accra: W.E Dubios Center, 1993.

_____. *Beatification of Area Boy*. Ibadan: Spectrum Books 1999.

2

The Logic of Disorder in Soyinka's Post-Nobility

FRANK UCHE MOWAH

Introduction

Already he has begun to shrink from the bewildered stare of the South
African, knowing that the supposedly free mind who once symbolized a
loophole for the dead-end of the South African dilemma has himself
become the creature of despair.
> —SOYINKA, 1967

The dilemma of the African at the dusk of the twentieth century and
the vision of a new dance in South Africa—these issues inform the
dominant themes of Soyinka's post-Nobel creative thrusts. Contrary
to our expectation, because the very notion of a demarcation suggests
a difference, (a difference between the pre-Nobel and the post-Nobel
Soyinka) that Soyinka of the post-Nobel era has perhaps overhauled
his creative engine to emerge with a completely new "thing" discon-
tinuous with his pre-Nobel tradition, post-Nobel Soyinka is one and
the same in essence with the pre-Nobel Soyinka.

Acutely steeped in Africa's history and inspired by the continuous socio-political malady in the continent, Soyinka's post-Nobel works, which include *Mandela's Earth and Other Poems* (1989) *Isara: A Voyage Around Essay* (1989), and *From Zia With Love* (1992) and *The Beatification of Area Boy* (1995), show a continuity with the imagery and symbols of African dilemma and history already contextualized in earlier works.

Mandela's Earth, echoing Soyinka's position in his Nobel speech, "This Past Must Address Its Present," indicates that he is taking seriously South Africa as the most important issue of the late twentieth century. It has gone beyond the prophetic insight of *Ogun Abibiman*—occasioned by the poet's interpretation of Samora Machel's symbolic decision of 1976 to place Mozambique in a state of war against white Rhodesia—to an avowal of faith and hope in what Mandela symbolizes. In *Ogun Abibiman* chances are that both a mythical god and a legendary hero of African history would fuse in the epistemological plane of Africa in defining a solution to a problem which began as a betrayal of the legend (Shaka the Zulu King) by his kinsmen; the result, a terrible curse on South Africa by Shaka.

> Did my dying words raise echoes in your hills
> When kinsmen matched broad blades
> With Shaka's shoulders? *The whites have come.*
> *And though you seize my throne, you will never*
> *Rule this land* (II).

In *Mandela's Earth*, "the hour [not only] presses now to full enforcement," but Shaka's terrible curse, which was fortunately exorcised by the silent one (Ogun) helping Shaka to reclaim his manhood, transforms into love for the country. But will this love "survive the epitaph?" Soyinka rightly wonders. Dennis Brutus, the South African poet and apostle of hope, has vested in this image a powerful metaphor of humanity's essence of being, just as Soyinka in *Ogun Abibiman* envisions a new role for Ogun and the Shaka incarnate (now Mandela):

> And tell me, you upon whose human heart
> Descends this fear, this shadow framed

Of the Apolycapse, say, pacific love
If loves survives the lash, contempt,
The silenced screams in blood-lit streets,
Say, if love outlasts the writing on the wall
In the hidden cells of Death's own masonry
Say, if love survives the tether's end
Whose weight, whose tale
Is yet another facelessness . . . .(20)

In a significant sense, therefore, *Mandela's Earth* contextualizes the South African predicament as well as the overall political dilemma of Africa. Mandela becomes a symbolization of all these. In his Nobel lecture, "This Post Must Address its Present," with an exceptional foresight, Soyinka foregrounds the "egregious" assault on Nelson Mandela, South Africa, and the entire African continent. In that talk, Mandela assumes a prominent focus after a painful contemplation of the brutal assassination of Samora Machel. This is an indication of the importance of South Africa to Soyinka's creative mind:

> That world which is so conveniently traduced
> by apartheid thought is of course that which
> I so wholeheartedly embrace—and this is my
> choice, among several options, of the
> significance of my presence here. It is a
> world that nourishes my being. One that is
> so self-sufficient, so replete in all aspects
> of its productivity, so confident in itself
> and in its destiny that it experiences no
> fear in reaching out to others. It is the
> hearthstone of our creative existence. It
> constitutes the prism of our world perception
> and this means that our sight need not be and
> has never been permanently turned inward.
> ("This Past . . ." II)

Mandela's Earth presents us with this montage of apartheid in an ironical humor, especially in the light of recent developments;

indeed, it "presents the last bastion of civilization against the hordes of barbarism from the North" ("This Past . . ." 12). The onlookers at the African predicament can no longer afford an indulgent smile. What happened in Nigeria in 1993 during the last days of Ibrahim Babangida in office, symbolized in the June 12 struggle for demoracry, shows that the world in which Mandela's endurance and logic are equated with a frightening logic is not an isolated one. It is also the world of Nigeria, Sudan, Cameroon, Somalia, Ethiopia, Zaire, and other countries on the continent where fascism and political degeneracy present us with a frightening logic of disorder.

This metaphor of fear, pain, and resistance provides the South African poems of *Mandela's Earth* a structural pattern of discourse, a system of contrast and opposition, which allows us insight into a thematic relation to other African worlds. The mode of discourse emphasizes the leadership problem of Africa and depicts Mandela's unusual steadfastness as a burden (of responsibility):

> Your bounty threatens me, Mandela, that taut
> Drumskin of your heart on which our millions
> Dance. I fear we catch fat leeches
> On your veins. Our daily imprecisions
> Dull keen edges of your will.
> Comprises deplete your acts repletion—
> Feeding will-void stomachs of a continent,
> What will be left of you, Mandela?
> (*Mandela's Earth*, 5)

The answer to what appears a mere rhetorical question comes firstly from *Ogun Abibiman,* where, as we know, "termites gnawed/the homeposts of our kraals even while we made the stranger welcome" (13). A political warning whose recurrence is already manifest in the legion of disagreements among the children of Shaka; and in a more philosophical sense, the last poem of *Mandela's Earth*, "Cremation of a Wormy Caryatid" allows for the cremation of what is left of African values as well as its unsavory past already being destroyed by angry worms (parasites? or revolutionaries?). Reflecting on mortality, this poem also deals with the question of permanence in our world. It furthers, even as it pursues other themes of time, corruption, betrayal, religious difference, and stresses the notion of vision and Soyinka Ogun's protégé:

> ... invisible in my gallery gloom.
> Threads heartwood, hours of skilled devotion
> Like spaces of the unknown creative
> Hands, now a womb of dust (63).

This image of (Soyinka) the artist is immanent in the primal artist who had etched the images of existence on the caryatid. Thus the images on the caryatid present us with the depressing montage of African history from the ancient times to the present. And the artist who is (at first) mortal forges a historical dialectics, a liberation narrative. The visionary who transforms the plastic art into a living poem becomes immortal as the pillar, metaphorically speaking, collapses. It is in this sense, in which the caryatid is a pillar, that the metaphor assumes poignancy and relevance. It is then not unlikely that Soyinka is foretelling the inevitable collapse of the worm infested (parasite-infested) Africa. That is the only way forward in the light of the virtual impossibility of self-redemption:

> Alas, what's gone is gone. The rain affirms the loss.
> Grace that was a fiery dying congeals.
> The skies have opened, gods and herogods
> Blot all traces of their erstwhile dance
> With mortals, uphold the love of pinpricks
> Mere woodworms may pronounce on golden realms.
> (*Mandela's Earth*, 69)

Symbolically, as in "Idanre," rain portends newness or harvest; but here it climaxes the destruction and termination of an order or disorder, which is aptly presented in *From Zia With Love*. What else can creep into a system better and deadlier than worms other than cocaine?

Indeed, even the logic which disorder ensures as evinced in Ogun's paradigm is overturned unapologetically in the context of *From Zia*

With Love by the irrepressible god of mischief, Esu. Is it that Soyinka the poet has grown impatient at last? Is it that Ogun, the god of endurance, has grown impatient surrendering hope to despair? Or is it that Africa now needs the action of a mischievous god to destroy, sorry, cremate its edifice before the rains in "Cremation of a Wormy Caryatid" can portend freshness and a new beginning?

Isara: A Voyage Around Essay is a significant invalidation of the conclusion (or the temptation to conclude) that everything of the past is a worm-eaten model that requires cremation. Some of them require more sacrifices to restore their value. By describing *Isara* as a chronicle of the events of the freedom movement in Africa, Bill Schermbrucker wittingly touches on Soyinka's interest in the betrayal of the ideals, which characterized the struggles of the Africans of the colonial period. He categorically describes his generation as a wasted one and *Isara* is an illustration of the zeal towards a cherished and ideal goal, which Soyinka's contemporaries and subsequent generation of Africans have allowed to be extinguished.

Isara is thus a post-colonialist discourse, which takes the totality of colonialism as its underlying *otherness* and presents an orderly tradition of Africa, celebration and humanity as instruments of its subversion.

It is for this reason that Essay's eventual meeting with his Pen pal betrays the term of reconciliation between the systems of option, but, more seriously, it further highlights the universality of Soyinka's historic vision as well as the *oneness* of all races.

Of course, by voyaging around Essay, rather than with Essay, Soyinka is reconstructing the value of historical artifacts as a contemporaneous and simultaneous source of quenching a burning thirst for action, change, and growth. The standard set by Soditan's generation should have been improved upon to the glory of Africa.

In other words, it is not all wormy caryatids that should be cremated. The content of the iron box bequeathed Soyinka by his father, even though infected by worms (roaches' eggs), tantalizes him and turns out to be for him a creative reminder of what had been and what should have been in Africa after the ravages wrought on it by the combined forces of colonialism and post-modern capitalism (and the capitalization of African weaknesses).

Told as a moral fable, as a fairy tale, as a myth, as a memoir, and as a tribute to a disappearing generation, Soyinka wittingly (or unwittingly) allows his mythical mind to construct logic to validate what would normally have served as an explanation of post-colonial disorder in Africa. It is not by accident that the images of Wade Cudeback's *Odyssey* on the rough wild of America and that of Soditan on the imaginary plains of his country (already in the hands of the colonial masters) fuse at some point.

Ten years before the Nobel, Soyinka had said in "The Writer in an African State" "a concern with culture strengthens society, but not a concern with mythology." This is because "the artist has always functioned in African society as the record of mores and experiences of his society and as the voice of vision in his own time" (13). This vague distinction between culture and mythology perhaps was necessary as part of his creative intent, but not because mythology can be isolated from any human culture nor can it ever be divorced from Soyinka's own vision of both personal and collective consciousness on the one hand, and on the other, as a means of wrenching the overall human society from its own depravity and illogicality.

The search for idealistic principles and harmony (symbolized in the Garden of Eden) in the human community is the reason for myth and religion, for mythical and religious extrapolation of historical and ethnographical events. Myth also offers, alongside history, explanation for similarities and differences by elevating socio-political problems into symbols, symbols that in turn are insight into the transcendental and the vision of the archetype, as Mircea Eliade puts it in *Images and Symbols* (174). Therefore, while it may be expedient to pursue local social problems and issues as literary themes, it is clear that it is only through mythology that we can reach the deeper discoveries that bind a community of people or even nations. By the same token, it is only mythology that can validate the racial reconciliation achieved between Essay and Wade in *Isara* at a point in the African colonial experience at which reconciliation was not permissible. At a different level, it can also validate the disenchantment, which clouds the dictatorial atmosphere of *From Zia With Love*.

As Soyinka richly explicates in *Myth, Literature and the African World*, the cultural and political hostility of the West towards Africa, which requires Africa to sublimate its existence to that of the West, draws from African writers

> the simultaneous act of eliciting from history, mythology and literature, for the benefit of both genuine aliens and alienated Africans, a continuing process of self-apprehension whose temporary dislocation appears to have persuaded many of its non-existence or its relevance . . . in contemporary world reality.

Myth ceases, at this point, to be a personal fad and becomes a necessary syntagmatic feature in the African artist's profound contextualization of the savagery that has been wrought on his psyche, essentially through a mytho-religious repudiation of his *being* and *becoming*. Yet as Soyinka's very strong and convincing espousal in his Nobel lecture shows, violence and destructiveness have been the inherent characteristics of the Euro-Christian and Arab-Islamic states while African societies in pre-colonial times had never gone to war with one another over religious differences. So if the goal of history is the complete liberation of man, then man's only chance lies, not in a religion or philosophy or mythology that is based on racism and violence but in the ethical precepts that spring from the worldview and authentic religions of the black races, "none of which is ever totally eradicated by the accretions of foreign faiths and implicit eurocentricism" (*Myth, Literature and the African World* 17). This is exemplified by the fact that African countries are easily disposed to forgive and collaborate with their erstwhile colonial masters in whose hands they suffered untold abominable fates as against the hatred and grudges still nursed by some European nations over their colonial nations of some two centuries ago.

The testing ground of this spirit of accommodation is Southern Africa. According to Soyinka, all lovers of peace must bring this spirit of accommodation into the modern world. It must be allowed into that spirit of human partnership, into a rational state of being.

It is only when this is done, only when that capacity for reconciliation simply demonstrated by every liberated black nation in Africa is achieved that the dilemma of the African in the post-modern African world can be resolved. And it must be resolved before the advent of the twenty-first century: "this and the end of racism, the eradication of human inequality . . . and the enthronement of universal suffrage—and peace" (20).

All of these are enunciated in the 1986 Noble Prize for Literature speech.

Works Cited

Eliade, Micrea. *Images and Symbols: Studies in Religious Symbolistic* New York: A Search Book Sheed and Ward, 1969.

Schermbrucker, B: "The Personal Fight for Freedom in Africa." Review of *Isara: A Voyage Around Essay. The Globe and Mail*, Saturday, January 6, 1990.

Soyinka, Wole: "The Writer in an African State." *Transition* 31, Vol. 6, June/July 1967.

_____. *Myth, Literature and the African World*. Cambridge: Cambridge University Press, 1976.

_____. *Ogun Abibiman*. London: Rex Collins, 1976.

_____. "This Past Must Address Its Present," 1986 Nobel Lecture. Statements: Occasional Papers of the Phelps-Stockes   F u n d , No. 3, March 1988.

_____. *Mandela's Earth and Other Poems*. New York: Random House, 1988.

_____. *Isara: A Voyage Around Essay*. Ibadan: Fountain Publications, 1989.

_____. *From Zia With Love*. Ibadan: Fountain Publication, 1992.

_____. *The Beatification of Area Boy: A Lagosian Kaleidoscope*. London: Methuen, 1995.

3

Wole Soyinka

Sixty Years Later into the Roads Taken

Kalu Uka

Two roads diverged in a yellow wood,
And sorry I could not travel both
And be one traveler, long I stood
And looked down one as far as I could
To where it bent in the undergrowth;
Then took the other, as just as fair,
And having perhaps the better claim,
Because it was grassy and wanted wear;
Though as for that the passing there
Had worn them really about the same
And both that morning equally lay
In leaves no step had trodden black.
Oh, I kept the first for another day!
Yet knowing how way leads on to way,
I doubted if I should ever come back.

I shall be telling this with a sigh
Somewhere ages and ages hence:
Two roads diverged in a wood, and I
I took the one less travelled by,
And that has made all the difference.[1]

—ROBERT FROST, 1874-1963

"All the difference" was made in the life of Akinwande Ishola Olu-wole Soyinka by his taking the "less travelled" roads in artistic creativity and its practical realizations in his society.

Robert Frost, himself an earlier Nobel Laureate, preceding Soyinka's arrival at that podium by more than twenty years, had tried to underscore the dilemma of choice for the artist in the symbolism of the road.

In all his works—be they essays on man and society or on art and politics; or on drama and cultural development; or on man and history; or on poetry, people, and places; or on the psychology of memories and growing-up—Soyinka set foot on many a path, before fixing on the *cerebral.* Certain densities developed in the complexity of his expression and his agonized engagement with discovering and making relevant what T.S. Eliot has characterized as the "objective correlate" of a given experience in the artist's sensibility.

Therefore, Soyinka has often been classified as "romantic" or "difficult" or "obscure." In the process, some of those who sincerely admire and would explicate his works in critical evaluations themselves become "difficult" and leave the uninitiated reader more baffled and frustrated than before such a reader came upon the supposed explication of Soyinka's art. At least this seemed to be the case, until critical doyens such as the late Donatus I. Nwoga came up with such essays as "Obscurantism and the Poet," which, while not holding up obscurantism *per se* as a virtue, urged greater effort in intellectual appreciation and perception of the socially relevant and linguistically experimental among Africa's artists as "children of two complex worlds"—the indigenous and the borrowed.

In his own "defence," as it were, often, Soyinka himself did not make matters easier. He took on a cynically contemptuous aspect; or became angrily ironical and sarcastic; indifferent or just plainly amused. All of which added to the controversy.

Examples abound in the *Art, Dialogue and Outrage* counter-pointed controversies—with J. P. Clark (now Bekederemo) after *America, Their America* (before the civil war), or again in *The Man Died* (post Nigerian civil war); then in the "era" of the formerly U.S.A-based critical "triumvirate" of Chinweizu, Jemie, and Madubuike via, as one "mediator critic" puts it, Achebe's *OKIKE*, thus instantly exacerbating the implications of variant critical approaches to creativity and comment. Then came the period of the "generational gap," "counter-valuation" theater and drama, when Femi Osofisan "countered" *The Strong Breed* with *No More the Wasted Breed*, backed by the "counter-valuation" criticism of 'Biodun Jeyifo in *The Truthful Lie*; thereafter reconciled and synthesized by the Nsukka school's Obi Maduakor's *Wole Soyinka: An Introduction To His Writing* and Jonathan Peters's *A Dance of Masks*.

Through all these it appeared as if the "roads" taken by Soyinka were undesirable; it appeared as if to be labelled "romantic" or "difficult" was in itself other than a label; for, as image, it did not stick; it appeared as if a critic's artificial and fancy classification could become an indelible cognomen; indeed, critics struggle as F.R. Leavis and the "New Critics" of that era struggled to outdo each other in claims of whose evaluation is the more valid, or acceptable.

Meanwhile, despite all these (or because of them?), Soyinka's brain, prolific as ever, and his pen, sharp as always, were feeding the field with more primary, creative fodder—so that secondary expedition of critical evaluation could continue unabated. At the University level, theater and drama departments had a surfeit of productions, performance tours, and discussions. For secondary schools, quick-witted, profit-seeking Certificate Examinations teachers were churning out Onibonoje-published "Soyinka-Made-Easys."

The high-water mark of critical views, commentaries, and exploitation of the Soyinka situation may have been reached in 1974, when Soyinka turned forty. By his fiftieth year, in 1984, 'Dapo Adelugba and other "Ogun children" were celebrating in a book of essays, *Before Our Very Eyes*, of that title. Then in 1986, when Soyinka turned fifty-two, comment, criticism, creativity, adverse and positive, coalesced into a world event—the Nobel Prize for Literature happened.

Soyinka had become the FIRST African to win the coveted Nobel prize in Literature. His chosen road had been recognized: the Yoruba matrix of his African vision had enlarged into an African highway, the original path through the Frostian "yellow wood"—or, as Africa's anthropological detractors used to call it, "the jungle pathways." It was not simply a matter of "something new out of Africa," but a matter of a twilight zone emanation, bringing together into a dazzling focus the victories of Soyinka in art, Samora Marchel in death; Dele Giwa in a fire bomb, and Nelson Mandela moving nearer to freedom for self, race, and continent. That October 1986 was a golden memory indeed.

Then came 1994. The Diamond Year. By the time of the Golden Jubilee in 1984, the road to the Nobel, if it existed, was perhaps only a chink. Its laser-like beam was sharp, but not yet flooding. Since the floodlight of 1986, the rhythms of the dance have changed their pattern. Controversies and uncertainties virtually turned into encomiums. Dissension turned into celebration; romanticism into realism, masks into faces, and pathways into roads.

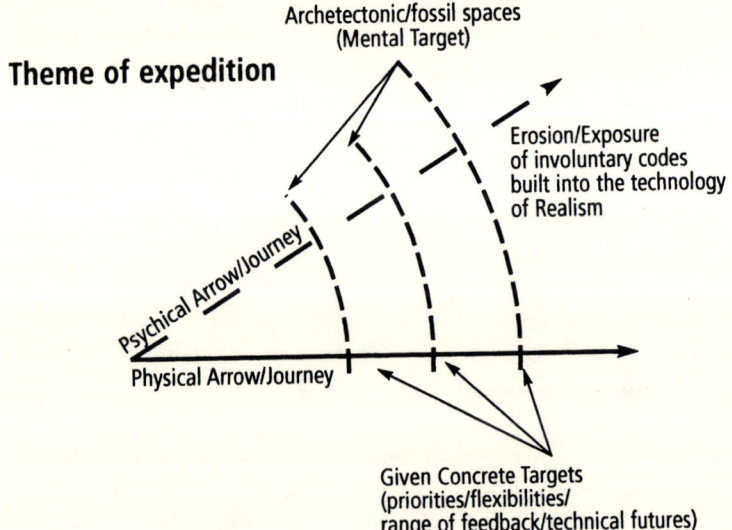

Theme of expedition

Archetectonic/fossil spaces
(Mental Target)

Erosion/Exposure
of involuntary codes
built into the technology
of Realism

Psychical Arrow/Journey

Physical Arrow/Journey

Given Concrete Targets
(priorities/flexibilities/
range of feedback/technical futures)

In the above diagram, Wilson Harris has expounded his idea of the "theme of expedition" (designed by Rutherford and Peterson)[2] into "resources for new (creative) writing in English coming out of heterogenous backgrounds, material and spiritual." Through such "exploration," one may now try to re-examine Soyinka's "Mobius Strip," take the tail of the snake out of its mouth, release Ezeulu's python from Oduche's box, and perceive (as Alexander Animalu et al[3] tried to) that "symbol of optimism . . ., that illusion of a kink in the circle and possible centrifugal escape from the eternal cycle of Karmas that has become the evil history of man . . ."[4]

The physical arrow represents the "expedition into society." In Soyinka's *The Road*, there are three crucial "protagonists of the road"—Kotonu, Professor, and Murano. They undertake the journey, partly as an actual physical journey (where Kotonu, the Driver, and Samson, his conductor started) and partly really as a spiritual expedition, especially for Professor (an expelled Christian Sunday School Teacher fallen from grace) and Murano (an Ogun Festival Mask Dancer supposedly killed in a road accident by Kotonu while a possessed dancer). The physical journey is also "the plot of the conventional play . . . the conscious structure" wherein Soyinka achieves the "concrete targets . . . which are involuntary codes (which) are in fact animistic though masked as social, religious and historical." In *The Road* there are codes of fear that lead to a number of drastic actions in the unfolding of the follies of man in his tragic violence: Kotonu is afraid after killing the god and donning the mask to save himself and Samson from the possible lynching the mob of celebrants would have visited on them (especially in Nigeria, a Driver must escape instantly from the scene of a fatal accident or there will be mob justice—as Achebe's poem, "Lazarus" shows, and Soyinka's Say Tokyo Kid poem also shows); then again, Samson is afraid, though not as nervous as Kotunu, that an accident is imminent because Kotonu had not killed a dog ("Ogun's meat"); again Say Tokyo Kid acts against Professor by stabbing him, out of desperate fear as Murano, the Mask and Dancer, begins to "come alive" and Say Tokyo Kid himself is smashed against a bench by the needly re-possessed Murono before he, Murano, finally dies. Fears here produce a heap of dead and dying at the end reminiscent of *Hamlet's* final scenes. For Professor, his nemesis is produced by the "code of cultural and spiritual superiority" which he had assumed over all the lay-abouts, apprentices, driver's license touts, and low-class Policemen like Particulars Joe.

From the diagram also it can be seen that the psychical arrow goes off at a tangent from the physical arrow, so that an area of space is created between them. "The psychical arrow is sprung from the subjective imagination (of the Author) as it seeks to cohabit with the actual physical journey and turn it into a visionary quest with a capacity to unravel self-deceptions and to sense eclipsed potentialities."[5]

If Wole Soyinka is called, not pejoratively, a romantic, it may well be deserved when one considers the level of the "visionary quest" immanent and eminent in his works. The "self-deception" of Professor in *The Road* is unravelled by such a quest. The reluctance to desist from the lure of the flesh in an Elesin-Oba in *Death and the King's Horseman* is unravelled by the quest which Olunde, spiritually superior, fulfills in the end; Daodu and Segi eclipse Oba Danlola in *Kongi's Harvest* when they stop his and Kongi's "royal drums" in mid-dance by such a quest, and, in their case, secure the future. This, then, is the role of the psychical arrow.

Rutherford and Petersen elaborates,

> . . . a major task of creativity is to penetrate complex self-deceptions as well as complex values with which we have invested objects or orders that we have come to take for granted. There are two ways in which it is possible to react to this penetration or 'erosion of values.' One is by submitting to it as absolute loss or oppression . . . . The other is by anticipating, in the logic of the creative imagination, an EXPOSURE of involuntary codes by which we are conscripted, and therefore digesting by degrees a state of change which, left to its own natural or unnatural devices, would overwhelm us in the long run . . . .[6]

Soyinka, it appears to this contributor, has seemed (and been classed as) "difficult" or "romantic" or both, because of people's poor appreciation of the meaning or significance of the "space created *between* the *psychical* and the *physical arrows.*" Within that area are "contrasts between cultural biases and the creative imagination endeavouring to free itself from those biases," in effect "representing a person's mind when his creative imagination seeks to break or revise the concrete targets." In *Death and the King's Horseman*, Mr. Pilkings, the ignorant British District Officer, almost like Captain Winterbottom in *Arrow of God*, is firmly locked within his own prejudices and limited horizon of a disparate irrationality which does not understand, nor cares to admit the possibility of other civilizations' irrationality. So, for him, neither Olunde's spiritual journey nor that of Elesin-Oba makes sense, and he can don the Death-Mask with perfect sarcastic aplomb and entertain his civilized guests in the Ball or Garden Party. Even the drums, the heartbeat of that Yoruba nation, touch him but superficially. If there is any contrast between his attitude and that of the women in the market place, it is only an observed dramatic irony on the part of the unprejudiced audience. Pilkings cannot dialogue with the primitive, jungle people over whom he is Her Majesty's District Officer in the middle of an international war—that is, violence of a technologically high order.

Notes

1. Robert Frost, "The Road Not Taken," culled from L. Perrine, *Literature Structure: Sound and Sense* (New York: Harcourt, Brace and World Inc., 1970) p. 594, as recorded by the Author on L.P. Caedmon TC 1060.
2. Anna Rutherford and Kirsten Holst Petersen, *The Enigma of Values—An Introduction* (Aarhus, Denmark: Dangaroo Press, 1975) p. 12.
3. Alexander Arimalu, et al. in an essay on Achebe's 60th Birthday "Event, "Eagle On Iroko," Nsukka, Feb. 1990.
4. Jonathan A. Peters, *A Dance of Masks* (Washington, D. C.: Three Continent Press, 1978), p. 10.
5. Rutherford and Petersen, *Enigma*, p. 14
6. Rutherford and Petersen p. 15.

Works Cited

Animalu, Alexander. Essay contributed to "Eagle on Iroko" on Chinua Achebe's Sixtieth Year Celebration, UNN, February 1990.

Chinweizu et al. *Towards The Decolonization of African Literature.* Enugu: Fourth Dimension Press, 1980.

Clark, J.P. *America, Their America,* London: Andre Deutsch, 1964.

Frost, Robert "The Road Taken" in L. Perrine. *Literature Structue: Sound and Sense.* New York; Harcourt, Bruce and Inlord Inc. 1970.

Jeyifo Biodun. *The Truthful Lie: Essay On The Sociology of Literature.* London/Port of Spain: New Bencon, 1985.

Maduako, Obi. *Wole Soyinka: An Introduction To His Writings.* Ibadan: Heinemann, 1991.

Nwoga, Donatus. "Obscurity and Commitment. In Modern African Poetry. *African Literature Today,* 6, 1982.

Osofisan, Femi. *No More The Wasted Breed.* In *Morountodun and Other Plays.* Ikeja: Longman, 1982.

Peters, Jonathan A. *A Dance of Masks.* Washington. D. C: Three Continent Press.

Rutherford, Anna and Kirsten Holst Petersen. *The Enigma of Values,—An Introduction.* Aarhus Denmarten: Dangaroo Press, 1975.

Soyinka, Wole. *Art, Dialogue and Outrage.* Ibadan: New Horn Press, 1968.

_____. *The Round.* London: Oxford University Press, 1965.

_____. *Death and The Kings Horseman.* London: Methuen, 1978.

_____. *Kongi's Harvest.* London: Oxford University Press, 1967.

_____. *The Strong Breed.* In *Collected Plays.* London: Oxford, 1973.

_____. *The Man Died:* Prison Notes. London: Rex Collins, 1972.

4

The Organization of Symbols in Wole Soyinka's *From Zia With Love*

SIMON OBIKPEKO UMUKORO

"Wole Soyinka is a play-wright and poet who in a wide cultural perspective and poetic overtones fashions the drama of existence."[1] This is how the Swedish academy presents Soyinka, the recipient of the Nobel Prize for Literature in 1986. The academy here reaffirms the literary and social/ethical values of the works of Soyinka which were published before he was awarded the prize, but the comment could have been made with equal truth of his works published after the award, especially his play, *From Zia With Love* (1992).

It is my purpose in this essay to examine this play and show that it possesses basic social values which are dramatized by the choice and organization of a number of symbols. In addition, I will examine the strengths and weaknesses of the play.

In a note to the reader/audience, Soyinka remarks that "the play (*From Zia With Love*) is based on an actual event which took place in

47

Nigeria in 1984, under the Military Rule of Generals Buhari and Idiagbon." He cautions, however, that the play "is an entire product of the imagination, and makes no claim whatever to any correlation with actuality."2

In other words, *From Zia With Love* is not a historical document and does not pretend to be a factual account of the events of the regime of Generals Buhari and Idiagbon. Although it utilizes those events as raw ingredients of creation, the play is an artistic, verbal imitation of life. It recreates and explores the dilemmas of life in Nigeria under the rule of Generals Buhari and Idiagbon.

This may be a suitable subject for psychological drama, but Soyinka treats it mainly as social drama. For the concern of the play is not so much to portray the interior life of individual characters, their personal and moral degeneration, as it is to illuminate and expose the immoral character of Nigerian society under Generals Buhari and Idiagbon. And this is done, to a large extent, through the exploitation of certain well-organized symbols, the most frequently used one being that of imprisonment.

In this play, Soyinka attempts to show that the Buhari-Idiagbon regime was a scourge on the Nigerian people. In particular, he tries to show that under their rule, Nigerians were condemned to an imprisoned and perilous life. He therefore employs the symbol of imprisonment to express, in very strong language, the disastrous impact of that rule on the masses of the Nigerian people.

For example, the setting of the play is a prison yard with a row of cells in half-arch on the one side and a large cell on the other. The inmates are encaged in those cells which are fortified by cell bars. The prison is separated from the rest of the world by a high stony wall and a lagoon which in recent times has become inaccessible as it has been covered by water-hyacinth weeds.

Attempts by the outside world to have contact with the prison community have all been aborted by the weeds. A good example is the attempt to use canoes propelled by paddles or outboard motors. The weeds "fouled up the propellers and the paddles couldn't fight them." As a result, "not one canoe has been able to find its way anywhere close to the wall" (27).

Even strong swimmers who tried to find a passage through the weeds with waterproof packs gave up; while the only Ijaw boy who persisted drowned one Sunday morning. His legs got: "more and more entangled in those slimy long roots (of the weeds) as if some hidden monster kept dragging him down" (27). Thus, the prison community is cut off completely from the rest of the world.

This is a symbolic representation of Nigeria in the days of Generals Buhari and Idiagbon. As in the case of all military regimes in this country, when the two generals took over power through a *coup d'etat*, they closed all Nigerian borders and no one could come into or leave the country. They therefore transformed the country into a cyst where no escape was possible.

As with setting, so with character and characterization. It is a constituent part of the symbolism of imprisonment in the play. The characters are the very types that operate well in a prison community. For example, there are prison officers such as Superintendent and Warders. There are prisoners who are also the focus of the play. They are the special inmates of the General Cell and those of Cell "C."

The inmates of the General Cell are a mixed-bag of criminals. They include "first offenders and hardened convicts, political detainees and awaiting trial." Some are "disabled, semi-crazed or eccentric as well as the restless and listless" (1).

Among them is a group of prisoners who govern the community. The group constitutes the supreme organ of government in the prison, which is called "The Eternal Ruling Council" (The Armed Forces Ruling Council in a thin disguise).

The Council is headed by the Cell Commandment who is called Commander-in-Chief. He has a deputy called Number Two and a Director of Security. Then, there are Civilian Ministers such as the Ministers of Labour, Agriculture, Health, Information and Culture, Water Resources, Home Affairs, and Education.

This organisational structure is a duplication of the structure and hierarchy of any military regime in Nigeria, with special reference to the regime of Generals Buhari and Idiagbon. What Soyinka has done in this play is to put Generals Buhari and Idiagbon in prison and make them rule over a prison community. Thus, the prison community is a metaphor for Nigerian society over which the two generals ruled. Put differently, the prison community is Nigerian society at large. Both of them are one and the same thing. As the Minister of Education puts it "outside or inside, the same thing" (16).

Once we respond accurately to the image of the prison, it becomes fairly easy to see what Soyinka is driving at. A prison is noted for the suppression of the individual's rights. In a prison, a large measure of an inmate's freedom and rights is suppressed. So, Nigeria is a prison because the government embarks upon measures which tend to suppress the fundamental rights of the individual, such as the freedom of speech and the right to justice.

Take, for instance, the promulgation of Decree 2 of 1982, gazetted as "State Security Decree." By the provisions of this decree, prominent politicians of the "Second Republic" were detained in prison custody indefinitely without trial. Even when government bowed to pressure, the politicians were tried not in ordinary courts of law, but by military tribunals, whose claim to the dispensation of justice was questionable. The argument here is not that the politicians were blameless but that their detention without trial as well as their trial by military tribunals is a violation of their inalienable right to justice.

The history of Decree 4 of 4th April 1984 is equally telling. Gazetted as "Public Officers (Protection Against False Accusation) Decree," Decree 4 set out to gag the Nigerian Press. The journalists, Nduka Irabor and Tunde Thompson of the *Guardian* Press, who dared to exercise their right, were tried on trumped-up charges and jailed under the provisions of the decree.

The dramatist is burdened by the suppression of the individual's natural rights in Nigeria exemplifies by such oppressive moves as the infamous Decrees 2 and 4 of 1984. Thus, he employs the symbolism of imprisonment that lucidly evokes the problem for the reader's condemnation, indirectly asking for an alternative Nigerian society in which the fundamental rights of the individual are respected.

However, the symbol presents an inherent contradiction, especially when faced with the demands of the reality in which the story is situated. In reality, a prisoner is under the control and authority of another person or persons, normally, prison officers. This is at variance with the office of Head-of-State whose authority is final and supreme. Thus, if we ask, "can the prisoner make a Head of State? The answer is no. But Soyinka affirms it in the play, perhaps to suggest that Generals Buhari and Idiagbon were caught by their own decrees. Whatever it is, the problem is how to unite two states of being which are mutually exclusive. Even so, it is insisted in the play that Generals Buhari and Idiagbon were not subject to their own decrees. Hence, their "power is even rottener (because) the very rule it makes it breaks" (92).

Furthermore, the symbol of imprisonment is rather severe and negative on the regime of Generals Buhari and Idiagbon, as it allows no room to accept any of their policies. Let it be noted that the Nigerian society which the two generals met was near anarchy. It was a society on the brink of collapse due to indiscipline in high and low places. In fact, the accusation of opposition parties against Alhaji Shehu Shagari is that his inability to discipline members of his cabinet led to the collapse of the Second Republic.

In that circumstance, some of Generals Buhari and Idiagbon's policies, such as the ones against smuggling, corruption, currency trafficking, and the whole concept of "WAI,"(the acronym for war against indiscipline) had merit and deserve to be appreciated. Yet, Soyinka rejects all as "banalities" (88). This total rejection is not objective enough and, in fact, is an example of throwing out the baby with the bath water.

The most important right of the individual which every free society strives to protect is the right to life. It is the very foundation upon which all other rights rest, as only the living can claim the right to speech and justice. *From Zia With Love* explores how the regime of Generals Buhari and Idiagbon violated this fundamental right of the individual. This act of violation is what Soyinka describes in the note to the reader as the "actual event" that inspired in the play.

In 1984, the government of Generals Buhari and Idiagbon promulgated "The Miscellaneous Decree," which prescribed the death penalty for a variety of crimes such as arson against public buildings; damage to public property, including electric cables, telephone wires, and oil pipelines; and dealing in hard drugs, like cocaine, heroin, and LSD. In pursuance of this decree, three cocaine convicts—Batholomew Owo, 26, Bernard Ogedengbe, 29, and Lawal Ojulope, 30—were tried and executed in 1985.

Soyinka's play is based on this incident, which it also recreates faithfully in the episode concerning the inmates of Cell "C." Thus, in this incident, Miguel, Domingo, Detiba, and Emuke are convicted and sentenced to deaths for drug trafficking. They are imprisoned in Cell "C," awaiting execution; and in the final scenes of the play, they are executed.

The incident is a classic example of a senseless, cold-blooded murder. This is because drug trafficking is not a capital crime like murder or armed robbery, which may require the death penalty. As *The New Nigerian* points out in an editorial, even though "drugs such as cocaine, heroine, LSD and even the home-grown Indian hemp are capable of doing great damage to the health of the individual and the society, yet it will be stretching the analogy much too far to presume that drug pushing is just as grievous as wielding a gun or a machete and shooting or hacking down a victim."[3]

Compare, for instance, the way drug traffickers are punished elsewhere. For example, the play informs us that in the United States of America, they do not execute drug traffickers. Rather, "they slap them on the wrist with a few years which they hardly ever complete as parole takes care of most of it." Also, the Americans turn a blind eye on the Mujihadeen peddlers in Afghanistan because they are fighting communist rule; and in North Pakistan, you can buy an armoured tank with a packet of stuff and collect your change with a mortar or two" (58).

The contrast is demonstrated further in the play in the first part of the allegory of a business deal in Kótópó and Kòtòpò which Sebe Irawe recounts for Wing Commander as follows: "Now let's say I make the same deal in Kótópó as in Kòtòpò. In Kótópó, the punishment is two years suspended sentence, while in Kòtòpò—gestures across his throat" (50).

In this allegory, Kótópó where the punishment is "two years suspended sentence" represents the United States of America while Kòtòpò where the victim is beheaded represents Nigeria under Generals Buhari and Idiagbon. The question which is posed by this juxtaposition of events is, why is it that in Nigeria the death penalty is imposed on an offense which carries "two years suspended sentence" elsewhere, or as Miguel puts it: "Why do we have to shoot one another here?"

The play seems to answer the question where Sebe says, "That's army government for you" (50). So, "we have to shoot one another here" because we are governed by a military law which is rooted in violence, a brutal law that thrives on the wanton destruction of human life. And Emuke adds, "na soja man de do de kin dabaru nonsense wey put we for this kin mess" (62).

What makes the case more objectionable is that the drug peddlers are convicted and sentenced to death by a retroactive law, "a law enacted to deal with an offence committed when such a law did not exist" (p. 92). The play offers an insight into the operations of this law in the second part of the allegory when Sebe says:

> When one started that very business deal, Alhaji Kótópó was in charge, but when you wake up the next morning and General Kòtòpò has taken over in Potopo and the rules are changed overnight. Everything becomes Kótópó-Kòtòpò-Kótópó and you find yourself floundering in pòtòpòtò. (50)

In the instance quoted above, Alhaji Kótópó represents Alhaji Shehu Shagari, President of Nigeria in the Second Republic, while General Kotopo is General Buhari who wrenched power from him through a *coup d'etat*. The allegory may therefore be recast as follows: the offense was committed when Alhaji Shagari was President and at that time, it was not a capital offense. However, when General Buhari took over from him, he not only changed the law, imposing a death sentence, he caused the presumed offenders in Shagari's period to suffer the supreme penalty.

The point which the allegory is designed to clarify, therefore, is that according to the law of the land, drug trafficking was not a capital offense. It became one only according to the will of Generals Buhari and Idiagbon. Their will is not reliable. It is a wayward will which goes "backwards and forwards in time" (78). Their patron god is Esu, that "small but potent god who throws a stone today and it kills a man next week" (78-79).

Soyinka's view on the issue is that the drug peddlers do not deserve to die because "no one has a right to take a human life under a law which did not exist at the time of a presumed offence" (93). Their execution therefore is an act of cold-blooded murder; and it pinpoints the immoral character of the regime. Emuke makes the point clearer when he says:

> All I know is dat dis na wicked country to do something like this. We know some country wey, if you steal they cut off your hand. But everybody know that in advance. So, if you steal, na your choice. Every crime get in proper punishment. But if you wait until man commit crime, then you come change the punishment, dat one na *foul*. Na proper *foul*. I no know any other country wey dat kin ting dey happen. (29)

However, the dramatist knows what his character does not know. He knows that "this kin ting" has happened in Pakistan, where President Zia concocted a law to murder his predecessor in office, Ali Bhutto, one of the incidents from which the play derives its title.

In fact, he offers a long list of global dictators (Sekou Toure, Pinnochet, Arap Moi, Idi Amin, Houphouet Boigny, and other Arab and Asian dictators). Soyinka's aim is to show that Generals Buhari and Idiagbon belong to this group because they are also murderous statesmen.

It is therefore proper to read the play as a sequel to *A Play of Giants* (1984). Not only because it repeats or updates the list of global dictators in the earlier play,[4] but also because it extends the story of that play to Nigeria, a story of "the terrifying evil of power and what happens when men acquire power over the lives of others."[5]

The other element in the structure of the drug incident is Wing Commander. He is linked to the drug convicts by polarity, the similarity of opposites such as day and night.

Wing Commander is a drug baron with business deals in various parts of the world, including Asia and Europe. The play tries to offer a record of his exploits in this business. For example, he was the key figure in "The Old London Exploit" in which two diplomatic bags of marijuana, intercepted by Scotland Yard, disappeared from the Nigerian Commission in London; and as a cover up, the Ministry of External Affairs back home was burnt down. He helped out in "The Affair in Milan." His minder at the embassy got through to the courier in prison and arranged his escape.

These are mere "peanut pickings of kindergarten days" (72) by comparison with the deal he is executing in the present world of the play. By this deal, he receives "a consignment of fifty kilograms of prime grade cocaine from Zia, the former Pakistani dictator, and ships same here for Sebe to sell and distribute, the other incident from which the title of the play is derived. It appears the consignment of drugs is lost in transit to pirates; hence, he temporarily suspends his studies in Pakistan and returns home to track down the pirates, retrieve his goods, and arrange an appropriate punishment for those responsible for the loss.

Here, then, is a person who more than anybody else deserves to be punished for drug offenses because he is doing more damage to the health of the society. But he is not punished. Rather, he is protected by the regime because he is a senior army officer and a member of "The Eternal Ruling Council." He tells Sebe: "We military stick together. We may settle scores among ourselves from time to time, even bloodily, but in the end, we close ranks" (74).

This is a contrasts to the way the regime treats the inmates of Cell "C": who are civilians. While it protects the military officer, it hounds the civilians to death by a retroactive law. Obviously, the regime is unjust as it governs by the law of discrimination.

I have argued that in Soyinka's *From Zia With Love*, the symbol of imprisonment is used as an element of structure and organization. The other dramatic elements such as setting and character derive their significance from this symbol and in turn reinforce it. The use of this symbol serves Soyinka well to attack the negation of ethical values in Nigerian society by the regime of Generals Buhari and Idiagbon and thus indirectly asks for an alternative society in which the fundamental rights of the individual are protected. However, the symbol is rather severe on that regime. It is also inherently contradictory. In conclusion, I wish to reaffirm that in regard to the organization of symbols, the strengths and weaknesses of Soyinka's play are intricately interwoven.

Notes

1. Quoted in Ronald Austin Wells, "Wole Soyinka" in *Statements: Occasional Papers of the Phelps-Stokes Fund*, Number 3, March 1988, p. i.
2. Wole Soyinka, *From Zia With Love* (Ibadan: Fountain Publication, 1992) Further page references are to this edition.
3. The *New Nigerian* in an editorial quoted in *Newswatch*, May 13, 1985, p. 12.
4. In *A Play of Giants* 1984; the list contains dictators such as Hitler, Pinochet, Galtier, Pol, Nguema, and Idi Amin.
5. Yakubu Nassidi, Review of Wole Soyinka's *A Play of Giants, in Saiwa: A Journal of Communication*, 3 (1985): 94.

5

Anarchism and the Nigerian State in Soyinka' *From Zia With Love*

Tanimu Abubakar

In his call for the suppression of the Enrages in 1793, the Girandian Brissot associated the action of the Enrages with anarchism and, in the process, defined the features of anarchy as:

> Laws that are not carried into effect, authorities without force and despised, crime unpunished, property attacked, the safety of the individual violated, the morality of the people corrupted, no constitution, no government, no justice, these are the features of anarchy.[1]

In the imaginative and polemical writings of Wole Soyinka, there is a consistent pillorying of Nigeria as a lawless society fast receding towards anarchy in the Girondinian fashion. In *From Zia With Love*, Soyinka adds a deeply penetrating and harassingly disturbing dimension to the ascension of anarchy in the Nigerian society.

In fact, Soyinka's encapsulation of the problematic of social chaos in *From Zia With Love* projects the paradox that those in authority are themselves criminals and yet use the force of authority to punish other criminals. This pursuit of the scapegoat, which Soyinka treats in the fate of Eman and Lazarus in *The Strong Breed* and *Interpreters* respectively, is succinctly conveyed in the conversation between the Wing Commander and Sebe over the "missing" bag of cocaine. In fact, the execution of Emuke, Detiba, and Miguel, the three convicted drug pushers, illustrates further Soyinka's general concern with the status of the scapegoat as a carrier of the guilt of others and as a testifier to the assassination of conscience and morality in the affairs of politics in Nigeria and throughout the Third World.

In Soyinka's *From Zia With Love,* we are thus dealing with dictatorship as the embodiment of the use of force to assert authority. This dimension of anarchy is rooted in the politics of the despot, the *Kongis,* of the third worlds who replace participation and civilized conduct with naked violence. Soyinka projects this criticism of political disorientation by making the principal character, the Wing Commander, the medium of collective self-confession. According to the Wing Commander, "between Sekou Toure, Zia, Pinochet, Moi, Boigny and other third world and Arab one party-state dictators," there is no difference. If we add the Bokasa of *Opera Woyonsi*, we get a universal variant of totalitarianism, which the bane of the crisis of under-development in the Third World. The specific Nigerian variant of anarchy in its strange totalitarian form is depicted in detail in Sebe's definition of the "country" in a conversation with the Wing Commander:

> My friend, we know how you people make, unmake laws to suit yourselves . . . . Not that we are complaining but, General, look at it from a businessman's point of view . . . . Now let's say I make the same deal in Kótópó as in Kòtòpò. In Kótópó the punish is two years suspended sentence, while in Kòtòpò) (*gestures across his throat*). That's Army government for you, all inside one country like this one. And it doesn't end there. When one started that very business deal, Alhaji Kótópó was

in charge, but then you wake up the next morning and General Kòtòpò has taken over in Pótókó and the rules are changed overnight. Everything becomes Kòtòpò- Kótópó-Kòtòpò and you find yourself floundering in pòtòpótó. Well, that's business life for you, but I mean, its not fair. It lacks stability and without stability you can't do business. (49-50)

Here, Soyinka uses tonal contrast and pun to demonstrate the solemn conversion of the attributes of civilized society into the language of organized crime. In between the undulating essence of Kótópó and the depth of the brawl in Kòtòpò, Soyinka paints the picture of a society in a perpetual state of confusion and retardation. This deformity assumes even a larger-than life posture in the final crush into pòtòpótó, a symbol of putrefaction. In the very lyricism of its rendition, the above quoted passage is an *oriki* of a society compelled to exist in a permanent state of childhood. The cynicism it raises is sharp and the despair concealed overbearing. Typical of anarchy, the rottenness of the wider society is conveyed in the manner in which the world of crime subsumes the civil society and distorts the parameters of ethical conduct into the accepted code of sealing deals. Not surprisingly, what the Nigerian society lacks (fairness, justice, and good government) the under-world possesses, not as attributes of cohesive social existence but as the very negation of humane values. Sebe's eloquent enunciation demonstrates the fact that the underworld itself operates on the principle of law and procedure and enforces discipline, ironically, on precedence. In this context, Sebe chastizes the student who dupes him and gives him a dateline within which to comply with the accepted convention of criminality in these words:

Your partner in crime has confessed his own part. You see your own type is stupid. That's the difference between you and your accomplice. He was tempted. He fell. Even Adam our forefather was not perfect. But your contact knows it couldn't last forever. He borrowed the stuff, that's what he did. Borrowed it. Made himself some bread. He knew he had to pay it back sooner or later. So when our people caught up with him, he tendered. Guilty with reason, he pleaded. But they told him, no, guilty with interest. They calculated the interest.

He paid back the capital. And he paid the interest. But you, what did you do with your capitals. (39)

In this passage Soyinka illustrates the fact that in anarchistic societies, method, order, socialization, and discipline exist in the realm of criminality. Also in this passage, Sebe teaches the youth the universal law of crime and, in doing so, appropriates the very language of religion and the basic foibles of man to convey the universality of temptation and ambition. In human terms, man is imperfect; Adam failed and therefore needed forgiveness. But in the world of crime, salvation lies in creative utilization of criminal opportunity, in making good bread without disrupting the equilibrium of the system.

In *From Zia with Love*, Soyinka also illustrates the fact that criminality, the epidemic that afflicts the Third World, is also sustained by a patterned order and by rat-race. In the world of the criminal force is rarely, but fatally when used to settle score. What is used in large degree is the trickster motif; the crafty and creative survive while the arrogant and forceful are destroyed. In other words, in the world of the criminal, we deal with the survivor and the doomed. The world of the hooligan is sufficient unto itself and operates in a chain of graduation. The Youth's testimony of his entrance into crime provides poignant encapsulation of the ontology of the species as this passage illustrates:

Youth: Yes, that was the start of my disaster. He used to fence us that's how I got to know him. We stole valuables from our parents, we left the door open for one another, it was easy. Sebe would buy the goods from us. Stereos, jewellery, even motor tyres and spare parts. Then one day he asked me if I would like to earn some really big money . . . well, from then on, it was one thing leading to another. We got on well. He treated me like a son. (69)

In *A Walk In The Night*, La Guma paints the picture of the society that disorientes its youth to the extent that children play "war game." In *From Zia With Love*, Soyinka treats this malaise of social dislocation as a function of anarchy. Matrimonial relations are here reversed so that children not only prey upon their parents, as their type do in

Orwell's *1984*, but associate, paradoxically, parental care with the materialistic exploitation of crime lords. In other words, the children that take to crime are internally generated and this shows a pathetic negation of the process of the regeneration of the human values. For Nigeria, this crisis of growth is tragic because it indicates a stultification that dangerously reminds us of an inglorious past or a despairing present a bleak future, and all of these questioning the authenticity of our independence. It is in this sense that Femi Ojo-Ade argues that, "the unfurling of flags and the chanting of anthems has not awakened the vibrant air of freedom but the wasteland of new slavery." (198)

Societies with anarchistic inclinations not only recede to their inglorious past but resurrect them in a histrionic fashion. *From Zia With Love* illustrates that Nigeria, which it consciously reflects, is fast receding into an enlarged state of barbarism and lawlessness.

The Youth's confession comes close to being an expression of angst, except that the sympathy it seeks to evoke is intended to secure leniency from the Youth's interrogators. It is in fact the Youth's capacity to manipulate situations that marks him out as the epitome of what anarchy institutes in the psyche of the younger population. This situation is similar to that of Shukov in Solzhenistyn's *One Day in The Life of Ivan Denisovish*. Both are survivors, masterfully cutting corners to reach their goals.

In the life of the survivor, there is no morality, only dubious expediency functions. As stated in the song of the social prophylactic, we are advised to "remember it is all basic: man must wack":

> Civil law or stern decree
> The private sector remains elastic
> Man must wack
>
> The question to be or not to be
> is precarious
> Leave all morals to the cleric
> Man must wack. (44)

Moral degeneracy, then, is a function of social and material deprivation and the pressure of existence dictate the need for elastic apprehension of chaos as the common denominator in man's social life. In this song Soyinka roots the immorality of the life of the "dregs of the city" who "merely try to earn a dishonest living" as Yusuf Idris does in "Waiting for Laila." As a survivor, the Youth does not only manouvres himself out of the deadly clutches of Sebe by getting himself arrested and detained, he also secures his life from the brutality of inmates by promising to inform them about the whereabouts of the 50 kg of cocaine in dispute between Sebe and the Wing Commander.

While the Youth is a survivor, the Wing Commander is doomed. He is officious and relies more on power than on wit and in the world of the criminals wit counts more than power. In an attempt to compel Sebe to disclose the whereabouts of the 50 kg of cocaine, the Wing Commander resorts to threat:

W. COMM: Just remember what is at stake. For me. And for you. We military stick together, remember that. We may settle scores among ourselves from time to time, even bloodily, but in the end, we close ranks. When we do . . .

SEBE: . . . We bloody civilians become the scapegoats.

W. COMM: I'm glad you know that. (74)

Paradoxically, the incapacity of the Wing Commander to play the game *diplomatically* makes him a prey to Sebe's incredible capacity to appropriate mythical equation to lure his victim into a trap. The Wing Commander is found dead on the road, some parts of his body removed for ritual purposes. His body is recognized not by his uniform or official car, the symbols of his power, but by the wrapper and the black cap, the symbols of expiating Esu.[2] The Wing Commander thus becomes the paradoxical victim of power—this time around, the power of cultism. Soyinka's inclination to associate bloodshed with sacrifice does not apply here precisely because in the Wing Commander's death, it is invidious rivalry that is settled. It is a case of elimination, as coldblood ritual murder. In projecting the use of ritual and juju to settle scores, Soyinka satirizes another dimension of anarchy: unbridled religious charlatanism. In *From Zia With Love*, the Jero-type[3] religious charlatanism is extended, this time around, to the realm of traditional religion. Esu is thus invoked as a patron, a source of protecting one faction of criminals against the other. In fact, Soyinka's satire of this charlatanism is poignant for the simple reason that all metaphysical forces are now subjected to perversion for the sole purpose of "making some bread." Sebe tells the Wing Commander that he is protean as far as the role of religion in the pursuit of wealth is concerned:

> There has to be some honesty in the world, whatever people say. How can I call myself Alhaji? It wouldn't be right. I went to Saudi, I went to Jeddah on pilgrimage, but it was strictly a business pilgrimage. (47)

Appropriating religious paradigm for the pursuit of "dishonest" living gives the Nigerian character a banal attribute. In other words, the moral perversion of Nigerian social life goes hand-in-glove with spiritual vandalization. The level of social and psychological decay is so deep that existence in Nigeria, which the play reflects, is equivalent to the herculean task of "finding peace in a place of heartache." Soyinka indeed raises a toast to an arid land:

> Let's raise a toast to our control free
> And so glorious
> Never-say-die-till-you're-dead Republic—
> Man must wack. (44)

In *From Zia With Love*, Soyinka deals with the collapse of the state itself, with a situation of total absence of authority, firmness, and order. The dearth of the attributes of civilized society and justice defeats the sense of purpose in each person, leading social life into a paradoxical negativity. The series of enactments in the general cell which mimics a cabinet meeting illustrates this negativity of social life. In the scenes enacted, "health" is equated with "death," "information" with "falsehood," and "security" with "tortures, detention." The irony involved in these depictions is not the presence of these social problems but the permanence of their "stability" in our collec-

63

tive existence and the abrogation of a future. Soyinka deliberately makes the prison a place riddled with extortion racket; it is a microcosm of the outer society. The pitiful image of the wider society is graphically captured in the wretched human salad that inhabits the prison. "The inmates," we are told, "are a mixed bag." First offenders and hardened convicts; political detainees awaiting trial, and a lot more. Soyinka's depiction of the prison as a microcosm of the wider society is achieved through the removal of social stratification, that is, through subsuming the dialectical image. What we thus get is a fluid milieu into which character and action fuse and separate according to the dictates, not of social conflicts, but of thematic trends which are geared towards projecting a society in a state of perpetual chaos. This fluidity gives a general picture of social chaos which goes beyond the usual political divide between civilian and military regimes. As the "Minister for Education" in the play tells us, the prison is a replica of the outer society:

> EDUC: This is a military regime so don't mess about. Even when we are doing the civilian style—because you see we try to conform to what is going on in the country outside—so before we changed to military, even then our commandant was still commander-in-chief as well as a civilian president. (15)

Soyinka is concerned not with the change of regimes but with the failure of government as an institution. This failure manifests itself not only in the inability of government to fulfil its obligation to its citizens, but also, and more disturbingly, in the reversal of the administration of justice and fairness. The trial and subsequent execution of Miguel, Detiba, and Emuke illustrates this enraging negation of the basic tenets of civilized society. Emuke succinctly makes their case in these words:

> We go see. All I know is dat na wicked country to do something like this. We know some country way, if you steal they cut off your hand. But everybody know that in advance. So if you steal, na your choice. Every crime get in proper punishment. But if you wait until man commit crime, then you come

change the punishment, dat na foul. Na proper foul. I no
know any other country way data kin' thing dey happen. (29)

Emuke's statement may as well be the ranting of a dying man desper-
ately searching for clemency, but it still reveals the *unjustness* of
retroactive *justice* and paints the state as an instrument of vengeance.
Yet, the same state fails to punish big men who are equally guilty of
crime and through its structure unwittingly provides succor for criminal activities. In this respect diplomatic relations and protocol are
exploited by top government officials to perpetrate the same crime
for which the underprivileged are severely punished. In this context,
the diplomatic bag is the symbol of official corruption and its concealment. The song of the diplomatic bag gives us an adequate picture of the way justice is traduced by power and authority.

> For a diplomatic bag
> Is a copious magic bag
> Its free from drug-free guarantee
> To contraband its free
> Its mouth is open wide
> To swell nations pride
> For though it stinks in foreign state
> The bag is a sovereign state (57).

The diplomatic bag is both a symbol of national disgrace and the
indicator of the legal status of the elite. It is an edifice, a sovereign
state in which state assignment coincides with state consignments.
The call for patriotism, as found in the W.A.I. jingles, thus draws our
attention not to the existence of authority and good governance, but
to hypocrisy. Soyinka indeed sustains the dialectical relationship
between illusion and reality through the sustenance, in the play, of
hypocrisy as a quality of state power. In doing this, Soyinka, like other
dramatists of note, attempts to "evoke and awaken in the observer,
listener or reader emotions and impulses to action or opposition."
These responses encapsulate Soyinka's disillusionment with dictatorship and anarchy.

In *From Zia With Love*, Soyinka encapsulates and restates, through coherent dramatic enactments, the deepening crises of the Nigerian society. Through this basic concern, Soyinka provides universal postulations about dictatorship, the collapse of civil society, the evaporation of state power, and the ascension of crime and charlatanism. These features of anarchy create a singularly memorable sense of despair, point to man's capacity for destructiveness, and raise serious doubts about the capacity of Africa to rescue itself from the shackles of under-development.

Notes

1. See George Woodcock's *Anarchism: A History of Libertarian Ideas and Movement* (London: Penguin, 1975), p. 8.
2. The figure of Esu, like other deities and mythological personages of Yoruba mythic order, features very frequently in Soyinka's works, especially in the plays. Esu is a very significant god of Yoruba pantheon. He is the trickster god who has close links with Ogun, god of the road and iron; the creative and destructive sparks of Yoruba creation myths.
3. Brother Jero is the memorable religious hypocrite of Soyinka's plays *Trials of Brother Jero* and *Jero's Metamorphosis*. Both plays are hailed as some of the most memorable satires on Nigeria's religious hypocrisy of our time.
4. W.A.I. is an acronym for War Against Indiscipline instituted by the military regime of Generals Muhammadu Buhari and Tunde Idiagbon. *From Zia With Love* chronicles the ills of this regime.

Works Cited

La Guma, Alex. *A Walk In The Night*. London: Heinemnann, 1962.

Ojo-Ade, Femi. *On Black Culture*. Ile-Ife: Obafemi Awolowo University Press, 1989.

Soyinka, Wole. *From Zia With Love*. Ibadan: Fountain Publisher, 1992.

Woodcock, George. *Anarchism: A History of Libertarian Ideas and Movement*. London: Penguin, 1975.

6

Liberation Narrative and Post-Modern Africa

FRANK UCHE MOWAH

I

"With God all things are possible". This is a significant, yet ambiguous assertion. This is because God reaches out of the statement (vision) of John in the New Testament of the Bible and naturalizes into a modern metaphor such as art, or money, or man. In other words, we could substitute God with any of the paradigmatic elements and have a post-modernist slogan: (a), with arts all things are possible, (b), with money all things are possible; and (c), with man all things are possible.

There are two fundamental points here. The first is hinged on the structure of possibilities, while the second is planted within the soil of the union of literature or art and God, especially in the context of meaning in the present capitalist colonization of the world, the former USSR included, and by implication the entire world.

The possibilities then can be seen as all things which can be grown and consequently harvested in the socio-economic and socio-political climate of the contemporary age theoretically referred to as the post-modern age. By implication, the post-modern age is the age of technology, the age in which the computer rules as god and which in literary denotation can be regarded as the information age. But this is describing a period by an attribute of its invention. Perhaps a more perceptive way of looking at this notion of post-modernism or the cultural logic of capitalism is to see it as Fredric Jameson (1984:65-88) has done as a "culture produced by multinational capitalism: a totality which is the effect of another totality". In effect, the possibilities result from the other possibilities of subversion or promotion. In one context, art could become a god as it acts as a mediatory force where all other things have been rendered impotent by the forces of capitalism. Or in another context, it could become an instrument of promoting the devastating demolition of salutary norms and values by the caterpillar wheels of capitalism.

Post-modernism then is, in a critical literary sense, a spinning signifier which produces endless metaphysical referrals. It is a reaction to modernism, and to any modern theory like structuralism and Marxism in which meaning is systematic. This reaction is borne by the uneasy assumption that our world has already become post-contemporary, by over-reaching itself through cultural evolution and huge strides in technology advancements. This state then becomes a signifier, of a type which spins off other signifiers, which in turn refer to such signifiers like (a) the obliteration of history and (b) the entrenchment of anarchy. (It also refers to such positive signifiers like the rediscovery of bedrock reality and the information technology).

It has been rightly argued that post-modernism relegates history to the dustbin of an obsolete episteme although, there has also been counter argument that history is not made obsolete but that it is being re-thought as a human construct. In other words, history which is supposed to be a revitalizing force of living experience is dead, existing only as a fossil in documents. Even when texts like Osundare's *Waiting Laughter's*, Soyinka's *Ogun Abibiman,* and Ibrahim Tahir's *The Last Imam* teach the lesson of history, the lesson is not salutary nor edifying but it is the lesson which is the consequence of an unknowable past. This signifies, in a way that history evinces, a negative notion of suppression and rejection of that which preceded it.

If post-modernism is not a continuation of modernism, what is it then? First let us consider the concept of modernism. Modernism can be loosely defined as the tradition of the new in art—usually experimental and containing elements of deprecation as well as creation. In viewing the meaning of modernism in relation to its practitioners, we can like Ezra Pound, can described artists as the antennae of the race who will never be trusted by many in society. The distinction here is one that is between salvation and the apocalypse. In other words, modernism is entrenched in superstition or religion as the case may be. For instance, modernists like Karl Marx and Sigmund Freud had tried very hard, in the negative sense of modernist religious perception, to shift the world from religious dogmatism in faith to that of the hermeneutics of suspicion. Accordingly, no knowledge could be taken as its face value. While Karl Marx struggled to expose the class structure of the world, Freud strove to expose the effect of the suppression of erotic desires. Civilization therefore is nothing more than suppression of truths. And since the traditional man of faith seeks transcendental truth, modern thinkers like Freud and Marx gave it to him in repressed impulses. What is important is that the truth is manifest all the same. But it is the modernist artist like Eliot in *Wasteland* and Soyinka in *Idanre* who have placed truth in organic cohesion as well as in transcendence. For Eliot, it is humanist catholic religious faith, and for Soyinka, the rediscovery of meaning though traditional system of belief, myth and religion.

Conversely, post-modernism quarrels with the modernist quest for meaning or transcendental truth. It rejects superstition by seeing religious residue in any way of thinking which affirms the truth. Similarly, it encourages the subversion of truth and meaning, even scientific truth to the extent that it contests any modernist discarding or recuperating of the past in the name of the future. This takes us back to our premise in which money becomes a substitute for transcendental value, a reaffirmation of the fact that it is a culture produced by multi-national capitalism.

The question then is: how is this applicable to the Nigerian context? Let us consider this in the light of our industrial and technological *nothingness*. The truth remains however that despite our technological backwardness, Nigeria is an apostle of negative post-

modernism, perpetrating the ill-traits of capitalism in its entire rami-
fication without apology for its acidic consequences on the people.
And the annual budgets since 1986 have fully affirmed this thrust.
What the budgets have signified is a culture of dog-eat-dog, a culture
of survival of the fittest, a culture in which any mediatory and salutary forces in favor of the under-privileged class is subverted. Yet it is
a known secret that our socio-economic and socio-political fate is
now tied to the tool of capitalism—the World Bank and the International Monetary Fund. Worst still is the fact that post-modernism (in
developed economics like U.S.A. and Japan) is dependent on the
power of the computer (technology). The relevance of the computer
to any economy cannot be contested. What may be contested is the
relevance of the positions of the computer age to an economy such as
ours which is still living in the pre-technological age as can be illustrated by the local and national elections (December 1990–June
1993) in which human heads were the ballot papers (open ballot system). Whatever argument is adduced for its advantage by our political pundits, it still points to our innate backwardness.

In any case, post-modernism or multi-national capitalism in our
own context has simply entrenched a conduit pipe through which
our natural resources are channeled to foreign economies. In this
sense, post-modernism then becomes a synonym for post-colonialism. And in our own case, it is neo-colonialism or the end of effective
political institutions. Jean-Francois Lyotard (1984) calls it de-ration-
alized capitalism, that is, the play of exchange and the primitive
acquisition of money as exchange will render unnecessary the discursive presupposition of institutions. It is for good reason that Lyotard
has seen this type of post-colonialism as dangerous and vicious. In
our instance, the inexplicable devaluation of the Naira has rendered
millions of Nigerians destitute, only producing a dangerously vam-
pire class known euphemistically as *money-bags*. What we have, in
other words, in a situation as the one described, is the entrenchment
of some variant of fascism or "Nazism".

Two examples will suffice: the first is the breakdown of the instrumental reason as well as mythic and traditional values. Thus, it is not
surprising, though shocking, that the African concept of *welfarism*
imbedded erstwhile in the extended-family system has now been sub-

stituted with an individualistic disregard of life—kinsmen's or enemies'. And with the effacing of Maroko from the earth, (in Nigeria)
that is, the *Auschwitzing* of brothers by fathers, the final demolition of
a system, legitimatized by the practice of post-colonialism has been
achieved. The second example reaches beyond the primitive practices
in our shores to the present impulse in the gulf region which threatens human existence on earth. The remote cause is rooted in multi-
national capitalism. Again, we have a situation in which brothers are
eliminated by their brothers and sons by their fathers. Achebe's powerful work, *Things Fall Apart* is a prime example to illustrate this
point. The story of Ikemefuna exemplifies the post colonialist tendency. It is no surprise that the situation in the text produced a salutary warning which was not heeded by the capitalist fascist
Okonkwo: "DO NOT KILL THE BOY, HE CALLS YOU
FATHER". The implication of Okonkwo's action is the same for any
post-modernist aggressor who places money or power or capital
before God and/or man. And that is, kill those who call you father.
Or kill those who call you brother. Or kill those who call you President, or Messiah, or Uncle. In other words, exploitation implies no
brotherhood, no fatherhood, and no god. Instead, it encourages the
running of everyone aground. Niyi Osundare's *The Eye of The Earth*
depicts how man, the ravager, is also the ravaged—a true picture of
dog-eats-dog situation. Nevertheless, if post-modernism did not
entrench a system in which the very fabric of our society is being
shredded, the salutary effect that it generates could possibly have
enhanced our well-being.

The negative aspect of post-modernism or post-colonialism
relates to literature in a sense that is more vicious than it manifests
itself in political institutions. In literature, it is a reversal of the casual
order (what we have seen as the obliteration of history), or the elimination of "difference" or the reversal of the hierarchical opposition of
the signs in the text. Besides explaining the working of capitalist
thinking and philosophy, that is the denial of any substantial meaning— such as the negation of fascism and demonism,—it also initiates the tendency (or mastery) of the art of double-speak prophesized
by Orwell in *1984*. Critical discourse ceases to be a source of meaning
or even truth. This fact (not contention) is borne out by another fact

that no literary theory in Nigeria has come out with a mastery of what I will term, for want of better term, Babangidaism.

Babangidaism will be a discourse in which utterance is an efface-ment of the thought process, in which the motive of the speaker is absent in the sound-concepts or signifiers. For instance, the signifier, "43 Local Government Areas" in 1991 budget speech ceases to be what it was and becomes a signified, "97 Local Government Areas" when the President had to address a group of soldiers in Enugu a cou-ple of days after the speech. The signifier has thus become a *problem-atic*. On a more serious note, literary scholars should, whether positively or negatively, define a cultural pattern in the flux of this state of post-colonialist de-culturalization. What is literature after all? It is not just narrative strategy or the explication of such narratives. Rather it is primarily a validation of the viability of history and its contextualization within the scheme of the socio-political set-up of societies. It goes further to assert itself as machinery which creates possibilities of salutary truth.

And how then do we get at this truth if signifiers are effaced? What Western metaphysics of destruction is simply affirming is the loss of order in Western society as well as the rejection of the chaos of mod-ernism. This loss presents us with a mood of multiple irony and end-less cynicism. In literature, cynicism is converted to despair and loss of faith in the structure which underlies reality. Above all, the belief that literature can create authentic meaning is seriously shaken. One of the possibilities already hinted at (especially for us in Nigeria and Africa where meaning appears to be impossible and where literature fails to yield systematic knowledge for our leaders) is the subversion of this tendency. This is necessary because we have nothing else yet but our culture to float on the sea of modern technology. Culture to us is a web of meanings that we spin in a continuous process of sus-taining our identity. And because of the chaotic mode of existence in less developed countries like Nigeria, new poets find it difficult to work out new ideas and fresh metaphors which could justify the pul-sation of culture. They let themselves be caught in the throb of post-modern mystification rather than creating demystifying signifiers which will challenge the failure of government and society. In Nige-ria, there are of course, new poets who hold up promises. Poets like

Afem Akeh, Onookome Okome, Olu Oguibe and Harry Garuba are examples: a true (positive, neo-African) post-modernist affirmation of fresh ideas and images and salutary values.

Indeed, post-modernism has both negative and positive implications. Its negative aspect which relates to literature Niyi Osundare describes as "an empty technology of the text". It is its positive aspect which Harry Garuba in his "Graffiti, Grammatology and An African University Experience" sees as capable of showing how the thought of a system are controlled by a continuous spinning off of signs from a primary one that is of primary importance here. But perhaps, the metaphor, the positive re-direction of signs towards useful signification rather than on the open license the wall declares open for discourse offers to the aggressors and strongmen of a disintegrating system. It is in this light that Babangidaism might perhaps be explicated as the production of a primary sign which then spins off endless arrows of signifiers which in turn could be arrested and contextualised. Perhaps the best example of this mode of ironizing a text is Prof. Nwabueze's "imperfect obligation,"a term which defines the Babangida administration's unwillingness to honour its obligations to its citizens even when such obligations were constitutionally backed by law. In fact, since 1985 when General Ibrahim Babangida wrenched power from General Buhari, every text he made (action and utterance) has been colored by his own skepticism, ambiguity and self-contradiction, a position which in turn allowed for a free-play of interpretations, all of which sought to unearth a hidden ideology (or *hidden-agenda* as his critics term it). This consistent slipperiness has earned the admiration of skeptical criticism (in other words, deconstruction) and it is this attitude in philosophical contemplation that has also caused Christopher Butler (1984:65) to assign to the author an inability to create any homogenous set of meaning in their text. As he points out, "Indeed, once the notion of free play of language is allowed to take over, he author, director of our attention to aspects of reality, and, for much else can be dispensed with".(66)

II

Essentially therefore, it is the positive thrust of the technology of signs in relation to the vision of under-development in Nigeria (or

Africa) that is the goal of this essay, especially in respect of the effect of the information age on the culture of the twenty-first century Africa. The information age is the contemporary period in which the information technology revolution is holding sway. What distinguishes it from the earlier agricultural and industrial technologies is that the former leverages the brain while the later focuses on man's brute sense of working technological inventions. But what is significant is the quantum, an almost infinite leap in leveraging afforded by information technology.

The argument on the relevance of advanced technology to developing countries is neither here not there, but the truth is that the consequences of not having it are devastating to our economic and political systems. Worse still is the fact that our policies are formulated with the assumption that development is driven by the combined forces of (good) economic policy and technological know-how. In reality however, nothing is ever done by us about the lack of technological knowledge despite the fact that the traditional comparative advantage that we (less developed countries) have had over developed countries have been eroded by advanced technology. For instance, despite low labor cost with less advanced technology, developed countries produce cheaper and better textiles and other products like coffee and fruit drinks with their automated machines. The implication of this is unemployment. This is beside the fact that the nature of international market economic activity has been altered to our disfavor. Some critics have made the point when they argue that to be in this global rat race, countries must maintain their respective comparative advantages.

Meanwhile, appropriate policies which will encourage the growth of advanced technology in less developed countries are yet to be formulated because of inept and corrupt leadership as well as a result of the forces of post-colonialism which divert public fund to private uses. This reflects in our literary business in two ways. First, in respect of the production. And secondly, the adverse effects of under-development which necessarily become the subject of literary imagination and criticism. What indeed the computer has contributed to the publishing industry is the down scaling of the price of publishing. Therefore, while there are more cheap books in circulation in Advanced

Technology Countries, in Less Developed Countries, the books are so expensive and well beyond the means of the average wage earner (that is if the books are available at all). The implication of this is that so many manuscripts are never published, new writers are stillborn, and the high level of illiteracy remains ever unchecked. With the computerization of arts and information, knowledge ceases to be an end for its own sake. It is now a marketable commodity as well as the principle force of production, to the extent that power belongs to the person, or institution, or government, who has assess to that knowledge (knowledge here could be formulaic variables to the factors of colonization). It is worth recalling that Less Developed Countries like Nigeria were caught slumbering when writing started (writing being one of the basis of civilization), which was then the best means of storage and retrieval of knowledge and information.

Nevertheless, what bestows legitimacy to social institutions in the face of this technological onslaught cannot then be scientific knowledge but *narrative* knowledge. This is also the contention of J. F. Lyotard in "The Post-Modern Condition". Various African scholars like Biodun Jeyifo, Chidi Amuta and Omafume P. Onoge see literature as weapon of liberation. Essentially, narratives like myths, legends, stories, songs, epics, define the expression and actions of cultural institutions. It is what is transmitted from the set rules of narratives that constitute the social bond. In other words, narrative knowledge derives its potency from the fact that it can certify itself without recourse to argumentation and proof. But since science, which is indeed the epic of technology (since it is used in obtaining public consent sought by decision makers) needs legitimacy; it has to fall back on narrative knowledge as an instrument for that legitimacy. In essence, if science is the epic of contemporary history, then our humanity that sanctions science is the "hero" of liberty. And liberty is the goal of all epics.

This brings us, at last, to the place of Nigerian (African) literature in the post-colonial age. Primarily, our writers have, of necessity, concentrated on the adverse effect of lack of scientific knowledge in our society. They must compensate for this lack with a metaphor of connotation, a narrative knowledge which will reconquer the right to scientific knowledge. In effect, Nigeria and other Less Developed

Countries resort to a narrative of Liberation as against the unusual narrative of freedom. This is also an aspiration for a discourse which is rooted in African epistemology—a respect for welfare system (taking care of relatives) and a deep-rooted respect for salutary values.

In any case, the features of post-modern narrative, whether of freedom or liberation, are similar except for a slight modification in concepts. Four significant features of post-modernism confront African poets. The first is the theme of creative or salutary transformation: this implies a projection of vision beyond the banal theme of change. The others are: the need to purge the system of superstition; the invention of fresh metaphors or alternatively a new language of narrative and the need for a significant contribution to local cultures, which in turn is a contribution to world literature and culture. This contribution will achieve the fact of narrowing the gulf between races and continents through the evocation of the archetypal theme of passion and endurance and the consequent triumph.

In a truly stupefying way, Soyinka and Achebe are Africa's prophets of post-modernism, especially with the monumental insight evinced in their *Dance of the Forests* and *No Longer at Ease* respectively. Both works have the motifs of freedom for man—the hero of liberty; both are concerned with the salutary transformation of the world through the transformation of post-colonial Africa. And both works demonstrate the possibility of eliminating the multinational capitalism reflected in neo-colonial images. Furthermore, both works uphold images of visions which manifest themselves as a need to raise the disconnectedness of the post-modern age. And while Soyinka gives us a signified, which is a reversal of meaning though the use of pun, irony, ridicule and the regurgitation of tyranny as against binary fusion—signifying the emptiness of contemporary sophistication—Achebe on his part, unearths an ironic character who preshadows the marginalization of contemporary middle class.

Indeed, as a literary significant, *No Longer at Ease* rather than *A Man of the People* is the prophetic novel. Nevertheless, the two visionaries presented in these novels of consequence always succumb to the cynicism which we have referred to earlier. While Achebe's cynicism is always total as with the failure of *No Longer at East* and its sequel *Anthill of the Savannah* to produce a redemptive metaphor for the system, Soyinka cushions his pessimism (i.e., the lack of certainty or epiphany in the system) with a temporary arrest of the wheel of existence with a belligerent and willful character—usually a symbol of the mythical god Ogun. This character as a literary hero has appeared only once. It is Mandela in *Mandela's Earth*. Yet largely because in a postmodern sense of doubt and skepticism, Soyinka, the liberation artist (narrator), has chosen first to discover where the "rain" of backwardness "started beating us" in the dawn of modern African moral history, a morality game used as weapon by the first-set of industrious Nigerians (see *Isara: A Voyage Around Essay*) in a set-up of colonizing influences but failed in providing the type of answers which could explicate the nihilist tendency in contemporary Africa—a tendency which in turn has eroded every imaginable human values encoded in the ten commandments. Soyinka's initial vision of an "honourable" Babangidaic Nigeria proved to be an illusion and as faulty as it has misled his (Soyinka) Nigerian, and indeed global, audience who shared in his vision. On the one hand, this failure of vision is possible because of his adoration for a scheming, self-willed, inventive and creative hero like Babangida, a hero who approximates to Ogun. But on the other hand, it explains his post-Nobel prize skepticism and apparent disillusionment with the viability of the literary text. This further explains his revisitation of the themes of the cyclical play of history and false consciousness in *Mandela's Earth* (see "Cremation of a Wormy Caryatid", "Doctored Vision" and "My Tongue Does Not Many Slogans"). It also explains his resort to the medium of television/cinema (See (Okome's 1995) a medium which allows a phonocentric and pictorial display of radical signifiers and authorial commentary. Whether this would succeed or not in dismantling the anarchy and nihilism in Nigeria is irrelevant, what is clear is that final acquiescence to the hypnotic influence of post-modern ideology of skepticism.

Nevertheless, it is with the products of the age of post-colonialism that we must search for the four features of post-modernism. Niyi Osundare meets these four qualities in his later poetry— *Waiting Laughters* and *Moonsongs*, and Festus Iyayi achieves an average. For instance, in Iyayi's *Heroes*, the subject of contemporary struggle for existence produces a salutary, transformatory vision for the society, an insight into the working of agents of multi-national capitalism. He succeeds in unearthing a hero of freedom metaphorized in a reconstructive history in which the genuine agents of nation-building are put in their right perspective and pedestal. Marx has indeed shown how history is usually written to the advantage of the ruling class. Historical materialism therefore strives to correct this anomaly. For Iyayi, the Marxian concept becomes a paradigm for understanding the carnage resulting from class conflicts in his *Heroes*.

It is Osundare who proves to be the master of the game in virtually all his works. In *Waiting Laughter* for instance, the metaphor, laughter, naturalizes into a feature of history, "our history of mountain that is being drained by thirsty oceans" (37). Nevertheless, the victims of this anomaly will have their "waiting laughter" since reality point to an inevitable change, some salutary change. Osundare recognizes that superstition is a veritable tool of conservatism and thus of the perpetration of anarchy and oppression in our society. He uses his narrative knowledge to purge the society of this ill in order to achieve salutary transformations.

In "The Seer" ("*Songs of the Market Place*"), he raises the issue of false visionaries and prophets which has become a troubling feature of our under-development. He reminds us that we all know those responsible for our draught and famine (that is under-development and its attendant suffering), we all know the corrupt politicians and inept leaders, yet we accuse the rainmakers. Thus in *Waiting Laughter's*, "waiting" ceases to be an image of religious glory or even doom but an apocalypse and subsequent triumph of the saints (i.e, the down-trodden). Religion is therefore any way of thinking that relates to truth. And certainty is undoubtedly reality. This certainty is the certainty of the beaks of the "New chicks breaking the fragile tyranny of hallowed hell" (96). While Iyayi fails in the invention of significant images and metaphors to serve as a gesture to a society which requires more possibilities, varieties and hope, it is Osundare who has created new metaphors, fresh language and fresh ways of telling the story of the dearth of that vision which would have led the Less Developing Countries into the information age. The reversal of cause and effect in *Waiting Laughters* is unwittingly post-structuralist for it significantly becomes a form which is achieved through another form: the production of a polyvalence of voices with each voice accounting for a different level of reality in the system. The authorial voice rises above these other voices with a lyric of symbolisms—symbols of our passion of untruth, half-truth, and lack of direction. And imagery too is personified in order that it speaks eloquently of our sensual and sensuous cycles.

In conclusion, since science is the epic of post-modernism, since narrative knowledge is more or less the hero of this epic, it is then understandable that in developing countries, the hero could be glorious as in the primary epic, or tragic as in African epics (see *Sundiata* and *Emperor Shaka Zulu*). Unfortunately, the African hero in the post-modern system is still a tragic one whose subject is of a dream-order, a dream of change, a vision of under-development and a distant future when humanistic values could be realized. Ironically, it is with the narrative weapon that these humanistic values might be infused into Less Developing Countries. It does this through signifiers that refer to themselves. Difference is thus achieved through what it is rather than through what it is not. What is an equivalence of the scientific knowledge? In essence, if scientific knowledge is capable of leveraging brain-power through the storage and retrieval of vital information, narrative knowledge or weapon will be equally capable of doing the same for Less Developed Countries. The question, nevertheless, is that of who has the monopoly of this knowledge. In Advanced Technological Countries, the computer is controlled by the agency of government or by power-brokers who use retrieved information to advise and/or invent for the advancement of the society. But in Less Developed Countries, even with narrative power, the equation remains unbalanced because the knowledge stored in literature (or narrative) is not retrieved by government or its agent. The system thus remains under-developed, uninventive, and in many ways retrogressive. The government's brain is not leveraged by any aid so it continues to spin off signifiers which continue to produce endless diabolical referrals. Refusing advice or not availing itself with information implies that the ruling class is confident of or is satisfied with the power and knowledge it has, for it is in its own selfish interest, to shut itself to progressive changes going on in other parts of the human community. This is playing god, and in such a game, all things are possible.

Works Cited

Achebe, Chinua. *Things Fall Apart.* London: Heinemann, 1958.

_____. *No Longer At Ease.* London: Heinemann, 1960.

_____.*Arrow of God.*London:Heinemann,1965.

_____.*A Man of the People.*London:Heinemann,1966.

_____. *Anthills of The Savanna.*London:Heinemann,1987.

Barth, John. "The Literature of Replenishment: Post-modern Fiction: *The Atlantic.* January 1980.

Butler Christopher. "Ambiguity and Self-contradiction" *Interpretation, Deconstruction and Ideology.*

Oxford Clavendon Press, 1984 rep. 1986.

Garuba, Harry. "Graffiti, Grammatology and of Grammatology: An African University Experience". Unpublished Seminal Paper of the Faculty of Arts, University of Ibadan,1987.

Jameson, Fredric. "Postmodernity, or the Cultural Logic of Late Capitalism" .*New Left Review.*July-August, 1984.

Lyotard, Jean-Francois. *The Postmordern Condition: A Report On Knowledge,* 1997.Trans.Geoff Bennington and Brain Massumi. Mineapolis: University of Minesota Press,1984.

Okome, Onookome. "Cinema and Social Change in West Africa". *IRIS: University of Iowa Journal for The Theory of Image and Sound.*N0 18,1995.

Osundare, Niyi. *The Eye of the Earth.*Ibadan:Heinemann,1986.

_____. *Moonsongs.* Ibadan: Spectrum Books Ltd.,1988.

_____.*Song of the Market Place.* Ibadan: New Horn Press,1987.

Soyinka,Wole. *Ogun Abibiman.* Ibadan/London: Rex Collins/Opon Ifa;1976.

_____.*Idanre and Other Poems.* Ibadan /London:Methuen, 1967.

_____.*Mandela's Earth and Other Poems.* Ibadan: Fountain Publication,1989.

7

Soyinka's Isara and the Myth of The Magic Box

Harry Garuba

Two years after the publication of *Ake*, Soyinka's childhood autobiography, the author opens a tin box belonging to his father, who had died about a decade earlier. Scraping away the cockroach eggs that had accumulated in it over the years, the author tells us that "a tantalizing experience" opened up for him as he "browsed through a handful of letters, old journals with marked pages and annotations, notebook jottings, tax and other levy receipts, minutes of meetings and school reports, programme notes of special events, etc" (VII). This is how Wole Soyinka's *Isara* opens with a prefatory note from the author.

Thus, so far, this reads like a factual account of a real event, the beginning of a biography or some genre of that sort, relying primarily on actual events and verifiable facts. But as rendered in the language of the "Author's Note" to *Isara*, the presentation is already thoroughly interlaced with the notion of myth and folklore. Two apparently neutral phrases—the "tin box" and the "tantalizing experience"—are, as we shall see, loaded signifiers pointing to a different order of experience than the factual.

For instance, the word "tantalize" has so much become part of the English language and our daily usage that we often forget that it is derived from the classical Greek myth of Tantalus, the son of Zeus, condemned (for revealing the secrets of the god) to stand in a pool of water beneath clusters of overhanging grapes. His punishment was that when he bent to drink from the pool the water ebbed, and when he made for the grapes they receded just beyond his reach. The author of *Isara*, in using this word, is subterraneously trying to connect the originary impulse of his narrative with this myth. What he is saying, just below the surface, is that the contents of the box opened just after the completion of his autobiography of his childhood excited a literary desire in him to again follow the path of biographical narrative. But the facts were simply not enough: having revealed the secrets of the tin box, he is briefly condemned to the fate of Tantalus. Reaching to fulfil the biographical desire, the fruits of its promise recede and trying to drink from the pool of his father's experience, the water ebbs. He therefore has to seek other avenues in memory and imaginative or fictional biography.

But the mythical connections do not end here. The materials that provide the basis for the narrative are stored away in a "tin box." The magic box is a recurrent item in mythology and folklore. The myth of Pandora, the woman through whom Zeus sought to punish man for the gift of fire from Prometheus, is well known from Greek mythology. The box given to her is said to be the source of all the ills of the world. Pandora's box has since become a cliche in English, but what may not be so well known are African folktales of magic boxes (or pots)—often in pairs—which either hold the promise of fabulous riches or of monstrous evil. The general pattern of these stories has to do with a deprived orphan who involuntarily sets out on a journey, some kind of rite of passage, at the end of which there are two boxes, of which he/she is supposed to choose one. The larger box—always, invariably, the evil one—tries to influence the orphan's choice by important entreaties while the smaller box is more muted in its solicitation. The orphan chooses the smaller one and reaps its reward of wealth.

There is no need to press the links any further or more emphatically than Soyinka has himself outlined them. In the very first paragraph of his author's note, he recalls his father's death and details the circumstances of the funeral at which he was unavoidably absent because of the political situation in the country at that time. When the exile is finally able to return home under a different dispensation, he takes his time before deciding to open the "magic" box—his father's bequest to him. His reward, on opening it, is—as every good orphan's moment of joy—a treasure of letters just beneath an overlay of cockroach eggs. For an artist, there could be no wealth or inheritance of greater value.

Wole Soyinka's compulsive mythopoesis has long been recognized as the always, already written pre-text to his works and its use in *Isara* sets the narrative on the familiar Soyinka terrain. And this pattern of transforming experience into myth or re-writing experience into the structures and codes of mythology runs right through the whole of this book. This transformational framework creates a multilayered narrative in which alternately myth is pressed into the service of mundane experience and the latter acquires a symbolic intensity that aspires towards the mythical.

Here again, a ready example will serve to illustrate this point. The story itself begins in Isara with the visit of the Elder Soyinka (Soditan Akinyode; fondly called "Essay" by his colleagues) who has come home for the "outing" of a lorry bought by his father's friend. The first "to be owned by an indigene of Isara" (3). This "out of season" visit, as different from the regular "seasonal" visits at New Year, Harvest, or Easter is significant not only for Essay but for the whole of Isara. This was not just one of those "return to sender," in the modest houses built at home by the sons of Isara who had travelled out and acquired success in whatever enterprise they had been involved in; this was different. This lorry was bought by Node, a resident of Isara, a stay-at-home who had metamorphosed from being a successful farmer to become a shrewd businessman. In a truly fundamental sense, Isara was making a slightly different kind of transition into the modern world—not asking its sons to go out and acquire its benefits, but bringing these benefits home through its residents.

The theme of transition, with which Soyinka has always been preoccupied, is at work at different levels here, encompassing both the slightly mythical and the downright realistic. At the first level, the book begins with the word "Ashtabula" (the name of a little town in Ohio in the United States of America) and ends with this same word. For an Isara man in the 1940s—even an exile—this place name in Ohio conjured visions of a new world of wonders. As Essay sits in the country quiet of Isara reading a letter from Wade Cudeback, his pen pal in Ohio, his imagination rises to meet the wonders described in this letter, and the name Ashtabula ceases to be a place name and becomes a repository of everything from success to fulfillment, to the experience of riches of the world across the seas. As the sacrificial ram bleats to arouse the coming "outing" of Node's lorry, Essay chuckles to himself saying, "All right, I give you till dawn tomorrow then Node will ride on your back to Ashtabula" (4). And later, as Wemuja, his childhood companion, comes out of the driver's cabin of the new lorry, Essay wonders with a touch of envy, "Had he reached his Ashtabula?" (27). Ashtabula, in Essay's imagination, is so thoroughly marked with the register of myth that its association with the wonders of the North American continent is extended to all the wonders of Essay's fertile mind. Beginning with Wade Cudeback's exotic handwriting through the even more exotic sights of his adventures such as the Magnetic (I almost said magical) Mountain, the realistic is so overlaid with the imaginative that the sights of Ashtabula and its environs begin to suggest to Essay and his circle of friends, the "twin-fantasy" to the tales of "A Thousand and One Nights" or the "Adventures of Sinbad the Sailor" (6).

Essay tries at every point to recreate this world of wonder in Isara. He searches for parallels between Ashtabula and Isara and in ruminating about the similarities, trying to find something local and fantastic to describe to Wade Cudeback in his reply, his mind pauses briefly on his own grandfather's name, which means "surrounded by sorcerers." Could this be a local equivalent for the "Witches House" in an Ashtabulan place called Salem? The name only directs him to history, first setting out from Isara to meet the railway and to enter a new world. From this moment the book records his and the exiles wandering through the world and their homecomings and comes back full circle when the world in the person of Wade Cudeback comes to Isara and the school teacher receives him with the words: "Welcome to Ashtabula!"

Essay's immersion in the fantasy world of Ashtabula is balanced on the realistic level by the pace of events in Isara. Node's lorry brings the benefits of modern technology and trade home to *Isara* and it is appropriately launched with a triple ceremony involving traditional rites, a Christian blessing, and Koranic readings by the local Imam. But Isara still remained steeped in its traditional ways, its institutions remained in the hands of a traditional elite impervious to change. However, as events begin to gather pace, the rivalry between the old elite and the new emerge into open conflict. The occasion is the selection of a new ruler (Odemo) for Isara. The traditional elite opposes the candidature of Akinsanya, a native son of Isara resident in Lagos, who has made a name in the new world as a trade unionist and nationalist. They see him as having been polluted with new ways and therefore not fit to occupy the seat of a traditional throne. The new elite, on the other hand, want an enlightened leader, knowledgeable in the ways of the world and also committed to progress. The political maneuvering is conducted both on the traditional level of charms and mysterious and occult rituals and at the level of making representations to the colonial authorities. In the end, it is decided that a vote be taken and Akinsanya wins. So again, at this realistic level, the book also ends with the world coming to Isara through a native son finally returning home to assume authority. It is important to recognize the interplay of the two levels here because the leader is, in this instance, elected in the manner of the Greek demos by a popular vote: a true merger of modern democratic methods and a traditional institution.

Wemuja, who acts as some kind of usher to the two events, the launching of Node's lorry and the launching of the horse on which Akinsanya rides into town, links both events, telling Alanko, his apprentice, that they will not be carrying tradition, on that day, but will be carrying history. He is right in more than one sense. The bringing of Akinsanya into the town and his installation as the Odemo was in itself a historic event. Its historical significance in the context of the book and of the Nigerian polity is however much wider. For Isara, it symbolized the ascension of the new elite and the coming not just of the mechanical apparatus of progress (the lorry) but also of its human embodiment. In the larger context of Nigeria, Professor Abiola Irele tells us, in a review in *African Commentary*, that "the stakes involve more than a simple transition from the traditional system to the new: the white horse on which Akinsanya, erstwhile trade unionist who becomes the group's candidate, rides into Isara to make good his claim to the throne is the price Sipe has extracted from an old Brazilian family for a debt, and signals the displacement of the first wave of modernizers, celebrated in Olinto's *Water House*, from the forefront of Nigerian development" (63). The event, therefore, also symbolizes the rise of a new local elite in Nigeria.

But, then again, even in so factual a historical record as this the lure of fantasy is never far from the surface of its realistic rendering. This lure is here embodied in Wemuja, who brings the horse into town accoutred in Western cowboy suit almost like a figure materialized straight out of Ashtabula. Wemuja is some kind of small-scale Don Quixote character who consistently transforms reality to fit his own fantasies; and even though he is a relatively minor character in the scheme the book draws, he shares an imaginative kinship with Essay, through whose eyes the story largely unfolds.

Isara represents Soyinka's most sustained attempt in his writing to recreate the physical and social details of an African world in the transitional period between the consolidation of colonialism and the rise of an indigenous middle-class nationalism. As we read through the book, we are brought more acutely in touch with a physical landscape, with its flora and fauna, than we get in most West African fiction. This mimetic thrust of the story is very striking because in most of the African writing that we are familiar with, there is often no meaningful attempt to evoke a physical world with its soil and seasons, its hills and houses, its streets and sounds and the details of daily life like the food and the smells of its delicacies. On the social level, the relationships and obligations, familial and cultic, the routine household activities, eating and entertaining are all recorded with a writer's fidelity, the complex multifaceted business of simply living. This descriptive adequacy is achieved through the use of a lucid, unobtrusive prose style with the words chosen to fit the occasion. The book begins with Essay's meditative perusal of Wade Cudeback's letter. The slow, measured cadence of the language matches the somnolence of the village of Isara itself until the bleating goat disturbs the quiet and we are gently nudged into the florid style of the letter which describes landmarks in other climes. The tempo of the narrative quickens at every turn with the pace of events until the language gathers breath-taking speed at the end of the book. The outer and inner worlds of the characters completely merge in the character of the man Agunrin Odubona, who regains his voice at a congress on the succession to the throne. From the rather placid beginning, the narrative, through its various meandering routes, gathers speed and arrives at a fascinating climax. It is as if from the various tributaries, the narrative streams meet, at a memorable watershed which sums up the aspirations and desires of all the characters. The last fifty pages or so in which this happens are an enduring feast of prose narrative.

Essay's "magic" box reveals a fascinating array of characters which include among others the enterprising Sipe, otherwise known as the Resolute Rooster, Essay's own grandmother obsessed with her burial rites, Goriola the fastidious sanitary inspector, Dr. Mackintosh who tried to teach his African students the wonders of classical music, and Ray Gunnar, the Trinidadian confidence man. All of these characters, comical, grotesque, and serious at various turns are all portrayed with sympathy and understanding. In delineating these characters the author shows a compassionate understanding of the circumstances of their lives. The material which Wole Soyinka uses in these character portraits could in the hands of a writer like V. S. Naipaul be turned to other uses. There are hardly any hints of satire in Soyinka's portrayal of these characters: even their most ridiculous ambitions and self-inflation are seen against the background of a colonial society trying to redefine itself in the context of a larger world.

This larger world, it should be noted, is a world with which the characters have only a textual relationship in the form of letters and newspapers. Hitler and Mussolini, the Salem Witch House, and the Reversing Falls, are real to them in the way only an oral society just developing a scribal culture can conceive of such people and landmarks. This is perhaps why the letter is used as a major structuring device in this book. The letter is both textual and personal. As personal correspondence, it is supposed to be private; but as written document it could also be publicly consumed. Portions of Essay's letters are read out by him to his pupils and his personal circle of friends. In these letters the private and the public are allowed to merge in a new way which is possible only in a predominantly oral culture.

Isara, the record of the personal lives of a few characters, also becomes a chronicle of public events; it becomes, so to speak, a genre of social history. By conducting a vigorous dialogue with the life and times of his father, Wole Soyinka is also able to recreate for us the life and times of a period in Nigerian history. It is no accident, therefore, that the personal and the public come together in the final celebration at the end of the book. It is also appropriate that at this event, Essay's pen pal, the scribal man of letters from Ashtabula, comes personally to Isara to meet his textual friend; and Isara and Ashtabula become one. In voyaging around his father, Soyinka also manages to voyage around the fathers of Nigerian history.

In the end, *Isara,* Wole Soyinka's tale of a magic box bequeathed to him by his father, becomes the story of a personal inheritance and a public legacy. What more can a review such as this say but recommend that we all pay a textual visit to Isara with the aid of Soyinka's magic box-book!

*This piece was first published as a review essay in the Nigerian daily, *The Sunday Times.*

8

Soyinka's Appetite For Sacrifice

Daniel Gover

Of all the dualities that run through Wole Soyinka's dramatic writing and reflect his shifting balance between the creative and destructive sides of life, one of the most instructive sets of contraries is the alternation of appetite and sacrifice. These two drives figure prominently in both the comic and tragic sides of Soyinka's vision from his earliest plays through his major tragedy, *Death and the King's Horseman.* They reflect the sometimes contradictory energies that drive his writing: the human needs to enjoy life to its fullest as well as to transcend it to a higher stage. Soyinka uses these conflicting drives to celebrate and satirize the human appetites for love, power, money, and glory by depicting the growth of appetite as either a vice or a virtue. The physical appetites are usually associated with egotism, while the spiritual drive is connected to self-sacrifice, social commitment, and artistic creativity. The continuous flux between these two forces of appetite and sacrifice produces the dramatic tension in Soyinka's plays. Human nature seems to be at war with its own conflicting needs both to fulfill and transcend the individual self, to dominate the community and to serve it through sacrifice. While there are only a few key characters created of pure self-sacrifice, like Eman in *The Strong Breed*, there are many composed of total appetite and self-interest, like Kongi in *Kongi's Harvest*. But perhaps most interesting of all are the characters interested in both appetite and sacrifice, like Elesin Oba in *Death and the King's Horseman*.

The origins of Eman's sacrifice in *The Strong Breed* are in his social concern to root out evil from the community. As an outsider, he questions the actions of the village in designating a sacrificial carrier of the year's evils who is killed before the New Year begins. By defending the idiot boy Ifada who has been selected as the scapegoat, Eman exposes the callousness of the village ritual. In placing their accumulated evils on an unwitting sacrifice, the villagers are avoiding and thus increasing their own evil. Eman asks them, "But why do you pick on a helpless boy. Obviously, he is not willing . . . in my home, we believe that a man should be willing" (*Collected Plays 1*, 128). Eman has identified the necessity for self-sacrifice in any ritual to remove evil from a community, but, unfortunately, by doing so he alienates the village elders, who finally select him as an alternative carrier. The elder Jaguna challenges him by saying, "There is only one other stranger in the village, but I have not heard him offer himself" (130). Eman rises to the occasion not out of an appetite for martyrdom, but because he is strong enough to oppose injustice and shelter the scapegoat Ifada from the village. In the symbolic terms of the play, Eman is born of "the strong breed," like his father who has chosen to carry the evils of the world down to the river where they can be cleansed. He also been born for sacrifice, having fled from his own village after his wife died giving birth to their son, a sacrifice his father told him was the identifying price of the strong breed. Yet it is in his blood to confront evil rather than to avoid it. Earlier in his life, when he was preparing for the ritual sacrifice of circumcision, Eman caught his tutor trying to blackmail young girls into satisfying his sexual desire. Even then he senses that genuine sacrifice must be purified of physical appetite.

By challenging the villagers to sacrifice their own evil, Eman seals his fate. He tells them, "A village which cannot produce its own carrier contains no men" (129). The ironic price for saving the unwilling carrier is to be cast in that role himself. After a chase, he is finally taken and killed. His sacrifice, like that of Christ, to whom he is compared, fills the people of the village with awe: "One and all they looked up at the man and words died in their throats" (146). Eman is the type of strong man who dedicates himself to defeating evil even if it requires self-sacrifice. He is certainly the strongest idealist among Soyinka's early characters.

The title character of *Kongi's Harvest* is exactly the opposite: a tyrant driven to insane proportions by his appetite. Soyinka's portrait of the kind of corrupt maniacal political leader with whom independent Africa has been cursed inspires his most vicious satire. Kongi is a dictator driven by such an absolute lust for power that he requires the sacrifice of all the moral figures in society. His tyranny devours the strong breed of idealists willing to sacrifice themselves in order to end political corruption and establish a better social order.

From the opening anthem of the play, we are made aware that a price must be paid to support the absolutism of a government stuffed on its own appetite. Power must be fed by sacrifice:

> The pots that will eat fat
> Its bottom must be scorched
> The squirrel that will long crack nuts
> Its footpad must be sore
> The sweetest wine has flowed down
> The tapper's shattered shins.
> (*Collected Plays*, 62)

The sacrifice will be made by the forces of rebellion that oppose Kongi. Though he already has power over the traditional king, Oba Danlola, Kongi wants a public demonstration of the transition to his power at the Harvest Festival. Since the Oba is reluctant to justify this new corrupt leader by handing over the New Yam, Kongi tries to manipulate him by promising the release of political detainees. The opposition leaders Daodu and Segi represent a political version of the strong breed; they are young idealists willing to sacrifice themselves to end Kongi's evil.

Kongi himself appears as a parody of a political dictator, somewhat like Brecht's caricature of Hitler in *Arturo Ui*. His ego is so monstrously swollen that he has the yearly calendar renamed for himself. For a photographer he poses like Christ in the Last Supper, then sets his Aweri lackeys to work on his next book as soon as they release his last one. Completely self-centered, Kongi wants the traditional Harvest Festival to become a celebration of his absolute power. When he learns that one of the detainees has escaped, he explodes in a paroxysm of revenge.

> I want him back—alive if possible. If not ANY OTHER WAY! But I want him back . . . And hear this! The amnesty is OFF! The reprieve is OFF! The others hang tomorrow . . . No Amnesty! No Reprieve! Hang every one of them! Hang them! (100)

When his ranting ends in an epileptic fit, it seems that his own rage threatens to destroy him before his enemies ever will.

If *Kongi's Harvest* were a more universal satire, the denouement might well produce the dictator's fall. But Soyinka appears to be making a bitter point about the excessive political appetites that have been engorging themselves on contemporary Africa. So Kongi triumphs easily over his opponents. The Harvest Festival becomes an orgy of Kongism, featuring pictures of Kongi University, Kongi Dam, Kongi Refineries, Kongi Airport, and a chorus from the Carpenters Brigade, who sing,

> We spread the creed of Kongism
> To every son and daughter
> And heads too slow to learn it
> Will feel our mallets' weight. (115)

Daodu, one of the young leaders of the opposition, identifies the role of sacrifice in a political context: ." . . we . . . hereby repudiate all Prophets of Agony, unless it be recognized that pain may be endured only in the pursuit of ending pain and fighting terror" (127). Just as Eman in *The Strong Breed* was willing to sacrifice himself to oppose evil, so Daodu and Segi are part of a new political strong breed, rebels who will risk everything to stop the tyranny of dictatorship. They recognize that sacrifice is needed to halt Kongi's insatiable appetite for power and the social pain it produces. Unfortunately, as political tyranny continues to feed on the sacrifice of progressive political forces, the Harvest Festival comes to a climax with a burst of gunfire which kills Segi's father while he is trying to assassinate Kongi. The dictator's triumph means the martyred sacrifice or flight of his enemies. But Soyinka is far too satirical to allow Kongi's harvest to be gathered painlessly. His victory speech turns into a parody of a political bacchanal in which the tyrant "exhorts, declaims, reviles, cajoles, damns, curses, vilifies, excommunicates and execrates" (131) until he foams at the mouth. Then Segi enters dancing with a copper salver, like Salome, and presents Kongi with her father's head on a platter. A blackout captures Kongi's mouth frozen open in speechless terror. It is a visual representation of the tyrannical appetite as a form of cannibalism. As he devours his enemies, so the dictator will destroy the people.

Kongi's Harvest is very different in form and tone from *The Strong Breed*, yet it does dramatize a similar point through satire rather than symbolism. The unchecked growth of social appetite, whether in traditional village or new centralized state, will require the tragic sacrifice of the strong breed of martyrs and rebels who rise up against evil.

In most of Soyinka's work, appetite is simply a life force that can be repressed, although at times it can be channeled into higher purposes than the purely egotistical. Physical appetites are the basic drives of life which manage to assert themselves no matter how people seek to control them. In fact, efforts made to sublimate the appetites can provide good material for satire. In Soyinka's early comedy, *The Lion and The Jewel*, the life force embodied in sexual appetite is celebrated at the expense of intellectual pretension. The young teacher, Lakunle, a representative of social change, wants to transform his love, Sidi, and his whole village into models of modern Europeanized culture. His antagonist is the local chief or Bale Baroka, the representative of tradition. Lakunle is a half-baked Europhile who has seen the world he wants in the new metropolis of Lagos. But he is also an over-reaching snob who looks down on the traditional villagers as "your race of savages" (*Collected Plays 2*, 5). The cultural tradition he hates the most is bride-price, because he can't afford to marry Sidi with only his exalted feelings of romantic love, but still refuses to work a farm in order to earn the money. He calls bride price "A savage custom, barbaric, out-dated, rejected, denounced, accursed, excommunicated, archaic, degrading, humiliating, unspeakable, redundant" (8), stopping his list only because he owns the Shorter Companion Dictionary instead of the longer one. It makes one think of Pope's line, "A little learning is a dangerous thing." At times one questions why Lakunle wants to marry Sidi at all because her insistence upon the bride price frustrates him to the point of shouting at her, "Bush girl you are, bush girl, you'll always be" (10). But, of course, Sidi is beautiful; and though Lakunle sublimates his sexual drive into his devotion to cultural progress, he cannot completely repress it.

Ironically, it is an instrument of modern culture that causes Sidi's vanity to overflow. A photographer has published her photos in a magazine which has brought her to the attention of Bale Baroka, the Lion of Ilujinle. After feasting his eyes on Sidi, the Bale decides that it is time to feed his appetite, noting that "it is five full months since last I took a wife" (18). The play develops into a comic merry-go-round of appetites. Sidi gets the notion that being a famous beauty makes her too good for both Lakunle and the Bale: the former she now regards as a "mere village school teacher" (12), and of the Bale she says, "I am young and brimming; he is spent/I am the twinkle of a jewel/ But he is the hind quarter of a lion!" (22). So, puffed up with vanity, Sidi is ripe for deflating, and the bale is able to trick her into bed by feigning the impotence of old age. Along with his senior wife Sadiku, Sidi celebrates the supposed end of Baroko's storied sexual appetite as a victory for womankind. She accepts his invitation to visit in order to crow over his impotence, only to be seduced as he slyly feeds her appetite for self-love. By co-opting some of the new culture, he intends to put her picture on a local stamp and reproduce it a thousand times, she becomes dizzy with the prospect as well as his power, which takes on the color of his sexual appetite as he tells her,

> . . . old wine thrives best within a new bottle. The coarseness is mellowed down, and the rugged wine acquires a full and rounded body . . . (49)

When she returns to Lakunle no longer a virgin, he thinks that they can finally marry without the bride price. But to his surprise, she throws him over for the older but still potent Bale, saying,

> I who have felt the strength, the perpetual youth zest of the panther of the trees? And would I choose watered-down, a beardless version of unripened man? (57)

Thus Lakunle, the modern man of learning but repressed appetite, loses out to the traditional lion of physical desire. As Soyinka suggests once again through Sidi's choice, we live in a world ruled by appetite rather than sacrifice.

In Soyinka's early plays the themes of appetite and sacrifice play off against each other to create shifting balances of comedy and tragedy. *Kongi's Harvest* is a satirical tragicomedy based on a parody of political dictatorship in which the satisfaction of appetite requires the sacrifice of moral opposition. In a different but related way, *The Strong Breed* is a symbolic tragedy in which idealistic opposition to evil is shown to lead inevitably to sacrifice. On the other hand, *The Lion and the Jewel* is a satirical comedy of appetite contrasting modern and traditional views of love. Because of its comic effects, very few in Soyinka's audience would compare it to his later tragedy *Death and the King's Horseman*. And yet a simple parallel connects the two plots: in both the desire of an older man blocks the relationship of a younger couple. Of course, the two works are so different in method and tone that this slight coincidence seems hardly significant at first. Yet it does point to the balance achieved in the later tragedy between appetite and sacrifice.

Not since Eman in *The Strong Breed* has a Soyinka character possessed an appetite for sacrifice like that of Elesin Oba. And yet, like Bale Baroka and so many of Soyinka's characters, Elesin is also dominated by his physical and egotistical appetites. He is something of a culminating character for Soyinka: a man whose appetites for transcendence through death and earthly fulfillment are both strong, though at odds with each other. And it is the collision of these powerful human drives that produces Elesin's great tragedy.

We are introduced to him at the peak of his life, when he is described as "a man of enormous vitality, [who] speaks, dances and sings with that infectious enjoyment of life which accompanies all his actions" (Soyinka: *Six Plays*, 147). At the same time, he is on the verge of transcending his life voluntarily through a life-giving self-sacrifice. Following the King's death he is going to join his master in the ancestral world. His final act of ending life seems to stimulate his sensuous enjoyment of its beauty. Elesin's celebration of life before leaving it is expressed in the most lyrical poetry of any of Soyinka's plays. As poetic as his professional Praise Singer, Elesin glorifies the physical side of life. The opening scene is set in the market at closing where the great variety of life's appetites are displayed and fed. His language is filled with images of feasting, for his life has indeed been a banquet: "That Esu-harassed day slipped into the stewpot while we feasted. We ate it up with the rest of the meat" (147). He is also confident that his death will be a gift to please the appetites of the living. He tells the Praise Singer that "My fame, my honour are legacies to the living; stay behind and let the world sip its honey from your lips" (148). The Praise Singer replies in kind: "Your name will be like the sweetberry a child places under his tongue to sweeten the passage of food. The world will never spit it out." For Elesin, fame and honor seem to reinforce his sensual enjoyment of life.

Yet even at this moment of climactic fulfillment a note of danger is sounded. After Elesin remarks that he has neglected "my women" of the market, the Praise Singer warns him of their influence: "They love to spoil you but beware. The hands of women also weaken the unwary" (148). Elesin's answer links the two worlds of physical and spiritual desire: "This night I'll touch feet with their feet in a dance that is no longer of this earth. But the smell of their flesh, their sweat, the smell of indigo on their cloth, this is the last air I wish to breath as I go to meet my great forebears."

Elesin Oba is able to join in a lyrical embrace two contradictory appetites because he regards death as life's ultimate experience rather than its end, a new beginning, for which one can develop eager anticipation. Elesin revels in the significance of his sacrifice in his proud, even boastful Song of the Not-I Bird, in which he mocks the universal fear of death that intimidates all living creatures except himself. The secret of his lyrical celebration is that he alone is brave enough to withstand the fear of death and glories in his triumph over it. There is none of the dark fear that surrounds Eman's sacrifice in *The Strong Breed*. Instead, Elesin displays comic scorn for all those who profess courage but quail when asked if they hear death calling:

> 'Not I', shouts the fearless hunter, but it's getting dark, and this night lamp has leaked out all its oil. I think it's best to go home and resume my hunt another day. (150)

Elesin mockingly compares this universal fear of death to his own confidence and courage: "Tell my tapper I have ejected/ Fear from my home and farm. Assure him,/ All is well" (152). He even mocks the gods who, though immortal, still fear to die, comparing them to himself:

> I am the master of my fate. When the hour comes watch me dance along the narrowing path, glazed by the soles of my great precursors. My soul is eager. I shall not turn aside. (153)

His proud dance will require no lonely sacrifice, for he says that "I go to keep my friend and master company." His language, however, remains fixed in his physical appetite, still infused with abundant images of food and feasting. After all, as a royal member of the court of Oyo, he has indeed feasted on life. He continues to view the world through his enormous appetite at the same time that he denies being imprisoned by it:

Who says the mouth does not believe in 'No, I have showed all that before?' I say I have.

> The world is a constant honey-pot.
> Where I found little I mad do with little.
> Where there was plenty I gorged myself.
> My master's hands and mine have always
> Dipped together and, home or sacred feast
> The bowl was beaten bronze, and meats
> So succulent our teeth accused us of neglect. (153)

Elesin recognizes that his time is ending and that he must now wind down his appetite: "The world was mine . . . But the twilight hour brings bats and rodents / Shall I yield them cause to foul the rafters?" Beyond a certain point satiation becomes fouled by scavengers who will later be associated with those who eat left-overs. One needs to know when to leave life's banquet, and for Elesin it seems to be with his final drink of honor that marks the end of his life. The Praise Singer addresses this point:

> I say you are that man who
> chanced upon the calabash of honour.
> You thought it was palm wine
> And drained its contents to the final drop. (154)

Elesin understands that to deny that life has an ending would be a transgression against respect:

> Life has an end. A life that will outlive
> Fame and friendship begs another name.
> What elder takes his tongue to his plate,
> Licks it clean of every crumb? He will encouter
> Silence when he calls on children to fulfil
> The smallest errand! Life is honour.
> It ends when honour ends. (154)

Yet immediately after this summative statement of nobility, Elesin's appetite re-asserts itself and threatens his delicate balance between life and death. First, he feigns offense to embarrass the market women for not clothing him in the royal robes of a great man of honor. Though only joking, he suggests that honor also feeds his vanity. He wants to be publicly acknowledged as a great man and seen wearing fine clothes. He laughs only when the women robe him richly. And then, suddenly, his eye is struck by a beautiful young woman who appears in the passage through which Elesin has come: perhaps a sign of life in the passage to death. Certainly she revives his appetite for sensual beauty and blocks spiritual thoughts. Just as suddenly his language shifts to the key of a different physical appetite:

Tell me who was that goddess through whose lips
I saw the ivory pebbles of Oya's river-bed. . . .
Not even Ogun with the finest hoe he ever
Forged at the anvil could have shaped
That rise of buttocks, not though he had
The richest earth beneath his fingers
Her wrapper was no disguise
For thighs whose ripples shamed the river's
Coils around the hills of Ilesi. (158-9)

En route to the afterlife, Elesin suddenly envisions a different and
more sensuous kind of heaven and an extremely earthbound, sexual
goddess. His keen appetite has led him back from the entrance to the
ancestral world to this heaving, panting earth where he becomes once
again a privileged sensualist:

. . . In all my life
As Horseman to the King, the juiciest
Fruit on every tree was mine. I saw
I touched, I wooed, rarely was the answer No.
The honour of my place, the veneration I
Received in the eye of man or woman
Prospered my suit and
Played havoc with my sleeping hours.
And they tell me my eyes were a hawk
In perpetual hunger. (157-158)

The hunger of his appetite has never left him. Instead of hungering
for honour in death, Elesin is suddenly driven to use his social honour
and royal standing to feed his physical appetite. He demands that
Iyaloja, leader of the market women, arrange his marriage to this
young woman, despite the fact that she is betrothed to Iyaloja's son.
By doing so, he shows an important confusion about honour. He
turns the world away from his transcendent sacrifice and back to his
physical wants by telling Iyaloja, "Then honour me. I deserve a bed of
honour to lie upon" (160). She replies that his honour now rests upon
fulfilling his sacrifice: "You are not one who eats and leaves nothing

on his plate for children." His people consider him a sacred provider, not a glutton, a giver of life, because he dares to overcome death, not an eater of left-overs. But since his appetite for verbal wit is equal to his other desires, Elesin can twist Iyaloja's warning into an assertion that his final act of fertility will be a blessing to enrich the world's abundance:

Then let me travel light. Let
Seed that will not serve the stomach
On the way remain behind. Let it take root
In the earth of my choice, in this earth
I leave behind. (160)

In language rich with fertility, Elesin makes it seem as if feeding his appetite will enrich the lives of the living. Iyaloja reminds him in his own imagery not to turn his blessings into a curse: "The living must eat and drink. When the moment comes, don't turn the food to rodent's droppings in their mouth" (162). Excessive appetite can become disgusting and turn life's feast into the excremental leavings of scavengers. Despite this warning, the scene ends with Elesin's face aglow with pleasure as the young woman kneels before him. One indeed wonders whether he is ready to leave a world that continues to feed his appetite, allowing him to charge it to the account of his honor. In his rich and sensuous language, Soyinka has established the physical rhythms to which Elesin dances along the passage to immortality.

If the first scene is a lyrical hymn to the appetite, then the second and third scenes represent a call to duty. They reaffirm another historical reality in Nigeria besides the Yoruba tradition. Soyinka has set the play during World War II, when Nigeria was an English colony and England was at war. Elesin's ritual, which follows the death of his king, coincides with a visit to Nigeria by the Prince of Wales. Thus, the English District Officer, Simon Pilkings, intercedes to have Elesin arrested so that he cannot perform his suicide. Pilkins and his wife, Jane, believe that it is their duty to keep Elesin from dying. But when his Sergeant Amusa and constables enter the market, they are blocked by the market women who drive them from the scene, mocking their impotence in the service of the white man. The girls "don't want the eater of white left-overs at the feast" (179). Their power over the colonial police is a sign that the English cannot truly determine the crucial events of Yoruba culture. Once again the term "eater of left-overs" is used to refer to a dishonored servant in league with the wrong master. Immediately after their departure, Elesin Oba consummates his marriage and then begins his final departure ritual. Though the market may seem an inappropriate location for his dance of death, we are reminded that his approaching end whetted Elesin's appetite for life. So first he marries and then he begins to die, and his transitional dance commences in a solemn but not sad mood. The Praise Singer asserts that Elesin's death represents a voluntary and heroic triumph over death: "It takes an Elesin to die the death of death.... Only Elesin ... dies the unknowable death of death" (184). Then Elesin dances into a trance as the lights dim. There is no reason to believe that his next encounter will not be with the ancestors. The English efforts to arrest him have failed and there seems to be nothing to stop him now.

The next scene, set at the English Ball to honor their Prince's visit, becomes the intellectual heart of the play by questioning whether Elesin Oba's self-sacrifice is a worthy one or a destructive feudal anachronism. The debaters are Elesin's son Olunde, who has returned from his medical training in England to bury his father, and Jane Pilkings. Olunde regards his father's death as self-sacrifice, essential to the continuity of his culture. Having been in England during the war, he has come to respect a similar strain in the English character: the willingness to sacrifice oneself for the communal good. The case of a captain who blew himself up with his ship when it endangered an entire harbor causes them to disagree. Olunde is inspired by the self-sacrifice, whereas Jane adamantly maintains that "life should never be thrown deliberately away" (193). That is exactly her opinion regarding Elesin's sacrifice. She regards it as a waste of life in service to the worst aspects of the past: "it is still a barbaric custom. It is even worse—it's feudal! The King dies and a chieftain must be buried with him. How feudalistic can you get!" (194). Olunde, on the other hand, represents the powerful idealism of Eman in *The Strong Breed*. He views his father's death as a sacred compact based on honor and tells Jane, "What can you offer him in place of his peace of mind, in place of the honor and veneration of his own people? What would you think of your Prince if he refused to accept the risk of losing his life on this voyage?" (194).

Of course, their points of view are different. Olunde's attitude echoes the words of the Praise Singer in describing Elesin's sacrifice as a victory over death and a denial of fear at the end of life. As a transition to the world of the ancestors, it is also an affirmation of the Yoruba belief in the afterlife. It is no accident that Soyinka makes it clear that the Pilkings are not believing Christians, and their negative views of Yoruba culture are particularly cynical concerning attitudes toward death and the ancestors. We see them for the first time tangoing in the costumes of the Egungun and mocking an ancestral masquerade in order to entertain the Prince at the Ball. Pilkings repeatedly expresses racist colonial views of Africans and his wife seems only to voice a more polite version. When Olunde expresses both pride and sadness in his father's presumed death, Jane blurts out, "You're just a savage like all the rest" (197).

The argument is abruptly halted by the sound of Elesin Oba's voice. Despite earlier expectations, Pilkings has managed to arrest Elesin. The drama is heightened when he enters in handcuffs and immediately begs for his son's understanding. But Olunde rejects him out of hand, employing the terms earlier used to condemn excessive appetite: "I have no father, eater of left-overs" (203). The son walks out, leaving his father sobbing on the ground. The proud horseman has fallen in shame before his son. Having failed to control his appetite, he has spilled the calabash of honor. But he is still not ready to die.

First he reappears in chains, imprisoned in a place that was once used to store slaves. He has become re-enslaved to both the Europeans and his own appetite for physical life. If he were only imprisoned by the English, he would feel anger but no shame. But Elesin dishonored the feast of his life when he failed to end it and became an eater of left-overs. At first he tries to blame others for his downfall, such as Pilkings and his new young wife, to whom he says,

. . . You were the final gift of the living to their
Emissary to the land of the ancestors, and perhaps

... and perhaps your
warmth and youth brought new insights of this
world to me and turned my feet leaden on this side
of the abyss. For I confess to you, daughter, my weakness
came not merely from the abomination of the
white man who came violently into my fading
presence, there was also a weight of longing on my
earth-held limbs. I could have shaken it off, already my
my foot had begun to lift but then, the white ghost
entered and all was defiled. (207)

Elesin admits that his appetite for life held him to the earth, yet he
claims that he would have surmounted this obstacle if the white man
had not intervened.

Iyaloja then enters to serve as Elesin's final teacher, returning the
focus of his shame back on himself. She reminds him of the excesses
of his appetite:

We fed you sweetmeats such as we hope awaited
you on the other side. But you said No, I must eat
The world's left-overs . . . No, you said, I am the
hunter's dog and I shall eat the entrails of the
game and the faeces of the hunter . . . You said No,
I shall step in the vomit of cats and the droppings
of mice. (210-11)

She reminds Elesin that his desire was once directed toward the afterlife as much as this earthly one. His failure thus signifies a betrayal of
his people and his culture. In replying to her warnings, Elesin confus-
es the role played by the English with his own physical desires:

What were your warnings beside the moist contact
f living earth between my fingers . . . the renewal
of famished embers lodged eternally in the heart of
man . . . It is when the alien hand pollutes the source
of will, when a strange force of violence shatters
the mind's calm resolution, this is when a man is

made to commit the awful treachery of relief,
commit in his thought the unspeakable blasphemy of
seeing the hand of the gods in this alien rupture
of the world . . . there might be the hand of the gods in
the stranger's intervention. (212)

Elesin feels that the intervention of the English was meant to be, that it was the instrument of the gods acting in accord with his own appetite. Perhaps the arguments of Jane Pilkings against ritual self-sacrifice were meant to have more of an effect on Elesin than on his son Olunde. Perhaps his physical appetite eclipsed his spiritual faith and he excused himself knowing that he could blame the English. In doing so, however, Elesin is complicated in the colonial subjugation of his people. As Iyaloja says to Pilkings, "This is the man whose weakened understanding holds us in bondage to you" (214). When a man's faith in his culture weakens, then he is most open to the divergent views of others. Elesin's own overwhelming appetite for life coincided with the idea that "life should never be thrown deliberately away" (193). If life itself is sacred, then all attempts to end it are either tragic or wrong. But we must remember that Elesin embraced his sacrifice willingly. He viewed it proudly as a triumph over the fear of death, as the basis of his honor and as a way of re-uniting with his king. He bid the world watch him dance by performing in the open market, and he danced into a trance without interference from the colonial police. In short, he really has no one to blame but himself. As the noble horseman he had the reins of the world placed in his hand, yet, as the Praise Singer says, "you watched it plunge over the edge of the bitter precipe . . . [until] . . . our world is tumbling in the void of strangers" (218).

Iyaloja enters for the final time, bearing the body of his son to Elesin. To rescue his father's failure, Olunde has sacrificed himself. Though it fulfills the burial ritual of the king, Olunde's death completes Elesin's shame. The son who replaces his father reverses the natural order of time. Iyaloja says, "The son has proved the father Elesin, and there is nothing left in your mouth to gnash but infant gums" (218). Initially the carrier of Yoruba tradition, Elesin Oba has proven to be an alienated and sensual man. Having failed to sacrifice himself according to tradition, Elesin finally commits suicide as a modern man, out of a profound sense of loss and shame. He suddenly loops his chain around his neck and strangles himself dramatically. He has lost everything: his honor, his title, and his son. Why not also his life? Tragically, his late suicide cannot reclaim what has been destroyed. As Iyaloja says,

> He is gone at last into the passage but oh, how
> late it all is. His son will feast on the meat
> and throw him the bones. The passage is clogged
> with droppings from the King's stallion; he will
> arrive all stained with dung. (219)

Elesin Oba is forever doomed to eat left-overs and be fouled with excrement. As for the English who tried to control Yoruba destiny, Iyaloja suggests that their victory might be as empty as Kongi's Harvest, based as it is on the tragic sacrifice and shame. She tells Pilkings, "The gods demanded only the old expired plantain but you cut down the sap-laden shoot to feed your pride. There is your board. Feast on it" (219). Beware appetite, she seems to say, because it can lead to disgusting excess.

So Elesin dies in tragic disgrace as a man who betrays his family and people because his appetite undermined his noble goals of self-sacrifice. In this he is like other appetite-crazed leaders of modern Africa such as Kongi. His excessive drives and ego cause the people's suffering. He is also an unfortunate African like Lakunle who has lost his grip on his own culture and opted for the call of the European-west. He leaves life filled with shame and loss rather than noble self-sacrifice. In the end both his death and his life have been diminished. And yet Elesin is a genuinely tragic character who brings about his own fall and causes the sacrifice of his son. For his part, Olunde reminds us of Eman, Daodu, and Segi: his youthful idealism keeps him truer to his culture than his father. For Elesin, the contradictory appetites for life and honor led him to a crossroads he could not get beyond. But nowhere in Soyinka's dramatic work has the conflict between sacrifice and appetite produced such powerful tragedy.

Works Cited

Soyinka, Wole. *Collected Plays 1*. Oxford: Oxford University Press, 1989.

_____. *Collected Plays 2*. Oxford: Oxford University Press, 1974.

_____. *Soyinka: Six Plays*. London: Methuen, 1984.

9

The Political Conscious in the Cinema and Literature of Wole Soyinka

ONOOKOME OKOME

The feeling among Nigerian economists and social analysts during the dictatorships of the *generals*—Ibrahim Babangida and Sanni Abacha—was that the crime of political misbehavior can be placed on the doorstep of the people. Critics have blamed the people of Nigeria for being docile and minimally opportunistic in their approach to prevalent political predicament. Since the first military *coup d'etat* in 1966, the Nigerian people have hopelessly watched their political life mangled. They did nothing.

Ken Saro-Wiwa, the slain minority and human rights activist, believed that the political problem in Nigeria is primarily that of follower-ship, not of leadership. Chinua Achebe, Africa's respected novelist and prose stylist, thinks otherwise. The problem with Nigeria, according to Achebe in his slim, controversial book on Nigeria's socio-political life, is principally that of leadership. He blames most

107

Nigerian political and traditional leaders for their shortsightedness, bigotry, and ethnic parochialism. Since independence in 1960, Achebe claims, Nigeria has not had the good fortune of a dedicated, altruistic leader.[1]

The case of Nigeria is the classic example of a country lost among its many natural and human resources. It is the obvious case of the squandering of a nation's resources by a small self-seeking clique of people who are indiscriminately parasitic or who, at best, occupy the unenviable position of an uncritical *comprador*. What was once perceived as the Nigerian Dream is now generally regarded as the Nigerian Shame. This shame is vast, destroying the collective and individual psyches of the nation and denying any true movement towards a democratic life. Yet, this is the only prerequisite to the full utilization of the human and material resources available to Nigerians.

Independence ushered in hopes in the 1960s. It was a period of political stability. The Nigerian nation was seen as a possible model for Africa's democratic march. Although this hope was dashed in the events of 1963 – 1966, which culminated in the Nigerian Civil War in 1967, all hope was not lost. This chasm was seen by many truly as one of the many obstacles of political integration that the country needed to surmount. After all, the nation did not come to be as a result of plebiscite. It was the arbitrary amalgamation of diverse ethnic kingdoms and peoples, some of whom share deep-seated historical pride. Soon after the Civil War, which lasted from 1967-70, new hopes and new aspirations were rekindled. It was as if the long expected *discursive centre* was about to be formed. The "*discursive center,*" which Foucault[2] sees as the *soul* of all plural nations, has consistently eluded the Nigerian nation. Nigeria came into being without a distinct *soul* of commonality among its culturally diverse ethnic groups, which according to Ernest Renan and Foucault is necessary for a viable political system.

The sudden crude oil wealth helped in no small way to prop up hopes among Nigerians. The Gowon Regime, a military government, which oversaw the war and its immediate aftermath, was said to have boasted that "Nigeria's problem was not that of money, but how to spend it." The 1970s provided vast potentials for young Nigerians. As soon as the young Nigerians grabbed their university degree, they were given good jobs, well paying; they bought cars, and looked forward to a rewarding life. Politically, the state was stable. Social life in big cities—Kano, Jos, Maiduguri, Lagos, Benin, Warri, Onitsha, Aba, Ibadan, Port-Harcourt and many more—was secured. One could move from one part of the country to another without fear of molestation. Ethnicity was not then a vicious political weapon. Corruption was not endemic. Real business flourished. The school system worked. Nigerian scholars, intellectuals, university workers, and teachers had respect in world literati. The army still had a semblance of public respect. Road network was good and expanding. There was a dream, there was hope.

By the 1980s, Nigeria's DREAM had become a "wasted opportunity." In the place of a stable political era of the oil-boom, a reign of anarchy was instituted. The degeneration began in the late 1970s with the overthrow of Major General Gowon. The brief purposeful Regime of General Murtala Mohammed gave way to Major General Obasanjo's regime of circumstance. Obasanjo's regime sat on the fence and did nothing decisive until 1979 when it voluntarily handed over to the "democratically elected civilian government" of Alhaji Shehu Aliu Shagari.

Shagari's reign was profligate, corrupt, and highly insensitive to the yearnings of the Nigerian-in-the-street. Brazen use of state power, corrupt enrichment, stupendous display of personal wealth, and an epic neglect of the public health system, education, and political life led to its demise in 1983 when General Buhari and his alter-ego, General Idiagbon, took over in a military coup. For a while, some sanity prevailed, but this was to be only a brief interlude. Within the two months that this regime lasted, a significant turn in the social attitude of Nigerians was recorded. A social orientation program called War Against Indiscipline (WAI) was launched and vigorously pursued. Attitudes towards public utilities changed dramatically and Nigeria seemed to be headed somewhere. This hope was dashed. Although many critics would criticize the Buhari/Idiagbon era for its austere attitude to public spending, its highhandedness in dealing with the vibrant, somewhat irresponsible Nigerian press, and the stoic radicalism of its leaders, Nigerians can now look back to that period of political reign with nostalgia.

In 1985 the Buhari/Idiagbon leadership was changed. General Babangida, a member of the Supreme Military Council (SMC) under the Buhari/Idiagbon regime, organized a carefully planned palace coup. This was in August, 1985. Since then the political and economic life of the average Nigerians have declined progressively and unabated. The Babangida Era, a period of political life noted for its slimy military politics, is a period of public life that most Nigerians would hate to relive. In what seemed like a nightmare, the economy plummeted, the Naira, the national currency, with a one-to-one exchange value to the United States Dollar, sank and by 1993, when Babangida was forced by huge public outcry to "step aside,"[3] the Naira had sunk to an all time low, exchanging at 40 to the US $1.

The Babangida Era will be remembered for many ills. But none of these will be more devastating to the national psyche than the profligacy of the regime's attitude to spending public funds. William Keeling, the British journalist who wrote for the London *Financial Times,* was deported when he reported that Babangida's misadventure in the small, war-torn African nation of Liberia amounted to US$550 million. This huge sum of money was the fallout from the Gulf War. Kept in special accounts, Babangida and his henchmen accessed it anytime they wanted. The Central Bank was made to report directly to Babangida's Presidency, and the First Lady, Mariam Babangida's prodigious spending outmatched Imelda Marco's epic taste. With the Better Life Programme in place, fully supported by the Federal Government under General Babangida, the First Lady was able to divert huge sums of money into her coffers. As if the drain on the national economy was not enough, Babangida set up white-elephant projects such as the People's Bank and instituted a process of a dubious transition to democratic rule in 1986. The People's Bank project (which was a copy from some Asian country) was conceived as a means of extending loan facilities to peasant farmers and the low-income industrialists. It turned out a jamboree of corrupt government officials. Operators of this bank grew richer and the Chairman, the late Chief Tai Solarin, a man of conscience, a social crusader, had to resign in the event of public outcry. When Babangida left office hurriedly for his 50-bedroom home in Minna, Niger State, little was left in the treasury. But before he left he set up an Interim Government. This government was headed by Chief Ernest Shonekan, a successful businessman from the Southwestern part of the country.

The Interim Government was the "child of circumstances," as some political analysts have termed it. On June 12, 1993, President Babangida was force to conduct presidential elections, after so many unkept promises and the winner of that polling was undoubtedly Chief M.K.O. Abiola. The Chief did not get the position. The President did not want him to. Babangida had not reckoned that the election was going to be peaceful and fair. He did not reckon that there was going to be a clear victor. He annulled the election and set up the Interim Government. What followed was unprecedented in the political and economic history of Nigeria. Civil and human rights movements sprang all over the country, demanding that democracy prevail and the rightful winner of the presidential elections be given the ticket. From July to November, 1993, commercial activities in many cities in Nigeria were paralyzed. Foreign nationals were advised to flee the country, as civil war was imminent. In November, the Interim Government was set up. Although this doused the flame of protests in the streets, it was not to last for long. After a spell of deep uneasy calm, protesters, foreign missions and pre-democracy movements started calling for the installation of the winner of the June 12 presidential elections. By November, 1993 there were clear signs that there was no government in place. The Interim Government was not respected. At this point, General Sanni Abacha moved in. He sacked Chief Ernest Shonekan's Interim Government and installed himself. The General had been part of Babangida's team. A dogged fighter and a strategist of great potential, he out schemed Babangida and remained as Chief of Defense Staff during the Shonekan-led Interim Government. When he found the time right, he acted. He reigned for a while as the eighth military leader of the battered Nigerian economy since independence.

When Abacha took over from the Interim Government, the economy had slumped; nothing worked, moral attitude had declined abysmally, and the national ethos—or what was left of it—was under severe public scrutiny. Coming from Babangida's politics of hatred and economic misrule, the public, sensitized since the 1980s, was violently critical of Abacha's take-over. To calm nerves, Abacha set up the Constitutional Conference. His aim was for this conference to decide the political future of Nigeria. His reason was that previous political options, the parliamentary and American democracy, had failed the nation. Hurriedly, old and dubious politicians were drafted to Abuja, the administrative headquarters of the nation. When the controversial conference kicked off, it was neither the nation that was discussed nor the June 12 issue. It was the welfare of conferees. Many observers consider the conference a political ploy. General Abacha was only buying time. He wanted to remain in Abuja for as long as he could manage it. The maddening spell of the detention of pro-democracy activists had proven this. June 12, a political watershed, the most eloquent testimony of Nigeria's greatest and boldest move towards popular rule, was annulled. What happened after the annulment of the elections of 1993 was a clean, unambiguous demonstration of the people's will— the desire to move with the democratic world. In the protest that ensued, a lot of people laid down their lives for the course of democracy. I cannot think of anything close to this in the recent history of any African State. It was a collective assent. The June 1993 riots were demonstrations for democracy, for hope.

Predictably, the economy of the country declined further in Abacha's time. There was a dangerous calm in the political atmosphere. All opposition seemed have been defeated, but this was only on the surface. Foreign missions in Abuja were careful about what they said about the Constitutional Conference, which was hurriedly set up to buy time for the General. There was a general attitude of what Nigerians would describe as "wait-and-see." Meanwhile, the art and act of corruption, abuse of office, ethnic chauvinism, and religious bigotry, which the Babangida years made official in Nigeria's social and political fabric, assumed deadly dimensions. To get along into government circles, you had to belong to the right religious block or ethnic origin, the alternative is to be the loyal friend of the General and/ or his friends. Corruption in Abacha's Nigeria was endemic, pervasive and openly admitted. The Nigerian *Shame,* which Jack E. White aptly spelled out in his article, "Shamed by Their Nation," in the September 6, 1993 edition of the *New York Times* grew hydra-headed, unchecked.

Even now years after this denigration, Nigeria lay prostrate under the rich African sun, waiting to fulfill the unspoken pledges which leaders in Somalia, Ethiopia, Angola, Liberia, and the former Soviet Union had inflicted on their political entities. Food is scarce. Wages are slightly below slave income and the paradox is a stunning picture: those close to the small military clique in power are living big. They flaunt their wealth: big cars, big houses, big parties.

In the midst of all the dictatorial madness, one voice, among a growing chorus of dissent, remained solidly devoted to a quick return to democratic rule. It was the voice of Professor Wole Soyinka, winner of the 1986 Nobel Prize for Literature. The Nobel citation captures precisely Soyinka's literary preoccupation. He is *the* African writer who "fashioned the drama of existence." Indeed, Soyinka has fashioned the drama of Nigerian existence since the 1960s. In his Nobel acceptance speech, Soyinka reiterates this major pre-occupation, merging the literary and social activism of his years before the Nobel into a synthesis, which is a pro-people and pro-Nigerian democracy for a country that has suffered strangely from the mis-rule of a small military clan. The theoretical underpinning of his literary work is supplied in these words: "justice is the first condition of humanity." Soyinka's literature, like that of his compatriot, Chinua Achebe, is a graphic description of the morbid transitional phases of Nigeria's social, political, and cultural life. His literature is life, sourced in the very turbulence of the Nigerian nation.

A chronological survey of Soyinka's dramas is in many ways a study of Nigeria's politics. As Dan Izbevbaye puts it, for Soyinka, "life is more important than literature; life is the higher form of art." Soyinka's art has always been art on behalf of his people, the struggles of the downtrodden, the *other* voice of reason, and the conscience of a wayward political system. In Soyinka's work, literature is not merely the verbal assemblage of social facts. It is, according to Izevbaye's, the "blueprint for social action." The "man dies who keeps quiet in the face of tyranny," Soyinka was quoted to have said once. This statement is explicitly sustained in his prison notes, *The Man Died,* was his reaction to his incarceration in solitary confinement for being suspected of having sympathy for the Biafran. Soyinka has, of course, suffered personal physical assault for his country and on behalf of its people. Suspected of having sympathy for the rebellious *Biafrans* during the Nigerian Civil

113

War, he was incarcerated for almost two years in 1967-69.

In the 1960s, when it became obvious that the first group of Nigerian politicians were irresponsible shadow-chasers who were more interested in swelling their pockets and their bank accounts, Soyinka cautioned the people of the dangerous development. Outraged by this apparent show of political recklessness, Soyinka had screamed, but nobody of substance listened. Those who consider his inauguration of the student body, the Pyrate Confraternity, during his university days at Ibadan an infantile exercise, need to rethink. With the motto which emphasizes objective resistance to crippling social conventions, Soyinka and other pioneers created a formidable body of enthusiast and patriots, deeply passionate and committed to the eradication of social vices and corruption. This body has moved out of the universities and now commands influential posts in the larger Nigerian society today. The idyll of this group is not far from what Soyinka has instituted in the radical thinking of Nigeria's social and political life: "justice is the first condition of humanity."

Soyinka's literature is a trenchant testimony of his social crusade, aptly summed up in his words, "justice is the first condition of humanity." Soyinka confesses that he became aware of his political *self* in a radical manner while he was in England in the 1950s. He saw the drifting political life of the new Nigerian nation as the new leaders jostled for political position prior to independence and was astonished at the show of outright recklessness of the new post-colonial ruling class. On his return to Nigeria, he had the opportunity to take a critical look at this political idiocy. In his play, *A Dance of the Forests,* commissioned for performance during the Independence celebration, Soyinka used the opportunity to show the drift of this new nation. Among the many metaphors which saturate the episodic structure of this rather difficult play, the image of the *half-child* (Abiku) [4] is very significant. The thesis of this play is simple: the nation is a still-born. It is in the process of becoming. This was proven right when the Eastern parts of the Igbo-speaking people attempted a break-away in the late 1960s. This resulted in the Civil War of 1967-1970.

Kongi's Harvest, one of Soyinka's early power plays, is a vehement attack on post-independence military dictatorship. The story is simply about the choice of political direction. The first coup had taken place in 1966 and there was a counter-coup. *Kongi's Harvest* criticizes both military and traditional rulerships. It accuses them of obnoxious cultural bigotry and instigates the "new people" to rethink their political life. While this play stops short of defining a clear political choice, it presents an array of political options. One of them is the brand of democracy, which is defined by the people for the people. Military autocracy and traditional feudalism are presented as two political options which must not be tolerated. What comes out in *Kongi's Harvest*, as in *From Zia With Love* or *A Play of Giants* for that matter, is an elaborate dislike for military autocracy. Nothing, according to these play texts, is more insidious and debilitating than military rulers.

In all his dramatic works, Soyinka has looked profoundly at one aspect of Nigeria's collective existence or the other. In *Trials of Brother Jero and Jero's Metamorphosis,* Soyinka takes a swipe at Nigeria's religious hypocrisy. In *The Road,* a very philosophical play, Soyinka is interested in examining the quest for the meaning of *Death*, which the Professor undertakes in this macabre drama. *Opera Woyonsi* is a triumphant indictment of the misrule of the Gowon Administration. *A Play of Giants* castigates the idiotic practices of African despotic rulers such as Idi Amin of Uganda and Jean Bedel Bokasa and all those who take political cues from these rulers. *From Zia With Love* is more specific about the cultural topography of dictatorship. It is the Nigerian political scene of the Idiagbon/Buhari era, which was abrogated by General Babangida. The preface to the text is very explicit about this. *From Zia With Love* is a straight attack on the Buhari/Idiagbon government which lasted two years, 1983-1985. This regime was noted for its high-handedness, its repressive opposition to the media, and its "dignified silence" to the plight of the people as Soyinka once puts it.

Soyinka's political literature is not restricted to the dramatic genre. In his novels, *The Interpreters* and *Season of Anomy,* he dissects the pattern of societal decay through true-to-life characters. His characterization is almost too real, situated within given social and political references of Nigeria's recent history. Soyinka has also written a dozen books of poems. While some emphasize the political, others look at the cultural.

Critics may complain that Soyinka's drama, indeed his literature, is far too elitist to make any immediate relevance to the politics of the nation. There is also the complaint that Soyinka is often esoteric in his deployment of language; that he mystifies ordinary and very mundane issues of social relevance. This is not altogether true. However, very these critics will fail to recognize the immense contribution that Soyinka's literature has had on the political development of the Nigerian nation.

Aware of the controversy surrounding his literature, Soyinka realized that to reach the teeming illiterate population, a more popular medium must be employed in the struggle against tyranny, political injustices, and moral depravity in contemporary Nigerian society. The Second Republic (1979-1983) proved to be a period critics of dictatorship described as charged with "uncertainties, fears, angst and perhaps, dread."[5] The point has been made earlier that Shehu Shagari, President of Nigeria from 1979 to 1983 was not in full control of his cabinet. Ministers held immense power, controlling a significant portion of national political activities. Reacting to this dicey situation, Soyinka realized that "book talk" (meaning intellectual talk disseminated through books) cannot solve the immediate problem. In 1983, there was to be a general election. Shagari, the incumbent President, was sure of victory. His political hangers-on were bent on giving the incumbent President a "landslide victory." Soyinka saw all the shenanigan of the show of political bravado and decided to act. He did using a popular a medium. He turned to the long playing record. He waxed and released *Unlimited Liability Company* just about when the general election result of 1983 was to be released. The long-playing record is a running commentary on the atrocious social and political records of that civilian rule in Nigeria. He castigates the Shagari regime, blaming it for gross dereliction of duty, official corruption, brazen power-show, and an unprecedented show of insensitivity to the plight of the common man. This record paints a gloomy picture of what is to come. It became an immediate hit. Its social satire is infused with popular lyrics from the popular highlife music maestro, Njamanze, who had thrilled urban audiences in Nigeria in the 1960s and 1970s. Predictably, the government of Shehu Shagari banned airing of the music in public. The Buhari/Idiagbon regime did the same. However, this did not deter its influence and popularity on University campuses nationwide. Some state-owned radio and television stations used it as *gap-song*. Soyinka scored a point here. However, that this did not deter the long waited "landslide victory." When the results of the 1983 elections were declared, President Shagari was said to have defeated all other candidates who ran against him by a controversial landslide majority, the so-called two-thirds majority *wahala*.

In his social crusade, Soyinka has also tried his luck with the film medium. In 1970, in collaboration with an indigenous film company, Calpenny Nigeria Limited, Soyinka made *Kongi's Harvest,* adapted from his play of the same title. This film is also a running commentary on dictatorship, especially of the kind that is debilitating wayward. He presents in this film the political choices that an independent African society is faced with. The political choices are wayward dictatorship, obtuse traditionalism, and a potpourri of the first two. Kongi, the dictator of Isma, is the exemplar of the first political choice, Oba Danlola represents the second choice, and the Daudu/Segi political coalition represents the middle point. The sad fact is that Soyinka does not assign a redemptive color to any of these. In fact, the Daudu/Segi coalition is not sufficiently grounded in the matters of the moment to make any significant input to the political debate engendered in the text. This text seems to suggest that the democratic impulse is a dynamic system which takes time to mature.

Pursuing his social crusade against corrupt government in the medium of film, Soyinka made *Blues for a Prodigal* in 1984. James Gibbs describes the social context of this film appropriately when he asserts that "this film is an occasional piece, a response to a particular government." This film, like the long-playing record, *Unlimited Liability Company,* is a virulent response to the Shagari administration. It is not unusual that Soyinka spends a great deal of time and resources to denounce the Shagari government. As a civilian government, Soyinka saw the possibility of a viable democratic heritage springing from it. It would be recalled that since the first republic, headed by Tafawa Balewa in the 1960s, no civilian government had gotten to power. It was the military all through, until General Olusegun Obasanjo[6] willingly handed power over to Shagari after a democratic election. Bitter that "bloody civilians" were messing up things, Soyinka became very upset. In a fundamental sense, *Blues for a Prodigal* is the first true underground film in the short history of indigenous film production in Nigeria.

For Soyinka, the Babangida regime, which promised to sanitize the social and political system, looked good. After the hated Buhari/Idiagbon, any thing would have been preferred. The hope which Soyinka had in the post-Buhari Regime was short-lived. Before he realized the fraud of the Babangida Regime, Soyinka agreed to take the position of Chairman of the Federal Road Safety Commission in that government. Critics railed at him, but he too maintained "a dignified silence," hoping that time would prove the critics wrong. One of the most persuasive criticisms against Soyinka at this point of his social crusade against military despotism was that he had done wrong to take any form of social work under the military. Soyinka said it was for the benefit of the people. He had set up a similar road safety campaign program during the regime of Governor Bola Ige of Oyo State. It was quite successful. Soyinka's primary aim was to reduce the volume of the carnage on the Nigerian roads. Soyinka had proven that it is possible to find a crop of Nigerians who were still selfless in the face of acute country-wide philistinism. Soyinka resigned his position as Chairman of the Federal Road Safety Commission in 1994, but not his enthusiastic support for the Commission. He could not cope any longer with the double talk of the Regime.

The Abacha regime has proven to be the most crucial period for democracy in Nigeria. It posed a set of new problems for the nation. During the chaotic end of the Babangida regime, Soyinka had witnessed some assaults on his fundamental human rights. In Abacha's Nigeria, these assaults assumed unprecedented dimension. The Abacha regime imposed all kinds of surveillance on Soyinka's Abeokuta country home to keep him in check. To counter the Abacha onslaught on the people, Soyinka opened up new political options, new strategies. The Abacha era has produced the African Democratic League (ADL), a pro-democracy movement in which Soyinka played a formidable role. But this was not the first of such organizations in which Soyinka had been involved in his career as a social critic and writer. It will be recalled that a similar body, with a different name, was inaugurated during the Gowon Regime. Tagged "Organization For Solidarity, Home and Abroad" (OSHA), its immediate aim in 1973 was to protest General Gowon's visit to England in the face of serious political and social problems at home.

The African Democratic League was Soyinka's special political device to counter the new regime. Under the auspices of ADL, Soyinka sought to prove to Western media why it was necessary for the West to help install democracy in Nigeria. Expectedly, this did not gone down well with the government of Abacha. On November 3, 1994, Soyinka was invited to the PEN meeting by the Czechoslovakian President-writer, Vaclav Havel. The Abacha Regime confiscated his passport, denying him the honor of attending the Sixty-First World PEN Congress at Prague which opened December 6, 1994.

Barely two weeks after this show of state terrorism, the United Nations office in Lagos issued Soyinka UN travel documents. In the face of an apparent show of power and a complete disregard for individual rights by the Abacha regime, Soyinka got "inside" information that he was to be *picked* up. Men of the African Democratic League got together and organized what one BBC reporter termed "a partridge shooting trip" for Soyinka across one of the porous Nigerian borders. Soyinka quietly slipped out of Nigeria on November 20, 1994, returning only after May 19, 1999, soon after Chief Olusegun Obasanjo was installed as the democratically elected President of Nigeria.

Wole Soyinka is a fine example of an African writer who has brought his literature to the street. Nobody living in Nigeria today can convincingly deny Soyinka his place as social crusader. For Soyinka, literature is not just a resurrection of a cultural past; it is not a personal excursion; it is a personal statement about a collective existence, our existence. Even in exile, Soyinka did not relent in the struggle for democracy and justice in his native land. In exile, Soyinka lived the Ogunian spirit of his patron god, Ogun. His literature is the life that we long for, the political *truth* that has so far eluded Nigeria.

Notes

1. This assertion is not only made in the small controversial *The Trouble With Nigeria* (Enugu: Fourth Dimension Publishers, 1993), but also in the many social novels that Achebe has published in his significant literary career. Among his novels where this point is stated clearly are *No Longer At Ease, Arrow of God, A Man of The People,* and, very recently, *Anthills of The Savannah.* In these novels, Chinua Achebe's search is not for the ideal politician, but for the culturally correct and politically upright leader of people capable of steering the badly mangled ship of state out of the terrible economic and political woods. Some critics are of the opinion that this has been the major contribution of Achebe to the political debate in Nigeria, indeed the Third World. See Chinua Achebe's "The Writer and His Community" (Achebe's *Hope and Impediment* [New York, Doubleday, 1989]: 47-61).

2. See also Ernest Renan's essay, "What is A Nation?" (in Homi Bhabha ed., *Nation and Narration* [London/New York, Routledge and Kegan Paul, 1990: 8-28) in which he explains that the "essence of a nation is that all individuals have many things in common, and also that they have forgotten many things" (11). "The nation," he says, "is a soul, a spiritual principle."

3. In General Ibrahim Babangida's final speech before giving up power in 1993, something akin to a valedictory speech, the General said he was "stepping aside" for the interest of the nation. To "step aside" has since become something of the nebulous in Nigeria's political jargon. In most cases, the phrase is used as a symbol of defeat.

4. *Abiku* is the half-child who torments its parents since it keeps coming into and out of being. The translation of the word *Abiku* as *half-child* is a representation of the middle-way which this being inhabits in the order of the Yoruba cosmos.

5. See Dapo Adelugba's "Yapping—A Form of Patriotism." *Before Our Very Eyes* (Ibadan: Spectrum Books, 1987), 183-211.

6. General Obasanjo is currently serving a second term as President of the Federal Republic of Nigeria after the horrific stint in General Abacha's jail.

Works Cited

Achebe, Chinua. *Hopes and Implements: Selected Essays.* New York/London: Doubleday, 1989.

_____. *The Trouble with Nigeria.* Enugu: Fourth Dimension Publishers, 1993.

Izevbaye, Dan. "Assets and Liabilities: Unlimited Liability Company As an Artist's Investment in the Popular Cause." *Before Our Very Eyes.* Ibadan: Spectrum Books Limited, 1987.

Gibbs, James. Review of *Blues For A Prodigal. Wasafari* (Autumn 1985).

Soyinka Wole. *This Past Must Address Its Present.* Occasional Paper, Stokes Fund, No. 3, 1988.

10

Mandela's Earth In Soyinka's Poetic Corpus

EMEVWO BIAKOLO

I t is of general cultural significance that the years immediately preceding the release of Nelson Mandela from jail in February 1990
witnessed a considerable outpouring of aesthetic works devoted to
the subject of the man. In Nigeria alone, besides Wole Soyinka's *Mandela's Earth and Other Poems,* the focus of the present essay, another
major writer, John Pepper Clark-Bekederemo, had at about the same
time published *Mandela and Other Poems.* Innumerable productions
of various lengths and under varying headings in different forms by
more or less minor literati pursuing the same theme also abound.

In popular music, Sonny Okosun's persistent concern with the
subject has been recently complemented by songs from, among many
others, Majek Fashek and, in a feminized variation, using the figure
of Winnie Mandela, Onyeka Onwenu. The situation with the fine
and plastic arts is much less familiar, but reflects the abiding romantic
and legendary attachments for any cross-disciplinary investigations
into the upsurge of *Mandelania* in Nigeria of the late eighties, at least

in the domain of aesthetic production.

If Wole Soyinka will be excused an infection with the Mandela fever at the time, it is not just because of the grandeur of the subject or the urgencies of the historical moment, but also because *Mandela's Earth* represents in some respects something of a departure from his earlier poetry. Admittedly, in *Ogun Abibiman* the substantive concern with the black condition had led to some sort of heroic miscegeneration of Ogun and Shaka, archetypes to be sure, of Nelson Mandela, with the latter of course coming directly from the same *earth* as Shaka.

Secondly, since the theme of Mandela is almost necessarily also the theme of apartheid, racism, and injustice, there are important ways in which Soyinka's pursuit, or rather this particular pursuit, in *Mandela's Earth*, is not new. But even in statistical terms alone, more than a full half of the collection (specifically the sections "Mandela's Earth" and "New York, U.S.A." along with "The Apotheosis of Master Sergeant Doe" in the section "After the Deluge") is devoted to subjects outside his immediate Nigerian environment. Evidently, this environment had been the main focus of Soyinka's earlier poetry in *Idanre and Other Poems* (1976) and *A Shuttle in the Crypt* (1972).

On the other hand, when we consider Soyinka's poetic oeuvre, it is *Idanre and Other Poems*[1] that seems strangely out of place. With the exception of the section "October '66" and possibly "Idanre," in another sense, the rest of the collection generally lacks the sense of dramatic engagement from a social perspective with *particular* events, people, and situations. As a general observation of Soyinka's literary technique, it is usually the particular which provides the pivot for metaphysical musings or social and political statements. When, as in *Id*, he wrestles with essentialist issues (life and death, growth and decay) unsituated within particular socio-historical contexts, the poems lack the dramatic vitality, not to mention irony of expression, customarily associated with Soyinka.

As an illustration, we may compare "Death in the Dawn" and "Post-mortem" (*Id*) with "Procession I" (*SC*). All dealing with the subject of human mortality, we may note several interesting features that link the *dramatic* irony of "Death in the Dawn" to the cold ironic distance of "Post-Mortem" and which serve to distinguish it from

"Procession I." The sardonic grin of:

> Let us love all things of grey; grey slabs
> Grey scalpel, and grey sleep and form,
> Grey images.

> . . . Brother,
> Silenced in the startled hug of
> Your invention (is this mocked grimace
> This closed contortion I?

Yet irony is present in both of them; in one, mere verbal irony, while in the other, the failure of the prayers, which constitute a spiritual sacrifice, as well as of the material offering of the cockerel's death, intensifies the sense of mortal necessity, of fatality.

But we must look at the functions of the ironic closure of "Death in the Dawn" to see its closeness in spirit to "Post-Mortem." The dramatic suddenness and twist in the ending seems more apparent than real for a variety of reasons. For one, we have been forewarned of this very possibility by the opposition in stanza two between the sappy stretch of dawn shadows and "twilight's death and sad prostration."[2] Then, in stanza three, a more funereal image emerges: "Swift, mute/Processions on grey byways . . .' From there on, the advent of death becomes more and more urgent and the poet's intention more and more obvious. So that by the next stanza, when he declares the cockerel's death a futile rite of propitiation, we are led inexorably to conclude that more wrathful marvels are a foot for the holy hour. Thus the impact of the closure becomes more diffused in the structure of expectation. The irony is no less poignant, but its momentary concentration is lost. It is only a little more concentrated, though very different from that of "Post Mortem" which signals its sarcasm from the very first line:

> there are more functions to a
> freezing plant than stocking beer . . .

If we compare these two with "Procession I," the descriptions of the first three or four stanzas in a sedateness of rhythm reflected in the regularity of stanzaic arrangement and indicative of the funeral march, tend to belie the potent drama undergirding this episode. Even the explosively suggestive one-line stanza which follows ("Tread. Drop. Dread. Drop. Dead) is tame by comparison with the later lines of "Death in the Dawn." The musings, fanciful flights, and declarations which follow do not really serve to demonstrate the dramatic nature of the subject.

Yet the issue is precisely that in this prison experience, a historical moment (a nation in crisis) is indissolubly embedded. Moreover, this experience provided the metaphoric space and justification for the poet's metaphysical quests after the meaning of evil, justice, and death (or life if you will). The personal in union with the social engenders the metaphysical. This is unlike in *Id* where there is often a direct leap to ultimate meanings. Occasionally, the *terminus a quo* is social experience, but social experience somewhat depersonalized.

The case of "Idanre" is a peculiar one in this respect. At first sight, the re-enactment of the *passage* of Ogun is another depersonalized exploration of the ontology of heroism. Many commentators have stressed, rightly, the dependence of the poem on the myths and legends of Ogun (Gboyega 1992) or the thematic implication of the narrative structure (Nwoga 1981). But the relationship of the narrator and hero is crucial to understanding the 'social engagement' of "Idanre." As I have argued elsewhere (Biakolo: 1991), a transformative actual relation- ship exists between Ogun, the hero, and Soyinka, the narrator- participant in what Gboyega calls the present event of "Idanre." Through this means, the narrator becomes also a quester and the experience becomes both remote/external/mythic-metaphysical and immediate/personal/social-historical.

Heroism and the heroic quest is never too distant from Soyinka's creative consciousness, of course. But the identification we speak of which occurs in "Idanre" is repeated in other ways in the group of poem called "Four archetypes" (*SC*). Here, however, the symbol of the suffering hero in collision with power takes place against the background of the poet's own concrete personal living history at the time of the composition of the poems. This actuality gives the poems a vitality and truthfulness to which any number of impersonal visions of martyrdom cannot approximate. The striving of "Idanre" to capture this vitality, and any success adduceable thereto, depends greatly upon the truth of this personal experience. It is this which makes even "Poems of bread and earth" (SC) so vastly different from "grey seasons" (*Id*).

When we turn to *Ogun Abibiman,* we are closer by far to what Obi Maduakor calls the subordination of the private and personal to the public voice (75). In many ways, the work is at one in spirit, if not in tone and merit, with *ME.* Here, two traditions (the Ogunian and the Shakan merge (Biakolo 1988:182). Although there exists a gap in narrative and thematic structure which makes the unification of Ogun and Shaka as one essential hero somewhat unsuccessful (Biakolo 1988: 183-191), the thrust, rare in Soyinka, is towards a racialized view of suffering and oppression. This is what justifies the redemptive action (or rather potential action, since in *OA* the preparations and rhetoric do not really issue in any shooting war) of the composite hero Ogun-Shaka.

More germane to the considerations which engage us here, *OA* signals two aspects of Soyinka's poetic career which have come to the fore in *ME.* Firstly, in so far as the earlier collections had been located in subject matter, theme, and sensibility in the Nigerian environment, *OA* represents a major shift towards a more continental and racial outlook. It is true that here, as in *Id,* Ogun, Soyinka's major poetic symbol, maintains a distinctive presence. But this is an Ogun whose "masculine energy is spent" (Maduakor 1991:74). As in "Idanre," his mute resoluteness, as he forges his weapons of war, is not in doubt. Also, the cause, after all, is just. However, by the close of the poem, the Blacksmith's forearm could just as well have gone on lifting, dancing, and swathing till doomsday. Ogun is about to engage his armies in battle in unfamiliar territory.

With *Mandela's Earth and Other Poems,* Soyinka well and truly embarks on a sojourn outside his usual Nigerian haunts. The title section, *Mandela's Earth,* begins with the poem "Your Logic frightens me, Mandela." This is an appropriate commencement in many ways. Written in the ironic panegyric mode which characterizes the "Oriki" of Ogun, many instances of which we have in "Idanre," the poem details images of Mandela's youthful hopes during the nationalist struggle before his imprisonment. It proceeds next to his suspicion of, disdain for, and rejection of "solutions" devised by apartheid rulers. But by far the central thrust of the poem is a playful probe into the secrets of Mandela's longanimity and godlike strength of will. The images deployed here and the way Soyinka uses them to carry forward the subject and theme is especially remarkable, reminding us of "Conservations At Night With A Cockroach" and "Gulliver" in *SC*, not in imagery or tone, but in spirit and subject. In stanzas four and five, specifically, he suggests that perhaps Mandela relied on crossword puzzles or chess or checkers or scrabble or monopoly to pass his monotonous days. But no, each is rejected in turn: "Subversion lurks among chess pieces. Structured clash of black and white . . . And equal board? No!" As for checkers, the "game has no respect for class or kingserf/ordered universe." Monopoly offers the only prospect. But the rules here are a different kettle of fish: "the Cards read 'White Only'/In the Community Chest. Like a gambler's coin/Both sides heads or tails, the 'Chance' Cards read:/Go to jail. *Go straight to jail. Do not pass 'Go.'"*

Next Mandela's vision and will occupy the poet, and in the imagery of moth and bulb we discern the intricate relationship between the black people, the apartheid rulers, and Mandela. In one reading, it is the moth of apartheid that must dash against the steely supernova of Mandela's scorching will. In another, the moth which is the black populace can come to no harm against the light bulb of apartheid. But poised between moth and bulb Mandela's gaze rests on the fluctuations of their constant encounter. In this wise, he becomes the "broken arc of tungsten" the light-giving metal which, trapped, can bend, but never break. He remains sensitive to the slightest political motions, though forced by incarceration to the slow pace of "earth's phlegmatic turns." Yet the poet fears for the generous heart which carries within itself the fate of millions; he fears that it may break from the weakness of will of this multitude.

But it is in "Like Rudolf Hess, the Man said" that the wit and sarcasm of Soyinka comes to the fore in this collection. The dramatic start of the poem sets the tone: "Got you! Trust the Israelis. I bet . . . It's he! Nazi superman in sneaky blackface!" Rendered in the first person, the poem fluctuates between an apostrophic monologue and a "dialogue" between a representative of the apartheid regime and the subject, Mandela, who remains mute throughout.

It details the discovery and capture of Mandela who is indeed Joseph Mengele, the Nazi eugenics experimentalist disguised (Ojaide 1991:739). Against this Mandela-Mengele is a deposition on a legion of the crimes of apartheid: the murders of Sharpeville and Soweto, Steve Biko, Ruth First, and countless others; the harassment of Dennis Brutus and so on. Under the satirical mode, Soyinka displays his gift of verbal irony as in:

> Stripping the "circumcised dogs" To buff and
> Searching secret parts for jewelry. And your love
> For gold teeth—ah yes, gold!
> Gassed them cold and questioned their anatomy.

The ironic play on the common Hebraic contempt for uncircumcised non-Jews achieves full weight first by the use of "buff" which follows and which in this instance does not merely mean a colloquial usage for bare skin, but more appropriately bare *animal skin*. Deeper still, jewelry in the next line is a *double entendre* for precious stones as well as Jewishness. Finally, a macabre touch creeps into the humour, reminiscent of the sardonic irony of "Massacre 66," in the line: "Gassed them cold and questioned their anatomy." Aside from the mortal seriousness of the reference and the accompanying macabre tone, the ironic play belongs to such poems as "Telephone Conversation." The poem could very well have been titled "The Metamorphosis of Mengele," a suggestion supported by the brilliant alliterative line by which Mandela is transformed into the Nazi butcher of Auschwitz:

> Mandela? Mandel . . . Mandel . . . Mengel . . . Mangele!

Between "Like Rudolf Hess, the Man Said" and "Funeral Sermon, Soweto," the next more extended poem is "So Now They Burn the Roof Above Her Head." It is a poem dedicated to Winnie Mandela. Its subject is the harassment of the hero's wife beginning with the *arrest* of her bedspread, on which the bulk of the poem dwells. But more fundamentally, "So Now They Burn" is about color, especially the color red, i.e., that of the bedspread which is also the color of the

African National Congress Flag. The red spread symbolizes love, birth, and regeneration:

> This bedspread knows the pangs of birth.
> Like earth in hope of our remarking, it is
> Generous in love, a feast
> . . . it wears the hues of hopes?

But it also symbolizes death, i.e., heroic passage, and revolution. Away from this color and context, the pre-eminence of color in the poem recurs in the refrain on white: "whited out," "Whited sepulchers." When red shows up again it is the color of fire by which the Apartheid regime enacts its inquisitorial rites on Winnie and the black people.

Judged by length alone, "Funeral Sermon, Soweto" ranks in higher order than "So Now They Burn the Roof Above Her Head." But this poem, which traces outlines of funeral rites among different cultural groups, thus signifying the impetus behind these obsequies, and by contrast reveals the bareness of life and dignity among Sowetans, is rather unsuccessful. The ironic ending where the mourners are treacherously slain, has come too late and too brief, swallowed up by what was after all only an ethnographic excursus. The pathos is entirely lost. What remains of passing interest towards the end are the intertextual codes: echoes of Oswald Mtshali's *Sounds of a Cowhide Drum* and Dennis Brutus' "A Troubadour, I traverse all my land" and "At a funeral" (*A Simple Lust*).

On the other hand, "No He Said" attains a peculiar grandeur. A poem in eight regular septet with an apt contrasting septet and a couplet, it is a dialogue between Mandela and his jailers. The dominant image suggested is that of a Promethean figure chained to a rock and subjected to a variety of temptations by his captors. One after the other he spurns suggestion of isolation, of compromise, despair, and capitulation into personal comfort. The consistent force of his character and will is underlined by his refrain which concludes each stanza: "No, he said." In the end, he establishes his godlike status in this supreme dare, and furnishes a closing vision of hope.

The next major section of the collection is "New York, U.S.A."

But between "Mandela's Earth" and the former is "After the Deluge," which consists of three poems in addition to the initial poem of the sub-title. These are "Apollodorus on the Niger," the masterly executed satire, "The Apotheosis of Master Sergeant Doe" and a strange badly articulated panorama of Nigeria in the eighties, "My Tongue Does Not Marry Slogans."

Composed in rhyming couplets, "The Apotheosis" retraces the path of the late Liberian upstart dictator, Samuel Doe. It is a familiar path trodden by a vast majority of the military "saviors" on the African political scene. The gradual degeneration is treated without any dramatic turns, a style aided by the regularity of the couplet form. The course is followed to its pathetic finish in:

> Your worthy predecessors raise a toast
> From exiled haven,or from the eternal roast

> Swinging Bokassa, Macias Nguema, Idi Amin Dada
> You sucked their teats, you supped from their cannibal larder,

> And belched in unison...

The satire of power and misrule is vintage Soyinka, but "The Apotheosis" is not in the mould of "Conversation At Night With a Cockroach" or even of "Four Archetypes." It belongs more to the style of *A Play of Giants*. Moral outrage is subdued by the consciousness of the banality as well as the risible absurdity of these evils. The optimism of the last stanza that Doe will go the way of his ilk does little to mitigate the dominant sense of ludicrousness of the entire proceeding.

On the other hand, moral energy is evident in "My Tongue Does Not Marry Slogans." At issue is Soyinka's grouse with leftist radicalism, which he accuses of cant. To underline its impotent sloganeering, he provides visual sketches of wrongs in society: the empty clinics, malnutrition, the abandoned dead, famine, Police brutality, and religious violence (none of which seems to arrest the thoughts of ivory tower radicals). Instead, dribbling "slogans a thousand safety/Miles away, holding forth by Staff Club/Swimming Pools," they are at bottom no different from devotees of buddhist nescience. Their quest for "One-Cure/Cure-for-All Eternity" leads them to regard all societal-meliorative efforts as diversions unworthy of notice or support. "My Tongue" is in a sense a poetic version of Soyinka's combative inaugural lecture at the University of Ife (now Obafemi Awolowo University), "Barthes, Leftocracy and Other Mythologies."

We come now to the section "New York, U.S.A." The title poem of this section calls to mind Wole Soyinka's put-down in the sixties at the publication of John Pepper Clark's (now Clark-Bekederemo) *America their America.* Compared to America and even New York herself, all men are small. Those who flay at her, to turn Soyinka on himself, are as children flaying at the giant, so that J. P. Clark-Bekederemo has the last laugh after all.

But in its Horatian manner, "New York, U.S.A." remains interesting as a satire and in some places re-affirms Soyinka as a withering satirist of unmatched status. Cast in the form of a travelogue, the poet provides us his impressions of New York at disembarkation ("Initiation"). Echoes of America's racialism and demented materialism are subtly hinted at in "FOLLOW THE SIGNS, WATCH FOR COLOUR CODES," as well as the next stanza, which compares the immigration process to a Roman amphitheatre. Soon enough the artificiality hits him: "New York loves you!" But this is only a prelude to fuller awareness of the emptiness and barrenness of language in the city, a view of which we get in sub-section II. Nevertheless, the full force of the meaninglessness of the language of love, friendship, concern, and family/community spirit is not felt until the poet's passage through the decrepitude, depravity, violence, and injustice of "subway, New York."

Then in "The Most Expensive Anchorman in U.S.A.," Soyinka puts his satirical gifts to devastating effect. The subject (Dan Rather of CBS?) becomes the prototype of American banality and insensitive media. The satire is more effective as a result of the direct speech attributions. This dramatic mode, with occasional commentary only from the poet, becomes a process of self-revelation of the subject to us. We are back here to the style and environment of "Telephone Conversation."

This section of the collection ends, however, on a happier note, a celebration of the boxing prowess and person of Muhammed Ali. "Muhammed Ali At the Ringside, 1985" is part narrative, part panegyric. It recounts the presence of the boxing legend at a fight. Soyinka situates Ali in what we may call his natural environment. The atmosphere of fanfare and festivity masks the very brutality of the sport—something not lost on the poet. But he is no weeping willow. When the cameras and the poem turn to Ali, the irony is poignant on the stillness of the man who hitherto epitomized the passion and the glory of this fervid social event.

But history is revisited here. Even as his legend dominates the present, the poet presents a vista of his most celebrated fights. And then, he bursts into an *oriki* in the penultimate stanza. On the strength of this stanza and the organization of the poem, "Muhammed Ali at the Ringside, 1985" must rate as perhaps the best in the collection. Certainly, this stanza must rank as some of the greatest lines Soyinka ever wrote, calling to mind not the poetry of the laureate, but the marvelous poetic lines of *Death and the King's Horseman* or even *Kongi's Harvest*.

It is not merely the aggregate of animal metaphor appropriate to this sport which exalts the stanza. The images of butterfly and bee for instance have a definite historical location already in the Ali lore and the poet's adaptation of them is exhilaratingly exact. The snappy incomplete declaratives of the *oriki* style and rhythm are concluded appropriately with the familiar crowd exclamatory shouts of "Ali! Ali!" This is followed by a vintage Soyinka technique, borrowed also from *Ijala* poetry of archetypal comparisons (e.g., Esu) or of short parabolic statements whose allusions are obvious:

> . . . He brings a message—
> Although through the messenger, the neighbourhood is roused
> Yet no one sees his face, he waits for no reply,
> Only that combination three-four calling card,
> The wasp-tail legend: I've been here and gone.

This poem, which shows clearly that Soyinka cannot only curse but eulogize as well, is at one in spirit with the Mandela poems in the collection, especially "No, He Said." They indicate a consciousness of race, expressed in the celebration of forms of black heroism. This consciousness had been sublimated earlier in the mythical/legendary form in the Ogun of "Idanre" or the Shaka and Ogun of *Ogun Abibiman*. What we have here instead is the personal historicization of this consciousness.

The rest of the collection are incidental poems dealing with sundry subjects (from reflection on the interminable arguments about this style ("Transitions"), to a mythologized landscape view of the University of Ife campus ("Campus, Ile-Ife"), to his humorous encounter with his optician ("Doctored Vision"). The collection concludes with the strange poem "Cremation of a Wormy Caryatid." Save perhaps Clark's "Imprisonment of Obatala," there is no African example to compare to this mediation on an architectural column. English competitors for precedence include Keats' "Ode on a Grecian Urn," Shelley's "Ozymandias," and the legendary figures of Tennyson and Browning.

Fundamentally, "Cremation" is a meditation on mortality. The sense of loss occurs at several levels. The primary loss is of the caryatid itself, eaten up by woodworm. Then there is the collapse, the "second deaths" of the royal glories sculptured so beautifully on the column by the artist, along of course with the picture of menials -slaves, no less than birds and beasts. If the *works* of the artist submit to this inner decay, it is indeed the artist himself that has thus died. This is the third level of loss. But there is a fourth—and perhaps a fifth too. The caryatid is destined for fire now because of the inner collapse from worms. This is a more merciless, total, irreducible, loss and it is no wonder that the poet hesitates, "Yet, the poised hand/Briefly trembles."

Somehow it is appropriate that this final loss be accompanied by a dirge, the song of the *gbegbe* leaves. And with this song we are at the core, the heart of Soyinka's aspiration in "Cremation." This song is the *cri de coeur* of all mortals, what Okigbo calls the "imperishable cries" for immortality of the human heart. All the new imaginary forms, glorious as they may seem, which the visions of the past assume in this fire, are finally futile "careful ruins on histories' sands." Even the rain which appeared to promise a reconciliation and recreation of the past merely "affirms the loss." But that aspiration remains in the last desperate line: "Yes, these stubborn/Scepters, exorcised, yet marrying earth to heaven!" It brings no real hope, though, only the clutching of a drowning man at straw.

This poem shows Soyinka at his most personal, meditative mood. Consequently, the language makes no aspiration (never much a Soyinka virtue (to common public access. Even the order of the description of the caryatid and its pictorial depictions reveals no attempt to present any clear linear picture to the reader. Instead "Cremation" gives us the image of the poet-persona as a great and sensitive mind, rather closed in on himself, ruefully pondering, without adapting to the rigors of any definite system, the impermanence of the human estate.

Mandela's Earth and Other Poems, then, is the work of an aging Soyinka, fully possessed still of the vigor of his mind and, even more than that, of his withering wit and a satirical spirit. But the moral outrage of *A Shuttle in the Crypt* has given way to a more benign view of human foibles. It is not a compromise with cant, injustice, and superficiality. Only a maturer, mellower, Horatian outlook, away from the Juvenalian disgust with evil of his younger days. This is also far from the metaphysical orientation of *Idanre and Other Poems* or the mythological disposition of *Ogun Abibiman.* This is Soyinka engaged in a personal assessment of contemporary history in a more public style. The subjects are in a sense commonplace (at least in the sense of public events); the poet's style presumes a communicative public with whom he shares his thoughts on these subjects; but the tone and voice remain those of one man, Wole Soyinka.

Notes

1. All subsequent references to this collection will be abbreviated as *Id.* References to the title poem itself of the collection will however occur as "Idanre." Similarly, *A Shuttle in the Crypt* will be rendered *SC; Ogun Abibiman* as *OA,* and *Mandela's Earth and Other Poems* as *ME.*

2. The ghostly suggestiveness of "shadows" in stanza two even leads us to the mortal vulnerability echoed in "apprehensions for/A naked day" in the next stanza.

Works Cited

A. PRIMARY MATERIALS

Soyinka, Wole. *Idanre and Other Poems*. London: Methuen, 1967.

_____. *A Shuttle in the Crypt*. London: Collings/Methuen, 1972.

_____. *Ogun Abibiman*. London and Ibadan: Collings and Opon Ifa, 1976.

_____. *Mandela's Earth and Other Poems*. Ibadan: Fountain Publications, 1989

B. SECONDARY MATERIALS

Biakolo, Emevwo. *Narrative Categories and Oral-to-Written Literary Transformations*. Unpublished Doctoral Dissertation. Department of English, University of Ibadan, 1988.

_____. "Transformation From Oral to Written Tradition: An Analysis of Soyinka's Idanre." *Gege* (March 1991) 163-177.

Gboyega, Kolawole. "On The Making of Wole Soyinka's Poetry: A Literary Inquiry into His Sources." *Journal of Asian and African Studies* 44 (1992): 119-130.

Maduakor, Obi. *Wole Soyinka: An Introduction to His Writing*. Ibadan: Heinemann, 1991 [Orig., New York and London: Garland, 1986].

Nwoga, Dennis. "Poetry As Revelation: Wole Soyinka." In *Critical Perspectives on Wole Soyinka* Ed. James Gibbs. London: Heinemann, 1981, pp. 173-185.

Ojaide, Tanure. "Ogun Widens His Haunt. Wole Soyinka's New Poems." *Callaloo* 14/3 (1991): 737-751.

11

Ogun's Hand

Social Order in Soyinka's *From Zia With Love*

CHUKWUMA OKOYE

The crises in the continent of Africa are evincible in all spheres of existence—social, political, ideological, economic, historical and cultural. Ambroise Kom passionately agonizes over what he sums as

> the multidimensional failure of our institutions: phantom States in search of an undiscoverable democracy; an extrovert economy which is almost entirely controlled by corrupt networks; a disjointed society whose essential services – schools, public health, personal safety in particular – seem irremediably compromised; young people who are crippled, left to themselves in a world without any ethics (2000: 3)

This grim picture of the state of contemporary Africa is by no means contentious. An objective view reveals even more horrid portraiture:

religious and ethnic motivated genocide, corruption, mismanagement, hunger, poverty, dictatorship, disease, foreign debt, and so on. The genesis of this appalling state of affairs is often traced to our colonizers who greedily and frenziedly tore out territories for themselves and arbitrarily hammered them into convenient nationalist contraptions in utter violation of the peoples' national identities, and also on ourselves who have failed to surmount the befuddling problems of postcoloniality decades after the advent of self-rule. It is however in the search for a functional institution, one that answers to the peculiarities of African needs and aspirations, that contesting discourses have emerged. The controversy that has trailed Ambroise Kom's essay is illustrative of the dynamism that has characterized the debate. Madeleine Borgomano, for instance, controverts Kom's Afropessimistic stance by citing many cases for 'Afro-optimism' (2000.). Similarly Bill Ashcroft contests his recommendation of a clean break from Eurocentrism as the path out of Africa's travails by insisting that there is "some way to use dominant technologies in a way that is appropriate to local conditions and local aspirations." (2004.)

Most African writers have displayed acute dismay with the problems of postcolonial African states and have indeed subscribed to contrasting strategies in the debate to resolve, according to Bill Ashcroft, the "conflict between a dominant discourse and a local reality." (: 1.) In their respective works they have not only reconstructed the jaundiced social realities of their environments but have often proffered some form of elixir. One notable radical option, akin to Ambrose Kom's, is the form of decolonization prescribed by such African nationalists as Ngugi wa Thiongo (1972): a total break from the expressive tools of the colonizer by the adoption of indigenous forms as the only medium of representation capable of narrating authentic African experiences. The opposing option is the insistence that cultural representations are still possible even with culturally alien modes through a process of appropriation and interpolation. Chinua Achebe, for instance, insists that "the English language would be able to carry the weight of my African experience." (1994: 434) Soyinka's position in the polemics is quite obvious. He writes in a foreign language and is, according to Patrick Chabal, "at once utterly modern in the Western sense but also fundamentally African in both inspiration and artistic sensibility" (1996: 4). [1]

Wole Soyinka is ineluctably one of Africa's great writers who have relentlessly focused on the social predicament of the continent. Through his fictional and non-fictional writings, discussions and actions he ranks as "one of the African continent's most vigorous fighters for social justice and most effective campaigners against human rights violations and abuses" (Biodun Jeyifo, 2001: xvi). His writings bear the ineradicable stamp of reformative social consciousness and patriotic zeal. Exploiting whatever medium at his disposal – drama, film, essay, novel, symposium, television, interview, radio – he has unsparingly lashed at the high and mighty and inevitably incurred the wrath of sundry personalities and institutions, resulting in frequent harassment, exile and incarceration. Yet Soyinka remains perilously undaunted. Femi Osofisan catalogues amongst the victims of his vitriolic criticism

> ... the rogues and predators ... the inept and corrupt politi-
> cians, the mimick men in uniform, the bribe-taking and
> indolent bureaucrats, the shallow, pretentious professors,
> and others, the whole gallery of our thieving myopic, and
> 'follow-follow' elite class. (1988:187)

In every respect Soyinka's crusade has indeed been for a stable and equitable society where the rights and privileges of the populace, especially the underprivileged, are guaranteed and social and human infrastructures function optimally. Onookome Okome observes that his art is "the art of his people, the struggle of the downtrodden, the *other* voice of reason, the conscience of a wayward political entity" (2001:59).

In Nigeria, which obviously is the immediate context of Soyinka's literary and critical interest, the African predicament is classic. The colonial bequeathal of geographical and political dislocations has left the country floundering hopelessly in the void of political and social afflictions. For over four decades of political independence the country still searches for a meaningful political institution which would guarantee a decent social order. Indiscipline, tyranny, injustice, starvation, political killings, human rights violations, moral decadence, lawlessness, crime, election malpractices, religious intolerance, and only one major civil war *yet,* mark the social history of the country. This woeful picture is perennial not because of a dearth of socially conscious voices, such as Soyinka's, but because these voices have consistently failed to pierce the concrete deafness of the institutions that be. *From Zia With Love* is yet another volume from these voices. With this play, published six years after the award of the Nobel Prize for Literature, Soyinka displays his typical hand in caustic social and political criticism.

A stylistic interrogation of some of the major plays of Soyinka reveals a pattern of transition from abstraction and obscure symbolism and mysticism to more immediate and aggressive accessibility. A gradual disregard of subtlety from the highly rarefied to the most elemental, direct and confrontational approach to social representation. From the almost impenetrably mystical, symbolic and mythical *A Dance of the Forests* (1960) to the more mundane "King Babu" is discernible a progressive initiative from obtuse allegory and symbolism towards pungent and aggressive social criticism. This pattern could perhaps be a response to his critics' accusation of self-conscious obscurity, or the consequence of his acute pre-occupation with evolving social and political landscape. Or perhaps it is the growing limpidity of the writer's subject. Soyinka himself denies "any attempt to mystify or create obscurities. … But complex subjects sometimes elicit from the writer complex treatments" (Biodun Jeyifo, 2001: 35). *From Zia with Love* for me exemplifies the quintessential Soyinka: a blend of the mythopoet and the elemental social critic; a nexus of the abstruce and the austere; between obscure symbolism and quotidian simplicity.

In this essay I undertake a reading of *From Zia with Love* positioned within what I consider Soyinka's stylistics. I critique the writer's archetypal preoccupation with social inanity – lack of functional social institutions and attitudes – and the nuanced proposition of a panacea metaphorically located in the mythical hand of Ogun, the Yoruba god of iron and war. I shall also observe that this play exemplifies Soyinka's dialectics in the postcolonial construction of African identity or knowledge.

From Zia With Love is set in a remote prison, a penal island surrounded by hostile waters, making it impenetrable and reducing the possibility of escape to the minimum. The entire action of the play takes place between two cells: a general cell and a more exclusive one known as Cell C. The inmates of the general cell comprise of all kinds of criminals. According to the Cell Commandant,

> Political detainee dey here. Manslaughter dey . . . Innocents dey over yonder . . . Mistake dey here. Even coup plotter e dey here. (*From Zia*: 12)

Add to these the Commandant himself who is imprisoned for cocaine trafficking and you have indeed a mélange of criminals. In Cell C we have three men who also engaged in drug trafficking. The action of the play is woven around these men. This action is divisible into the actual and the simulated. The actual action happens in the actual time and place of the prison; while the simulated action is re-enacted by the inmates of the general cell in a 'play-within-the-play' mode. Through these re-enactions the playwright creates a convenient window through which the larger reality of the external world is narrated to the reader. This reality, although spatially and temporally distanced from the prison, is highly influential in the actual time, place, and action of the prison.

The plot of the actual action is very elementary, even familiar. It is about three persons who are arrested and later executed for drug trafficking. However, they were arrested before a death sentence was placed on their crime. Thus the sentence is retroactive. In the actual time and place of the prison nothing much happens. But the prisoners narrate scenes from their pasts, and much of the play's movement depends on these re-enactions. Through multiple role-playing and incidental makeshift sceneries these prisoners re-present the seedy realities of the typical African nation in the throes of military dictatorship; they project images of acts of lawlessness, manic corruption, and scenes of inhumanity. Miguel's song clearly presents the genesis of this lawlessness:

> Power is even rottener . . . But rottener than rottenest
> . . . Is power that makes and breaks—. . .
> The very rule it makes and breaks.

It makes and breaks. (*From Zia*: 92)

Thus the reader is treated to all forms of disgusting images of total abuse of power. The very description of the opening scene gives the reader a literal hint of the kind of action to expect in the play. The sign "Abandon Shame all who Enter Here" (: 1.) prepares the reader for a display of arrant shamelessness. Soon enough the play opens with one of the inmates, Major Awam, presenting his *curriculum vitae* which we understand within the context of the play to mean

> . . . Name. Age. Profession. And then, most important of all, wetin bring you here? What crime you commit? How much sentence they give you? . . . . (*From Zia*: 16)

The dramatic mode of presentation of this *curriculum vitae* is remarkable. According to the "Minister of Information and Culture,"

> . . . in presenting your Curriculum Vitae, you turn it into *ewi* for us and recite it, or you can sing and dance it . . . Or you can preach it like a sermon . . . And last but not the least . . . you can play it for us . . . The play is our favourite of course . . . . (*From Zia*: 16-17)

In these re-presentations the other inmates usually offer assistance by appropriating some of the characters in the story. Thus what is dramatized in this opening scene is the narrative of Major Awam who is officially detained for conspiracy but who in fact only dared to be idealistic in a military dictatorship: "Me, I don't plot coups. I believe in the power of truth." (: 12) It is through this very ingenious dramaturgy that the reader is conducted through the scenes of social and political decadence, through the ridiculous manner by which decisions are made by the people who rule over our lives.

The most significant of these flashbacks in which the *curriculum vitae* of inmates are 'played' is that of the young student who acted as a drug courier for Sebe Irawe, a versatile, ruthless and inventive criminal. The student wittingly committed a crime and got imprisoned just to escape the death sentence passed on him by Sebe Irawe, his devious

boss. Through his narrative one sees how a highly placed military officer, a Wing Commander and member of the Eternal Ruling Council—the highest governing body in the land—connived with the
government of Pakistan under the military leadership of General Zia
to import fifty kilograms of cocaine into the country. His trusted contact in this racket was Sebe Irawe. However, Sebe double-crossed the
Commander and stole the bag of cocaine. This student knows everything about this conspiracy and of Sebe's treachery. He even knows
where the sack of cocaine is hidden. Sebe caught him eavesdropping
on him and decided to hunt him down and kill him. To escape from
this death sentence, therefore, he walked his way into prison.

With this profound technique, Soyinka conveniently narrates
tales of social disorder. Such abuses of power and consequent breakdown of law and order are manifest in the framing and detention of
military personnel who dare to possess opinions contrary to those of
the leader and his cohorts; the wanton destruction of public property
to cover up cases of fraud and embezzlement; molestation and
oppression of the populace by the leadership; widespread injustice
and detention without trial; bribery and other forms of corrupt practices, especially by highly placed persons, and so on.

In *From Zia With Love* the outside world and the prison are set
apart such that the only contact between the two worlds is through an
illicit and precarious racket via an animist water-way which is endangered by the ominous and relentless growth of water hyacinths.
When the play opens, the sea weeds are impenetrable, thus completely isolating the prisoners from any contact with the outside world.
This severance of contact is of grave concern to the prisoners, for they
usually transacted business on that route. According to Detiba,
"Those weeds have made life miserable for everyone" (*From Zia*: 29).

It is possible to identify the prison as a symbolic representation of
contemporary Nigerian society and the water hyacinths as the various
social problems that have placed order beyond the reach of collective
experience. The fight to cut through the water hyacinths, therefore,
represents a desperate and courageous, even futile, effort to forge
social order out of the severance. However, it must be pointed out
that the society is itself partly responsible for this menace. The invasion of the water hyacinths is the consequence of society's irrationali-

ty and callousness. The very society has wittingly nurtured the ominous growth of this divide between itself and social order. The weeds, according to Sebe Irawe, will keep on growing because the society itself supplies nutrients in the form of human waste poured into the lagoon (*From Zia*: 36). It is not by chance that the two arch-criminals in the play are related in name to the water hyacinth. *Sebe* (which is the name of a poisonous snake) and *Irawe* (leaves on the ground) come together to illustrate how truly dangerous Sebe Irawe is. He explains to the Youth that Sebe hides under the camouflage provided by the leaves on the ground until someone steps on it. Then it strikes its unsuspecting victim:

> . . . But suppose it is not that kind of *Irawe*? Suppose the leaves we are talking about, what soja-man calls camouflage, suppose it is not leaves of the ground at all, but that other kind which covers up the lagoon? Suppose that is the kind of *Irawe* under which *Sebe* is hiding. (*From Zia*: 38)

Sebe and his sort are clearly responsible for the state of chaos in the country. If we accept that the water hyacinth is metaphoric of the very forces which have severed the country from social order, then we must see Sebe and his ilk as the instruments of this dislocation. They hide under the chaotic system and take advantage of it. Sebe connives with the high and the low criminals. Like a truly sly snake he lures his military companion into the bush and strikes him dead. He also engages in drug peddling, which is easily one of the greatest ills of the contemporary Nigerian society.

The other criminal, the Cell Commandant, whose real name is Hyacinth, is equally as devious as Sebe Irawe. He boasts:

> Ask the Police—when they booked me for my very first impersonation, over thirty years ago, I fooled them into locking up the genuine person in my stead. (*From Zia*: 17)

Like Sebe, he also trafficked in cocaine. And it is obvious that his status as Cell Commandant is articulated through brute force and ruthlessness. Perhaps the only difference between the two 'weeds' is that one is in prison and the other is not. But soon enough the two of them are bound to meet. Hyacinth has teamed up with the young student to go after the sack of cocaine which Sebe hides in the cushion of his armchair as soon as he breaks out of prison.

It is therefore clear that as long as these high and low criminals continue to operate the crisis in the nation would continue to grow. What Sebe says of the Youth is also true of Sebe himself, the Wing Commander, Hyacinth (Cell Commandant) and all the other criminals:

> . . . As long as the water weed has plenty of your type to feed on, all those so-and-so marine specialists or whatever they call them, they are wasting their time. There is far too much shit like you, waiting to pass through the sewage pipes and nourish the hyacinths. (*From Zia*: 36)

A certain familiarity with Soyinka's debt to Yoruba mythology and his adoption of Ogun, the courageous and ambiguous Yoruba god of iron and war, as his creative essence makes a mythological indexing of *From Zia With Love* absolutely irresistible.

In Yoruba mythology it is related that a certain dangerous primal growth severed the gods from their human subjects. It was Ogun who, at great risk to himself, fashioned an instrument of metal ore and cut a path through this growth. By this action he re-united the gods with their subjects.

Through this grossly simplified myth one can surely recognize the hand of Ogun in the play and exclaim, like Emuke: "Na sign, I swear, na sign from heaven" (*From Zia*: 30).

The chaotic nature of the society of *From Zia With Love* is symptomatic of the "primordial disquiet" or "the severance in transitional ether" which Soyinka describes in "The Fourth Stage" (1988) as the condition in the cosmic order which prompted Ogun's redemptive action. This disquiet is a consequence of the ominous growth that separated the world of the gods from that of the living, in exactly the same way the water hyacinth separates the prison from the outer world. A chaotic growth which severed man from his essence of being; a severance which Ogun himself heroically engaged and subdued, that man may be re-united with his essence.

145

This throbbing animist vegetation called water hyacinth symbol-izes the primal cosmic powers which resided in the growth between the two worlds of Yoruba mythology and which now lies between the two worlds of the play. It is a potent and wild force that can only be tamed through the offering of human sacrifice. Soyinka observes that this gulf that lay between two realms of Yoruba cosmic existence

> must be constantly diminished by the sacrifices, rituals, the ceremonies of appeasement to those cosmic powers which lie guardian to the gulf. ("The Fourth Stage": 23 – 24.)

Detiba's description of the drowning of the courageous Ijaw boy vali-dates this ritualistic reading of the water hyacinth:

> . . . Just watched his legs get more and more entangled in those slimy long roots. It was as if some hidden monster kept dragging him down. (*From Zia*: 27)

This obviously conjures the image of some diabolic cosmic essence inhabiting and guarding this transitional territory; a vicious power which wrenches human sacrifices for its sustenance. In this context, however, the power wrests the sacrifice from the unwilling or reluc-tant other world but remains largely insatiable because even with the death of the Ijaw boy the sea weeds continue to grow. What is needed to curb this menace is the hand of Ogun, wielding his long, double-edged, destructive/creative instrument of iron ore. Miguel seems to express this when he greets the courageous effort of the last man on the boat who tries to break through the menace of the sea weeds with these words: "what he needs is an assistant wielding a giant pair of water shears, maybe five yards long." (*From Zia:* 30) This instrument of iron is clearly an instrument of Ogun, and the prescription is rem-iniscent of that pristine bravery of Ogun when he plunged into the chaotic abyss and cut a path through it by which man and his essence were restored and order and stability reigned in the universe.

One should not, however, conclude from this that Soyinka is hop-ing for divine intervention, some kind of *deus ex machina* solution from heaven in the figure of Ogun, to restore peace and stability in the country. It is not the god himself that the playwright prescribes but a collective human archetype of his bravery; an action—revolutionary, heroic and rebellious—that

> . . . channels anguish into a creative purpose which releases man from a totally destructive despair, releasing from within him the most energetic, deeply combative inventions which, without usurping the territory of the infernal gulf, bridges it with visionary hopes. ("The Fourth Stage": 25.)

To conquer the growth of the water hyacinths the society needs to undertake a dangerous physical, rebellious, but purposeful and redemptive action. To conquer the menace of military leadership—or leadership in general since we infer from the 'Minister of Education' that the civilian is not really different from his military counterpart:

> Even when we were doing the Civilian style . . . so before we changed to military, even then our Commandant was still Commander-in-Chief as well as a Civilian President. (*From Zia*: 15-16)

—the community must engage in a heroic and concerted revolutionary action. The overzealous and brave soloist can only end up inconsequentially like the ignorant lone Ijaw boy. This submission is validated by Emuke's excited optimism:

> E go do am. If not today, then tomorrow. The others go join am try if e no manage reach us tonight. (*From Zia*: 31)

and Detiba's

> You'll see, he'll be back tomorrow. With others. They'll finish the job together. (*From Zia*: 31)

This optimism is, however, dampened by Miguel's pessimism. He intones rather mournfully:

We are all trapped where it will never happen. And if it does, we won't be here to see it. (*From Zia*: 31)

True to his words, the three prisoners are soon executed.

But even at this Miguel's grim prophecy still holds out a strand of hope. It is true that the revolutionary action does not happen in their life-time. But will it happen at all, even after they are dead? Will it happen before our very eyes? Miguel's cynicism provides the ambivalent other necessary for the launching of revolutionary initiative, the other side of the debate which serves to foreground Soyinka's social optimism. In the schema of human experience contrarieties often proffer a springboard for positive action. Indeed, Soyinka submits that in the corpus of Yoruba knowledge dislocations are often essential factors in the articulation of social and cosmic harmony. In his words,

> . . . a rupture is often simply one aspect of the destructive—creative unity, offences even against nature may be part of the exaction by deeper nature from humanity of acts which alone can open up the deeper springs of man and bring about a constant rejuvenation of the human spirit. ("The Fourth Stage": 31)

The implication is that one may emerge out of this social anarchism with wisdom and superior knowledge for the fashioning of a better society. This experiential triad that we speak of can be constructed along the three stages of existence which Soyinka recognizes in the Yoruba world: the past, the present, and the future. The past is inhabited by the deified ancestors and the anthropomorphic gods; the present is peopled by the living; and the future belongs to the unborn. In this fashion one can examine the fate of society in three stages: crime, penalty, and redemption. For the folly or criminal acts of man in the past, he is punished with a present social rupture. But if man pays the penalty of sacrifice or action he shall be redeemed in the future.

In the light of this analysis, one can see that the present chaos in the society represented in the play, *From Zia With Love*, is not utterly hopeless. The society is responsible for the continued growth of the water hyacinth through its folly—witting or unwitting—or its crime. The society pays the price of this folly in the form of social dislocation, and even sacrifice, represented by the menace of the hyacinth and the death of the Ijaw boy. But through positive action man shall emerge from this menace anew, stronger, and wiser. Through the metaphor of Ogun's hand a path shall be cut through the menace of social and political dislocations and the link re-established between man and social order.

From Zia With Love displays yet again Soyinka's relentless commitment to the pursuit of ideal social and political institutions in Africa. Just like his other socio-political plays (*Kongi's Harvest, A Play of Giants, A Dance of the Forest,* and *Opera Wonyosi*) this play explores the gross abuse of power and violation of humanity that has characterized African leadership. In this effort, published six years after he received the Nobel Prize for Literature, Soyinka proves that his wit, mythopoesis, drama and, above all, his deep commitment to the human predicament have remained robust.

Notes

1. In response to the agitation for African legitimacy in knowledge through a total excision of all forms that are 'Europhillian' or alien to Africa Soyinka says

   "There's no way at all that I will ever preach the cutting off of any source of knowledge ... There's no way anyone can ever legislate that once knowledge comes to one, that knowledge should be now buried as if it never existed (Biodun Jeyifo, 2001: 123)

Works Cited

Achebe, Chinua. "The African Writer and the English Language." *Colonial Discourse and Post-colonial Theory.* Patrick Williams and Laura Chrisman (eds.). New York: Colombia University Press.

1994: 428-434.

Ashcroft, Bill. "'Legitimate' Post-colonial Knowledge." *Mots Pluriels*. no. 14 – June 2000. http://www.arts.uwa.edu.au/MotsPluriels/MP1400akfr.html.

Borgomano, Madeleine. "A Few Arguments Against "Afro-pessimism.'" *Mots Pluriels*. no. 14 – June 2000. http://www.arts. uwa.edu.au/MotsPluriels/MP1400akfr.html.

Chapal, Patrick. "The African Crisis: Context and Interpretation." *Postcolonial Identities in Africa*. Richard Werbner and Terence Ranger (eds.) London/New Jersey: Zed Books. 1996.

Jeyifo, Biodun. *Conversations with Wole Soyinka*. Jackson: University Press of Mississippi. 2001.

Kom, Ambroise. "Knowledge and Legitimation." *Mots Pluriels*. no 14 – June 2000. http://www.arts.uwa.edu.au/MotsPluriels/MP1400akfr.html.

Ngugi wa Thiong'o. *Decolonizing the African Mind: The Politics of Language in African Literature*. London: James Currey. 1986.

Okome, Onookome. "The Social Crusade of Wole Soyinka." *No Condition is Permanent: Nigerian Writers, Democracy and the Struggle for Civil Society*. Hodger G. Ehling, Claus-Peter Holste-von Mutius (eds.). (*Matatu 23 – 24.)* Amsterdam/New York: Editions Rodopi. 2001.

Osofisan, Femi. "Soyinka In A Forest of A Thousand Revellers." *Perspectives on Nigerian Literature: 1700 To The Present*. Vol. 1 Lagos: Guardian Book Ltd., 1988.

Soyinka, Wole. "The Fourth Stage (Through the Mysteries of Ogun to the Origin of Yoruba Tragedy)." *Art, Dialogue and Outrage*. Ibadan: New Horn Press. 1988.

_____. *A Dance of the Forests. Myth, Literature and The African World*. London: Cambridge University Press, 1976.

_____. *From Zia With Love*. Ibadan: Fountain Publications. 1982.

12

From Zia With Love

Soyinka's Graffiti On The Nigerian Walls

EDDE M. IJI

Soyinka continues to write...with considerable interest.
—BIODUN JEYIFO (1988)[1]

Even after the Nobel, Soyinka's writings continue to echo his fervent concern for the dignity of man, a feeling gathered from the deep recesses of his humanistic vision. The degree of his consistency before and even after his Nobel Prize award is quite notable. This aspect, no doubt, has the tendency to douse any fire of lingering doubts about the unquestionable merits in the decision, character, and stamina of Soyinka in delving into the kernel of what has become our endemic national question. More and more sophisticated, biting, and effectively venomous, Soyinka has sharpened his parodistic thrusts into contemporary political life in Nigeria, unearthing all that is dubious. Parody, he had earlier asserted, is the most lethal weapon available to a satirist?[2]

Even though this paper attempts to zero in only on the endemic

151

Nigerian problem vis-à-vis their negative consequences on our national psyche and human development, as it has pre-occupied Soyinka's literary endeavor, it is not far-fetched to highlight, briefly, his other literary achievements before his Nobel-Laureateship. The main purpose of such a review is to adumbrate the aforementioned consistency of his literary vision.

In this regard, it can be suggested that if *Ake: The Years of Childhood* (1981), the unmythicized autobiography recorded from the perspective of a child prodigy, is regarded as a significant clincher to Soyinka's Nobel award, among other considerations, *Isara: A Voyage Around Essay* (1989) comes out illuminatingly as a masterpiece sequel to *Ake*. In this aspect, *Isara* is a mature adult's perspective, recapturing the socio-historical experiences, tears, glories, and paradoxes of his native land, literarily documented for contemporary and future readers. *Isara* thus helps to confirm the assertion that Soyinka is "a master, whether he chooses to write in the medium of poetry, drama, novel or autobiography." *The Man Died* (1972) had already established him as a virtuoso prison diarist/war chronicler, or historian of great repute; perhaps in the manner of Winston Churchill. Similarly, *Myth, Literature and the African World* (1976) had consolidated him as a classic essayist and comparativist of highnote, culminating in his attainment of a professorship of comparative literature. Thus, the compilation of earlier varied published or unpublished essays into a book, *Art, Dialogue and Outrage: Essays on Literature and Culture* (1988), can be regarded as a post-Nobel Laureate reaffirmation of his established essayistic and comparative high marks. His poetry harvest, *Mandela's Earth and Other Poems* (1990), a memento to Nelson Mandela's revolutionary fervor and heroic struggle for black freedom against the obnoxious apartheid policy, can be regarded as a collection of political odes that in many ways advance the mythic and mythicized vision of *Idanre and Other Poems* (1965), among others.

In consonance with this chronology of achievement, *From Zia With Love* is Soyinka's graffiti on our nation's walls or national psyche, recapitulating the stigmas that have become endemic problems of this country. In this sense too, it is in the parodistic tradition of most of his earlier well-received plays. In similar manner, *From Zia With Love* graphically recaptures and ameliorates some of the dramatic and aesthetic characteristics of Soyinka's earlier plays; while engraving further, very pungent socio-political statements of most of these plays of pre-Noble Laureation.

In character with *From Zia* are also, remarkably, some of Soyinka's post-Noble-award works in the areas of the filmic and electronic media (radio and television or video), and here one can briefly review the broadcast of his telemovie, *Giant on Trial,* produced on BBC-TC 2, courtesy of Independent Image Production in December 1992. Soyinka is both the scriptwriter and presenter of this audio-visual play, wherein Nigeria is literarily "put on one-sided trial" before the British viewers after the third abortion of the promised birth of the Third Republic. Focusing on similar parodistic jibes on Nigeria is his radio play, "The Scourge of Water Hyacinth" (1992). Here the problems of water hyacinth in all their ramifications; the pollution of Nigeria's coastal or Lagos water ways, *vis-à-vis,* the destruction of the eco-and hydro-system or threats to navigation, were highlighted as a metaphor for the hydra-headed problems of corruption in Nigeria.

All these are series of vintage Soyinka in cumbersome language, character, parodistic pungency and down-to-earth jabs and jibes. *From Zia With Love* is also refreshingly vintage Soyinka in many ways. First and foremost, this play characteristically memorializes prison experiences, courtesy of Soyinka's own direct suffering, and as is now well known to Nigerian readers, thanks to their confirmation as severally narrated by the irrepressible trio of Gani Fawehinmi, Femi Falana and Beko Ransome-Kuti, following the annulment of the June 12th Presidential election.[3]

Through the mouths of Inmates—First offenders, hardcore convicts, political detainees, awaiting trials, among others—we are able to emphathize with the grim and hell-like nature of Nigerian prisons. Ken Saro-Wiwa has also described this prison situation.[4] The shambles in our food-production, health-care, education, national security, transportation, and other aspects of Nigerians' daily struggles have been adequately portrayed through the words of the characters in the play such as the Ministers of Agriculture, Health, Education, Home Affairs, and Directors of Security. We learn also that water hyacinth is not only a threat to navigation, but, by their destruction of marine lives, they are hazards to fishery and thus to food self-sufficiency, food riots, among other problems, the numerous advantages of the water hyacinth nonetheless.

From Zia With Love derives its title inspiration, most probably, from Ian Flemming's novel, *From Russia With Love*. On the other hand, the subject matter or theme of the play is anchored on the mysterious disappearance, in transit, of about 50 kilograms of heroin or marijuana well-packed and shipped from Pakistan to Nigeria, courtesy of the late Zia Ul Haq, one-time President of Pakistan. This is Soyinka's recapitulation of such illegal drugs and other contraband trade booms or transactions existing through the connivance of very top government officials and co-operative diplomatic missions of two or more countries; their embassies and collaborations of top security personnel. The present disappearance can be traceable to an unknown dishonest courier. A lot of information is revealed through the dialogue of the Wing Commander, a Nigerian Student officer in Pakistan; he is a great contact person and one of the big brains behind the drug deals between two countries:

Wing Comm:	Your Scouts Either they're incompetent or they're dishonest. Such a heavy consignment cannot simply have vanished into thin air.
Sebe:	Of course, it cannot, my dear friend. It is somewhere on firm ground hidden away. Waiting . . . . (46)[5]

Sebe, it must be noted, is a great conduit, a great agent and courier recruiter. His personality fits the character of a faceless person in all such deals:

I am a moslem. But I am also a Christian, Buddhist, traditionalist, worshipper . . . everything you like, and none of them at the same time . . . . (47-8)

The Wing Commander reveals the core of the whole transaction, and one is hardly shocked as he asserts:

... what I mean is ... the people involved over there, my counterparts, they are in government. To deal with them on an equal level I had to make them believe that it was government to government affair, that there was cooperation here at the very highest level . . . . (48)

Soyinka calls the other people involved members of the Eternal Ruling Council (AFRC?). These people actively participate and promote the drug and other contraband trade as he hastens to say:

Even though the Wing Commander went to Pakistan on one of those military courses, as a student officer, I am on the Ruling Council . . . I had the full VIP treatment. But the real stroke of luck was getting on with President himself . . . . (49)

Thus, it was directly in intimate relationship with President Zia Ul Haq that facilitated the drug connection deals. Soyinka does not mince words on the historic-political reference as he broaches on wider subjects. Sebe confesses:

... Commander, that Zia man impressed me! the way he ignored everybody's protests and actually hanged a Prime Minister of his own country . . . This Bhutto was even his own country's representative to the United Nations. (49)

As a fascist leader reputed for his misrule, Zia justified this murder through trumped-up charges, and might have deserved the poetic justice as he himself ended very melodramatically. Soyinka's catalogue of fascist rules around the world is noteworthy: President Sekou Toure's trumped-up charge led to the imprisonment of Mr. Diallo Telli, "The first ever Secretary-General of the Organization of African Unity (O.A.U.)," implying that the military as well as the civilian regimes can be equally guilty of such dictatorial misrule, injustice, and selfish ends:

... Between Sekou Toure and General Zia or Pinochet or Arap Moi and Houphonet Boigny and other one-party Arab and Asian dictators . . . just what is the difference?

It is significant to note that to camouflage the marijuana, Zia was convinced to have the drug concealed in a shipment of fertilizer bags as a gift to Nigeria.

> . . . I said to Zia, why not send us a fraternal gift of a thousand bags of fertilizers . . . as a gesture of friendship. A contribution to our Operation Feed the Nation. Of course, he agreed. The rest was easy—special consignment. Privilege cargo, no inspection. The Generals took care of their end. I was to do the same with ours. (51)

This is reminiscent of the charges and counter-charges *a la* Jenifer Madike, who connived with top echelons of government to dupe the State. The elusive nature of tracking down the culprits is no longer disconcerting because of the ever-looming sophistication of criminality around the transactions. Sebe admits the level of sophistication among the Military circle in this regard:

> . . . when it comes to the Big League, we civilians are simply outclassed. Fifty kilograms at one stroke . . . . (52)

Soyinka emphasizes that it is under the silhouettes of the military regimes, particularly, that such drug trade usually thrives most successfully.

It is characteristic, therefore, that such regimes often devise superlatively draconian measures to ostensibly contain or curb such crimes, as exemplified in the Buhari/Idiagbon death penalty that saw the conviction and first public execution of Owo, Ogedengbe, and another convict in 1985. It is equally remarkable to note the rate of tactical elimination, hired killings, and assassinations that accompany the epidemic of double-crossings and short-changing as suggested by Soyinka in the play. Other related crimes also abound with such epidemic of government-to-government drug and other contraband trades:

> when you promise to deliver, you deliver. And you cover

your tacks. Even if it means burning down the Ministry of
External Affairs back home . . . . (55)

This reminds one of the often inadequately explained, though ostensibly investigated, fire and other unnatural disasters that occurred
with recurrent rapidity in Nigeria in the 1980s. A few such human-
inspired, provoked disasters include the fire outbreaks in the Federal
Ministry of Defense, Lagos and Federal Ministry of Finance, Abuja
and the crash of Military Hercules C-130 at Ejigbo, in which more
than 200 of the cream of Nigeria's young army officers and their
friends unavoidably died. These human-caused disasters were off-
handedly characterized as "acts of God" by the government. The
words of the Wing Commander in the play appear elucidating:

> If somebody could replace the entire contents of a diplomat-
> ic bag with Indian hemp, why couldn't that someone plant
> an incendiary device in another bag. You know how it works.
> (56)

It is with such graphic details that Soyinka attempts to engrave his
graffiti on the Nigerian "walls" and thus on the national psyche. They
are all emblematic of the Nigerian character, the seamy sides of our
endemic problems of corruption and misrule in high places.

On the other hand, through the words of the victims and convicts
such as Miguel, Detiba, and Emuke, we could glean other details,
representing voices of the victims of the so called national malaise. To
Miguel, who is on death row, the penalty of death for any drug
offender caught is "sickening" and is being done to gain favor with
Ronald Reagan, referred to as the "bloody hypocrite!"

> Those damned hypocrites know where the stuff is traded like salt,
> where it changes hands like local currency . . . . The American turn a
> blind eye on the mujihadeen in Afghanistan because they are fighting
> communist rule. In North Pakistan, you can buy an armoured tank
> with a packet of stuff and collect your change with a mortar or two.
> So why do we kill one another over here? What the hell are we trying
> to prove? (57-8)

Discussing the recurrence of *coup d' etats*, and the loss of lives when young coup-plotters are dastardly executed, the convicts assert:

Emuke: Make all of dem de shoot one another. When no soja lef, the people go get chance rule dem-selves without dem wahala.

Detiba: Well, the way they carry out may be. They are trying to carry out your wish. Coup today, casu-alties right and left, executions tomorrow. Then another attempt the day after . . . . (p. 61)

The recklessness of the executions in the words of the character is that "Sometimes, you don't even know who is really guilty of something . . . or someone . . . trying to settle old scores . . . ." As to the general political mess, civilian or military, the verdicts of the death-role inmates appear succinct:

. . . Anyway, for civilian mess and soja mess give me civilian mess anytime. At least civilian no fit do de kin dabaru non-sense wey put we for this kind mess. (pp. 61-62)

Soyinka's jabs at the military regimes are particularly reverberating. But we can readily identify which of the regimes, military or civilian, he addresses each time, for instance, when he says:

. . . this is a military regime, so don't mess about. Even when we were doing the civilian style because . . . we try to con-form with what is going on in the countries outside—so before we change to military . . . . Our commandant—was still Commander-in-Chief as well as a Civilian President. So no matter what style we are operating, you must address him with due respect and full protocol. (pp. 15-16)

Meanwhile, the youth, a drug courier, already in very hot water with Sebe, who recruited him, reveals a mode of recruitment of courier agents for the drug trade as he reminisces:

yes, that was the start of my disaster. He used to fence for us—that's how I got to know him. We stole valuables from our parents' colleagues while our own friends would rob our parents. We left the door open for one another, it was easy. Sebe used to buy goods from us. Stereos, jewelry, even motor tyres and spare parts. Then one day, he asked me if I would like to earn some really big money. . . . (p. 69)

As Sebe and the Wing Commander quarrel over the mystery surrounding the disappearance of the drug consignment, one could learn a lot about the nitty-gritty of their varied responsibilities in the criminal business. Sebe's role is to serve as a safe conduit for whatever the consignment may be, without knowing much detail:

> . . . I usually do not know the detail. "It could be guns and ammunition for another coup," or "for sale or hire to armed robbers" or "it could be gold or diamonds or contraband like ivory tusk."

As for the Wing Commander, he says:

> . . . I never leave anything to chance—never! I consign a top officer to clear the consignment and transfer it to the armoury. The formal presentation by the Pakistani ambassador was to await my arrival. I made sure of that letter of friendship from President Zia is right in my brief case . . . with the Presidential seal . . . .

All in all, when the chips are down, the Wing Commander reveals,

> We military stick together . . . . We may settle scores among ourselves from time to time, even bloodily, but in the end we close ranks.

In this process, he further admits, "bloody civilians become the scapegoats," but always mindful of "the fatted calf" rather than "just any scrawny scapegoat" (pp. 73-74).

Further revelation in character with military politics is that a top military officer who is really embattled or about to be caged in a tight corner could stage a coup to save his own neck or reputation:

> . . . didn't the one and only Idi Amin stage his coup to cover his ivory and diamond smuggling? They say Obote was about to put him on trial when he struck. (p. 75)

To Sebe, the conduit and intellectual clearing house of the drug and other criminal trades, anything can be done to protect not only the key personalities involved but, much more, to recover a valuable consignment that disappeared in transit. So either a *coup d'etat* as earlier suggested, or a draconian tightening-up of security is instituted, including the declaration of a state of emergency, to among other measures, "Close all borders, tighten up customs or bring up a stop—and search authorization—of . . . uniformed services." Any measure, including Esu-like reprisal and vengeful propensity like enforcement of retroactive laws, well-known to the military regimes, appears appropriate. Other such practical measures could include even ritual sacrifice to propitiate a wrong wrought even by government. Any measure taken according to this argument is in line with the moral equivalent of war, as enumerated below:

> Slackness, rigidity, forgery, cannery, venery, revelry, smuggling, ogling, laziness, apathy, telepathy, intolerance, permissiveness, academia, kleptomania, cultism, nepotism, nudity, drunkenness, superstition, godlessness, loitering, muttering, rioting, malingering, romour-mongering . . . .

The use of such interminable string of seemingly contextually meaningless words has become a part of the vintage Soyinka and serves, among other aspects, a dramatic effect of shocking or exciting the audience into alienation consciousness and intellectual alertness, deepening, in the process, active, imaginative participation. What is more, they are all epithetic graffiti, descriptive of aspects of the current Nigerian character, elitist, nouveau riche; top people in government and socio-economic management.

In much of this play, Soyinka's dramatic camera focus shifts to what the Wing Commander calls "Campaign of Reforms," characteristic of well-known and fake messianism. The reforms are encapsulated in retroactive laws to "tighten" the noose around drug dealings. These include redistribution, refining, sniffing, buying, inspection, tasting, injection, among other obnoxious drug practices. To effect control, a military tribunal is instituted *with immediate effect* with the power "subject to confinement, no bail, no option of fines . . . no right of appeal nor delaying device." The measures are as draconian as are well-known to Nigerians. Retroactive, the offenders are to "be guilty as charged, acquittal to be conditional on surrender of passport," reporting every morning to the nearest police." As for fugitive suspects, there must be seizures of every spouse and children as hostage, with a price. Other offenses include the possession of the tiniest of doses to wholesale vendor/habitual user or first-time offender. The punishment for the laundering of earnings from operations shall incur something worse than life incarceration. It must be forfeiture of life by firing squad, and forfeiture of property at home or abroad and liquidation of assets. The retroactive rules are also meant for the settling of old scores. The directness of Soyinka's parodistic thrusts is quite evident:

> . . . the army is now in charge,
> Shape in or shape out . . .
> We are building a new nation,
> Clearing out the rot.
> Ending your civilian torpor
> Striking while it's hot.
> And remember we're the breed
> Whose bullets, fired the day before,
> Hit their mark the previous year
> And penetrate your door. (83-5)

The target of attacks becomes much clearer as the revolutionary impetus coalesces. Soyinka's targets are quite explicit. The aim of the regime here also includes rooting out any lingering philosophical mission, suppression of new ideas and independent judgement, reminiscent of the earlier plays *Madmen and Specialists, Kongi's Harvest,* and *The Road.* Even though the Buhari/Idiagbon regime was suspicious and hostile to radicals and iconoclasts, it was actually Babangida's that codified, defined, and effected the most vicious and repressive measures against what it called "extremists," radicals, and human rights activists:

> There's too much thinking going on,
> We'll put an end to it.
> We've had enough of dissidents,
> They must conform or quite.
> We're rooting for the radicals,
> Rooting them out.
> There ain't room for them and us.
> We're putting them to rout. (pp. 85-6)

Only time and history can recount who becomes more successful in routing the other, the so-called extremists or their exterminators!

The extent, however, to which the Wing Commander regales at the exploit historically visited on what he called the "Chief Kalakuta Priest" is quite revealing: copious references are made to the so-called travails, tortures, and framing of the late music maestro, Fela Anikulapo-Kuti, whose reputable music shrine was burnt down as tribute to "Unknown Soldiers." Reference is also made to the damaging effect of the tortures of Fela's irrepressible mother. Fela was eventually framed on currency violation and imprisonment during the Buhari regime. Perhaps the clincher in the regale is the Wing Commander's remorselessness:

> This cat's mother fixated
> why the obsessive worry?
> She fell out of the window:
> soldiers don't say "sorry"
> . . . Resurrect her if you can,
> build another Kalakuta!
> You'll learn the brutal truth
> of power . . . . (87)

It must be remarked that, as a political effect, Fela's surprise charge on violation rather than on pot-smoking appeared to have produced greater effects in terms of its diversionary strategies, as it left the music mega-maestro almost abandoned and dry. The Wing Commander regales further as he orders:

> ... Lock him up!
> Yap him
> Enough years to scare 'im.
> Muffle up his Afro-beat
> And scatter wide his harem
> Let him file for bankruptcy ...
> No airwaves may vibrate
> Except to army symphony. (pp. 86-87)

Here, again, only time and history have now proved how effective the incarceration of Fela has been in an attempt by the dictatorship to castrate and curb his symphonic radicalism.

Meanwhile, the Wing Commander reframes the controversial theme of the military regime's messianic crusade that continues, each time, to turn Nigeria into socio-economic nightmares with each recurrent cycle of *coup d'etat*:

> This nation is caught in a moral crisis. The road shall be hard to disciplinary bliss. This new broom is set to sweep with all its strand of steel. No taking 'No' for answer.

Remarkably, it is in line with this "new-broom-sweeps-clean" philosophical rationalization that the Battle Against Indiscipline (BAI), the equivalent to Buhari's "War Against Indiscipline" (WAI), was set up. Babangida's model of this is the Structural Adjustment Programme (SAP) with all its inhuman pills:

> ... subversion can sprout in unlikeliest places ... Root out!
> Fight the drug menace. Drug dealers are national saboteurs.
> Sniff them out! Root them out. Forward with B.A.I; the vanguard of national redemption. (88)

To the death-role inmates and general criminals, mixed with hard-core ones, such "campaign of banalities" can make no citizens and patriots. However, the retroactive laws that have roped in so many people condemned to death on even frivolous drug charges have been widely condemned, but apparently to no avail. Life under a law which did not exist at the time of a presumed offence. If ever there was a clear case of a verdict directed from above, it is again seen in the rhythmic constance with which history keeps repeating itself in our socio-political experience, as we observe in the monkey justice carried out against General Zamani Lekwot and others of the so-called Zango-Kataf conflict who were formally condemned to death for religio-ethnic violence. The reverberating echoes of protests against the executive lawlessness were almost equal to the outcry against the condemnation and execution, by firing squad, of Nigeria's most historical drug convicts, Ogedengbe, Owo, and the other.[7]

In most cases, the judicial process is tantamount to a travesty of justice, a rape and prostitution of democracy. In this regard, all death-row offenses are treated with levity and against the rule of law as:

> . . . verdicts delivered by the political tribunal are no longer subject to a decision of the Court of Appeal. The Head of State has taken over their function . . . . (95)

Reminders of this executive high-handedness abound in various instances in the socio-political history of Nigeria. Soyinka describes the gory and heart-numbing nature of the execution stakes, indicating the barbarity of such practice, legitimate or not:

> We take down the bodies and put in those cheap coffins. After that, we still have to take down the stakes again, scrub them down for the next round. (100)

No less abhorrent is the last scene of the play, wherein Soyinka describes the vulturism of the execution attendants and cleaners of the execution arena. These people scavenge on the available possessions of the executed victims:

Sound of distant machine guns fire out single shots. The
Trustees place their loot in the bucket, begin to gather up
their spades, scrubbing braces and buckets. In the background, the prisoners' voices rise in a dirge. (p. 101)

All these stranger-than-fiction recapitulations of actual events invoke
impressions of savage comedy rather than of melodrama. What is
more, they create pictures of the scenes of the theatre of cruelty rather
than of national tragedy. For while the latter beautifies and enriches
the human sensibilities through the sublime, the former uglifies and
creates psychic numbing that dehydrates and debilitates individual
and collective image *vis-à-vis* creative vision; constraining varied
developments.

Remarkably, Soyinka's use of rhythmic odes, chants, varied prisoners incidental labor songs, dirges, or repetitions of seemingly meaningless litany of abusive words here are particularly refreshing. Some
of these inventions, though not really un-Soyinkan, appear here in
their episodic recurrence. They are used to create, separate, and connect loosely independent scenes to which they can also, at times, provide contrasts. In the process, they could help to occasionally create
comic relief to the depth of savagery, tragedy, and melodrama, or chorus chants, comments, or for rhetorical bombast. Examples of these
abound in:

"Ode to Commodore Ayacinth" (pp. 18-20),
"Prison chants" (p. 21);
"Speakers Military Voice" (p. 24) and (p. 31);
"Song of Social Prophylactic" (pp. 43-44);
"Songs of the Diplomatic" (pp. 56-57);
"Chorus of Campaign for Reforms" (p. 83-84);
"Songs of State Assignment" (pp. 77-78);
"Songs of Displaced Moralities" (pp. 96-92);
or the Rhythmic "Sinanmaniac Dance to the tune
of Zombie" (p. 96).

These and other refreshing techniques, borrowed or modified show
clearly that in spite of all his distinct, albeit tedious styles, Soyinka is

still wide open to other aesthetic and dramatic innovations. It is for this reason that Biodun Jeyifo's statement quoted earlier in this paper becomes particularly meaningful: "Soyinka continues to write with a lot of considerable interests."

Undoubtedly, *From Zia With Love* is a work of a "graffiti" virtuoso. It is Soyinka's post-Nobel masterpiece, still in the tradition of Soyinka's activist humanism, altruistic defense of human rights, and the preservation of the dignity of man in a humane world of "live and let live." This play is deliberately overloaded with apparent dramatic tautology to further emphasize Soyinka's consistency and irrepressible spirit of commitment. Soyinka remains one of the most committed writers of our time.

Notes

1. Biodun Jeyifo, "Editorial Note" in Wole Soyinka's *Art, Dialogue and Outrage: Essays on Literature and Culture* (Ibadan: New Horn Press, 1988), p. vii.
2. Wole Soyinka, "Ideology and Social Vision," in *Myth, Literature and the Afican World* (London-New York: Cambridge University Press, 1976), p. 102.
3. The three human rights activists were imprisoned by General Babangida (Rtd) but were released as a "gesture of goodwill" by the Head of Interim National Government (ING), Chief Ernest Shonekan. See also their accounts of prison experiences in "Walls Have Ears," by Gani Fawehinmi, and "The Struggle Has Just Started" by Femi Falana in *Tell Magazine* 36 (September 13, 1993), 21-28.
4. Mr. Ken Saro-Wiwa also charged with treason for speaking against the oppression of his minority ethnic group, as the President of the Movement for the Survival of Ogoni People (MOSOP) was also released after a long and painful incarceration. See "The Ethnic Question" in *African Guardian* 8, 37 (September 20, 1993): 14-15. Ultimately, Mr. Saro-Wiwa was hanged on November 10, 1995 by the General Abacha Government.
5. Wole Soyinka, *From Zia With Love*, (Ibadan: Fountain Publica-

tions, 1992), p. 46. All subsequent pages references as indicated are to this text.

6. The acronym, AFRC, means Armed Forces Ruling Council and this was adopted during the regime of Generals Muhammadu Buhari and Tunde Idiagbon. General Idiagbon died recently and General Buhari still worked for the military authorities in Nigeria as the executive chairman for the Petroleum Trust Fund.

7. The three young men convicted on drug-related offenses were publicly executed by firing squad with a trail of public rage and outcry against the execution. That has been so far, the first and, so far, the last of such execution of drug charges in Nigeria. It was therefore most historical. Soyinka was among the fervent voices of protest against the executions in 1985.

13

The Value of Things

Soyinka's *Cremation of a Wormy Caryatid*

CHRIS DUNTON

Mask, drum, and statue have long since been adopted by West African poets as images of cardinal significance. Senghor, Bebey, Okigbo, and many others have drawn upon the vivid sense stimuli—visual, aural, kinesthetic—these images provoke. At the same time artifacts such as mask and drum provide a powerful field of reference, through which can be articulated the poet's reading of history, his or her fears for the present, and a sense of communal identity. The power of mask, drum, and statue to call up this social-historical understanding has everything to do with the nature of the aesthetic in African art, with the recognition that aesthetic value is often indivisible from an artifact's function. Here I am using the word function not in its narrowest sense (usefulness as tool, appliance, furniture) but as a way of referring to the structured and socialized impact an art-work has on effect.[1] What is at issue is the dynamic presence of the artifact—mask, statuary, drum—within a specific realm of human experience. These artifacts both express and enable contact with—variously, and intersectingly—ancestors, gods, and history. In other words, they exist as a powerful and tangible realization of the process of contact, that process through which an individual, a community, engages in the moment of self-realization, of apprehending its present condition.

For Senghor, in a poem such as "Prayer to Mask," the artifact provides an affirmation of—or even the means towards—a sense of self, and that sense of self can only be arrived at through a sense of origin and togetherness with the community. Through a series of association—and association in the tightest, closest sense, not through random images that just happen to make contact with each other—Senghor moves from his opening invocation, "Masks! O Mask!" to the idea the masks speak for history, for ancestry, to the idea that history has formed him, Senghor, and his responsibilities (as a poet, expressing his community) to the realization that the mask can be called upon for guidance, for intercession:

> Mask of unmasked faces, stripped of all dimples, a wrinkle,
> Who have formed this image, my face bent over the alter of
> blank paper
> In your image,
> Hear me.

It is the close binding of image association here—Senghor's face mask-like, his writing-paper (medium of expression) a shrine—that gives these lines their potency.

Musical instruments—artifacts that often have in Africa a pronounced visual as well as aural appeal (a carved drum, for example)—appear frequently in Senghor's poetry, though usually the reference has little elaboration. Tamtam, flute, and drum feature again and again in exclamatory invocation, a brief notation of the effects reproduced by their social function. Okigbo, though, in "Lament of Drums," is much more explicit. Here there is an extended, multi-voiced articulation of drums as the voices of the community's ancestors. As with the mask in the Senghor's "Prayer to Mask," the drums speak of the sense of continuity, but here that sense is acutely sharpened, as the community enters into crisis (the poem refers to events such as Awolowo's arrest, leading to the political storm of Nigeria's mid-1960s). The artifact, the drum, here provides a vital point of reference within a cultural field; the voice of certainty that renders all the more painfully apparent current uncertainties.

For J. P. Clark-Bekederemo, too, the artefact exists within a critical field, focusing our attention on the process of history. Mask and drum become prisoners of history, but articulate ones. The poem "Ivbie," subtitled "a song of wrong," tells how "rare works of art" are discovered in the Plateau tin mines, in Benin, arousing "great historical/interest in London, Moscow, New York." Clark-Bekederemo's marginal gloss to the poem reads here: "Interest abroad is only aesthetic, not being aware of the mysteries behind. The expropriation of art-works becomes paradigmatic of the contemptuous windowing of Africa by the West: of its disdain for human experience, its extraction of material goods."

In a much more recent poem, "Lament of the Images," Ben Okri takes up this recognition and expands on it. Here too, artifacts are shipped out of Africa, reduced to objects of study, "purified" of ritual significance, and then designated "Art." That is they are forcibly divorced from the realm of human experience within which and for whose profound benefit they were designed. Okri goes on to show how, though imprisoned, the masks still speak: their access to living community is so fragile, though, and so few have the presence of mind to connect with them that present becomes alienated from past:

And the spirits
Hunger
For our touch
Our contact
The spirits
In their
Loneliness
Have begun
To go insane . . .

Sharing Okigbo's fears and, like him, hearing the voices of the artifact, Okri sees the community careering into anomy, self-denial, violence. His poem ends unequivocally, with a Birago Diop-like recognition, and one that I want to take up in relation to Soyinka:

> The makers of images . . .
> Dwell with us still
> We must listen
> To their speech . . .
> Recharge the psychic
> Interspaces
> Of our dying
> age . . .[2]

Finally, like Okri, Niyi Osundare sees the artifacts as speaking the past. Here, though, that speaking may be distorted, misleading, and so for Osundare the artifact becomes an object of scrutiny, suggesting the need for a critical reading of the way in which history is presented and a critical attitude towards social hierarchy established. In "A Dialogue of the Drums," Osundare offers words of warning to a court praise-singer, suggesting that the traditional function of his craft—including the use of his drum—is to project a sense of continuity, to bolster institutions that may in fact not deserve to survive:

> . . . If you listen properly
> To the dying echoes of your drum,
> You will hear this resounding fact:
> The people always outlast the place.

That questioning of the function of craft, art, of artifact, is another important element in Soyinka's most recent poetry.

In "Cremation of a Wormy Caryatid" (in the 1989 collection, *Mandela's Earth*), Soyinka follows the poets quoted above in focusing upon the artifact as means of access to a sense of continuity, of cultural-historical identity. The poem closes the *Mandela's Earth* collection, a marker perhaps of the significance Soyinka attributes to it (the collection itself has an inbuilt, projected significance, as Soyinka's first post-Nobel prize publication).

"Caryatid" is an elusive work, and what I want to do in this essay is to offer a tentative reading only, opening up questions about it rather than attempting a firm interpretation. I shall concentrate on: how Soyinka develops the idea of an artifact, in this case a Yoruba carved housepost,[3] as articulating object that enables a sense of contact between present and past; what critical field opens up in so relating past to present; how Soyinka evokes the poet's own imaginative construction/fabrication as means of enabling a sense of history and—the most interesting and trickiest issue—how Soyinka applies irony to the above questions.

A longish poem, "Caryatid" is made up of thirteen strophes, which average—with a solid, chunky look on the page—thirteen lines each. Two of the strophes open out into Yoruba songs, the Yoruba lines alternating with English translation.

In the first six strophes, Soyinka shows how the housepost has been eaten away, invisibly at first, by woodworm; he describes the structure of the post, the figures it depicts and the physical damage the worm has inflicted, reaching out then to reflect on the worthlessness of the artifact now to acquisitive collectors, and on the nature of power and hierarchy (the post depicts both kings and slaves). A middle section (not marked explicitly as such) shows the decision taken to burn the post, to stop woodworm spreading ("To save the grove, we isolate the tree"); though ownership of the post has been established at the beginning of the poem (Soyinka refers to "my gallery"), it is here in that strophe that the poet enters as a more tangibly present, reactive, formulating consciousness. Strophes 9-11, the most elaborately worked section of the poem, describe in vivid and beautiful detail the fire in process of destroying the post. At the end of strophe 11, rain begins to fall and the two final strophes comment on the action of this rain as "arbiter," quenching the fire, "marrying earth to heaven."

As with Ben Okri's "Lament of the Images," Soyinka rejects any false use-value for the artefact as art-object: here there is the bitter satisfaction of seeing the caryatid rendered next-to-useless to collectors because of its poor condition:

Peace, peace, acquisitor heart.
Still your pangs of greed, quit longing.
Douse hunger.

In a key line that will be repeated later in the poem, Soyinka observes that, "the woodworm have scooped the substance," leaving behind a hollow post, "mere form."

Soyinka's wry dismissal of the claims of the collector here is quite discrete, occupying the second strophe, before he moves on to another theme. It might on first reading seem incidental to the rest of the poem, but in fact is not. Its significance becomes clearer when Soyinka returns to the theme of acquisition in the penultimate strophe, his tone more openly contemptuous as he suggests the burnt and rotten remnants of the post might be marketed as relics, as he imagines in a museum or commercial gallery a "Display of wooden tibia,/Mildy charred authenticated." At this point Soyinka's revisiting of the idea of expropriation more clearly relates to the main argument of the poem, a complex, multi-stranded debate over the actual value of the caryatid and over the process of evaluation.

Evaluation must take into account the purposes for which an artifact was intended. At a very early point in the poem, Soyinka speaks of the housepost's "Votive claims," suggesting an effect close to reverence, or at least—in the religious sense—to observance. The post here is endowed with connecting force, providing access at the (symbolically potent) threshold of the building to ancestors and hence to a confirmation of the living community's cultural-historical identity. A little further on, Soyinka notes how the figure depicted on the post has over the years gradually rotted away: grand personages such as "sages, warriors, lords" and, Soyinka adds, in parenthesis, "the ancestor presence too?" This is a tentative observation, but a potentially devastating one: that what is at stake here is not just the final deterioration of an artifact, but an actual shift in social being, a loss of contact with ancestry. At the end of the strophe, Soyinka notes how woodworm attacks unobserved at first, so that this is not an overt, easily objectifiable assault (like colonialism), rather, "the thrust of enemies within." Is Soyinka here referring to the corrosive effect of an abandonment of inherited values? If so, his poem relates again, though perhaps obliquely, to Okri's "Lament," with its quasi-negritudinist plea for a return to those values. How then does Soyinka orient himself to inherited cultural values? How does he read the processes of culture and history?

Certainly, reading the past is a problem close to the center of the poem. At the end of the second strophe, Soyinka observes that in attacking the post the woodworm have "left mere form, and scooped the substance." Around the middle of the poem, with the post on fire, he expands on this line, noting:

The cinders of past epochs sink—but slowly.
Lack of substance clings tenaciously
To form.

Again, as in his comment on the tenuousness of ancestral presence, Soyinka seems to be querying here the strength of the record of the past, suggesting that our continuity with cultural history is less substantial than we sometimes assume/claim it is, suggesting that perhaps there is a problem here of distorted evaluation.

An argument for a re-evaluation of history can be read in Soyinka's description of the destruction of figures on the post. Hierarchy here is confounded as, in a slightly hackneyed observation, reminiscent of Hamlet ("a may go a progress through the guts of a beggar;" "the noble dust of Alexander…stopping a bung-hole"), Soyinka points out "The Woodworms' evenhandedness has spared / Neither king nor beast." And there is more here than a simple bringing down to earth or reminder of the last things. The hierarchy in question is one built on oppression: royal feet rest not on a stool but on a "headstool"; there is a slave parade on the lower levels of the post, slaves whose necks are not depicted as such, but Soyinka reads as being "halter-ornamented raw." The point is made quite deftly and Soyinka resists drawing an extended argument here. But the court depicted on the caryatid echoes that of Mata Kharibu in *A Dance of the Forests,* and the recognition of the realities of a slave society echoes one of Soyinka's main initiatives in his reworking of *The Bacchae.* In both of these works, as it seems in "Caryatid," Soyinka is suggesting a revision of current assumptions about our relationship with the past, warning that the past should not be idealized, least of all through the abstracted, fossilized signifiers that represent it in a work of art.

There is in fact a fairly constant strand of irony in the poem (remembering that irony has to do, broadly, with the gap between assumption/expectation and the true *avoirdupois* of experience); the reader's problem lies in judging at what point and how forcefully that irony is offset and constrained. The opening period of the poem—a beautifully constructed statement, lightly organized through alliteration that is never too conspicuous—sets the tone:

> Ancient caryatid, too long a host
> To woodworms browsing deep within
> Your charitable mass, keen mandibles
> Have proved your outward piety, aired hidden
> Histories through a million perforations.

The phrase that strikes me here is "outward piety": even without the qualifier "outward," the word "piety" has accrued an aura of irony, often used to suggest a slippage between appearance and reality, used here to help build up an uncertainty. What constitutes now the real, dynamic relationship between past and present?

A sense of dramatic irony enters quickly afterwards, when in the same breath Soyinka mentions the "unknown creative hands" that carved the post and the "industry" of the woodworm that have destroyed it. A little later then Soyinka suggests that our sense of loss, seeing the post crumble, is perhaps slightly deranged ("what futile sighs the heart exhales"): hypnotized by dust, entranced (or idealized?) in sense of history, mind and eye are seen to be "enslaved." When the decision is taken to burn the post, Soyinka's irony comes into full play. Hesitation is depicted (if I am reading this right) as maudlin sentimentally:

> . . . the poised hand
> Briefly trembles. A passing chord in air,
> Choral disquiet, hovers, plucks at heartstrings,
> Pleads a stay of execution.

Even resolution is comic, as Soyinka imagines himself, Nero-like, in the act of decreeing execution ("Thumbs/Down-pointed urge the fate of porous caryatids"). The significance of the deed is punctured by bathos: this may be "Sacrilege," but it is carried out with "match and kerosene." Looking back at this point, even the title of the poem, with its somewhat musty over elaborateness, seems to devalue the significance of loss, to suggest this is not after all such momentous timber.

And yet, despite the poem's extensive play with irony, despite its questioning the real nature of the past and—importantly—questioning the value we place on that past, "Caryatid" does not suggest the past is sundered from the present, that at each new moment consciousness invents itself, simply making do in an existentialist non-continuum (free of the fourth stage).

There are two strands in the poem that off-set critique and irony. First, the recognition of permanent reference points that are independent of the artifact, despite the fact that both the creator of the artifact and the present observer share recognition of these. Second, the recognition of the creative power of the human imagination and of the plasticity of the language it deploys. Soyinka's development of the first of these ideas seems to me easier to understand than the second.

Over and above the hierarchy depicted on the post, beyond ancestry and beyond the time-span managed by any individual consciousness (all of which Soyinka addresses in this poem with, at best, uncertainty), stand the gods. In that highly ironic strophe in which the decision is made to torch the post, Soyinka observes "Healthy gods . . . disdain weak intercessors"—the suggestion being that a sentimental attachment to the post is misconceived. The ancestral presence may be tenuous (because of cultural-historical transformation?), but either the gods remain—or the subject wills that they remain "healthy." Perhaps, even, the ancestral presence is not that tenuous, but still effectively bound into the relationship between gods and living community. In *Ake* (pp. 2-5), Soyinka makes much of the igneous rock outcrops, the "omnipresent rocks" that stud the landscape around his birthplace, around which the parsonage was built (the building "Fenced . . . by tumuli of rocks in overlapping, interleaved planes, sheet rock-face drops"). Here in "Caryatid" these rocks reappear, in a strophe (number 5) that at first sight, like the strophe on acquisitive collecting, appears to be discrete and marginal to the main line of the poem. The "igneous outcrop" here is identified as "ancestral plinth," and what it is does is to contain, denote the permanent; arbitrating earth and heaven, death and gods. Its level of inclination is different from that of the post. Unlike the vertical line of that impermanent artefact, it veers off, obliquely "From ... mortal planes," constituting "at tangent ... demonic lift that stands in qualifying contrast, not in the sense of opposition—against the mortal column" (the caryatid).

Not everything in this strophe is straightforward. In its final line, for example, Soyinka introduces a sense of lesson, of uncertainty about cultural continuity, in his use of the past tense verb, referring to the "cycle symmetry that ruled the carver's world" (does it no longer rule?). But the setting of the rock outcrop, arbitrator between earth and heaven, in contrast to the—ingenuous—vertical of the post, suggests a contrast between different levels of truth. This is, I think, the dominant strain in the poem's two closing strophes, when rain comes—that word again—as "arbiter," when, while there is no redeeming the post itself (what's gone is gone) or the false readings made of its significance (whatever relationship the present determines with past, this must be critical and dynamic), there is here, through the agency of rain, a marriage "of earth to heaven," an acknowledgement of permanent and accessible truth that demands a more adequate and critical consciousness of the realities of the present moment.

The other positive, redeeming strain in the poem lies in Soyinka's demonstration of the power of the creative intellect. Associated with this, I would place the Yoruba songs—the ten-line song on mortality that appears about half-way through the poem, and the little fragment on water dousing fire that comes towards the end. Certainly in the first of these I see no trace of irony: in this song's tender, wistful recognition that the day gently passes, that the soul adapts to strange lands, Soyinka seems to me to introduce an outlook that is entirely attractive in its sincerity and sensitivity, in order to offset images of false consciousness. At the same time, the poem moves towards an increasingly dramatic demonstration of a different type of mental activity, of word usage. In the early strophes, Soyinka impresses with the immaculate balancing of clauses (into periods that have a classical beauty), with the wise, just-short-of-caustic wit he can turn on the greedy and insensitive, with some unforgettable imagery (enhanced through the very careful placing of word in clause):

> . . . The stallion's heaving chest caves
> Gently inward at a finger's touch.

It is in the middle of the poem, though, as the post burns, that Soyinka's language really takes off:

> . . . Protean are the stallion's
> Shimmering thighs. A cinder ruptures; as fanned
> By hot winds, desert blown, the arches sway,
> Reform as careful ruins on histories' sands.
> Horsemen, groom, lance and standard
> Slew half-circle, subsumed in subterranean
> Fires. The field of gore glows golden,
> Glory-hued to the last hurrah.
>
> Dissolute in the dance of fire, acolytes
> Abandon vestments, paraphernalia, soar
> Upwards on instant flames, sink back to earth.
> Kaleidoscope unflagging, a brace of peacocks
> Fan new-hazed triumphal arches where
> Slaves in loincloth earlier knelt in homage.

Not the entire poem is as eloquent as this: in some places familiar mannerisms emerge to deaden effect. But the quotation above is an example of the stunning word mastery this poem can achieve, a virtuous performance in forging visual and kinaesthetic imagery. I am not sure that Soyinka has produced anything as rich as this, or as luxurious: and in demonstrating this particular kind of eloquence I think Soyinka is contributing another strand to the central theme of the poem, that here he intends again to provoke questions about the process of evaluation.

What he is doing here is recreating the carver's vision, producing verbal signifiers as affective as the visual ones (or possibly better, since it isn't clear the carving on the post is especially proficient). This strength to recreate may be the twin hope of the poem—twin to the acknowledged power of heaven—since while artistic products may die, artistic skills will always be renewable. This idea makes sense in relation to the poem's impatience with fetishization, with fixation on the material rather than on human potential (and with its insistence that human action, social structures, be judged critically). Or these lines may be underpinned with irony and Soyinka may be demonstrating how easy it is to be seduced by one's own creative potential, in language as beautiful and as impermanent as the carvings on the caryatid and perhaps as much a product of false consciousness. Look, after all, at the kind of triumph Soyinka's triumph of language celebrates in the lines quoted above. If there is no irony here, then the poem demands the kind of critique that has been carried out on, say, *Death and the King's Horseman*, with its celebration of the verbal brilliance, the dynamism, of members of the Oyo hierarchy. But perhaps the creative process Soyinka is demonstrating here is neither free from irony nor undermined by this, but living on a precarious balance, always inviting complicity, always provoking critical distancing: that is, after all, the permanent condition with Ogun.

Notes

1. African artworks have often been interpreted by way of a more reductive functionalism (recognizing no value beyond the way they are wielded, beaten, or sat upon). On this, Soyinka comments:

   house-post sculptures, stone heads and enduring bronze . . . have no 'functional' values in that sterile sense to which such works are now reduced by puritanic aberrants. A blacksmith's poker, an egungun dance, an Ifa prognostic, or a royal stool may simultaneously express the history of its makers, their concept of beauty, their propitiation of unseen forces, a statement of cosmic relatively and a mode of experiencing all of these, of harmonizing them with the challenges of existence. ("Aesthetic Illusions," 90)

2. In the central episode of Francis Bebey's *Concert Pour un vieux masque*, also, an Africa mask finds itself imprisoned in a museum-

case. Here, like Cesaire in "Return to my Native Land," Bebey undertakes an investigation of black consciousness, reviewing the experience of the diaspora in relation to the experience of Africa, prodding at questions of self-knowledge and the same of history. While Okri's images go insane, Bebey's mask commits suicide, apparently insisting on a drastic rupture of continuity. Yet, through its self-immolation, the mask is seen to make regeneration possible—perhaps because an understanding of what has happened, of what the masks has done, opens the way for a less compromised self-knowledge:

The power of the word is beneficent a father respected and obeyed not destructive. Thanks to this the death of an old mask is the beginning of a life which will no longer suppress anything (my literal translation).

3. Less often found now than fifty years ago, these houseposts at one and the same time make a strong visual statement and give structural support to the veranda-ends of Yoruba roofs (they are alternatively referred to as veranda posts; the word "caryatid," from the Greek, through Latin, designates a carved supporting figure). For examples, showing the multiple figures and depiction of hierarchy that Soyinka's housepost features (see Fagg et al. 1992:43, 183). The same author's note shows how support of the roof becomes both "aesthetic and moral opportunity," the concept of support being "expressed in both its metonymic and metaphoric significance" (182). "The function of the veranda post as a structural support of the house provided the artist with an opportunity to present images of persons and roles upon which life in the house depended. The carvings were not merely decorative. They presented figures as models of cultural values, and shaped the attitudes and perceptions of those who passed by in pursuit of their daily domestic activity" (84).

4. How does this relate to a marriage of heaven and hell (see the Blake poem): to the sense of necessary contraries, passive wisdom, and

creative energy? Blake's thinking here is close to Soyinka's speculations on Obatala and Ogun. A useful reference point may be in trying to assess what Soyinka has to say in "Caryatid" about the role of the creative imagination.

Works Cited

Bebey, Francis. *Concert pour un vieux masque.* Paris: L' Harmattan, 1980.

Clark, J. P. *A Decade of Tongues: Selected Poems* 1958-1968, Harlow: Longman, 1980.

Fagg, William, John Pemberton, and Bryce Holcombs. *Yoruba Sculpture of West-Africa.* London: Jonathan Cape, 1992.

Okigbo, Christopher. *Labyrinths.* London: Heinemann, 1971.

Okri, Ben. *An African Elegy.* London: Jonathan Cape, 1992.

Osundare, Niyi. *Village Voices.* Ibadan: Evans, 1984.

Senghor, Leopold Sedar. *Selected Poems.* Trans. Craig Williamson. London: Rex Collins, 1976.

Soyinka, Wole. *Ake: The Years of Childhood.* London: Rex   Collins 1981.

_____. "Aesthetic Illusions" in *Art, Dialogue and   Outrage,* Ibadan: New Horn, 1988:86-109.

_____. *Mandela's Earth.* London: Andre Deutsch, 1989.

14

Ola Rotimi and Wole Soyinka at Unife

A Newspaper Controversy

BERNTH LINDFORS

Theater history is beginning to emerge as an important new discipline at African Universities. Master's theses and doctoral dissertations on aspects of local theater history have already been produced by scholars from Nigeria, Ghana, Cameroon, Tanzania, Malawi and several other countries with strong theatrical traditions. The first of these professionally trained theater historians did their advanced degrees abroad, but today an increasing number are completing their studies at home, investigating phenomena that can be researched more exhaustively in an indigenous setting. These pioneering young academics are recovering Africa's theatrical past.

One problem in carrying out such research is that of locating reliable documentary records. Even relatively recent events will be remembered by various witnesses differently, so the theater historian must make an effort to cross-check oral interviews by consulting written materials and other tangible records produced during the period under scrutiny. For a history of a stage company, for instance, he or she would have to examine printed programs, contemporary newspaper reviews, published interviews, and whatever photographs or films of performances might still survive. Some of these materials will be housed in convenient archives or held by individuals active in the company concerned; others will be lost or scattered and will have to be sought out by resorting to techniques reminiscent of those employed by Sherlock Holmes. It is entirely possible that vital records will elude even the most intrepid scholar simply because they appeared in media regarded as too ephemeral or too fragile for preservation; they may be remembered and talked about, but copies can no longer be found.

This is often the case with newspaper items that made a sensation in their days but were never systematically recorded, collected, and archived. How does one get hold of such data? If there are no newspaper indexes to refer to and no well-stocked newspaper libraries within an easy travelling distance, the researcher may be faced with the proverbial problem of hunting for a needle in a haystack—and a faraway haystack at that. It may be useful, therefore, for academic journals to reprint important documents that are now extremely rare or inaccessible to most researchers. As an example of what I have in mind, I am offering for reproduction here a set of interesting cuttings from 1983 issues of the *Nigerian Tribune,* a newspaper published in Ibadan. Though these are relatively recent materials, the *Nigerian Tribune* is not held in many African newspaper collections, so the important theater debate stirred up in its pages a few years ago will be unknown and unavailable to the vast majority of scholars interested in contemporary Nigerian theater history.

The controversy focused on the University of Ife theater and on two distinguished Nigerian playwrights who had directed productions there: Ola Rotimi and Wole Soyinka. Rotimi, after returning from undergraduate and graduate theater studies in the United States in 1966, was attached briefly to the University of Ibadan before moving on to the University of Ife to take up an appointment as Director of the University Theatre, a position he held until 1977. Soyinka, based at the University of Lagos from 1965 to 1967 and held in detention from 1967 to 1969 during the Nigerian civil war, spent

1970 to 1975 in self-exile in Europe and Ghana. Upon returning to Nigeria, he accepted an appointment as professor of Comparative Literature at the University of Ife and soon became involved in dramatic productions there. When Rotimi left, he took over as Head of the Theatre Arts program and Director of the University Theatre, positions he held until he opted to take early retirement in 1985. During their twenty years at Ife, these two talented directors, who also had become Nigeria's pre-eminent playwrights, made the "Unife Theatre" into one of the most exciting centers of theatrical activity on the African continent.

Inevitably, people compared them—as playwrights, as directors, as men of the theater. Each had compelling theatrical vision and a distinctive professional style. Each had a strong personality. And each had devoted backers and detractors who argued interminably about the respective merits and demerits of both. When one of the Soyinkaphiles ventured to publish in the *Nigerian Tribune* a brief account of the Unife Theatre that belittled Rotimi's achievements there, it was only natural that the Rotimites should respond. Indeed, the response came from Ola Rotimi himself, who offered a lengthy rebuttal in three installments. This prompted a "correction" from Soyinka, which in turn led to a series of rejoinders from both sides. The whole *palaver* is reprinted here, starting with the first salvo, which was fired on February 12th by Kole Omotoso, then a Lecturer in Arabic at the University of Ife and a good friend of Soyinka:

Unife Theatre

The University of Ife Theatre has always realized itself, in its more than ten years of existence, within a larger unit of the University of Ife. At its inception, it was part of the old Institute of African Studies and it expressed itself in the Ife Festival of the Arts. When in 1977 it was thought that an African University should be in its totality an Institute of African Studies, and so the specific Institute of African Studies was dissolved to create four departments, the University of Ife Theatre became an arm of the new Department of Dramatic Arts. The process of this change and the trend of the continuity are complex and anyway need not be related here. Suffice it to say that the first part of the history of the theatre ends with Ola Rotimi's move to Port Harcourt and

Wole Soyinka's assumption of responsibility for the theatre from 1977. If there is need to give an example of the continuity in different dimensions, it is in the initial composition of the company, consisting as it did then, of enthusiastic amateurs, be they farmers or carpenters or school teachers and the guerilla theatre activists.

This initial composition of the company was to help seal the relationship between the University and the town of Ile-Ife just as the guerilla theatre takes instant theatre to the streets of the town and the open spaces of the University. If it has taken this long time to see the linkage and continuity, it is because the story of the theatre had been viewed from the perspective of the directors—the founding director. Ola Rotimi, and his successor, Wole Soyinka, instead of being viewed from the perspective of the theatre itself, as something growing, expanding, changing like all living organisms.

The University of Ife Theatre premiered all of Ola Rotimi's plays until his departure from the University in 1977. More than the experience of these premieres was the absorption by the company of a particularly rigid mode of production. Ola Rotimi has an epic hand in the dispersal of characters, props and set on the stage. He could get a hundred things going on the stage without one duplicating another. He was meticulous in working out for each person on stage the particularity of their movement on the stage.

This rigidity could be partly explained by the fact that many of those who were members of the company at the period he headed it were sometimes no better than enthusiastic green hands for whom things must be spelt out or else everything would spill out.

While Ola Rotimi produced the plays of other playwrights, using the University of Ife Theatre Company, he never allowed any other play director to work with the company as long as he was heading it. Some of the plays of others which he directed himself include *The Family* by C. Ekiye and *The Curse* by Kole Omotoso. This attitude must have strengthened the rigidity of the company for those years he headed it. It is perhaps, in the spirit of this rigidity that Ola Rotimi decided against having anything to do with the hall that later came to be known as Oduduwa Hall. He saw it as a monstrosity that could not respond to the handling of a director of plays, more so since the University authorities did not consult him in the planning of the hall.

Perhaps because of his epic production style, the space most usually favoured by Ola Rotimi was and is the courtyard, preferably, of split level rather than something that seems to give the impression of a proscenium.

When Wole Soyinka took over in 1977, he saw no reason why attempts should not be made to rescue what could be rescued from what the Italian builders were doing. He therefore went ahead and cooperated with them, made suggestions and virtually took over the hall on behalf of the University of Ife Theatre. This takeover and use of Oduduwa Hall, along with the Pit Theatre located in the African Studies buildings, meant the virtual abandonment of the building at Arubidi in the town of Ife where Ola Rotimi used to produce his plays. At Arubidi, the theatre was visible and seen to be doing things whereas in Oduduwa Hall and in the Pit Theatre the public was shut out. Space therefore, and attitude to space, played a part in that complex process of making change and producing continuity within the University of Ife Theatre.

Finally, the directorial approach of Wole Soyinka is different from that of Ola Rotimi. Soyinka works with both the script and the actor, changing the lines and the movements as both come to share a relationship of understanding and identification. One invariably remembers the performance of Soyinka's plays those which he directed himself, by the characters as interpreted by actors and actresses to the extent that the names of such roles tend to stick to those who played them at the first performance. This type of directorial approach expects much from the individual actor and actress. When we remember the medley composition of the company under Ola Rotimi and the different levels of formal education and theatre experience, it was certain that the theatre which Soyinka took over would not be adequate for his purposes.

For quite some time since 1977, Soyinka has used students, members of staff, as well as members of the University of Ife Theatre in his productions. This could be only a temporary solution. With the establishment of the Department of Dramatic Arts, a slow process of training for the members of the company began through the one-year certificate programme in Dramatic Arts. Along with this programme for those who were thought capable of benefiting from the training went the re-deployment or outright dismissal of those who could not cope with the new requirements. While all these complex moves were taking place, the University of Ife Theatre continued to premiere the plays of Wole Soyinka as well as other playwrights.

The result of the training, of the diversified production styles, the inculcation of confidence in each actor and actress is paying off now and it is bound to increase in the future. The University of Ife Theatre began as a pioneering experiment, being the first of its type to be attached to a University in Nigeria. The theatre has not abandoned that pioneering spirit. It has come a short way to be such a formidable unit which will go a long way in the history of theatre performance in Nigeria.

Rotimi, stung by some of these assertions, tried to set the record straight in a three-part reply carried in the *Nigerian Tribune* on March 19th, 23rd, and 26th:

> Since my departure from Ife I've been silent. Resolutely silent because I wanted time to think—think of how I could be far more relevant, more relevant to this nation through my calling.
>
> Because I yearn for fewer distractions, but seem to find this ideal permanently elusive, I have become more conscious of the value of time. I must admit, too, that I'm inclined to being more cynical of forums that tend to further claim what little time I may have for my own. In this respect, I have refrained from taking up membership of organizations, even of such as the Association of Nigerian Authors, or what-have-you. I've been keeping myself to myself—only scurrying out on occasional sallies with a new work or other, and retreating quickly to my unshackled condition with its everlasting administrative usurpation of my longing to be left alone to just teach, research, write, publish and produce.
>
> Impotent in my toothy dependence on that monthly salary—which, I hear, Vice President Ekwueme and Governor Aper Aku are even now threatening to halve in the name of a cure for our ravished economy—I find my dilemma growing more disconcerting in its mind-numbing details.

The greater reason for wanting to keep myself to myself, and fetishly protect my time and peace.

But it seems I can't even have that peace. Dr. Kole Omotoso's article in the *Nigerian Tribune* of Saturday, February 12, 1983, for instance, is a clear case of what, in pidgin, we describe as "trouble de sleep, monkey go wake am!"

Before I set to, I have this one and only regret to express. Wole Soyinka's name has been invoked—for reasons best known to Dr. Omotoso—into the said article in a manner which I consider most unfortunate. My relationship with Wole Soyinka (for those who might want to know) has been most cordial. Indeed, brotherly, I would say.

Well, there was a time—just before I left Ife University—when certain persons in high places in that institution would have succeeded in causing friction between us. I must say that, in the height of those ominous moments, it was Wole himself who took the initiative of advising that, no matter the provocations, we both must try to save our relationship from external abuse.

Since my departure from Ife, Wole has, in a number of ways, made me feel that his plea for mutuality between us, was sincere. I would like to think that he, too, has had cause to confirm my openness towards him.

Sadly, however, it would seem that, for reasons best known to them, some persons in the same Unife Department of Dramatic Arts are becoming dizzy with a free-wheeling sense of history to a degree that is clearly insidious.

Since I know something about the Unife Theatre that has been the cause of a spate of press publications in recent times, and since my name was particularly juggled with in Dr. Omotoso's own write-up, I owe it to history to correct some of the patently grovelling outpourings. So now . . .

Essentially, the publication by Dr. Omotoso set out to compare the character of the Ife University Theatre under my directorship (i.e., 1966 to 1977), with what it is now under a different management of which he happens to be a part. Fair enough. And this is not my gripe.

Comparative studies are normal in scholarship to which Dr. Omotoso and I make claim. My gripe is simply that Omotoso has treated this norm with amazing levity, glorifying trivialities and celebrating untruths. This, to me, is most dangerous because the Doctor, like me, is a teacher—a dispenser of knowledge to trusting minds. It is dangerous to possess the capacity for feeding high-protein trash to such trusting minds, just because one prefers the ease that goes with lazy research.

To start with, some fundamental corrections are necessary, at this point. The learned writer claimed that "the Institute of African Studies at Unife was dissolved in 1977 to create FOUR Departments . . . ." Misinformation! The Institute of African Studies was not dissolved in 1977, but in 1975. Second. The Departments that emerged from that dissolution were not FOUR, but two, namely: Music and Dramatic Arts.

It is probable that Dr. Omotoso also had the Department of Fine Arts as well as the Department of African Languages and Literatures in mind in his conclusion on FOUR department outgrowths. But the truth is, the sections of Fine Arts and Languages and Literatures evolved from the Institute to become a degree-awarding Department as far as in 1973 and '74, respectively. Not '77. Anyway, let that pass.

Other points. I don't know how Dr. Omotoso got the idea that I did not want to co-operate with the "Italian" builders who constructed Oduduwa Hall. Nor can I fathom the basis of his concluding that it was Soyinka who redeemed that majestic theatre building from neglect. To begin with, I did undertake the planning of Oduduwa hall with the architects. But, as is usually the case with such multi-purpose ventures, there came a stage where technology took over, and the artist's interests had to tolerate other needs. Even so, I never was going to abandon Oduduwa Hall. As a matter of fact, we did stage *Kurunmi* in the Oduduwa Hall amphitheatre in 1974 or thereabout.

The true position was this. With four other venues

(including the Pit!) for play-production at my disposal on Ife University campus, and another one in downtown Ife, I had no real urgency for the inner theatre of Oduduwa Hall. The open air allure of traditional African theatre was my preference. All the venues, excepting the inner hall of Oduduwa, had that allure—as Dr. Omotoso himself seemed to have observed.

Be that as it may, there was yet another reason why I wasn't too much in a rush to use the inner Oduduwa Hall. It was that railing. I can't remember noticing it in the initial designs I planned with the architects. But, there it was in the building upon completion. That railing. That 20-odd inches high, galvanized pipe barrier on the stage-floor separating actors from spectators. I had meant to quietly dismantle that metallic apartheid someday, so that both actors and audience could flow into one. I never got round to that. The railing is still there—as cheerfully redundant as ever!

All told, there were no major modifications that the Hall required after it was built. Nothing structural, at any rate. And contrary to Dr. Omotoso's hint, I don't think Wole Soyinka undertook a crucial "rescue" work on the Hall either. The changes I recall noticing being made were on the exterior decoration of the Hall. Facade touches mainly in which white emulsion sweeps replaced the original, ill-matching purpose on the same abstract designs. That's all. Functionally, rather scant to warrant chronicling.

But then, to a hustler in the field, such flimsies too, must count as epochal index to contrastive studies in Theatre History. Anyway, now to other matters in that publication. Dr. Omotoso argues that the actors whom the present managers of Unife Theatre inherited from me suffered from a major handicap. He diagnoses this as a certain "rigidity" in their acting habit. He then goes on to ascribe the cause of that "rigidity" to the monopoly I had, as artistic director, over the actors throughout my stay at Ife.

Coming from someone like Dr. Omotoso who was one of the more regular visitors to the old Unife Theatre at work, this statement is plain wicked. Kole Omotoso knew that I never monopolized the handling of those actors. With me from 1968 to 1977 when I left Ife, were two other senior academics who were also full-time artistic directors of the group. They were Dr. Akin Euba and Miss Peggy Harper. There was yet another equally able colleague—from 1970 to 1972/73—Dr. Sam Akpabot. We all worked with the group at will.

A more seasoned coterie of artistic directors is yet to be found in this land. Which speaks more for the vision and mature sense of mission of Professor Hezekiah Oluwasanmi—the second Vice-Chancellor of the University that flaunts "Learning and Culture" as its motto.

Granted, Akin Euba and Sam Akpabot are specialists in music. Nonetheless, they both also worked with the group in idioms as markedly theatrical as mine. They both directed the actors in musical dramas. For instance, Akin Euba, assisted by Peggy Harper, handled the actors in such works as *Chaka* and *Obaluaiye*, and Sam Akpabot, in his own *Jaja of Opobo*.

The crucial point here is that Akin Euba and Sam Akpabot also handled those actors in exploring the realms of acting, movement and directing. More can be said of the involvement of Petty Harper whose special area is choreography and movement.

Dr. Omotoso's picture reducing those actors to histrionic fossils is, therefore, hardly borne out by the dynamics of the actors' circumstances during my years with them. Let's examine the circumstances further.

For the sake of argument, let's even believe that no one else but me, handled the actors to the extent in which their acting became stereotyped.

To start with, Dr. Omotoso graciously concedes in his article that I did stage the plays of other authors. Not just my work. He mentions *The Family* by Comish Ekiye, a modern, middle-class, social drama. He also cites his own *The Curse*. But what the learned Doctor fails to tell the reader—as expected of a true theatre scholar—is whether the acting and directing styles for staging my more traditional *The God...* or *Kurunmi*, are also the same for *The Family*, or his own allegorical fantasy, *The Curse.*

Certainly, Omotoso knows that the genre, time-setting, and cultural matrix of a play do determine acting style as much as directing approach. Elementary theatre knowledge, this. Well, then, how can he talk of "rigidity" in acting response, when the same actors, as he himself tells us, were exposed to plays of intrinsically varied acting and directing styles? Confusion?

If Dr Omotoso is implying that the old Unife actors were used to my kind of artistic vibrations, one would agree with him, even though he would be saying nothing new. You can't work with another human being—even an animal—let alone a corporate body of beings, and not expect some degree of mutuality in sensory tuning. Even then, transferred to new hands, what such actors require is a period of re-orientation in which the "new-comer" director must take the lead, inspiring faith and confidence. If no director is prepared to go through this strain, it is unfair to blame "rigidity" on the actors.

Like the fellow who came from Ibadan, eager to work with the group soon after I left Ife. He plunged straight into business, then soon realized he couldn't cope, gave up in a matter of days, and scuttled back to Ibadan, self-righteously wondering how anyone could achieve things with those kinds of actors! But the answer is simple. Patience. The trouble is, most so-called Nigerian theatre directors bustle forth, wanting to USE actors. This is wrong. A good director does not USE actors. He works with and shapes them. Or as Goethe puts it, he "advance(s) them in their art." Acutely true in our developing Nigeria.

Another point. The Doctor attributes what he calls "rigidity" of the actors they inherited from me to yet another factor. This is that I never allowed any theatre director from outside to work with the group. What logic! Stanislavsky must be squirming with guilt in his grave for having dominated the Moscow Art Theatre with his own directing vision! So must be Goethe and his monolithic presence over Germany's Weimar Theatre; Laura Keene and America's Chestnut Theatre.

Perhaps, I am invoking the ghosts of distant cultures. Let's be homebound then. Directors Ogunde, Baba Sala, your actors are doomed to "rigidity," they say, unless you make way now for all comers!

Anyway, back to the point. Perhaps the questions should be: Did any outside director come forward, offering to work with the Unife Theatre, in my time, and was put off? To my recollection, no one approached us. Which was just as well, anyhow. As far as I know, there were only two theatre practitioners in Nigeria at that time who I could have welcomed to handle the Unife group in dramatic production. Only two persons whose knowledge of theatre directing I trusted. Unfortunately, they never approached us.

Of course, quite a number of people think they know what directing is all about. Fine. Everyone is entitled to private delusions. But those who really know about directing, do appreciate the fact that it is a science that goes beyond mere transmission of content through actors in a series of configurations on an action-space. Thank goodness, "outsiders" who ogle at the director's science didn't venture to embarrass themselves by offering to work with the Unife actors in my time. That theatre had no room for dilettantes! More especially when such dilettantes think that a Ph.D dissertation on some tangential work in drama submitted for, say, a degree in Arabic or French studies, does qualify them for work with actors who take the business of acting as their life! No way.

In his desperation to establish a base whereon to highlight—if prematuredly—the qualities of the Unife Theatre under the new management, in contrasts to the old theatre, the Doctor describes the latter as "consisting . . . of enthusiastic amateurs . . . farmers, carpenters . . . school teachers."

The hint of educational lapse is implicit in the Doctor's

spotlight on the more artisan background of the actors in the old theatre. The hint is deliberate. It serves the biased intentions of the Doctor, to the extent that the description is lopsided. In the old theatre were carpenters, bicycle-repairers, farmers, teachers, painters, tailors—and their wives too! True. But in addition to, and working as actors or staging-hands in close partnership with them, were University staff of equally assorted background. Professor Michael Crowder (Historian), Professor H. L. Moody (English), Dr. Adebona (Lecturer in Botany), Femi Robinson (Chemical Technologist), Margaret Folarin (Lecturer in English), Leke Owolabi (Senior Accountant), Dr. George Reid (Lecturer in Philosophy) and more.

I am using the adjective "old" pointedly, because there seems to be a piteously strenuous effort by persons of the Omotoso ilk to draw red line between everything that the Ife Theatre was, up till 1977 when I left, and the wonders that the Omotoso proclaim to be happening to it ever since.

As far as I am concerned, the University of Ife Theatre, in my time, endeavoured to create a unity between the University and the Nigerian people, through art. We called that policy "integration of town and gown." I strongly believe that the University of Ife Theatre today is still capable of fostering that aim. And I also believe that it is possible, quite possible for Nigerians to advance a cause without first effacing the identity of the precedents that had nurtured that cause.

Dr. Omotoso's insular focus on farmers and carpenters cannot but be deliberate, as it provides desired leverage for the learned doctor's innuendo on the mental inadequacy of those actors whom he ascribes to the "old" Ife Theatre.

His description also sees them as "enthusiastic amateurs." Clearly, Dr. Omotoso's idea of amateurism is at variance with the dictionary acceptation of that word. Let's analyze his inference. Among my early actors were people like Muraina Oyelami and Tunji Buraimoh, and Tijani Mayakiri. They had been full-time actors under the late

Duro Ladipo, before coming to me at Ife. There was also Gboyega Ajayi, former leading actor in the Adejobi Theatre Group. Certainly, Dr. Omotoso is not implying that the Adejobi Theatre or Duro Ladipo Theatre is an amateur group—if he is being sincere about his claim to knowledge of Nigerian Theatre History.

When the Murainas and the Mayakiris, and the Gboyega Ajayis and the Ogundepos and the Ayantuji Amoos and the Peter Badejos came to assist in my search for contact with our artistic roots, they were early master-performers in their own right. They joined the University of Ife Theatre at its inception (then called Ori Olokun Players) and received monthly stipend. What was so amateurish in the make-up of the old group that doesn't exist in the new?

In another paragraph of the publication, the Omotosos would have the world believe also that involvement of students is one salient feature of the composition of the present Unife Theatre. That's a lot of baloney, as the Americans say! At the same time that carpenters were bustling with farmers and me in the old Unife Theatre, University students were also an integral part of that theatre's acting personnel.

The students at that time included Bode Sowande (now a lecturer at Ibadan University), Tony Obilade (also now a lecturer at Ibadan University), Akin Sofoluwe (the Agricultural Engineering student, who was the first Kurunmi), Seinde Arigbede (then a medical student at the University of Ibadan). Again the list could go on, and on. Yinka Oke-owo—now NFA Secretary—in his student days, was the first Ifa Priest in *Ovonramwem Nogbasi*; Ade Onigbinde—now NFA Chief Football Coach—was one of the early Balogun Ihikunles in *Kurunmi*. The Sholu sisters—both lawyers now. Mrs. Yinka Anjorin. Where does one end?

To talk less of notable outsiders like Segun Akinoba, who resigned his post of Senior Executive Producer at NTV, Lagos, to work full-time with the group, satisfied to earn a lower salary because of his belief in the philosophy and artistic orientation of that kind of theatre.

True, the "students" referred to above, were not formally enrolled in the Department of Dramatic Arts. But our talk is not on Theatre Historians, or Theatre Analyst, but on acting and actors. Talent then, not paper qualification, must be the crucial measure here. Drama schools do not implant talent in students. They only stimulate and discipline talent in the perfection of skill. With the right teachers helping, of course! The deduction is that, to be a good actor, you either have IT (i.e., talent) or you don't. And with that basic stuff called talent, the rest is up to a sensitive director to induce the desired skill from it.

That those students in the old Theatre played their roles in ways that have made a memorable impression throughout Nigeria, Ghana, in France and in Germany in the mid-sixties and seventies, is a testimony of their ability to match any Drama School snippet on the brass-tacks of acting. Granted, the Drama School student of Acting would excel when it comes to citing the theories of acting from Stanislavskian technique across to Agnes de Mille's; would certainly excel in mouthing Aristotelian unities—if irrelevantly! But in the matter of down-to-earth, acting know-how, the type that spirals organically from felt sensations within, to kinetic realizations, without? Let's not kid ourselves.

A classic story comes to mind here. The name Faye Dunaway is quite familiar to the film fan in Nigeria. For those who might not know, well, Faye Dunaway is one of America's top film actresses living today. See *Chinatown, Eva Peron*, etc. Of course, that also means that Faye Dunaway is a millionaire. I saw a coverage on her in *Time Magazine* a few years back, saw her lolling uncaringly by a personal swimming pool which I'm sure costs as much as would pay the salaries of all the staff in Ife and Port put together! Austerity or no austerity!

Well, actress Faye Dunaway was my classmate at Boston University's School of Fine and Applied Arts. I was studying playwriting and directing then. Faye was doing straight acting. Both of us, undergraduates, acted in class scenes together. All of a sudden, with an extra year to go for the Bachelor's degree, Faye said she was quitting—going to New York; just quitting, heading West California, anywhere. She said all she wanted was a chance to get her teeth fully into the real thing: acting. She quit.

We all shook our heads, good kids, and went ahead, piously filing our applications to continue studies at graduate level. I landed Yale, attracted by the John Gassners and Alois Naglers—big names in the study of Theatre History and Dramatic Literature. Returned home three years later. Loyal Nigerian! Now Diane Schultz.

Diane Schultz was one of the brightest at Boston. Like Faye, she too was studying acting. Extremely bright in the theories. But Diane Schultz had no acting "umph," let's face it. Anyway, Diane too went straight to do graduate work. She is now a top-ranking academic in one of America's Universities. Teaches Theatre History which, I'm sure, is being updated to include contemporary American Theatre History.

This in turn means that, as one of the queen bees who make the American theatre scene tick today, Faye Dunaway is being studied in Diane Schultz's seminars. So much for the fallacy about Dramatic Schools as automatic instillers of acting talent. In further groping for distinctions between the present Unife Theatre and the old, Dr. Omotoso makes some comparative passes between my directing style and that of Wole Soyinka. He concludes that members of the Old Theatre couldn't cope with the requirements of Soyinka's directing approach which, as he puts it, "expects much from the individual actor and actress." And what is the singular mark of Soyinka's directing regimen? Dr. Omotoso explains that "Soyinka works with both the script and the actor, changing the lines and the movements as both come to share a relationship of understanding and identification."

Again, the man has said nothing. Just another effluence of inanities, as far as knowledge of theatre theory and practice goes. I'll prove this later. For now, let me say that if this, indeed, was really the test applied in re-deploying and dismissing some of the old actors who, as we are told, "could not cope," then one wonders whether Dr. Omotoso's revelation gives credit to Wole Soyinka himself for adopting that kind of narrow test. Or should we now say that, this explains why, for instance, someone like Ayan Amao—the superlative bata-drummer of the old theatre got "re-deployed" from the position of bata-drummer, to being a bartender at Oduduwa Hall?

Well, like the true artist that he is, good old Ayan Amao had his pride. He rejected that gracious "re-deployment" (or was it humiliation), grabbed his bata-drum one morning, and headed South-West for Lagos where the University of Lagos quickly recruited his drumming expertise into its Centre for Cultural Studies. Some price we pay in Nigeria, in the name of "polish by the script"!

Back to the argument. As a criterion for testing the competence of performers in a group that strives to exemplify contemporary African theatre with roots in content, music movement, etc., the insular focus on actors' response to script simply doesn't make sense.

However, this is not to say there is no merit in "working with both script and actors, changing lines and movement . . ." Of course there is. Now, here is the rub: the business of "working with both script and actor, etc" is a common chore in play-directing. Not an innovation. Certainly not a discovery! What else is a play director supposed to be doing with a script under his nose and actors before his eyes?

One doesn't have to look far to know that the practice of "working with both script and actors, changing lines and movement, etc. etc." is a directing convention that dates deep into theatre history. What, for instance, does the learned Doctor think 16th Century theatre was demonstrating through the opening passages in Act III, Scene II of Shakespeare's *Hamlet?*

For Dr Omotoso to have displayed "working with both script and the actors bla-bla-bla" as a distinction of the Soyinkaesque directing acumen is simply laughable in its nothingness. It's like saying Sunny Ade's sound is different from Victor Uwaifo's in that Sunny uses the guitar and conga drums! What does Victor use? This is not even lazy research. It is no research at all. The difference between Peugeot and Datsun is that Peugeot uses Petrol and tyres, and is meant to cover distances. Some distinction!

Certainly the learned Doctor can do better than that, in probing what really are the precise trademarks of Soyinka's or any other practitioner's craftsmanship in play-directing.

If it appears that I am being too hard on Dr. Omotoso, it is because this is not the first time I have to draw his attention to the need for proper research before submitting work of informative value for publication. The first time was in 1977. Then, my communication to him was done in a private letter. It would seem that, six years after, the fellow is yet to appreciate the essence of research in addressing a subject of educational purport.

In a sense, one doesn't blame him. About time our real theatre historians and analysts—the Adedejis, and the Ogunbas and the Ogunbiyis—started looking into the dynamics of play production in our land. We've just about had our surfeit of the customary re-cycling of Western ideas on Brechtian techniques and Stanislavskian method into our students' skulls. Such fixations only serve to further nurture the kind of mulish commentaries on Nigerian theatre practice which one has been encountering here and there.

The English Departments may continue their monocled preoccupation with text if they like. But the theatre analyst/historian must begin to sit beside and watch how the Soyinkas and the Kalu Ukas, and the Adelugbas and the Zulu Sofolas and the Otis and the Maddys and the Ogundes grapple with their visions in directing. Essential to such investigation is the question as to whether these visions are aiming at something new, something relevant to African cultural expositions.

To start winding up, there is a point for which one must thank Dr. Omotoso. He did admit that (I quote) "the University of Ife Theatre began as a pioneering experiment," being first of its type to be attached to a University in Nigeria. The Theatre has not abandoned that pioneering spirit" (unquote). Amen. This much is heartening. And one is assuming, of course, that the "pioneering spirit" of which we are being reassured is that of commitment to a sustained communing with the people inside and outside the natty walls of our University campuses, through the medium of institutional theatre.

This is where the news that the new Unife Theatre would soon be going out on such missions—as of old—is most heartening. Especially, in these times when austerity and FEDECO and sudden fires and surprise arrests are most unworthily claiming our minds.

The only thing though, if one may proffer some advice, is this: drama (for it to get to and be part of the people) means and takes a lot of endurance. Running an itinerant theatre in an institutional setting, whether in a University or in a State Arts Council, is perhaps one of the most trying of theatre experiences. A fundamental reason is that those centres lack that secret which helps to sustain cohesion among theatre members, and which in turn ensures the kind of longevity which groups like Ogunde and Alawada theatres enjoy.

This central secret is the family unit, acting as the hub of a theatre's organization and practice. Institutions can still evolve a viable substitute for the family unit, through other patterns of personnel organization and group commitment to shared concerns. The ten-year life span (1967-1977) of the old Unife Theatre has shown that ideas in that regard are workable.

This is not the place for details, but suffices to say that the old Unife Theatre's lifespan was insured on four principles, the knowledge of which I'd be most willing to share with whoever is so interested. Unfortunately in Nigeria, people don't seem to want to ask questions about the past with a view to improving on necessary points of departure. Rather, new builders prefer to destroy the past in an unnecessary drive for absolute credit.

The result is usually that the new building—not having benefited from and understanding of the contours of the land or the texture of materials—gets stunted at the DPC level. Like the Unibadan Travelling Theatre and its still sputtering efforts to move, after over two years of noisy proclamations about intentions of reaching out to the people.

Anyway, better luck to the new Unife Theatre. In this task, my friend, Wole, will certainly need the help of his colleagues—the Omotosos and the Ogunbiyis who must try to see their function as not dominant only in the proclamation of intentions from the rooftops of the *Nigerian Tribune* and the mountaintops of the *National Concord*.

Drama, as we know, derives from the Greek word *dran*, which means "doing." And when the *doing* actually gets going, pray, the theatre managers should not preempt the Nigerian public of their right to be ultimate judges of the drama they see, either. Things get rather incestuous when the very *doers* of the drama also arrogate to themselves the role of public interpreters.

Let's leave the self-advertising game to the Obeyas trying to tell Nigerians "what to think" about Mercedes Benz or no Mercedes Benz deals. After all, Plato may be right in maintaining that those who "produce" may know less about the value of the matter produced than those who "use" it. That could be true in Nigeria too. If only we would give it a try!

Three weeks later, on April 16th, Wole Soyinka offered some conciliatory remarks as well as "a correction":

Ola Rotimi's three-part series on Unife Theatre must have saddened many readers—they certainly had that effect on me. I intend to stay out of the controversy—apart, of course, from being cast willy-nilly, as a passive principal. Nevertheless I feel compelled, solely for the sake of the practicalities of theatre, to correct one erroneous understanding of Professor Ola Rotimi, obviously drawn from my "redeployment" of one musician, Ayantunji Amoo. I do not want the public to be left with the incorrect notion that traditional artistes have been given the boot in favour of "academic" artistes, any more than I would like bartenders to feel that their profession is looked down upon, and used as a dump for putting old theatre rags to grass.

The drummer in question was not "redeployed." I actually dispensed with his services, which were no longer required. The responsibility of the Artistic Director of a company with limited resources is to balance the various expertise within the company, not make it top-heavy in any one direction. Amoo was not the only casualty. At present we have three first-class drummers with the company, one of whom is illiterate in conventional language. But the language which he does speak—the language of dundun, gangan, etc.—is the language we need in the theatre. He is also disciplined, does not fall asleep during rehearsals and does not come late to performances—so he fits into the company. I do not know if he is an inferior or superior artiste to Ayantunji but he is more than adequate for our dramatic needs.

Amoo was re-employed by Oduduwa Hall as a barman some time afterwards and this was only as a result of passionate pleading by the late Ayansola who was Amoo's mentor and patron. Ayansola said, "Listen, you are punishing me, not him. The responsibility for him and his family will fall on me if you leave him jobless." So I gave him a job as a barman in Oduduwa Hall with a promise to recall him if the fortunes of the company improved to such an extent that I could afford to give him another chance. There are no hard feelings between Amoo and myself; he has been here to say hello to me a couple of times since he left for Lagos.

Even more to the point, I do not see redeployment as a barman, particularly when the bar is an integral part of the entire theatre organization, as a humiliation. One lesson which I try to impress on all members of the company, including students, is that no activity connected with the theatre is beneath them. If a bar is required to make the theatre pay its way, then the artistes in that company must be prepared to serve drinks, mop the floor and flush the slop. I took over the bar myself during the performances of *Dream on Monkey Mountain*, directed by Caroll Dawes, a role into which I slipped naturally because of my post-graduate education as a barman-cum-bouncer, among other jobs. An excellent artist here whose painting decorates my wall runs a bakery on the side. Seven "academic" artistes bit the dust in my last few months as Head of Department, and a very well-known Visiting Artiste who has been with me off and on since the early sixties was recently given a two-month suspension by the new Head of Department for unprofessional conduct. If he had asked for job as barman in Oduduwa Hall during his suspension, I would have done my best to accommodate him.

Famous actors and artistes all over the world, no matter their country's ideological policy towards the arts, take on the most bizarre assortment of jobs during "laying off" or slack seasons. There are indeed restaurants and bars which specialize in part-time vacancies for theatre artistes—this is the sort of tradition which we have tried to emulate here by our special symbiotic relationship with Oduduwa Hall, a relationship which, incidentally, gives our Bursar sleepless nights and some dons here bouts of apoplexy.

There are far too many other errors of thinking and reading of facts in what Ola has written so let me just end by advising that, all in all, it is safer to leave the internal organization—which includes matters of discipline—of any theatre company to the on-the-spot leadership of the company, as events often wear deceptive looks—rather like the profession of acting itself. I can only hope that the present dust settles down quickly so we can get back to the normal business of collaborating on creative projects.

I wish to recall Ola to the fact that when Unife theatre acquired its video recording equipment three years ago, our first project was to bring him back for a spell so that he could recreate his former triumphs and put them on tape. Unfortunately, he had already completed plans to go to the U.S. on sabbatical and the project was shelved. Now, this was not just a personal decision by me but the collective goal of the department which embraced the idea enthusiastically. Surely, this is a far more accurate gauge of the attitude of staff here to Ola Rotimi's work, than any critical incidentals in an essay by a colleague. Other collaborations since his departure should be placed at the forefront of Ola's assessment of the genuineness of appreciation of his work both by his former actors and his erstwhile colleagues. Like all genuine appreciation, it is not an uncritical one, I wish Ola would try to read genuine critical interest where now he appears to read nothing but bad faith.

To this Rotimi responded on April 27th with a statement he called "My Last Word":

It is convenient for Professor Wole Soyinka to excuse the misrepresentations in Dr. Omotoso's article breezily as "critical incidentals." To me, and I should think, to the Nigerian public at large, among whom Theatre/Literature are students, accuracy of research data is no matter for cavalier scoffing. This thinking has nothing to do with tardiness to critical assessment, either. It is a matter of not playing dumb in the face of mass misguidance against which one happens to have a chance to react. Anyhow, times change. But yesterday, it was Wole Soyinka in a stout fight against what, to him, were misconceptions and misrepresentations in "Neo-Tarzanism: The Poetics of Pseudo-Tradition." Today, my own reaction to a similar "outrage" has become much ado over "critical incidentals."

Just as baffling is Wole's claim in the opening paragraph of his contribution. He says: "Ola Rotimi's three-part series on Unife Theatre must have saddened many readers..." It is indeed, tragic, if readers can be saddened at my calling a teacher who trivializes facts to order. The only consolation then seems to be that a number of students and staff of the very Ife University have since thanked me for finding the time to put an aspect of their history in proper perspective. The results of an opinion poll as to which side enjoys the greater sympathy would mean nothing to me, since my objective in this debate was neither to gladden nor sadden hearts, in the first place.

Now to the Ayan Amao matter which evoked so much sermonizing on the dignity of labour. So, discipline also had to do with the case. Fine. But why wasn't that intimated before? Instead, the aptitude for script-work was emblazoned in the original publication as the measure whereby some of the old Unife actors were knocked out. That was the 'cue line' given. I only reacted to it and deduced that, in such circumstances, illiterate artists like the bata-drum expert Ayan stood small chance. The latest revelation only serves to prove my contention that the original dish on the Unife Theatre was not painstakingly prepared. Too many vexatious flakes of raw onion and unground *egusi*.

Of course, I'm all for discipline. More poignantly, discipline imposed not only on the rank and file, but also one modelled in the moral and mutual leadership of the bosses themselves. That is one of the secrets of the 10-year longevity of the Old Unife Theatre.

One would have expected Wole, if he meant his contribution to be meaningful, to call staff-member Omotoso and tell him candidly that his article had some gaffes. Which done, if Wole had anything to say to me, he knew how to get in touch. We do correspond from time to time. But then, the question could be asked: why must Wole contact me? After all, did I contact Dr. Omotoso before bearing down on him? The answer is: yes, I did. As stated in my rejoinder, I had privately cautioned him on his approach to facts in another article: in 1977.

This time around, not only did he repeat the same tendency, but also decided to publish the result in a national newspaper. Not stopping there, he further went ahead— with the blessing of his Department, I now have reason to believe—to publish the stuff again in a pamphlet. Hundreds of copies of that pamphlet were churned out, carted along on a tour, and distributed North, South, East and West of the Federation as part of the programme notes for a play. The "critical incidents" and all— in the name of comparative study which really was more like a narcissistic rhapsody played in vitiation of someone else's past.

Having, I suppose, made my points clear, well, I agree. We should let the dust over this matter settle quickly. The dust needn't have eddied in the first place—with a little consideration for the consequences of biased chronicling.

Kole Omotoso, whose newspaper article had kicked off the whole controversy, came back on June 1st with a brief rejoinder entitled "On Unife Theatre: Ola Rotimi's Last But Not Lasting Word":

All I wish to do in this response to Rotimi's long reaction to my short piece on the Unife Theatre is to reiterate the facts that I mentioned in that piece, to mention a few others about Ola Rotimi's work and to elaborate on one particular issue.

It is a fact that Ola Rotimi did not permit any other director to direct the Unife Theatre while he ran it. It is a fact that Ola Rotimi's style of directing is dictatorial and there is nothing strange about this. Different directors have their different styles of directing. It is a fact that the Unife Theatre has grown beyond what Ola Rotimi left behind, whether he likes it or not. Some of the people he used to summon with whistles now direct their own productions and manage productions.

Other facts that can be asserted about Ola Rotimi's work include his conservative and backward historical attitude in his historical plays. There is also the unimaginative use of specific foreign nationals to play themselves in his plays. Here the Unife Theatre had gone beyond him. In productions such as *Biko's Inquest, Death and the King's Horseman,* and *Requiem for a Futurologist,* we have used black people, Africans, to play the roles of South African Boers, British DO's and Indian loonies where Ola Rotimi would have gone searching for such nationals. The performance of these black people in these roles has been convincing and successful.

Ola Rotimi's production of my play, *The Curse*, for which he would expect my eternal gratitude, demonstrates his static sense of space on the stage. Against my advice, the cages were made of heavy iron and made stationary, instead of being mobile and light. This play was also produced more successfully by Dexter Lyndersay.

Sometime in 1975, I was approached by a European Theatre journal to do an article on adaptations of Sophocles' *Oedipus Rex* in different cultures of the Third World. I picked on two Arab playwrights—Tawfiq al-Hakim and Ali Ahmad Kathir, one Egyptian, the other from the Hadramaut—and one African playwright, Ola Rotimi. All these three playwrights have attempted to adapt the story of Oedipus into their cultures. In the case of the Arab Muslim playwrights, one could see the influence and hand of their culture and religion on the situation of the Greek king. But this is not so in the case of Ola Rotimi's *The Gods Are Not To Blame*. What Ola Rotimi has done is to simply transfer the story of King Oedipus to Yorubaland with Yoruba names without permitting Yoruba culture to influence his adaptation. In reading the original and Ola Rotimi's adaptation, one finds that but for the names there is no difference. One particularly major problem is that Yoruba gods are not as implacable as the Greek gods. Something would have to be done to avert the horror of a man killing his father and marrying his mother. Ola told me that some Yoruba lady with royal connections in one of the Yoruba ruling houses had told him of a similar incident in Yorubaland. I said I would like to know this lady and source of her information. That information is still to be provided.

The other issue I mentioned in that article is that the fact that Ola Rotimi's language trips when he moves from Yoruba to English, which he did not like. He has since produced a Yoruba version of *Kurunmi* which he insisted we should do instead of the English version.

It is to be noted that I am not the only one to have made

these points about Ola Rotimi's work. And if I were to state now that Ola Rotimi's latest play *If* seems to take after *Moon on a Rainbow Shawl* (1958) by the Trinidadian (West Indian) playwright, Errol John, Ola Rotimi would want to know how I got to know of Caribbean playwrights when all I studied was Arabic!

As for Ola Rotimi's abuse of me in his articles, as well as in a personal note to Dr. Yemi Ogunbiyi, I leave that to the care of time. Time will take care of him. Miracles never end, Ola Rotimi might still grow intellectually. For Ola Rotimi's problem is his intellectual pretensions, not some mythical enemies who are supposed to have prevented him from getting his own at the University of Ife.

Rotimi did not bother to reply to this new provocation, but on July 13th Yomi Hussein, a former student at the University of Ife, offered some words "In Defence of Ola Rotimi."

It is very interesting to read all the intellectual pettiness being displayed on the pages of newspapers; only God knows who started it!

As a one-time student of Ife University, this writer had many opportunities to watch both Ola Rotimi and other performers like Wole Soyinka on stage. I cannot but conclude that Ola Rotimi is a first among equals. In his stage productions, his choice of language cuts across the societal spectrum and this makes both an unlettered man from Ife town and the overlettered University professor understand him; unlike those who are not even understood by the social class they profess to be dealing with.

To perceive Ola Rotimi from another angle, here is what commentator Yvonne Nerverson of the *Africa Magazine* (May, 1978) has to say: " . . . An African courtyard with a shrine for worshipping the gods. . . chanting begins off-stage . . . thus the play *The Gods Are Not To Blame* by Ola Rotimi opens and the set is filled with a colourful spectacle of SERIOUS (emphasis mine) African theatre."

On Ola Rotimi's use of "specific foreign nationals in his plays," what is a dramatic art? If the audience cannot be completely carried away as to believe that they are actually witnessing the events live, those who make do with a normal-sized man where the play requires a midget are only settling with the second best and cannot be regarded as having done justice to what should be. We would want Wole (sic) Omotoso to tell his readers whether this is his own idea of nationalism, or another version of the quota system.

As to whether the Yoruba gods are more implacable than those of Greece, a little digression may be necessary here: in this writer's home town in Ogun State, an old man (now dead) consulted the Ifa Oracle in what is normally called "Isepenwo" (i.e., getting a glimpse into what the life of a new born baby will be). It is important here to add that the mother of this new child died during child-bearing. The Ifa priest, without mincing words, told the father that his new child would be an instrument of the father's death. As would be humanly expected, the father asked whether the incident could be averted and some rituals were performed. But as was earlier predicted, the child later poisoned his father in an ambitious move to inherit his property. Unfortunately for the murderer, though, the poisoning effect was slow and the dying man changed his will giving a hopelessly small portion of his property to the desperate son.

As a matter of fact, the authenticity of the will was contested in a court of law and the dispute lasted several years. The case cited above may not be as horrifying as King Oedipus', but one thing stands clear: that little or nothing can be done about prophecy.

Academicians all over the world believe that real intellectual greatness abounds in the ability to research into foreign cultures and bring out what is relevant to the researcher's own culture; if this widely-held opinion is anything to go by, then one begins to wonder why Kole Omotoso is picking bones as to the similarity between Ola Rotimi's *If* and Errol John's *Moon on a Rainbow Shawl*. Art, they say, is not only the ability to create a new horizon, but also improving on what has already been created.

Those who had the opportunity of watching the play *If,* both in Ife, Ibadan and the National Arts Theatre in Lagos, confirmed that it is indeed a masterpiece. The Oduduwa Hall of the University of Ife was packed for the four days (Thursday-Sunday) that the play was staged there in 1979. Whether people of Kole Omotoso's creed like it or not, Ola Rotimi is an undisputable King of serious playwrights who deals effectively with both the societal vices and virtues in a way as to leave his audience speechless for hours after leaving the play arena.

The full capacity crowd that watched *If* on that Saturday in 1979 was vividly shown the nakedness of helplessness of our decaying society and people left the hall like mourners dispersing from a burial procession. This magic of mind control, I would say, is possessed by few artists. Any objective analyst of *If* cannot but marvel at Ola Rotimi's accurate prediction of not only the result of the 1979 general election, but the behavioural pattern of the ruling caucus at the centre.

In the light of all these, one wonders whether Kole Omotoso wants us to take him serious about his reference to Ola Rotimi's "intellectual pretension." This phrase is not only misdirected but quite inappropriate when one talks about Ola's works. It is a fact all over the ages that no group of people or individual has ever succeeded in suppressing genuine intellectual greatness; a Chief Justice has been moved from office here in Nigeria only to be re-engaged by a higher international law body that knows his worth.

Again, if some of those whom Ola Rotimi used to "summon with whistles" now direct and manage their own productions, as claimed by Kole Omotoso, this would have been a point in favour and not against Ola Rotimi as he would want us to believe. The joy of every lecturer is the number of successful students that pass through his hands. Which, I think, should be the case of Ola Rotimi. Objective analysts who know Ola Rotimi's worth are happy at his not-too-new job at the University of Port Harcourt. And may he continue to grow in strength.

Future historians of Nigerian theatre will no doubt seek to reconstruct what really happened at the Unife Theatre between 1966 and 1985, when Ola Rotimi and Wole Soyinka held sway there and made unique contributions to the development of African performing arts. In assessing the claims and counter-claims made by scores of participants and eyewitnesses, scholars will need to consult what a few interested parties said about those days in the pages of the *Nigerian Tribune* between February and July of 1983, for among the "critical incidentals" and "biased chronicling" recorded there, they may discover clues that will lead them to a more balanced interpretation of contested facts. As every historian knows, any documentary evidence that gives us added insight into the past is too important to be ignored. If truth be asleep, common newsprint could well become the "monkey wey go wake am."

15

Beyond Biography

Characters and Journeys In Soyinka's
Isara: A Voyage Around Essay

CHARLES BODUNDE

I

If the criticism of literary biography must aspire beyond mere restatement of historical details, then it requires for this purpose, a reasonable degree of fictivity. Soyinka's brief authorial note to *Isara* provides hints on the creative relations, which informs the production of the text. The author tells us: "I have not only taken liberties with chronology, I have deliberately ruptured it" (vii). Of course, this rupture of chronology releases the text from time specificity and encourages the critic to interpret temporal elements according to his/her own scheme. The prefatory note also contains evidence of fictionalization of characters and setting. Soyinka tells us that his decision not to use real names as in *Ake: The Years of Childhood*, his authobiography "is to eliminate all pretence to factual accuracy" (viii). He confesses that Ilesa and Isara, two places where 'Essay' (the author's father) and his friends make their leap into the external world are fictionalized to accommodate this compelling memory.

213

Soyinka uses a metalic box as the premise to interpret the life lived by 'Essay' and his friends. The box, owned by 'Essay', contains letters, journals, minutes of meetings etc. Thus, the box is a kind of relic, a condensed piece of information or knowledge, which the author approaches with the eagerness of a voyager. Two fundamental meanings are derivable from this tin box symbol. First, the box is a body of history. Second, as an epiphanic object, it strikes the writer with a sudden urge to assemble the cockroach-ravaged documents into an artistic whole. In a way, this explains the interlink between history (existing in scattered pieces of documents) and literature which attempts to transmute and transmit it. The voyage into the metallic box also achieves two purposes. It unveils the experiences of a father and other characters associated with him. It also reveals the difficulties in a self-imposed journey into artistic creation from the maze of biographical materials. The author describes the latter voyage as a literary experience, which "came close to being abandoned more than once" (viii).

The effort so far has been to establish the literary condition, which makes an exploration into the journeys and characters in *Isara* a reasonable critical enterprise. The author's deliberate fictionalization of characters, time and place is taken as a significant artistic process which elevates the text from mere history to an art product which, like the fictive genre, provokes critical discourse. This fictive colouring is identified by Bryce, who describes *Isara* as "a semi fictional memoir" (*West Africa*, 26).

The journey experience is central to the processes of the production of *Isara*. Characters in a journey artifice are usually portrayed as voyagers in search of self discovery and in this, they must interact with others within a much wider world of experience. Blake (1991: 192) describes a journey as "a wanting to know based on human desires and emotion." This description expresses the attitude and intention of the involved voyager. Mortimer (1991: 169) asserts that "journeys normally involve experiences of discovery and/or experiences of spiritual growth." He stresses that the most important aspect of the voyage is that it "holds out a promise of transformation of broader horizons and deeper knowledge." The journey experience, for Nnolim (1975: 192) is a structure of individuation that involves two processes which he calls the physical and the metaphoric types. Kunene (1991: 210) also contends that journeys embrace the spatial, the temporal, the intellectual as well as the psychological levels.

There is the need to emphasize that the author enlists himself as a voyager who makes his passage through the materials of the box to tell the story of other voyagers. Thus, the attempt in this paper is to explore the ways in which the complex journeys in the text contribute to the shaping of the characters that are recognized in this discussion as adventurers, exiles and homecoming voyagers. The study also involves a discussion of the ways in which Soyinka employs symbols to expand ideas connected with the theme of journey and the nature of the characters in his fictional biography. In this, some of the theoretical points expressed by Kunene and others with regards to the journey archetype are engaged in the study of *Isara*.

II. The Adventurers

A discussion of the journey motif in Soyinka's works necessarily compels a link with the much popularized myth of Ogun, particularly the god's primordial voyage across the abyss of transition. In *Myth, Literature and the African World*, Soyinka describes Ogun's journey into earth, the courage and heroism in his celebrated triumph over cosmic obstacles and the genius of his instrument of passage:

> There had to be a journey across the void to drink at the fount of mortality though, some myths suggest, it was really to inspect humanity and see if the world peopled by mortal shards from the common ancestor was indeed thriving. But the void had become impenetrable. A long isolation from the world of man had created an impassable barrier which they tried, but failed, to demolish. Ogun finally took over. Armed with the first technical instrument which he had forged from the primordial jungle, plunged through the abyss and called on the others to follow. (1976: 28-29)

From myth figures to contemporary characters, Soyinka's adventurers link each other like a chain. For instance, Soyinka provides the ground for a link between Ogun and Chaka in *Ogun Abibiman*. Here, Ogun's traversing of cosmic space and his battles and inventiveness find a historical parallel in Chaka the Zulu, the 19th century adventurer and warrior-king. There are at least two characters in Soyinka's *Isara* whose actions reflect the Ogun-Chaka journey pattern. These characters are Wade Cudeback and Sipe Efuape.

Cudeback (Essay's pen-friend) is captured in Soyinka's book as a compulsive traveller. Essay describes the name as rough and rugged, evoking the jagged rhythm of the landscape he traverses. Caught up in the restlessness of the adventurer in him, Cudeback fondly looks forward to another voyage even before he ends the story of an accomplished excursion. Soyinka gives the signature tune of his passion:

> I never see a map but I'm away
> on all the errands that I long to do
> up all the rivers that are painted blue
> And all the ranges that are painted grey. (6)

Cudeback supplies the image that underlines his adventure when he describes himself and Essay as men "smitten by travel bug." (7) His adventurer's anthem, imbued with the desire for new experience speaks for itself:

> Take the adventure,
> heed the call now
> ere the irrevocable moment passes.
> 'Tis but the banging of the door behind you,
> a blithsome step forward, and you are out
> of the old life into the new. (7)

The metaphor of the transition from the old to the new as indicated in Cudeback's anthem underlines the essence and purpose of a journey. This pattern reveals a new discovery, a form of knowledge which also validates the voyager's mental transition. This discovery is also accompanied with the desire to reveal. For instance, Cudeback's adventures give him knowledge on the Ashtabulan landscape. He uses the letter medium to transmit this discovery to his friend. This traffic of knowledge becomes a treasured tangible entity in Essay's possession:

> Ashtabula was a private world, one which he kept secure even from the close Circle of the ex-Iles. From time to time he would "lend" them a portion of that world, a portion too immense to keep within Isara. The magnetic Mountain was one- no one could be expected to guard such a miracle selfishly beneath his pillow. (7)

Cudeback's journey around Ashtabula constitute the first phase in the fulfilment of his voyage plan. Having conquered this space, he leaps into the second phase which is continental and wide-flung like Ogun's cosmo-terrestial voyage. Like all journeys, the Ashtabula-Isara voyage records its own hazard. Sipe, Cudeback's alter-ego in the lust for adventure reports that Cudeback "had taken ill in the high seas" (232). Of course, Cudeback has much to gain from his voyage to Isara. He arrives during the tense moment of the tussle over the throne of Isara. As he sits down in Pa Soditan's room inspecting the space with unnatural intensity, Cudeback is already recording his experience in a culture where adventure has tossed him.

Soyinka describes Sipe as "the other adventurer, the would-be merchant prince" (7). Cudeback and Sipe are connected by a readiness to take challenges and the mustering of will as machinery for the accomplishment of adventure urges. Akinyode links these characters by relaying those aspects of Cudeback's Ashtabulan tales that may guide Sipe in his adventure into the chaotic world of business. The characters are however different in their expectation from adventure. Cudeback enjoys the tingling romantic sensation of the exotic landscape he traverses but for Sipe, the motivation for adventure is basically material.

Sipe's journey efforts are of two kinds. One is physical and therefore involves actual movement through space. The other is mystical in nature and affects him mentally. On two occasions, Sipe's will power is tested by the strains and hazards of voyage. Sipe's decision to board a passenger lorry in order to attend his friend's wedding is consistent with his unbridled fondness for adventure. The lorry is one of the objects that test his will. When it moves through the dusty road, Sipe's suit ordered from a catalogue with a silk lined waistcoat becomes "shrouded by the dust of voyage which had seeped steadily through floor boards and loosely welded joints" (53) When the lorry breaks down, it chooses "the most arid sector of the road for its final rebellion." (53). There is a similar but much earlier experience with water traffic. Sipe's Ikorodu bound ferry has its propellers "twisted into a shapeless hulk by a drifting log" (55) and barely "limped into Lagos". (55)

Sipe refuses to yield his will to the moralism and regimentation of St. Simeon's Seminary. He is expelled from the Seminary following an examination malpractice but "like a fallen angel", (59) he renews his will and accepts his fall as a passage into the world of freedom, a space in which his spirit of voyage (into wealth) becomes liberated. To fulfil his dream of material success, be begins an adventure into mysticism. He urges his friends, the ex-Iles, to be part of a collective business venture and for this purpose, they must throw off "the shackles of salaried existence" (61) and be prepared to make a voyage "along the path of thorns...." (61) into prosperity. When it becomes apparent that no meaningful support will come from his friends, he turns to Onayemi, his childhood acquaintance, who has already recorded some success in business. Onayemi will not however cooperate until two of them agree to engage a mystic agent to ensure that the business thrives. Sipe endorses this approach having been convinced that it does not endanger the life of the partners. The mystic service entails the employment of a medium to invoke the spirit of the dead and the sacrificial offerings are dead or living partridge, living lilly and a white young pigeon. These items are to be turned into powder some days before the ritual and they must be wrapped with white cloth. This ritual also includes taking virgin earth from the graveyard. The sacrificial preparations are to be thrown into deep water while citing a curious sign. The mystic voyage latter draws Sipe into a chaotic dream in which he assumes a Faustian image standing in trial under a convocation of church ministers figured as Rev. Beeston (Sipe's former teacher at St. Simeon's) and other clergy men. In Sipe's physical and mystic adventures, we discover a man whose life is conditioned by the restlessness of an uninhibited voyager. This is the kind of vision that drives Cudeback, his American counterpart.

III. The Exiles

Sam Asein's description of the exile personality as "conditioned alien and outsider treading cautiously the precarious fringes of existence" ("Troubadours" 125) is quite relevant in the study of exile state in *Isara*. There are two characters whose journeys into exile and final harmony provide interesting study. One is the obscure Ray Gunnar and the other is the more developed character, Wemuja. Soyinka describes Ray Gunnar as a Trinidadian of Indian origin. Other details in the text position him as a fugitive forced to work as a deck hand, a condition which Soyinka says is "barely above the status of a stow-away". (157) Gunnar's sea voyage is hazardous. His very existence is threatened not only by the possibility of shipwreck but even more so by the pervading presence of Hitler's bomb and invisible torpedoes. The danger of a sea journey under a war atmosphere forces Gunnar to begin life as an exile in Liverpool:

> When his ship docked... and he felt the firm, secure contact of good mother earth beneath his feet, he knew that he had sailed on his very last voyage for a long time. Ray Gunnar jumped ship. The Liverpool air was a dirty fog but it smelt infinitely healthier than the mists and squalls of the open seas, whose depths were constantly threaded by invisible torpedoes seeking out his heart... (157)

Wemuja, the other exile, makes his journey into exile because of a crisis at home. Soyinka tells us that the Edo boy "left Benin, fleeing a task master of an uncle". (11) The author captures the boy's state at the difficult moment of arrival:

> The fare that brought him to Isara had been saved, despite days of hunger, for such a final act of desperation. He had sought no destination, merely entered the lorry that rumbled towards its take-off as his own stomach signalled its pangs of privation, and the limits of its endurance. The lorry stopped at Isara; Damian [Wemuja] disembarked, and lay across the road. (11)

What we find in the experiences of the two exiles is the spirited quest for harmony lost in the original home. The new found world is expected to provide this lost harmony. However, this expectation remains elusive until the exiles overcome their alienation through physical and psychic integration into the new community. New physical and mental journeys are therefore required to effect proper initiation into the new world. Gunnar, the double exile (as a Trinidadian of Indian ancestry and an outsider in London) experiences initial wanderings across the new land, moving across Birmingham, Hull and Glasgow until he finally finds harmony in London.

Wemuja's journey into integration and harmony is more harrowing. He has entered Isara hungry and emaciated. The Isara night guards suspect him to be a thief and keeps him in confinement. When the people later confirm his real identity (that of a desperate exile), he is sent to the king's household in his first journey within Isara. Disturbed by the pantheon carvings around the king's palace, Wemuja later pleads to stay in Pa Josiah's household. Within the moment of transition between the king's palace and Pa Josiah's household, Wemuja experiences the surging feeling of alienation, a mental torture that drives him into death-craving, that psychological state which Bodkin (1948: 66) says arises from "deep organic need for release from conflict and tension." In a suicide mission, Wemuja has attempted to purchase caustic soda from a retailer whose vigilance has stood between him and death. Wemuja's survival of the painful experience of death-craving initiates him into a transition to a new life.

The singular event that symbolizes Wemuja's complete integration and acceptance within the new environment is the fight between him and a layabout youth. Wemuja abandons self boasting in his native Edo and verbalizes his battle readiness and contempt for his opponent in Ijebu dialect. "Wemuja" (meaning "you know nothing of fighting"), the battle cry he produces in crude Ijebu becomes the magic word that attracts the other boys to his side and the name he is subsequently called. Even though the fight is even, Wemuja is carried shoulder high and celebrated as a hero by his new friends. Both Gunnar and Wemuja undergo a positive transformation after their journeys of integration. From the position of a menial job seeker in Black centres, Ray Gunner makes dubious but comfortable living by duping education hungry West Africans. Wemuja progresses from the status of a desperate exile to a timber lorry driver who is assigned a role in Akinsanya's journey to the throne of Isara. Both characters establish self transformation and harmony as typical patterns in a journey achetype.

IV. Homecoming Voyagers

More than any other character in *Isara*, Akinyode best illustrates the journey artifice in its physical and intellectual dimensions. As Soyinka indicates, the book reflects a voyage around him. Apart from this, he is connected with the other voyagers in different ways. Wade Cudeback and Sipe, the two adventurers are his intimate friends. Wemuja, the exile has lived with Pa Soditan, Akinyode's father, since his flight into Isara. Like Cudeback, he has journeyed through rugged landscape to ensure his own education. The author penetrates his mind to capture his journey experiences:

> ...in his youth had he not often traversed grounds, those bat-tle-contested grounds of Yoruba kingdoms? From Isara to Ilesa- at least four times a year- twice only as he grew older and become innured to a prolonged exile passing through Saki, Iseyin and the ancient city of Oyo, walking, cycling, entombed in dust-filled rickety transport. (9)

His epic train journey to the Seminary, made in the company of Wemuja, the guide and protector, typifies the compelling voyage into knowledge hidden in the external world. The train, which is mysteri-ous in its motion, becomes a metaphor for an expansive outward experience. It strikes Akinyode emotionally and engages him with the tingling sense of exhilaration:

> The noise, the chaos of every station enruptured him, the railway bridges, the water-pumps at which the railway [train] stopped to "drink", the piercing whistle which was almost drowned by the rhythmic, measured grind of wheels

accelerating and decelerating down and uphill, the ceremonial approaches and departures from stations. (11)

Akinyode's first journey to Ilesa covers the winding rail route from
Abeokuta to Ede and from this point to Iwo largely on footpaths. The
labyrinthine journey continues through major towns like Oyo,
Iseyin, Shaki and finally to the small town of Ilesa. The voyage is
emblematic of a quest for a wider mental horizon in which discovery
and knowledge become the ultimate rewards. Akinyode's journey
also reveals elements of a ritual experience. The physical and mental
hazards of the involving traffic on train, bicycle, donkey and foot sig-
nify an initiation into knowledge beyond the narrow confines of
Isara. Soyinka alludes to these journey patterns in a subtle manner.
For instance, he exploits a ritual context to project Akinyode's prepa-
ration for the epic journey:

> Going to St. Simeon's Seminary, leaving home for the first
> time and for such a prolonged period was a rite of passage; he
> would not return the same child as he went. Had his father
> not called him and told him: You are going into a man's
> world? Remember that. You must make your world there,
> your friends, your future companions. (14)

Akinsanya enters into Isara in the manner of a ritual procession. The
author enacts a mythic aura in his description of Akinsanya's motion
down the hill through the streets of Isara on horse back. This resem-
bles Soyinka's picture of Ogun (in *Idanre*) as he descends from the
Idanre hill into Ire to be crowned king and warlord. Again, a kind of
parallel can be drawn between Ogun's pilgrimage on Idanre Hill as
"hermitage in rockshields" (*Idanre*, 70) from where he returns as king
and Akinsanya's voyage to Lagos and his homecoming as the most
likely candidate to occupy the throne of Isara. As Akinsanya rides
through "the troughs and serpentine streets of Isara" (232) trailed by
his friends and assisted by Wemuja who plays the equerry, the gruesome images of disease storm Akinyode's eyes:

Akinyode Soditan turned his attention to Saaki's ramrod figure on the horse, yes, this was indeed homecoming. But would he truly "return to sender"? The tasks were daunting. Beneath the finery that surrounded them, the teacher was only too aware of bodies eaten by yaws, a fate that seemed to overtake an unfair proportion of Isara inhabitants. The children's close-cropped heads did not all glisten in the sun, tracks of ringworm ran circles through stubs of hair... Within that crowd, Akinyode's eyes caught sight of a goitre round a woman's neck, the size of a paw paw.... (234)

Thus, the problems at home are enormous. The enomity requires the combative force of the new order represented by Akinsanya and the new generation of Isara citizens who by virtue of their journeys have become men of knowledge, vision and power.

Isara's transition from its obscure status to an open and receptive community cannot be attained until it sheds the old tradition. The perfect symbol of that old world is Agunrin, the old and senile Isara warrior who, according to Pa Josiah "does not even accept that the railway or motor lorry exists in this world". (155) The journeys of the younger generation have endowed them with a new consciousness, a new tradition which is completely in advance of the world represented by Agunrin. The contest between Akinsanya and Erinle is less significant compared with that which exists between Agunrin and Akinsanya. The Agunrin-Akinsanya contest operates at the symbolic plain. Through deft interior monologues, Soyinka renders Agunrin's opposition to change. Opeilu's account of the involvement of the Awujale in the Isara politics strikes Agunrin with a magical effect. His head "jerked up violently, and sounds issued from his throat". (212) Agunrin, whose voice has not been heard for almost ten years exclaims "Aaa-wu-ja-le!" and follows with the statement: "O ti fo n'oju!" (meaning, it is smashed beyond mending). His death immediately after these statements is an appropriate climax. Soyinka's vision of death or transition as continuity is quite familiar (see for instance, Soyinka's *Myth, Literature and the African World* and Bodunde's "Tributes Censures and Transitions"). Agunrin's death at the moment of the coming of the new generation illustrates an aspect of the journey artifice described by Kunene (1991: 218) as "a rite of passage [which] ultimately leads to the birth of a new life through the death of the old." Akinsanya's impressive homecoming and Agunrin's exit are epiphanic of the changing phase of the social and political history of Isara. Thus, an important aspect of this transition is the return of the ex-Iles, the new force that for a long time have been cast away from Isara as exiles.

V. Journey Symbolism

Soyinka creates the condition for a wider perception of the journey motif in *Isara* by the deployment of certain symbols. For instance, the numerous footpaths and the ring-road round Isara evoke motion and active life. In one of his descriptions of human trafffic, Soyinka reveals the sense of motion in a typical new year homecoming: " A mere trickle to begin with, the human flow through footpaths and surrogate roads would swell gradually into a torrent over the remaining days before the New Year". (142) The ring-road symbol connects characters and setting and therefore provides the platform of relation, indeed, a bond between Isara and its citizens some of who are cast into spaces beyond this home. A picture of this road is given by Soyinka in his description of the epic voyage of Akinyode and Wemuja to Ilesa. The two negotiate a ring-road which the author says is "no more than a footpath which circled Isara, then joined up with the track that would take them into Egbaland...". (11) The reader is constantly reminded of a town that disperses its people into the external world. However, the dispersed citizens never forget to "return to sender" as a mark of communal and psychic reintegration. Characters like Akinyode, Akinsanya and Sipe have experienced the exile-homecoming phenomenon which the ring-road symbolizes. The ring-road symbol assumes a journey circle, a traffic construct which could be seen in the light of what Kunene (1991) describes as passage ritual which follows the pattern of a movement through space and time and leads from experience to wisdom and new form of behaviour. (211)

Soyinka makes repeated reference to the train. Within the historical context of the text, the train as an object of traffic evokes mystery. What Akinyode sees in his first encounter with a train is a monster that "steadily belched out its own entrails and was in turn swallowed by them". (13) The monster image expands into a mythic vision as Soyinka links the train's descent into the darkness of tunnels and bridges to emerge into light with the journey of real humans into the sacred *igbale* forest to re-emerge as *alagemo* masquerades. (14) With this mythic dimension, Soyinka reinforces the idea of journey as a transition into new life and power.

The timber lorry driven by Wemuja and the horse used by Akinsanya in his entrance into Isara are symbols which are central to the interpretation of the journeys and the characters in Soyinka's biography. The lorry is owned by Node who is paralysed. The vehicle however replaces the motion which his physical incapacity denies him. Node's vehicle is the first of such object bought by an Isara man. The people reconstruct the initial ceremonial reception of the lorry into Isara to accommodate the horse in the new ceremony of passage. The lorry carries the white horse which Akinsanya later rides to Isara. The two symbols, the lorry and the horse, are connected with Isara's motion into a new order, a point expressed by Wemuja in pidgin: "We dey go carry history." These symbols enhance the interpretation of characters and journeys as the dominant moving agents in *Isara*.

Works Cited

Asein, Sam. (ed.) "Troubadours, Wanderers and Other Exiles." *Comparative Approaches to Modern African Literature*. Ibadan: Department of English, 1982.

Blake, Susan. "Travel and Literature: The Liberian Narratives of Esther Warner and Graham Green". *Research in African Literatures*. 22.2 (1991): 191-203.

Bodkin, Maud. *Archetypal Pattern in Poetry: Psychological Studies of Imagination*. London: Oxford University Press, 1948.

Bodunde, Charles. "Tributes, Censures and Transitions: Soyinka's *Mandela's Earth and Other Poems*." *Wasafiri*. (1991): 205-223.

Bryce, Jane. "Voyage of Recovery." *West Africa* (21-27 May, 1990): 26.

Kunene, Daniel. "Journey in the African Epic." *Research in African*

Literatures. 22.2 (1991): 205-223.

Mortimer, Mildred. "African Journeys." *Research in African Literatures.* 22.2 (1991): 169-175.

Nnolim, Charles. "Jungian Archetypes and the Main Characters in Oyono's *Une Vie de Bay.*" *African Literature Today* 7 (1975).

Soyinka, Wole. *Idanre and Other Poems.* London: Methuen, 1967.

_____. *Ogun Abibiman.* London: Rex Collings, 1976.

_____. *Myth, Literature and the African World.* London: Cambridge University Press, 1976.

_____. *Isara: A Voyage Around Essay.* Ibadan: Fountain Publications, 1989.

16

The Role of Face in Wole Soyinka's *From Zia With Love*

A Study in Literary Pragmatics

Obododimma Oha

Most extant studies on the concept of face, for instance Goffman (1955, 1967) Brown and Levinson (1978, 1987), and Lim and Bowers (1991), focus on its function in natural discourse, particularly conversation. There is currently an emerging understanding that face practice could be studied outside the domain of conversations, especially in those other domains in which verbal interaction is implied and which involves much use of politeness strategies. Thus Chilton (1990) has done an interesting study of facework at the macro-level of discourse, with particular reference to political rhetoric and diplomacy. Drama, as a form of discourse (both in terms of verbal interactions among characters, and in stage-audience relations), also involves face-oriented communication especially in conflict situations; it would therefore be worthwhile to extend the study on face practice to the genre. This, coupled with the peculiar nature of Wole Soyinka's play, *From Zia With Love* (1992) (henceforth *From Zia*) as a play that satirically addresses the manipulations of power by individuals, serves as the motivation for this study.

We focus on Wole Soyinka's design of role relationships and goals of interactants through verbal and non-verbal actions that have special implications for face. We also show how, as implied discourse, the play serves as a face-threatening statement on military dictatorship. We call attention particularly to the fact that, since face-threatening is a prominent feature of satirical drama, the performance of a satirical play on stage needs the appropriate realization of linguistic and semiotic elements that carry the face-threatening potentials. Also, in the teaching of the satirical play text in the classroom, paying attention to the role of face in the play would assist in the better comprehension of the relationship between style and message.

II

Before carrying out an analysis of the role of face in *From Zia*, let us explore the theoretical knowledge available on the concept. Undoubtedly, this would clarify the understanding of the concept upon which the study is based.

Face in popular discourse is often taken to mean "integrity" or "honour". For the Chinese, however, face diverges into *mien-tzu* and *lien*. *Mien-tzu* refers to "a reputation achieved through getting on in life, through success and ostentation", while *lien* "represents the confidence of society in the integrity of ego's moral character, the loss of which makes it impossible for him to function properly within the community", which then implies that *lien* is "both a social sanction for enforcing moral standards and an internalized sanction" (Hu, 1944: 45). Ho (1976: 868) has also pointed out that *mien-tzu* has moral content as well, and that in some cases, both *lien* and *mien-tzu* are interchangeably used.

However, the differences between *lien* and *mien-tzu* are clear in Chinese social relationships. While *lien* is "something to which everyone is entitled by virtue of his membership in society and can be lost only through unacceptable conduct" (Ho, 1976: 870), *mien-tzu* is a possession of those with high social status. Ho adds this important clarification to the status constraint on *mien-tzu*:

How much *mien-tzu* a person has is, in general, a function of his social status. But the quantity of a person's *mien-tzu* usually varies according to group with which he is interacting. Thus a leader in the Chinese Triad society has *mien-tzu* within the underground, but such *mien-tzu* should not be given a recognition, at least under proper circumstances, by law-enforcement agents; a military officer should have *mien-tzu* before the men he leads, but may have little *mien-tzu* in the company of a group of intellectuals; again an academic may have *mien-tzu* among his colleagues, but this *mien-tzu* may not be of much utility in the business community. How much *mien-tzu* a person has, therefore, is not fixed in amount but varies largely according to the social situation in which he is interacting. (p. 869)

Furthermore, Ho explains that the status basis of *mien-tzu* may be ascribed, or may be secured through "competition and individual effort". In the latter case, further distinctions are possible: ". . . it is possible to differentiate *mien-tzu* which rests on the personal qualities underlying achievement from *mien-tzu* which derives more directly from non-personal factors, such as wealth, social connection, and authority, obtained through personal effort" (p. 870). Thus while one could talk of losing and gaining *mien-tzu*, it seems absurd for one to talk of gaining *lien*, which every member of the society is naturally expected to possess.

Apart from the basic differences between *mien-tzu* highlighted above, the relationship of *mien-tzu* to social behaviour and control is another issue dwelt upon by Ho. The individual who possess *mien-tzu* "is in a position to exercise considerable influence, even control, over others in both direct and indirect ways", and apart from this power-potential in *mien-tzu*, the individual who has this type of face "is under strong constraint to act in a manner consistent with the requirements for maintaining his *mien-tzu* as well as for reciprocating a due regard for the *mien-tzu* of others" (p.873)

The traditional view of face as "right" or honour differs from the technical view of the concept in discourse analysis. Face, in the Goffmanian sense, is redefined as a "want" (or desire) that participants in a discourse have, and not a right as such (Brown and Levinson,[1] 1987: 67). For Goffman (1955: 214), "the person's face is something that is not lodged in or on his body, but rather something that is diffusely located in the flow of events in the encounter and becomes manifest only when these events are read and interpreted for the appraisals expressed in them."

Brown and Levinson (1978, 1987), based on Goffman's perspective, categorize face into *positive face*, which is the want to be approved of by others, or to be seen as a desirable person, and *negative face*, which is the want for autonomy, or to be free of impositions from others. These face wants are easily threatened in discourse, for instance through the performance of such elocutionary acts as criticizing, commanding, querying, etc. Also, efforts are made by efficient communicators to use verbal forms that mitigate face threat. Thus, politeness is an attempt to protect the other's face in discourse.

In respect of politeness strategies, Brown and Levinson (B & L) argue that avoidance of face-threatening act (FTA) is more polite than the performance of FTA off record. Furthermore, they explain that positive politeness strategy (i.e., with redress to positive face) is geared towards the satisfaction of the addressee's positive face, and is approach-oriented. Negative politeness strategy, on the other hand, satisfies negative face; the addresser acknowledges the addressee's desire for autonomy or assures respect for it. Negative politeness is therefore an avoidance strategy (i.e., the addresser avoids infringing on the addressee's desire for non-imposition).

Lim & Bowers[2] (1991) have identified the limitation on the B & L model as the concentration on speech acts that threaten negative face (e.g. ordering) and less attention to those that threaten positive face (e.g. disagreeing and criticizing) (p. 417). L & B convincingly argue that positive and negative politeness are not all that "mutually exclusive" as B & L have tried to show, since, for example, "a speaker may alleviate the threat to negative face by avoidance (minimizing the imposition) and at the same time promote (approach) positive face (with expression of in-groupness), affection, or respect)"; and, in the same vein, "In an act threatening positive face, . . ., a speaker may alleviate the threat to positive face with both mitigating (avoidance) and promoting (approach) strategies" (p. 419).

Alternatively, L & B establish a tripartite model which comprises (a) "fellowship face" or the want to be included (desire for belongingness), (b) "competence face" or the want for one's abilities to be respected and/or recognized, and (c) "autonomy face" or the want for non-imposition on self. Fellowship and competence faces are derived from the B & L concept of positive face.

In addition, L & B identify the following kinds of facework (i.e. "ways in which people mitigate . . . face threats) as addressing the types of face wants mentioned above: (a) **Solidarity**, which addresses fellowship face; (b) **Approbation**, which is a demonstration of appreciation for the other's abilities, minimizing blame and maximizing praise, addresses competence face; and (c) **Tact**, which expresses respect for the other's autonomy or "freedom of action", often through being indirect and tentative, and providing options for hearer, addresses autonomy face. Also, the social factors identified by L & B as affecting facework are *intimacy, power difference,* and *rights.* Among the important findings of L & B (1991) in the use of this model is that relational intimacy increases the use of Tact and Approbation when speakers are performing acts that carry high degree of face threat. Thus relational intimacy is seen as the strongest predictor of facework.

It is against this theoretical background, therefore, that we proceed to discuss the strategic role of face in Soyinka's *From Zia.*

III

The nature of the social situation presented in *From Zia* (especially role relationships, power differences, pragmatic goals and cultural system) determines the ways that verbal and non-verbal acts that affect face are performed by interactants in the play. The play is set in the prison-yard, just like Segun Oyekunle's *Katakata for Sofahead* (1983).[3] The prison is itself set in a country (Nigeria) that is under military dictatorship (a macro-context that is conceivable as a kind of prison too). In other words the play is set in *prison-yard within a prison-yard,* and, in fact the (non-verbal) behaviours in the "micro" and "macro" prisons resemble, showing that the micro-prison signifies the macro, and vice versa. Thus the micro-prison as a sub-cultural context of dictatorship, is subtly used in criticizing the military dictatorship at the macro level.

In the prisoner-prisoner interactions, the major features are role playing, acculturating or initiating (or "welcoming") of new mates (technically referred to in prison studies as "prisonization"),[4] reflecting on immediate prison situation, and satirizing the events in the government of the wider society. The adoption of the dictatorship model in the cell governance is not only for the sake of indirectly condemning the military rulership, but also a way of showing that rulership is a matter of setting example for the whole society to follow. As such, a bad example when copied would mean greater problem for the society. With the cell government designed after the military dictatorship outside, we have a rigid high-low hierarchization in the cell, with Hyacinth in possession what the Chinese call *mien-tzu* (discussed in section II) and which other prisoners must respect. Hyacinth is the cell commandment (COMM), the commodore, and Commander-in-Chief. Ministers responsible to him include those of Health, Security, Labor, Agriculture, Water Resources, Home Affairs, Education, and Information and Culture. Others are Hyacinth's Number Two and the ADC. These social roles, however, seem to have overlaps which bring about confusion and conflict. The switching of roles by inmates is used in portraying the hypocrisy and evils in the military government in the society outside.

In a situation of rigid hierarchization and distribution of roles, we would anticipate the use of face-threatening devices, especially, for instance, where giving orders and calling to order are concerned. In the same vein, defensive or protective face strategies could occur. It is likewise predictable that, given the nature of relationship between the military government and the cell society, the switching of roles by the prisoners to what is happening in the outside society cannot be put up to favour the face of the military government and its agents.

Furthermore, the high-low relations in the General Cell determine who performs what kind of elocutionary act. Certainly, since Hyacinth is given the social role as supreme head, it would be strange to see any of his subordinates addressing him in coercive illocution. Rather, we would expect constant attempt at mitigating face threat when his subordinates address him. Also, Hyacinth, as the supreme head, is likely to invoke the right to speak and be listened to, and of truthfulness, which cannot be challenged by his subordinates.

It is not only that Hyacinth exercises control over his subordinates, such exercise of control applies down the ranks. In other words, dominance and subordination characterize the prisoner-prisoner interactions, reflecting the intersubjectivity of the cell society to the wider society in which dictatorship prevails.

What is particularly significant is the way elocutionary strategies are deployed in making this prison subculture realistic as an intersubjective world. The prisoners in the General Cell, in their parody, present us with the coercive nature of illocutionary acts performed by the military dictatorial ruler, or rather the tendency for such ruler to threaten the other's face with no redress whatsoever. In other words, the dictatorial ruler is identifiable partly from the kind of illocutionary acts he performs in his interactions with his subordinates. (By their acts you shall know them!) Hyacinth, in order to exercise total control, as well as to make the other feel the presence of (superior) authority, performs FTAs. In the following exchange, which occurs during a session of the External Ruling Council (a name that suggests an inclination for totalitarianism and power-drunkenness), he performs such acts as commanding/ordering, questioning, and authorizing to encode his power:

(1) COMMANDMENT: Minister of Health!

      HEALTH: (*Leaps up, salutes briskly*) Present sah!

      COMM: Make your report

      HEALTH: Seven dead sah!

      COMM: Seven dead? You mean between yesterday and today?

      HEALTH: In the last twenty-four hours, Your Excellency.

      COMM: Which Local Government?

HEALTH:	Katanga Local Government two; Aburi, one; Soweto, two. And another two in your own constituency, Amorako (*Pointing in the direction of the tossing figure on the mat*). At my recommendation, the Minister of Housing has relocated him to maximum Fresh-Air security by the door, but I think it's too late. Unless they take him to hospital.
COMM:	So, we have epidemic.
HEALTH:	Permission to speak sah.
COMM:	Permission granted.
HEALTH:	Your Excellency, yessah, we have epidemic. (*From Zia*, p. 2)

The invitation of the Minister of Health to make a report is rather an act of commanding, as is typical in military subculture in which a senior commands a junior. In the actual spoken discourse, this is to be marked by a rise in voice. In the printed text, as could be seen in except (1) above, this is signalled by the mark of interjection (!). Certainly, an actor performing the Comm's role has to observe this intonation requirement so as to communicate the illocutionary act appropriately and effectively.

Also, the appropriateness of voice and intonation would make the Minister of Health's response (the non-verbal action of leaping up and saluting briskly, and the verbal action, "Present sah!") also appropriate. That is to say that the nature of the preceding act (commanding) predetermines the nature of response, all other elements of situation being taken into consideration also. A command naturally reveals the commander as superior and invites submission and/or compliance from the addressee. Rebellion would therefore register non-compliance; in other words, the response to the act of commanding either confirms the presupposed power relations or refutes it. In the COMM-HEALTH verbal interaction, superiority is confirmed (and total submission also conveyed).

That act of commanding or ordering threatens the addressee's autonomy face—the want for non-imposition, to be left undisturbed. The performance of the act by the Comm is an attempt to express a claim of lordship over the addressee.

The act of questioning, as performed by the Comm in excerpt (1) above, and in other cases in the internal fictive discourse, is also strategically deployed to impose authority, not just as a way of seeking information. Even in terms of seeking information, the act of questioning in the excerpt satisfies power demands. It agrees with the situation of X (junior) being "answerable to" or "reporting to" Y (a senior).

The occurrence of the power-oriented FTA, *questioning*, after *ordering*, shows the awareness in the playwright that there is the need for such FTAs to co-occur and in a specific order. In "Make your report" there is also an implication of "X reports to Y". So, the questions that are asked by Y later appropriately consolidate the information-flow condition provided by the discourse context. In the rare cases in which the Comm is questioned by his subordinates, there are clear and effective uses of Tact—the facework that shows the avoidance of threat to autonomy face. In excerpt (2) below, a subordinate avoids questioning the Comm directly, to prevent the later from processing the questioning as face-threatening.

(2)   NO. 2:   Come on Chief, you know he's good. Look at the way he handled the last student riots.

        COMM: Nothing to boast about. He is just another of them after all. He even thinks like a student.

        DIR: *But Sir, you commended my handling of the workers' demonstration.*

COMM: Yes yes yes, and you don't let us forget it. Maybe you should change Ministries with Danlako. You handle Labor and let him switch to Security.
(*From Zia*, p. 4; emphasis added).

The statement underlined in the excerpt is tactical. It is a question that *pretends* to be a statement. The statement on the surface conveys the act of reminding. But it could be rephrased (i.e., transformed) to read, "But sir, didn't you commend my handling of the workers' demonstration?" The two sentences (the original in the excerpt and the question transform) actually have the same D-structure. For the question, ". . . didn't you commend my handling of the workers' demonstration?" to emerge at the S-structure level, at least three kinds of transformation are required: do-support, Neg-insertion (to insert the negative particle "not"), and NP-Aux inversion or I-movement (which would move "do + Past + Neg" (didn't) to the COMP-position as required in the formation of Yes-No questions).

Thus, in the question transform, the DIR would be threatening the Comm's fellowship face through the implication of unfairness on the part of the Comm. The DIR, therefore, opts for the statement that would obscure the threat. The strategy used by the DIR is Tact, or negative politeness (as it is called in the B & L model), which is an avoidance strategy. The Comm does not use such avoidance strategy at all. His assertion that the DIR is "just another of them after all; he even thinks like a student" is a bald threat to fellowship and competence face wants. A student, in the midst of such prisoners, or before a military government, would not have *mien-tzu*, what with all the idealism about better society students are known to agitate for. And, generally, students are no friends to military (dictatorial) governments, at least in Nigeria. So, referring to the DIR as a student is a tactic of alienation.

Generally, the Comm does not attempt to "clothe" his utterances with threat mitigators when addressing members of his council. Even some of the references to the Council members are decivilizing. For instance, the lexical choices like "bickering" and "you bloody civilian"

236

in excerpts (3) and (4) below.

(3) WATER: (*Protesting*) My portfolio sir—
             Water Resources.
     AGRIC: No, mine. Agriculture.

     COMM: Silence! Any more of that ancient
             bickering and I'll merge both min-
             istries into Agriculture and Water
             Resources then abolish both in
             one stroke instead of two . . . (p. 5)

(4) COMM: (*Waves his arms grandly*) Now that
             is the sound of stability. And secu-
             rity. (*Sits*) *circumnavigations* or
             poaching in other people's ponds and
             fishing in troubled waters. Give us a
             professional sitrep. (*Looks round*)
             Sit-rep. Situation Report, for *you
             bloody civilians.* (p. 6) (emphases
             in speech added)

Other stretches of language emphasized in the Comm's utterance in
(4) above are also insulting to the referent, and therefore face-threatening. No other prisoner dares use such choices in referring to him.
Instead, address tags that acknowledge the addressee's superiority are
used in referring to the Comm. For instance, "Sir" (or the more illiterate form "sah") and "Your Excellency". The word "Sir" in Nigerian
English conveys a recognition of the superiority of the referent, and
in the language of the military, such recognition is obligatory, partly
as a form of the military claim to maintaining discipline, and in more
dubious cases, an evidence of dictatorship as in the context of the discourse. In the "welcoming" ritual for instance, a non-recognition of
the implications in the use of the address tags is identified and correction is given to the new-comers:

(5) COMM: Educate these refugees.

237

EDUC: Yessah, Commodore and Commander-in-Chief. (*Turns to the kneeling men*) Now you! you had your ears open just now. I hope you heard me when I addressed the Commander-in-Chief. Right? What the Sergeant- Major was complaining about was that you addressed our Commander like a common man. When you address the Commodore, you say "sir." Is that clear?

MIGUEL: Oh yes, thank you. We're very sorry Sir.

EDUC: Yessah. No Sir. I beg your pardon Sir. I understand Sir. Permission to speak Sir. Permission to fall out Sir. And so on and so forth. This is a military regime so don't mess about. Even when we were doing the civilian style—because you see, we try to conform with what is going on in the country outside—so before we changed to military, even then our Commandant was still Commander-in-Chief as well as a civilian President. So no matter what style we are operating, you must address him with due respect and full protocol. (pp. 15-16)

238

The fact that the Comm is addressed with respect, but he does not care whether he threatens any person's face wants or not, further reveals him as a total dictator. He has the higher tendency to perform FTAs.

Apart from the types of FTAs examined so far, the COMM, as could be seen in excerpt (3), also performs other FTAs such as warning and threatening. Warning and threatening put the addresses at disadvantage as well as reveal assumptions of the addresser's superiority. Conditions for threatening, as specified in Fraser (1975: 179-180) are:

C1   The speaker intends to convey a proposition p which specifies a future action.

C2   The speaker intends that p be taken as I presenting an action which
(a) is going to occur (perhaps conditionally)
(b) has consequences disadvantageous to the hearer.
(c) the speaker recognizes responsibility for carrying it out.

C3   The bearer recognizes the intentions stated in C1 and C2.

Also following Gingiss (1986: 153), we could see the threats in excerpt (3) as "direct", since they are of the form, "I will do X". The directness of the threats again shows the Comm's lack of interest in redressing face threat.

The relationship of the prisoners with the prison officers (jailers), such as the warder and the superintendent, shows mutual inclusion. Such exclusion, which generates threats to fellowship face particularly, seems to originate from distrust. The prisoners do view the jailers from the angle of us-versus-them that is typical of the *Homo hostilis* (Keen, 1986: 17). Since the warder is not a member of the cell society and sub-culture, he is regarded as the "outsider", an agent provocateur who could pose a threat to the government of the cell, and to the territoriality of the cell. Thus in a satirical song, decivilising vehicles are used in addressing him:

(6)   PRISONERS: Oga warder, Oga warder!
                       Craw-craw warder, Oga warder
                       Sobia warder, Oga warder
                       Gonorrhoea warder, Oga warder
                       Appolo warder, Oga warder
                       Syphilis warder, Oga warder
                       Leprosy warder, Oga warder.
                       . . . (p. 22, ellipsis mine).

There is contempt for (any) authority that exists outside the cell. In excerpt (6), the Nominators (Nouns functioning as modifiers) which describe the warder are all dangerous sicknesses. The warder, as an "enemy", an agent of contrary authority, becomes a *sick* person and, what more, the type to be avoided (i.e. denied company). Thus the fellowship face of the warder is highly threatened.

In the proceedings of the Eternal Ruling Council, which are modelled after those of the military Government in the wider society (parodying Ibrahim Babangida's Armed Forces Ruling Council), we have overwhelming presence of face-threatening devices (ie, against military rule). Military rule, as typified in the Comm and his cabinet, is portrayed as dehumanizing, confused and confusing, and generally against the good of the society it is supposed to work for. The last point—military rulership being against (civil) society—seems to be a central issue in the play. We will therefore comment briefly on the kind of face-threatening semantic and pragmatic devices used in that regard. We will use excerpts (7) to (9) below in discussing the face-threatening nature of the devices.

(7)   DIR: Do I have permission to move on Sir?

        COMM: Permission granted.

        DIR: The hyacinths are still a hazard to
                  navigation.

COMM: That's why everybody calls me Hyacinth, so what?

(*DUTIFUL LAUGH FROM CABINET*)

DIR: The fishermen can't get at the fish . . . (p. 5)

(8) COMM: You left out what should interest your portfolio—security. While you were drifting from portfolio to portfolio, minding other people's departments, you missed your boat. And that boat is—security. With the water hyacinths spreading through the harbours, the nation cannot be invaded by sea. You cannot have any secret landings on unguarded beaches. Those sea-borne mercenary and guerilla incursions have ceased— that is security for you. Even our waterside prisons have become more secure. Ita Oko Penal Island, for instance. There has been no escape from there in the past year and a half—that is security, your portfolio. Cheap, natural, security barrier . . . (p. 6)

(9) NO. 2: My dear young major, your problem is lack of experience. You must forget all your funny ideas in here, you understand? On this council, security means only one thing—counter subversions. Counter subversive talk. Counter rumour-mongering. Counter incitement to subversion.

And you have been given powers to
deal with all that . . . (p. 8)

Negation (of responsibility) is adopted by the Eternal Ruling
Council as an ideology.[5] For excerpt (7), we could use Relevance Theory to determine the meaning of the COMM's response, "That's why
everybody calls me Hyacinth, so what?" The response is (naturally)
difficult to understand as the proper response to the utterance proceeding it. It does not have any direct link with the report made by
water Hyacinth (mere weeds) to navigation and Hyacinth, the name
of an individual? How can the hazard lead people into calling somebody "Hyacinth?" Certainly, a direct connection does not exist, so it
may be indirect. In this respect, to establish the relevance of the
Comm's utterance, we may use the instruments of para-logic, what
Chilton (1988) call "metaphor morphism". The morphism requires
the mapping of the problematic domain onto the known domain
which helps in clarifying the link, then back to the problematic for
interpretation. That is, seeking the clarification of X_1 by referring to
simpler (more familiar) understanding provided in Y_1 and Y_2. Thus,
with the morphism, we understand the Comm's response as implying
a symbolic link between him (his attributes) and the stubborn water
Hyacinths. His name therefore suggests his character.[6] Being a military figure, it becomes a serious indictment for his kind of rulership.
Judging from excerpt (8), it seems that the water hyacinth metaphor
morphism actually refers to the ideology of the military rulership—
the ideology of negating and impeding progress in society in order to
protect the rulership (note the ambiguity of "security barriers" in
excerpt (8).[7] This selfish pursuit, along with the hypocritical smuggling explicit of the military satirized in the Wing Commander and
the missing diplomatic consignment, more clearly portrays the military as incompetent in rulership.

The forms of indirectness used in satirizing military rulership,
which include ironies (on military goals and actions), metaphors, and
proverbs, tend to draw our attention to how far literariness can go in
addressing face.

IV

In the foregoing discussion on the management of face we identified the satirical portrait that the playwright has painted through the prisoners as particularly threatening the fellowship and competence faces of the military dictatorship in Amorako. The competence face of the military rulers is threatened by the prisoners' satirical dramatization of the participation of such rulers in smuggling, their confusion and duplication of offices, and the (mis)interpretation of the goals of government to their own selfish advantage. Portrayals of military rule as being dictatorial, lacking concern for human lives, and inconsistent (as witnessed in the military changing laws when and as it likes), threaten the fellowship face of the military.

The reader's attention was also drawn to the nature of some of the important verbal devices deployed by the prisoner-satirists in the face threats mentioned above. Among these devices were coercive illocutionary acts which correlate with power difference and pragmatic forms of indirectness (which intensify the satirical power of the discourse).

It is obvious that the main pragmatic purposes of dramatic communication (and, indeed, all artistic forms of communication) are teaching or imparting of ideals, as well as entertaining. The ways the ideals are imparted are often indirect. In fact, in such communication, we witness what Roman Jakobson (1960; and in Allen & Corder, 1973: 56) refers to as the metalingual function of language—the focus to the various techniques, which strategically communicate meaning.

Satirizing, as a macro-act, is generally face-threatening since the entity being satirized is put at some disfavour before the audience. Acts that threaten fellowship and competence face wants are highly alienating. The satirical play, as a mode of face-threatening, thus seems to have alienation as a covert objective. Distancing the audience from military rulership (i.e., discouraging such rulership) could be inferred as the goal of Soyinka in *From Zia*.

The satirical play has the rhetorical power of *persuading* by virtue of the verisimilitude of the image being presented. The semiotic power of the entire portrait is indeed what determines how far the attitude of the audience is influenced by the act of satirizing. And, covertly, the playwright would want to get the feelings of the audience (towards what is being satirized) to agree with his.

The objective of distancing military rulership of course needs not be overtly expressed. Following Habermas (1984, 1987), we could see communication action *From Zia*, in which the goal of influencing the attitude of the audience is not made explicit, as "strategic" communication. It is, as we have indicated, quite typical of artistic communication to prefer indirectness to directness. And indirect communication seems to be more effective since the audience is given the impression that no idea is being imposed but merely being suggested. In other words, the autonomy face wants of the audience are fully respected. Such tactful respect for the right of the audience contrasts sharply with direct forms of regulating behaviour ("do this" or "do that") which are also aspects of communicating dictatorship.   On the other hand, forms of indirectness in *From Zia* seem to be equipment for face redress, as L & B (1991) suggest—that indirectness is an avoidance strategy. However, it seems that the technique of indirectness could merely suspend the processing of the act as face-threatening.

Furthermore, the fictiveness of the experience presented on stage could be seen as militating element to face threat. In this case, an excuse is being offered by the artist—as if to say, "You see, it is untrue after all, even though I had to refer to social experience. But then, there was nothing I could do; I just had to borrow in order to tell the lie in a truthful way.[8] Thank you for not being a resemblance of the lie". This, however, does not cancel out the face threat in the satirical play. It merely provides some protection for the artist in the discourse (against censorship). The management of face in *From Zia*, therefore, highly enhances the purpose(s) and power of the dramatic communication.

The essay has also shown that in directing and performing Soyinka's *From Zia*, or in teaching it in the classroom as a literary text, attention should be paid to the vital role(s) of face, especially in characterization and the structure of relationships among characters. Also, the general communicativeness of the text may not be well-comprehended if the face strategies the text producer has used are not well studied and comprehended.

Notes

1. Hereinafter shortened to "B & L".
2. Hereinafter shortened to "L & B".
3. This style of using prisoner-characters to comment on social life through inset dramatic episodes has also been used in Segun Oyekunle's *Katakata for Sofahead* (1983), a pidgin play that very effectively presents the violent and almost "fictive" nature of prison life in Nigeria.
4. Donald Clemmer (1958:300) explains that: "Acceptance of an inferior role, accumulation of facts concerning the organization the prison, the development of somewhat new habits of eating, dressing, working, sleeping, the adoption of local language, the recognition that nothing is owed to the environment for the supplying of needs, and the eventual desire for a good job are aspects of prisonization which are operative for all inmates."
5. The function of negation as an ideological method is very typical to totalitarian rulership as we see in George Orwell's novel, *1984.*
6. This paralogic on naming seems to play on Ferdinard de Saussure's argument (1915) that there is no relationship between the *signifie* (signifier) and the *signifiant* (signified).
7. "Security barrier" could be read as "that which obstructs security" (i.e. that (barrier) which provides security)). The playfulness here points to the fact that in totalitarian contexts, what the ruler regards as security paradoxically amounts to insecurity for other citizens. His security agents in such a case become insecurity agents for the oppressed other.
8. 'Biodun Jeyifo has captured this paradox in drama with the playful title of his book, *The Truthful Lie.*

Works Cited

Brown, P. and Levinson, S. (1978). "Universals in Language Usage: Politeness Phenomena" in Goody (ed) *Questions and Politeness: Strategies in Social Interaction.* Cambridge: Cambridge University Press.

_____. (1987) *Politeness: some Universals in Language Usage*. Cambridge: Cambridge University Press.

Clemmer, Donald. (1958) *The Prison Community*. London/New York: Holt, Rinehart and Winston.

Chilton, P. (1988). *Orwellian Language and the Media*. London: Pluto Press.

_____. (1990) "Politeness, Politics and Diploma". *Discourse & Society*, Vol. 1(2), 201-224.

de Saussure, F. (1915; Rep. 1959) *Course in General Linguistics*. New York: McGraw Hill.

Fraser, B. (1975) "Warming and Threatening", Centrum 3, 1969-180.

Gingiss, P. (1986) "Indirect Threats". *Word*, Vol. 37, No. 3, 153-158.

Goffman, E. (1955) "On Face-work": An Analysis of Ritual Elements in Social Interaction". *Psychiatry*, 18 (August), 213-231.

_____. (1967) *Interaction Ritual*. New York: Anchor.

Habermans, J. (1984) *Theory of Communicative Action*, Vol. 1, Boston: Beacon Press.

_____. (1987) *Theory of Communicative Action*, Vol. 2, Boston: Press.

Ho, D. V. (1976) "On the Concept of Face". *American Journal of Sociology*, Vol. 81, No. 4, (January), 867-884.

Hu, H. C. (1944) "The Chinese Concept of Face". *American Anthropologist*, 46, (January-March), 45-64.

Jakobson, R. (1966) "Closing Statement: Linguistics and Poetics". In T. A. Sebeok (ed) *Style in Language*. Mass: The M. I. T. Press; 350-377. Also in Allen, J. P. B. & Corder, S. P. (eds.) (1973) *The Edinburgh Course in Applied Linguistics*, Vol. 1, Readings in Applied Linguistics. London: OUP.

Jeyifo, Biodun (1985) *The Truthful Lie: Essays in a Sociology of African Drama*. London: New Beacon.

Keen, S. (1986) *Faces of the Enemy: Reflections of the Hostile Imagination*. San Francisco: Harper & Row.

Lim, T. & Bowers, J. W. (1991) "Facework: Solidarity, Approbation, and Tact" *Human Communication Research*, Vol. 17, No. 3, 415-450.

Oha, O. (1991) "Discourse Strategies in Isidore Okpewho's *The Last*

Duty". A paper presented at a symposium in honour of Prof. Isidore Okpewho, Ibadan, 9 November 1991.

Orwell, G. (1980) *Nineteen Eighty-Four*. London: Heinemann.

Oyekunle, S. (1983) *Katakata for Sofahead*. London: Macmillan.

Soyinka, W. (1992) *From Zia With Love*. Ibadan: Fountain.

17

From Metaphysical Profundity To Ferocious Topicality

The Paradigm Shifts in *The Beatification of Area Boy*

IMO BEN UBOKUDOM ESHIET

A startling evocation and convergence of themes and forms that have haunted Soyinka for more than four decades of playwrighting, *The Beatification of Area Boy* evinces all the characteristics of its author's formidable cerebral talents. Consistent in thought and attitude, particularly in relation to Soyinka's reasoning on Africa's failed states, the play appears to hint at a movement away from the dour cynicism of earlier plays to a certain progressiveness in outlook. Furthermore there appears on the surface to be a certain paradigm shift from the playwright's recurrent Ogunian metaphysical evocations to a more ferocious topicality often associated with Nigerian dramatists who cut their teeth long after the Nobel Laureate had carved his phenomenal niche in world dramaturgy.

Enriched by decades of literary competence and experience in prodigious outpourings of artistic creativity, Soyinka in his new play seems to make some departures from the ubiquitous mythological motifs and ritualistic framework upon which the ordered diversity of his earlier plays like *A Dance of the Forests* and *Death and the King's Horseman* are structured to embrace a theatrical aesthetic which stresses the immediacy of an on-going experience. With this departure, Soyinka seems to align himself with latter-day Nigerian dramatists whose guiding principle, as one of them, Olu Obafemi qualifies it, is:

> . . . to demystify the theatrical medium – to create art that is close to the popular mode in terms of language and directness of purpose – and to make theatre effect some measure of social change. (Claude Schumacher, 1982: 235).

From the innovative communicative patterning of *The Beatification of Area Boy,* including its sustained cultivation of a subvariety of English registers and idioms the urban masses written about could identify with, it would appear that the playwright is committed to a popular mass oriented drama. In addition, he appears positively keen to reverse damaging criticism avidly marshalled against him for what has largely seemed to be an unrepentant obsession with turgid, obscurantist and convoluted modes of dramatic delivery.

Fueled by outrage, *The Beatification of Area Boy* is a trenchantly bitting interrogation of a cocktail of adversities including the free fall to anarchy resulting from military usurpation of political power in Nigeria. Showcasing the country as being engulfed in a spiral of military ambushes and economic decay, Soyinka allegorizes the aberration as an evil of pandemic proportions in Africa. To paradigmatize the disastrous missteps of soldiers in power, the playwright uses the synecdoche of Lagos as a coat hanger upon which he paints a murderously annihilating picture of a failed state, a diseased political condition marked by a complete dearth of fiscal prudence, parlous economic situations, massacre and rapine, alienated state assets, unmitigated poverty, misery, indeed, a sorry saga of cultural, political and social defenestration.

Illuminating this abhorrent condition as an "abyss of social anomie", Adebayo Williams telling remarks that:

> This is not a metaphysical affliction but a verifiable social phenomenon. A failed state is one that has been over-

whelmed by man-made disasters, characterized by wide-spread alienation and a comprehensive institutional collapse. (Kayode Soyinka 1999: 6).

This is the situation which Soyinka transforms into social metaphors as he weaves his compelling spell-binding narrative. In delineating the most obnoxious manifestations and purulence of military dictatorship, Soyinka, certainly with an alternative social order in mind, analyses not only the castrating irregularities of military rule but, indeed, the entire gamut of the explosive tensions of antagonistic and fanatical forces which subvert the oil on the wheel of social progress.

Accordingly, the portrayal of the setting of the action aptly approximates the very dysfunction of the system. It does this by emblematizing the byzantine complexities of the social incoherence engendered by the limited programming of inflexible autocratic military rule. By canvassing action on a dangerously uncertain and apocalyptic landscape, the dramatist succeeds in objectifying in concrete terms a fundamentally flawed system bogged down by a grim tide of skewed and unsustainable human and material development. In this landscape, abject poverty exists side by side with obscene affluence.

Consequently, brutality and violence, pervasive fear and upheaval, voided institutions and a paralyzed citizenry whose social behaviour continually tilt towards the treacherous constantly gnaws the sinews and fabric of society itself. Furthermore, forced expulsion and mayhem, calculated and wanton, entrepreneurially orchestrated to achieve a maximum accumulation of wealth exacerbate a human condition which the playwright furiously depicts as a bizarre and frenzied dash among deplorable rodents. In sum, the setting becomes a veritable metaphor for a land and a people enamoured by a rendezvous with disaster.

Abbreviating the traumas of a country prostrated by its military rulers, Emeka Anyaoku, one of Nigeria's most illustrious sons starkly witnesses:

Nigeria has been under military rule for 28 of its 38 years of independence. This has proved costly to the country's economic, political and diplomatic standing. Government by coercion and the absence of public accountability over so many years have combined to breed a culture of corruption and general incompetence in public and private sectors. The state apparatus was turned into an instrument of patronage and personal enrichment for the ruling elite rather than of public service. It has now been established that in recent years vast sums of money disappeared from the public treasury and the country's resources were so poorly managed that petroleum products which the country is so richly endowed, were in short supply on the domestic market. Nigeria's transport and telecommunication infrastructure as well as its educational and health services, all so vital for economic development, were neglected. All this was accompanied by serious violations of human rights and fundamental freedoms and disregard for the rule of law on the part of the state and its agents, which led to Nigeria's suspension from the Commonwealth in 1995 and to the institution of international sanctions against the country. (Kayode Soyinka, 1999: 9).

The maladroit management of public affairs and the consequent crippling social disorders that have retarded the progress of the nation and turned it into a laughing stock are the materials from which Soyinka fashions the formidable arsenal and structures of the dark comedy of . . . *Area Boy.* Comedy is a sub-genre in which Soyinka has distinguished himself so much so that Oyin Ogunba (1975: 68) remarks that "Soyinka's genius is really for comedy and satire rather than tragedy". Such plays as *The Lion and the Jewel, The Trials of Brother Jero, Childe International, A Play of Giants* and the play of our study all powerfully exemplify his dexterity and flair for comic action.

Soyinka's expertise as a deft designer of comic action even when handling issues of grave import is everywhere articulate *in The Beatification of Area Boy.* Witness the irreverent imbalance in the title of the play to start with. The schizoid titular items not only disintegrate into mutually contradictory and even antagonistic values, but also invite irony, satire, enigma and even confusion. To beatify as The Oxford Advanced Learners' Dictionary puts it, is the Pope's prerogative "to honour a dead person by stating officially that he or she is specially holy". The term Area Boy is a Nigerian speak for bums, miscreants and cranks. Taken together, we cannot but be jolted by the dramatist's strange but vibrant juxtaposition of discordant materials in his evocation of a rheumatoid world standing on its head.

Thus from the very initial textual signals the playwright, through a puzzling but mordant humour, zestfully stirs up a palpable mood of alienation and spiritual dislocation. This feeling is in turn sustained in the rest of the play by the bizarre lunacy displayed by the characters and by the wild and zany atmosphere of the action itself. Using the machinery of dark comedy with its disorienting gallows humour and jolting contrasts, Soyinka ranges far and wide in his thematic constellations synthesizing graveness with considerable comic action in his relentless portrayal of bewildering discordance. The artistic combination of the incongruous with the beautiful has the literary impact of intensifying contrastive effects and of highlighting objective observation, a cardinal feature of realism. The mode aligns Soyinka with such revered 20th century avatars of the theatre as Shaw, Pirandello, Chekhov, Shepard, Albee, Stoppard, all of whom are adept at the technique.

In the opening salvo of the comic onslaught, Soyinka brings down his gauntlet to unnervingly engender an emotional jarring through a disconcerting contrast overlaid with bitterly ironic overtones. From the aesthetically intriguing and clashing choice of artistic items in the title of the play to the sagacious but grating siting of action on a street where death is substituted for life, the dramatist uses keenly incisive and blatant style to advance his comic discourse.

The brazen framework of black comedy further serves to enhance the maximum shock value of the form and in epicly emphasizing through contrasts the schisms in the cultural and political institutions which the playwright depicts as emasculated and effete. Through unlikely metaphors and inverted conceit, the expository scenes aggregate to intensify the absurdities elaborately caricatured in the rest of the action. Notice how the first stage direction dramatizes the ironic disjunctions the play lampoons:

> The broad frontage of an opulent shopping plaza. Early day break . . . when the door slides open, the well stocked interior of consumer items . . . contrast vividly with the slummy

exterior. Frontage consists of a broad pavement . . . lined by
the usual makeshift stalls, vending their assortment of
snacks, cigarettes, soft drinks, household good, wearing
apparel, cheap jewellery, etc. (5).

In this terse frame of reference, the playwright skywriting his
intent gives an overview of his action's milieu, his major thematic preoccupation and the venerable comic mechanism keyed up in the
body of the play. Beaming with exquisite suggestions and captivating
hints, the stage direction conjures up a world of crass indulgence for a
powerful few and a miserable treadmill world of stress and strain for
the vast majority of people. Thus the queer street where action is set is
animated by a hybrid mixture and jostling together of the grandiose
and the tawdry. Broad spaces are counter-pointed by dingy pausity
while glittering shopping malls are off-set by even grittier surround-
ings. The street thus provides a reference point for the asymmetrical,
the incongruous and the ridiculous in the dramatic situation.

The visually evoked humour takes on a malignant and sinister hue
when the miss en scene expands to show 'The Barbar-stall' and 'Mama
Put's food corner' in every close proximity. In this cramped existence,
waste matter and human consumables coexist. By arranging the content and form paradigms of the initial action into a pattern which foregrounds the rest of action, Soyinka with great economy of means
wraps mood, atmosphere and even the core significance of his action
into a total configuration. His gritty description of the cityscape powerfully crystallizes the conceptual image of the malignant excrescence
he interrogates and exposes to thoughtful laughter.

With his operational technical thrust thus established, Soyinka
proceeds with theatrical acumen to lay bare the bizarre psychological
afflictions that castrate lives on the queer street. Characterized by
inventive comic details reflective of the sleazy social and political climate, the dialogic action is initiated by an eccentric vagrant apparently suffering from delusion of grandeur. The wild dialogic
transaction and the failed communication between this character
called Judge and Trader affords Soyinka the means to expose the
superstition, sorcery and inefficiencies eclipsing the system and to
demonstrate why the system fosters so much evil among its citizens.

The absence of congruence and effectiveness in communication between both characters enables the playwright to demonstrate how a distorted social order blights the minds of its people. The 'Early day break' which marks the beginning of action is an inverted conceit structured to accentuate the crank Judge's perception of the country as "a kingdom of lost souls" (p. 7), especially as the vitalities and regeneration often associated with that time of the day are replaced by the harshness of an irradiated hellhole which the entire play turns out to be.

In skillfully delineating the unhinged conditions and displaced figures in his play, Soyinka intricately weaves into the fabric of action a comic gear vibrant with crispness and spontaneity, compelling local references and accessible allusions vivaciously expressed through *wordsmithing*, wise cracks, obscenities and stony, pitiless mockery. Using these devices as a launch-pad for critical laughter, the seasoned dramatist ruggedly delves beneath the veneer of mundane anxieties to confront the terrors and unspeakable atrocities of a swashbuckling kamikaze dictatorship. The significant content of the play attempts to understand why dictatorship operate the way it does, why it breeds so much evil and why the detestable system is unsustainable.

One of the modes of interrogation Soyinka employs is the literary device and social weapon of satire, a means of expression which he recurrently turns to in a career that has spanned some of the most tumultuous times in his country. Thus with a profound sense of anxious concern, Soyinka directs virulent darts at a debased and debasing army which though masquerading as a redeeming corrective force is itself a venomous cankerous pestilence direly in need of scything. The scurrilous songs of the prisoners lampoon the army as a full blown disaster. Denounced for living on pillage and ransom, the military is shown as a band of brigands with brains in the boot who constantly breaks new grounds in notoriety. Its unbroken history of preposterous savagery is recounted in Mama Put's ordeal and in the adversities of the evicted Maroko dwellers.

The scathing implication immanent in this presentation is that if the army that has usurped the leadership of society is steeped in unqualified villainy then much could not be expected from other miscreants up and down the ladder. Thus imaged, the army seems to outclass and snatch the business of wanton criminality from the much maligned Area Boys. The brutal rape of Mama Put and the callous murder of her brother who died defending family honour and the violent seizure of Maroko are social and structural metaphors coordinating and intensifying related motifs in the action, typifying and illustrating the analogous rape and alienation of state assets by a sedentary, freebooting army.

The big wedding ceremony which is the trigger that detonates much of the play's humorous mass provides the dramatist a spectacular means to make his social comments on moribund traditions, and to direct attention to the obscenities of ostentation. Through this event the dramatist scorns the abuse and conversion of state machinery to personal gains and self-aggrandizement. His outrage at profligacy is poignantly and compelling articulated in the dismal but surprising failure of the wedding. The unexpected ending is a grand projection of Soyinka's revulsion at stupidity and the nemesis that rewards a people's unanswered yearning for clear leadership. Through it, Soyinka registers his strong protest against the use of state machinery as apparatus for patronage especially when it engenders in the disadvantaged masses a feeling of losing the ground from beneath their feet. The unexpected twist in the wedding is not only steeped in high drama but is also an eloquent statement of the playwright's sympathies and antipathy.

The dramatist's repudiations of ravenous greed and carvenous obsession with crass materialism are based on the problems of economic leukemia they create for the rest of society. The sly and streetwise Trader cues us into the lack of balance between segments of the milieu's economy especially between costs and prices. Remarking the inclemency of the socio-economic situation especially in regards to how inflationary pressures erode and outstrip buying power he groans:

> . . . Look, na early morning. I dey prepare for my customers and I wan' think small. We currency done fall again, petrol dey scarcity, which mean to say, transport fare done double. As for foodstuff and other commodity, even garri wey be poor man diet . . . (Stops as he observes Judge looking at him with total mystification) I just dey explain why I need small time to put new prices for all these goods (Judge looks even more bewildered).

This disequilibrium creates an "eternal nightmare . . . into which one wakes everyday" (p. 103). Unamendable to sustainable development, the chasm between the affluent over class and the downtrodden dwellers of "derelict spaces and makeshift hovels" (p. 63) makes the later seethe with fury, deep seated anger and restlessness all of which configurate in Mama Put's iconographic bayonet. Fatally undermined by the absence of good governance and macro-economic stabilization, the people and nation flounder on an economic knife-edge. Illegitimacy in the system as symbolized in perennial coups has deleterious impact on social conduct by intensifying the levels and ever rising tide of criminality and anomie.

With careful craftsmanship the dramatist uses aesthetic alchemy to translate social disorders into dramatic imagery. By the end of the play, the flaming dawn which much attention is focused on throughout the play, becomes symbolic of the existential fires and brimstone scourging the lives of the people in real life. Through a complex but incisive interrelationship of dramatic symbols, images of incineration are relentlessly evoked to heighten the unremitting inclemency and pervading atmosphere of annihilation which envelops the play. The enigmatic and incendiary dawn therefore emblematizes the roasted hopes, thwarted aspirations and scourged landscape.

A device for teasing–a dependable comic mechanism for deferring information, priming action or creating suspense or "when characters are intentionally placed in embarrassing or awkward situations" (Theodore Hatlen, 1987: 140) – the symbolism of the dawn is divested of its traditional signification of vitality and regeneration. Thus subverted, the imagery is travestied into aborted expectations, brazen rancidity, indeed, a grosteque representation of a degrading orgy of waste analogous to the obtaining social order. The choreography of symbols here echoes "Death at Dawn" and "October '66" where death in both poems stands in for life.

Commenting on the above poems in a manner vigorously relevant to *The Beatification of Area Boy*, Eldred Jones observes:

> Like *A Dance of the Forests*, a grim warning of how easily man could destroy himself and transform his potential for life into negative channels, these poems gaze with horror at man,

the victim of his own power, substituting death for life.
(1988: 177)

As *hors d'oeuvre*, the teasing and alluring dawn immerses us in
what would later turn out to be abrasive and devastating events. With
massive mangling of values and paralyzing deterioration of infrastructure, the point of reference for character and action becomes a
kaleidoscope not only of incensing sights and sounds of the fires of
misery, but also an open sore and insult to human decency.

Yoking medieval ritual practices and end-time anxieties together
with a damning portrait of rampant criminal activities, the play helps
us to recognize the scope of the evil bedeviling the nation and the bold
re-orientation the situation demands. Dramatizing a well patterned
anecdotal structure consisting in masking burning issues by presenting
what superficially appears as casually connected fables, the playwright
festoons his episodes with clusters of loosely-linked social metaphors
which cohere, however, in formal and thematic preoccupations.

In his searing exploration of the intersection of the alienated
Lagosian with an even bleaker landscape, the dramatist consistently
sustains a spiraling image of the macabre, the gruesome and generally fear and death causing—events as he attempts to crystallize the pictures of a thoroughly traumatized and battered humanity. The
imagery is exacerbated by references to truncated and castrated bodies. Listen to the grim frankness and ghoulish evocation of the dark
cannibalistic passions that haunt the land by day and by night:

> BARBER: You see all those corpses with their
> vital organs missing – breast in the
> case of women, the entire region
> of the vagina neatly scooped out.
> And sometimes just the pubic hair
> is shaved off for their devilish mix-
> ture. And pregnant ones with the
> fetus ripped out. Male corpses
> without genitals or eyes. Some-
> times they cut out the liver . . .
>
> TRADER: And what of hunchbacks? Dat na

> another favourite for making
> money. They take out the hunch,
> sometimes while the man self still
> dey alive. (. . . *Area Boy,* p. 14).

In all these weird tales, Soyinka comports himself as a disciplined artist and as a devastatingly incisive social commentator who strips stark naked all incarnations of evil, greed and corruption. The Lagosian kaleidoscope he splashes presents the city dwellers as gropping in a darkened actual desert and in the inner desert of the soul fraught with monstrous upstart scams, booby traps, deplorable man eating rodents and fatal ambushes. As Judge graphically describes it, Lagos is "A no-man's wilderness inhabited by phantoms" (p. 74). This view is validated by the extended dream and nightmare motifs in the play.

The catastrophe and misery of this voided existence are mimetically realized in the melancholic desolation and fittingly depressing atmosphere of the play, especially in the bleak aura enveloping the endless cortege of more than a million weary men, women, children and animals callously evicted from their Maroko abode and stranded on the streets. They playwright's human rights background and experience of forced exile provide ample first hand conviction to fuel his acid pen against the rank indignities heaped on the alienated urban masses. He images in singularly unforgettable metaphors his indignation at pompous hardhearted villains and the injustices they perpetrate on the masses.

Observe for instance how the avid emotive power under-girding his stark engraving of the Maroko exodus pithily illustrates his vehement political protest against privation and other forms of man's inhumanity to man:

> A ragged procession is reflected on the doors. Men, women
> and children carrying baskets, boxes, rolled-up beddings,
> bed-springs, cupboards, chairs, clutching all kinds of per-
> sonal possessions. Interspersed among them are the occa-
> sional lorries equally laden to the top, with people perched
> precariously on top and among the loads. Wheelbarrows,
> omolanke, a tractor with trailer, also loaded with human and

domestic cargo, the odd television set and antenna protrud-
ing from among baskets and sacks – An animated 'battered
humanity' mural of a disorderly evacuation, maybe after an
earthquake, from which an assortment of possessions have
been salvaged. (*Beatification* ... 74).

A consummate caricaturist, Soyinka's virulent satiric sketch of this
desolate, deracinated throng, especially as he brings alive the smallest
details about the "seemingly endless" (p. 75) procession conveys the
dramatist's natural empathy for the ruthlessly exploited victims of the
urban hell. The presentation of the above action embodies an occult
extension of injustice and failed leadership as universal archetypes.
Soyinka's immense talent as an eclectic and innovative dramatist is
everywhere present in the ease he transfers sign systems from the general fund of cultures available to him.

One of the chef d' oeuvre of his many years of artistic experimenta-
tion and formal innovations, *The Beatification of Area Boy. A Lagosian
Kaleidoscope* is an apotheosis of his comic gifts nourished by a blend of
traditions drawn from his indigenous heritage and socialization in rec-
ondite modes of dramatic mediation. This brilliant synthesis gives
added depth and sinews to the deceptively simply comedy.

The play's fundamental plot integrates ancestral aesthetic and a
sound understanding and application of contemporary conception
of the comic plot. According to Jan Kott, "The oldest and most
enduring kind of comic action, from ancient comedy to *commedia
dell' arte,* from popular farces to Moliere, is a clash between two houses" (Hatlen, 138) Soyinka invigorates and dramatizes with freshness
these diametrically opposed houses of authority and appearances on
the one hand, and that of ill repute on the other hand. In character
formation, he returns as he does again and again in his other plays to
some folk modes characterization.

Thus though implacably challenged by the terrestrial fires of existential terror, his characters vibrantly brim with startling native intelligence. In the characterization of Sanda, we perceive the
transposition of sign systems drawn from the African trickster motif.
Explaining the device Kofi Awonoor (1975: 75) writes that these are
folk heroes "chosen for possessing certain primordial qualities of cun-

ning necessary for survival in an uncertain world". Elaborating, he adds that the trickster is "the archetypal hero who succeeds or fails by his guile or preternatural wisdom or when aided by benevolent spirits or his personal deity".

Similarly, Isidore Okpewho (1972: 117) remarks that the motif is a vivid example of how oral literature is "designed to teach specific lessons of behaviour". He adds, "Little animals such as hare dupe the big ones such as elephant, demonstrating that everything should be given its due respect or recognition, however small it is". The essence of the character of Sanda answers to the delineations above.

Soyinka expands the traditional parameters of the motif to admit some sterling essences of his favourite deity, Ogun, in his casting of Sanda. In his creative mediation of existential contradictions, Sanda is modelled after the primordial god, Ogun. Revered as an explorer of uncharted territories, this mythological god of war and creativity is also worshipped by the Yorubas as a restorer of rights, a bridge-builder over gulfs. Okepewho (319) adds that "for his solitary withdrawal from both gods and men so as to reflect on his acts, Ogun represent for Soyinka the ideal of the meditative intellectual as well as the artist". Sanda's character in the play is consistently congruent in deeds and disposition with this thinking.

A contemplative individual often screening his face with some reading materials, Sanda leaves the comfort of the ivory tower for the harsh concrete realities of the streets. Though solitary in tendency, he is like the battle hardened Ogun, very alert to everything happening around him. Armed with a fertile native intelligence which he uses to deflate pompous and arrogant asses, and to outwit authority, he teaches creativity and organization to the dispossessed. He welds a tremendous and positive influence among this group of the vulnerable in the society of this play. An appreciative TRADER says of him: 'The neighbourhood owe you plenty. Until you come here begin organize everybody, we just dey run about like chicken wey no get head' (65).

Thus like his model deity, Sanda acts as a buffer against the continued emasculation of the weak, the unprotected and the beleaguered. Like Ogun, he is a pathfinder in his exploration of alternatives to uncritically accepted status quo. Okpewho (222) writes that "Soyinka exploitation of oral tradition" in this context, "consists essentially in reordering its facts in the service of his radical vision of the contemporary African struggle".

The Beatification of Area Boy is thus a search for meaning and the need for bold re-orientation in a wasteland of lost souls. It is a devastating barrage of dramatized criticism against the obsolescence of autocratic political systems represented in the play by a military dictatorship which empty of vision, paranoid of unrest and out of touch with the masses absurdly resorts to ring-fencing dissent and strangulating it in a ring of steel as a means of control and governance. In examining the diverse disorders manifest in the innumerable military rules that have afflicted the country and arrested its development, the playwright comes to the reasoned conclusion that military rule not only lends itself to extremes but also is a by word for cruelty, degradation and sharp precipitous decline into barbarism.

In construction and discourse the play inspires us to look back at the past and present. Furthermore, it raises salient questions about the horizons of future development. By looking intensely and unblinkingly recording pressing social and political dilemmas of the day, Soyinka answers to his best convictions that:

> The writer has always functioned in African society as the record of the mores and experiences of his society and as the voice of vision in his own line. It is time for him to respond to this essence of himself (Per Wastberg 1969: 17)

At the end of *The Beatification of Area Boy*, the playwright eventuates a union between enstranged elements. He seems to envision a social order where the gown would provide the town with enlightened leadership, guidance, instruction and direction. This arrangement not only testifies to the talent of man in shaping his living space according to his wishes and needs but also exemplifies the dramatist's repugnance at and desire to put an end to the prolonged and unbridled deprivation of the dispossessed masses.

By taking us on a journey through darkness and dingy places of increasingly cynical political manipulations, Soyinka appears concerned to exorcise the inner demons and dark forces of our social lives. Abiola Irele observes that:

No serious consideration of Soyinka's writing can fail to perceive the central position and even the explicit character of
the social awareness that runs through all his work . . . And it
is the logical development from this fundamental interest in
the realities of social experience implicit in his writings to an
active sense of social responsibility, that seems to define the
relationship of Soyinka himself to his own work as well as the
elements of his individual career and indeed, of his personal
drama.

Steeped in nightmarish violence and drained of mercy, the obtaining order Soyinka delineates seems to spur him with ecumenical
hatred and a desire to kick-start a revolution of the dispossessed.
Scripting his comedy with unyielding foreshadowing and dramatic
irony, Soyinka appears desperate for meaning in a society made prostrate by a lurid array of crimes against humanity.

In his search for meaning, Soyinka avails himself of the inexorable
amenability of myth to creative re-invention. Hear him:

You must know of course about my fascination with the
symbol figure of my society – Ogun. He represents this dual-
ity of man: The creative, destructive aspect. And I think this
is the reality of society, the reality of man, and that one
would be foolish not to recognize this. I cannot sentimental-
ize revolution. I recognize the fact that it very often represents loss. But at the same time I affirm that it is necessary to
accept the confrontations which society creates, to anticipate
them and try to play a programme in advance before them.
The realism which pervades some of my works and have
been branded pessimistic is nothing but a very square, sharp
look. (John Agetua 1975: 39)

Soyinka's fascination with the symbol figure of Ogun transcends the
metaphysics of the deity to a trenchant evocation of the deity's mythic capacity for shaping and transforming society. Through this subtle
mythic evocation he gives active voice and teeth to his sense of commitment. Through the activities and perceptions of the protagonist

of comic action, the playwright aims at re-educating the minds of his compatriots especially in shaping their ways of looking at social processes and in taking their collective destiny in their hands. In disposition, Sanda parallels Femi Osofisan's claim for Soyinka that he is Nigeria's:

> . . . first modern incarnation of the Malvarian idealist and activist, the romantic who voluntarily risks his own security and even survival in a daring physical intervention in political violence.

Though this assertion effectively qualifies the quintessential Soyinka, yet in the *Beatification of Area Boy*, the celebrated playwright goes beyond the celebration of the insightful individual to situating him in an arena of conscientization and collective struggle staged by indomitable and resilient though dispossessed characters. Evidently he seems to have shifted from "a very square, sharp look" engagement to a very square and sharp concerted action and participation in the suggestion and formation of a prototypical social order more relevant and humane than the presently obtaining institutionalized decadence, vulgarity, brutality, drift, obscenity, arrogance and sycophancy which the military bourgeoisie has engendered about. Herein lies the paradigm shift in the new dramaturgy of Soyinka, a shift which realized with supreme talent and clarity endows the play with precious artistic beauty and enduring value.

Works Cited

Anyaoku, Emeka. "Nigeria: Back in the Commonwealth; looking to the future", Kayode Soyinka ed. *Africa Today*, Vol. 5, No. 11, pp. 9-10, November 1999.

Hatlen, Theodore. *Orientation To Theatre*. Englewood Cliffs: Prentice-Hall International, Inc. 1987.

Irele, Abiola. *The African Experience in Literature and Ideology*. London: H.E.B. 1981, p. 198.

Jones, Eldred. *The Writings of Wole Soyinka*. London: Heinemann

1988, rev. ed.

Kott, Jan. "The Eating of the Government Inspector. *Theatre Quarterly*, 5, No. 17, 1975. Cited by Hatlen.

Obafemi, Olu: "Political Perspectives and Popular Theatre In Nigeria" Claude Schumacher ed. *Theatre Research International*, Vol. VII, No. 3, Oxford University Press, 1982, pp. 235-244.

Ogunba, Oyin. *The Movement of Transition*. Ibadan: University Press, 1975.

Osofisan, Femi. "Tiger on Stage: Wole Soyinka and Nigerian Theatre", in Oyin Ogunba and Abiola Irele, eds., *Theatre in Africa*. Ibadan: University Press, 1978, p. 1555.

Soyinka, Wole. "The Writer in a Modern State", in Per Wastberg ed. *The Writer in Modern Africa*. New York, 1969, p. 17.

Soyinka, Wole, "Interview with Wole Soyinka in Accra, Ghana, 1974" in John Agetua, ed., *When the Man Died: Views, Reviews and Interviews on Wole Soyinka's Controversial Book*. Benin City: Bendel Newspaper Corp., 1975, p. 39.

Williams, Adebayo. "Matador In Abuja" Kayode Soyinka ed. *Africa Today*, Vol. 5 No. 9, p. 6-9, September 1999.

18

Reparation, Reconciliation and Negritude Poetics in Soyinka's *The Burden of Memory, The Muse of Forgiveness*

USHANG P. UGOR

I

Wole Soyinka, Africa's most prolific and accomplished poet, dramatist and novelist has never left anyone in doubt about his commitment to the use art in national and political struggle. He uses art from time to time when the stakes on political matters are high in his country or when the stakes have something to do with the African continent. He has done this since his early plays, *The Swamp Dwellers* and *Camwood On Leaves*. This is also what he does with the highly controversial play, *A Dance of The Forests,* commissioned for Nigeria's independence celebration in 1960 and in all of the post-independence satirical sketches and full length plays dealing with dictatorial megalomania that was (and still) visible on the African continent. Examples are *Opera Wonyonsi, A Play of Giants, Before The Blackout* and *After The Blackout* sketches of the 1960s. The point he makes over and over again in these plays is that art is a utilitarian vehicle in the struggle to put right the continent's political disorder. He argues in these plays that art must be put to use for political purposes; it should be used to free the people from the shackles of oppressive governance and debilitating spiritual and culinary hunger. In doing this, Soyinka does not distract from his commitment to aesthetics. Indeed, as J. A. Adedeji points out, it is Soyinka's consummate commitment to this idea in his works that always reveals the depth and profundity of his theatre (1987: 104-129). This commitment has led him elsewhere lately. Soyinka has changed strategy once again, preferring in this instance to employ the strategy of essayistic writing to put forward his latest assault on tyranny. This latest drive is found in the book of essays, *The Burden of Memory, The Muse of Forgiveness.* This is certainly not his first foray into the art of essay writing. Soyinka is much an essayist as he is a playwright. Not too long ago, New Horn, the Ibadan based publishing outfit, brought out a huge compendium of Soyinka's essays that he wrote since the 1960. This is a valuable source of Soyinka's critical responses to matters ranging from arts, society, culture, politics and economy. This collection of essays, *Art, Dialogue and Outrage,* is an important source for the scholar who is interested in the early essays of Soyinka. *The Burden of Memory* presents a different but interesting facet of Soyinka's essayistic thrust, where Soyinka confronts a number of global issues from the position of one of the oppressed of the world. He takes on race and race problems, international politics and racial dichotomy and discusses the issues arising from them from the position of victimhood as he tries to come to terms with Africa's peculiar post-colonial condition from the bottom of the so-called global system. In other to do this, Soyinka's turns to his familiar mode of strategic probing, the art of soul-searching, a strategy of inquiry, which he demonstrates with astuteness and precision in *The Credo of Being and Nothingness.*

Polemical and illuminating as the *The Burden of Memory* is, we ought not to ignore the political reasons that compelled the foray of Soyinka from the fort a prolific literary artist to an international essayist with a mission to fight for the freedom of the continent and of all marginalized people in his country. Nigeria, his home country, has only recently gotten out of the quagmire of military dictatorship, which lasted for fifteen of her forty years of independence. The high point of this was the last five years of General Sani Abacha's dictatorial rule from 1993 to 1997 characterized by official murder, arson, lack of press freedom, repulsive and corruptive practices in high places, torture and many forms of inexplicable social torments. Obsessed with the struggle for justice and fair-play, Soyinka launched himself into the popular (though by government rating then, notorious) opposition to dictatorship in order to fight for the actualization of the annulled June 12, 1993 election, acclaimed to be the freest and fairest in the annals of Nigeria's election history and to re-establish democratic principles in that once great country—the so-called "giant of Africa." This effort was laudable as it was perilous. It was an action that led to Soyinka absconding from the shores of his country into a period of self-exile in the USA. He experienced a similar fate during the late 1960s when he objected to the Nigerian civil war and was incarcerated for along time. He eventually left for a self-imposed exile after his release to Ghana. *The Burden of Memory, the Muse of Forgiving* comes out of the contemplation of his latest foray into the wider world that brought him face to face yet again with a number topical global issues. *The Burden of Memory* tries to deal with some of these issues, privileging the contradictions and shortfalls of those who had tried to deal with the issues before him.

Soyinka raises fundamental questions in *The Burden of Memory*. Here are some of the most basic questions that he poses in this book of essays: does mere truth from an oppressor, a longtime oppressor for that matter, entitle him/her to forgiveness from and actual reconciliation with his victims? Should truth be a "prelude" to forgiveness or a "justification" for forgiveness and eventual reconciliation? The latter is what Soyinka believes "constitutes a stumbling block in the South African [TRC] proceedings" (*The Burden of Memory* 13). If the victims of prolonged human deprivation must forgive and reconcile with their tormentors, there must be some basis for the justification of the act of reconciliation; some reciprocity, call it recompense from the denigrating human monster who decreed such momentous human suffering. The fundamental question for the Truth and Reconciliation Commission (TRC) can then be reposed in this way: have all the elements of truth been laid bare in the South African case? Is apartheid really a thing of the past? Can reconciliation really be effective in a society that still harbors pockets of groups who still sanction the apartheid policy? To drive the point of his doubt home, Soyinka sites the example of the activities of an American political bohemian, Mr. David Duke, in Southern Africa. While the then South Africa government led by the indefatigable freedom fighter, Nelson Mandela, was genuinely pursuing the policy of reconciliation between the Boers and black South-Africans whom they have marginalized for decades, Mr. David Duke, an American presidential aspirant, daringly continued to show "solidarity with a self-declared independent free Boer republic" of some white unrepentant minority. Lest we forget, Soyinka argues, the United States of America from where Mr. Duke hails had rejected the transfer of over a million dollar made by the Libyan Government to Minister Farrakhan's Nation of Islam, labeling it "terrorist money". So where does the basis for forgiveness and reconciliation lie when an overture of reconciliation is reciprocated with a boisterous show of unrepentant action as it is with the case with the small supremacist white South-African Boers?

Beyond South Africa, this example sets a standard for the reconciliation and forgiveness by peoples of nations who have suffered untold hardship under notorious and evil leaders. Is it based on sheer "truthful confession" that the victims of the Abachas, Mobutus, Amins, and Nguemas must forgive them? Surely no! For the victim to forgive, he pays a price. He sheds off some incalculable bulk of a painful past to free his mind. The seeker of forgiveness and reconciliation should not just show remorse but must reciprocate by paying a price—return the wealth siphoned from their victims' vault, give it back to the oppressed so as to relieve them from the burdens of impecuniousness. This is indeed where truth and reconciliation become an elixir for restoration of peace between the oppressor and the oppressed. That process of truth and reconciliation, which consistently requires only the victim's forgiveness, Soyinka argues, is as unjust as the events that led him to be a victim. This is the position that is unequivocally enunciated in *The Burden of Memory, the Muse of Forgiveness.*

II

The debate of "righting the wrongs" that was brought against African peoples will continue to rage. Soyinka dwells on this issue extensively in parts of *The Burden of Memory*. Two examples are presented for attention, one is the remote but not forgotten history of slavery on the entire continent and the other is the immediate case of the Black South African people who were oppressed until the obnoxious apartheid policy was abrogated in 1990. In Soyinka's view, it is the South African paradigm that most immediately merits attention because "The victims are alive and in need of rehabilitation while their violators -as a recognizable group—pursue a privileged existence, secure in the spoils of a sordid history" (*The Burden of Memory* 24). Since the wounds of oppression are still fresh, there is the need for an immediate and more practical therapy.

But how can this atonement be properly done to achieve national purification in that enclave called South Africa? Can national healing and eventual reconciliation be achieved because some old scoundrel ruler has openly confessed his involvement in already known crimes? Soyinka draws numerous examples to contest the South African reconciliation process. Should the mere armchair confessions of Pot Pol of Cambodia, for instance, guarantee him freedom and forgiveness amongst the people whose humanity he degraded? The devious activities of the likes of Hastings Kamuzu Banda of Malawi and Miriam Mengistu of Ethiopia provide quintessential models in this regard. Whether these rulers are tried and acquitted, the society is purged not only by hearing of truth of their devious machinations against hapless people but also by the ignoble reduction of this once untouchable human-gods to the same soup that they had once served the people. Of necessity, "some measure of restitution is always essential after dispossession". (*The Burden of Memory* 36). Soyinka argues that this is an indisputably imperative, especially for the South African healing process.

Soyinka also discusses the issue of reparation in *The Burden of Memory*, reparation for the entire African continent that was at one time subjected to slavery. This issue, he admits, is as complicated as the biophysical structure of an octopus but a lot of questions can be raised around it, one of which is: Were the freed slaves in America properly reconciled and reintegrated into their society? The answer is not in the affirmative. The vestiges of racial discrimination are still visible in America today. In his opinion, this lack of thorough and genuine restitution to an oppressed people is largely responsible for "the culture of impunity in race relationship" (*The Burden of Memory* 37) that is still prevalent all over the globe. If the entire process of reconciliation is not properly done, it could set the precedence for other impulses of the degradation of humanity elsewhere.

Undoubtedly, the entire African continent has a right to reparation because as Soyinka argues, there exist, "distortions in her organic development that are still traceable to the ravages of slavery". (*The Burden of Memory* 38) However, the critical but unresolved question is who is more entitled to this recompense if it must be given at all? Is it to the present blacks in diaspora whose pedigree were physically uprooted from their cultural base or their black brothers back home in Africa whose great grandparents actually partook in the forced exportation of their kinsmen. Who is to pay what, to whom and for what? Complex as the issue of reparation to the African continent is, the African continent will remain a reminder of the sheer lip service to the idea of "European humanism". The catastrophe unleashed by Europe on the African continent was of a magnitude that cannot easily escape human imagination. Apart from the millions of souls lost, apart from the crass material exploitation that sapped the continent of its needed human resources and eventually "imposed a rapture in the organic economic systems of much of the continent" (*The Burden of Memory* 39), there exist till date, within the continent, a backlash in that single dehumanizing phenomenon. The entire continent is restless and pockets of violence erupt from North to South, East to West. For corrupt reasons, current African leaders find it reluctant to redress some of these basic issues. The imposition of nationhood among disparate ethnic groups, and the "partitioning of Africa" still have their toll on the continent today.

The issue of religion is also important for Soyinka in this book of essays. He argues here that the entire spiritual landscape of the continent was polluted by colonialism. Though the Moslems argue that their religion shares affinity with the African traditional spiritual values more than Christianity, Soyinka contests this view strongly, insisting that "Both religions came and subverted the organic systems of belief that pre-existed their arrival, religions older and, in many aspects, more humane than the manifested tenets of their own". (*The*

Burden of Memory 52) This is not the first time that he has made this point. The telling evidence from *The Credo of Being and Nothingness* is plain for us to see. Surely no traditional African spiritual value enjoins her adherents to shed human blood in exchange for eternal bliss such as Islam does. And this religious dimension in the reparation issue calls for a redefinition of the payers of compensation. Is it only Europe that should pay compensation to Africa or any other inculpated partaker of that inhuman experience even if the culprit is from within the continent itself? This question surely implicates Arab nations who had engaged in the trans-saharan slave trade long before Europeans landed on the shores of Africa.

Undoubtedly, the issue of reparation is justified and deserves attention and vigorous pursuit but the African continent itself needs to re-assess its own system of governance and must create good governance for her people. As the saying goes, he who goes to the altar of justice must do so with clean hands. What justification is there in asking for reparation for a continent whose own brother-rulers subject them to the most unimaginable human terror, worse than that for which they ask compensation? Not only must we learn to govern ourselves through refined, acceptable and civilized patterns, our indigenous enslavers must atone for their political and economic sacrileges. Based on this genuine sense of social purification, truth and reconciliation can then bring healing and reconciliation.

III

Early in its beginning, Soyinka had shown his lack of faith in the African cultural re-awakening tagged negritude pioneered by Léopold Seda Senghor and made popular by a brand of energetic scholars from Africa and its diaspora. This lack of faith was not so much in the message that advocates of negritude preached but in the actions of the messengers themselves who shouted more than they acted. It is for this reason that Soyinka once declared, "The tiger does not profess its tigritude, it pounces". In *The Burden of Memory*, once again Soyinka turns the search-light on the philosophy of negritude, x-raying the ironies and controversies that engulf its poetics on one hand and the philosophy of cultural awakening it was noted for on the other hand.

273

Senghor, a Senegalese and arch apostle of negritude enjoyed the advantage of scholarship in Paris because of France's "benevolent" assimilation policy. Though he desired to be a priest, he became a soldier, teacher, poet, politician and scholar. But of all of this, it does appear that it is the priestly vocation that influences his poetry the most. Senghor unabashedly confesses his love for France, exhorting whoever cares to read to forget the past and forgive the "best enslavers" on earth. For a scholar who had denounced the evils of colonialism and racism, this "quality of accommodation" which he proposes is not only incomprehensible but near intolerable. Soyinka notes that although Martin Luther Jnr, another priest, preaches the same forgiveness in his *Letter from Birmingham Jail,* "Martin Luther King Jnr's "love" is more accessible" (*The Burden of Memory,* 100). Senghor pleads for Europe's pardon for slavery not only from the oppressed people in the continent alone but also from God. Yet, Senghor proceeds to intervene on behalf of the oppressor, begging for the forgiveness of those who "turned his princes into sergeants, "who made houseboys' of his servants', "who hunted his children like wild elephants", that we must "forget those who stole ten millions of my sons in their leprous ship" and also forgive those "who suppressed two hundred million more". As Soyinka argues, Senghor "seizes the poetic privilege of presuming the confession of his sinners, treats their *mea culpas* as already intoned, and then grants them absolution". (*The Burden of Memory* 113). If Senghor truly appreciated the philosophical movement he and Aimé Césaire pioneered, a philosophy that was then adopted by poets and writers of the Harlem renaissance such as Langston Hughes, Countee Culen, Sterling Hayden, Claud Mckcay and Paul Vesey, then he should have understood that "such special pleading ... was frankly irreconcilable with the historical context that made negritude, a movement of protest, rejection, and racial discovery, inevitable". (*The Burden of Memory* 123).

We may endlessly engage in disputations about the special conditions surrounding colonialism in Francophone and Anglophone countries and how such conditions affected the tone of poets on either side of the divide, but the point that must never be missed is that both sides of the colonies experienced some form of political, cultural, social and religious deprivations, even adulteration and for this reason they exist no excuse for special atonement for any enslaver. They all need to pay reparations, Soyinka argues. In any case, Soyinka sums up, Africa's current economic backwardness is in dire need of reparation.

Works Cited

Adedeji, J. A. "Aesthetics of Soyinka's Theatre". *Before Our Very Eyes.* Ibadan: Spectrum Books, 1987.

Soyinka, Wole. *The Burden of Memory, The Muse of Forgiveness.* New York: Oxford University Press, 1999.

_____. *The Credo of Being and Nothingness.* Ibadan: Spectrum Books, 1991.

_____. *Art, Dialogue and Outrage.* Ibadan: New Horn Press, 1989.

_____. *A Dance of the Forests.* Ibadan: Oxford University Press, 1963.

_____. *A Play of Giants.* London: Methuen, 1984.

_____. *Opera Wonyosi.* London: Rex Collins, 1981.

_____. *Before the Blackout,* Ibadan: Orisun, 1960.

_____. *After the Blackout,* Ibadan: Orisun Acting Editions 1960.

_____. Camwood *on the Leaves.* Orisun Acting Edition, 1987.

19

Transition From Essence To Manifestation

A Study of vision in Soyinka's
The Road and *Beatification of Area Boy*...

B. ASODIONYE EJIOFOR

I
Introduction

The notion of vision in the life of a rational being assumes a structural rhetoric. Its engaging manifestations may even be archetypal to the extent that one becomes receptive of, and conditioned by the shape of one's cultural realities. Vision therefore is the essential impetus which structurally organizes a man's reception of the circumstances of being and becoming. Like the hub of a bicycle wheel, which disposes a multitude of inter-relating and inter-acting spokes, vision is the mind-set which acts upon man's reception of reality, and conditions all his interacting responses to the problems of existence.

Soyinka has consistently defended transition as a vision, which expresses the Yoruba reception of reality, being and becoming. Controversial as this mind-set may seem, its strongest persuasion believes existence to mean a continuing cyclical transition from the world of the dead and ancestral past, through the present living world, to the unborn future. At least, such is the conviction informing the 'Alage-mo' poem prefacing Soyinka's *The Road*, part of which is quoted thus:

I heard! I felt their reach
And heard my naming named.
The pit is there, the digger fell right through
My roots have come out in the other world
Make away. Agemo's hoops
Are pathways of the sun.
Rain-reeds unbend to me, Quench
The burn of cartwheels at my waist!
Pennant in the stream of time – Now,
Gone, and Here the future. (*Collected Plays*, 150)

Soyinka himself volunteers that 'Agemo is simply a religious cult of flesh dissolution' (*Collected Plays* I, 149) among the Yoruba. 'Alage-mo' comes then as the song of transition, chanted by devotees in worship of Ogun. If one conceives of the world around us, then the poet-persona's 'Agemo hoops' are actually rings whose arcs interlock in interrelationships through the stream of time between the past, the present, and the future. This conviction seals the case for transition as a cultural mind-set, controlling and conditioning Soyinka's every initiative including writing.

The word transition affirms change. Change in turn implies difference which may be essential or formal. Depending on the form, every transition involves change from life to death, light to darkness, literal to literary, etc. However, as concerns Soyinka's reception of transition, life continues in the endless cycle of birth, death, and rebirth. The thrust of Soyinka's theory of transition lies in the gulf of transition occasioned by an alienation of divinities of the Yoruba pantheon and man; and this can be explained in the distinction in Hegel's 'RELIGION' between consciousness and self-consciousness. Alienation is explained to mean that distinction in the distance between consciousness which lacks contact with true spirit, and self-consciousness which knows itself as true spirit and being in itself. In the Yoruba world-view, according to Soyinka, both the divinities and man suffer alienation because each would be missing a complement in the other. This last position is reflected in the following:

> ... to reassume that portion of recreative transient awareness
> which the first deity Orisa-nla possessed and expressed
> through his continuous activation of man images – brief
> reflections of divine facets just as man is grieved by a con-
> sciousness of the loss of the eternal essence of his being and
> must indulge in symbolic transactions to recover his totality
> of being. (*Myth Literature and African World View* 144-145)

Soyinka's submissions above are summary of Ogun's tragic plunge
into the gulf of transition in order to bridge the gulf and reconcile
man with the Yoruba divinities. This is akin to Christ's reconciliatory
initiative between man and God (2 Corinthians 5:18-19).

Suffice to mention that Soyinka's preoccupation with transition in
his writings unfolds in metaphysical, cultural and ideological dimensions. All invocations of Ogun in Soyinka's plays are often symbolic and
representative. Noteworthy is the fact that in all cases in Soyinka's writings, transition affirms change. The preoccupations of transition as a
visionary impetus remain the focal engagement of this essay with particular reference to Soyinka's *The Road* and *Beatification of area boy* ....

1. Synopsis of the Plays

(i) The Road
The story of this play is woven around a sixty year old man who is
seeking metaphysical power to enable him control his universe. The
avenues of the search for what Professor calls 'the unbroken word'
include the Christian Church, the "road" where he causes accidents
by rooting up road signs, and the "aksident store" where he entertains
touts, drivers, thugs and even the Police with palm-wine. Eventually,
Professor reaps judgement by being murdered by Say-Tokyo-Kid in
the end.

(ii) Beatification of Area Boy
This play is built around the victims of oppression in Nigeria. Most

of the people are destitutes of Maroko whose abodes have been demolished by government. However, among other details of the episodic style, the play institutionalizes forgery, extortion and robbery, and reaches a climax when Miseyi, a bride to be, abandons her groom to be in favour of Sanda her old schoolmate, and the leader of the AREA BOYS in Lagos.

2. Settings of Transition in the Two Plays

A cursory reading of Soyinka's *The Road* and *Beatification of Area Boy* shows a setting differential which records a transition from the metaphysical universe of Professor's world in *The Road* to the full representation of cosmopolitan Lagos airs, values and mind-set. It is inferred that *The Road* is set in Lagos particularly since the closest indication is from the representation of Lagos airs in the 1960 era. Other shots at Lagos are obscure references in invectives. Samson snaps: 'That man not only stinks like Lagos lagoon, he lies like a Lagos girl'. (*Collected Plays* I, 177) Samson also refers to Kokol'ori – Kotunu's father – as the 'first of the truck-pushers and the randiest between Obalende and Agege' (189). Also remarkable is the reference to Lagos mammy-wagons by Samson.

On the contrary, in *Beatification of Area Boy*, not only is the setting specified in the sub-title – A Lagosian Kaleidoscope – which stipulates Lagos, the spirit of Lagos is also captured in this play in the evolution of all the airs of Lagos, well beyond the limited representation in *The Road*.

In *Beatification of Area Boy* the representation of Lagos re-enacts the Y2K compliance of Lagos touts, impostors, businessmen, socialites, armed robbers, mobbers, ritual killers, fraudsters, oppressors, the military, political strategists, tribalists, extortionists and vagrants. If anything, the synchronic invocations of Lagos airs in the Port Harcourt and Ikot Ekpene by Minstrel, after tasting Mama Put's illicit gin (kain-kain), establishes the Lagos setting more than all. The re-enactments of Lagos in this play emphasize the fact that, when any stranger encounters Lagos, he has seen the entire country – Nigeria. Besides, by the use of poetic liberties, Lagos has been abstracted in

Beatification of Area Boy into groups of attitudes, fads, behaviours and values migrating from all the corners of Nigeria. In Lagos, all the above mentioned groups suffer transformation in transition, and are eventually routed back to other cities and towns of Nigeria. By extension therefore, one can say that Nigeria is the setting of this play.

3. Transition As Essential Path to Changes

Soyinka's dramatic objective in the words of Oyin Ogunba has been that of determining the 'stage between being and not-being'. According to Ogunba:

> If this is so, then Soyinka conceives THE ROAD also as a kind of spiritual transition in which a whole community is moving relentlessly towards a new consciousness. (*The Movement of Transition* 139).

The context presented above suggests an essential road through which 'a whole community is moving' The question then is what is the essence of transition in *The Road* and *Beatification of Area Boy*? It is notable that essential transition as we have stated before hinges on 'Agemo's hoops' whose time distribution spans the dead and ancestral spirits (past), the living (present) and the unborn (future) worlds. Of crucial interest is the fact that a continuous flow of being and becoming pervades all the worlds spiritually.

In spiritual terms, the road initiated in *The Road* reaches beyond the frontiers of that particular play, and assumes astonishing transformations in transition in *Beatification of Area Boy*. It is a spiritual road whose essential rhetoric remains 'silent but deep' and Murano, according to Soyinka, is the visual suspension of transition as he is trapped between life and death. His big left toe is said to 'rest on the slumbering chrysalis of the word'. Unfortunately, he is dumb, and cannot communicate the sensations of the road under his big left toe.

In both plays, Soyinka demonstrates a remarkable flow of vision in transition. The use of the concept of transition to re-enact 'Agemo's hoops' in time and space is unmistakable. Like Lagos analyzed above, times, attitudes, and the receptions of reality have suffered changes in the process of transition. Thus, the diachronic vision of a cradling Lagos where 'Senior Service' middle class men ride bicycles, while the mass of body odours scramble in mammy-wagons and molue's re-enacted in *The Road*, acquires synchronic sophistication in *Beatification of Area Boy*. Where *The Road* barely explores contemporary and homogenous Lagos life of the 30s, 40s, 50s, and 60s, *Beatification of Area Boy* captures that past in the resurrection of the 'white horse' bicycle by the Cyclist, and contrasts with the chrome consciousness of present day Lagos where the oblivion of bicycles is displaced by ostentatious taste for flashy cars and aircraft.

When Murano walks out of the shack every morning, he does more than tap palmwine for Professor in *The Road*. He is actually a vagrant in spirit, seeking pasture. He is a victim of a transition caught in the transformations of becoming, migrating at the end of *The Road* into the million vagrants from Maroko, and the prisoners in *Beatification of Area Boy*. Thus, there is a remarkable flow of vision in the transformations of becoming represented by Murano, the mute, between *The Road* and *Beatification of Area Boy*. In *The Road*, there is a quest for the 'unbroken word' conceived of as the treasury of truths. It follows that the 'word' is a rhetoric of supernatural force, controlling movement on the road. Transition therefore is man's inexorable surrender to the changes which occur in transition; to the transformations, constituting and characterizing the spiritual path of transition. Transition is the consequence of the whims of the 'word'. More relevant is the contemplation of the transformation of transition on the living community trafficking the road. Murano or the soul, which he represents, transforms into daring argumentations of Judge, the political stratagems of Sanda, and the irrepressibility of the minstrel and the prisoners. It would be recalled that Professor looked upon 'dead souls' with curiosity in *The Road*. It would seem therefore, that because of the privilege of having one leg in both worlds, Murano on symbolic resurrection in *Beatification of Area Boy* has shed the fears of Kotonu, Say-Tokyo and Professor himself in *The Road*. The victims of transition in *Beatification of Area Boy* are not dumb. Murano – a dead soul in transition – remains the rallying visionary impetus of being and becoming and of silence or dumbness and vocalisation in the two plays.

4. Time Transition: Milestones of Change.

This involves a dual engagement with time on the parallel levels of
the milestones of time in dramaturgy, and those of the evolving life of
the cosmos of the plays. These classifications will be expatiated upon
individually for clarification.

Milestones of time in dramaturgy concern the inherent time plan
which determines the location of actions in the play, within a specified and unified performance time frame. On the other hand, milestones of the evolving life of the cosmos of a play is not limited by the
time plan of the play. Whereas the latter may span a 24 hour day, the
former may be one hundred years old depending on the ages of the
dramatis personae.

Both *The Road* and *Beatification of Area Boy* each operate 12 hours
dramaturgical time plans. The markers of these plans vary with the
play. The markers of time transition in *The Road* begin at dawn shortly before a confused Professor meets a 'millionaire', and records the
time in the following words.

> Almost a miracle . . . dawn provides the greatest miracles but
> this . . . in this dawn has exceeded its promise. In the
> strangest of places . . . God God God but there is a mystery in
> everything. A new discovery every hour – I am used to that,
> but that I should be led to where this was hidden, sprouted
> in secret for heaven knows how long . . . (*Collected Plays*,
> 157)

The above evidence of dawn is Professor's witnessing word of the time
plan of *The Road.* Hereafter, events continue to overlap each other in
the play until noon when Salubi returns to demand a licence of Professor. Murano's first arrival and departure in the early evening at five
o'clock coincides with a requiem procession towards the church
involving the drivers and touts. At about thirty minutes past six that
same evening, Murano arrives finally with a gourd of palm wine to
water the communion throats of Professor and hangers-on at the
shack. At this point Professor volunteers a composed:

Hearken! (First softly, gradually building up, the sound of organ music.) Observe the saintly progress of the evening communicants. (222)

The play ends later that same evening with the blood-letting of Professor by Say-Tokyo.

The markers of the time plan of *Beatification of Area Boy* include details of dawn highlighted by most of the dramatis personae, one of which is Judge whose observations are recorded thus:

It is the kind of day when unbelievers are shamed and the faithful exalted. Look at that horizon – there, where the sun is just rising. Have you ever seen a dawn the likes of that? (Grandly) Do you see how its opening up the rest of the sky? (*Beatification* 8).

For Trader who is indifferent to Judges insinuations above, here is a dawn which exposed 'all those dirty roofs for Isale-eko'. Beyond the foregoing markers establishing the opening time specification of the play, readers are left to figure out the noon day entry of Miseyi as illustrated here:

Exit TWO-FOUR. Sanda picks up a journal, makes some notes inside, and ticks off a column with a flourish. He resumes his reading. Enter Miseyi, accompanied by her housemaid, heading for the store entrance . . . (46).

The above stage directions conjecturally place Miseyi's entry at about noon. It is this entry which occasions the reunion of Sanda and Miseyi who are actually long separated undergraduate classmates. In the afternoon proper of the time plan of *Beatification of Area Boy* one encounters a scene of alleged missing genitals on page 51 of the text. But for Police intervention, the person accused of being responsible for the 'disappearance' of the genitals would have been lynched by an irate mob. By late afternoon, Judge arrives in style with his hair made precisely to resemble an attorney's periwig, and promptly ushers himself to the Barber's swivel-chair for sifted ash to be poured upon the hair. At evening commenced the wedding as planned according to the following report by Sanda:

> . . . banquetting-hall is booked for tonight. Plus the entire courtyard of the plaza. Big wedding ceremony. Broad street is closed to traffic – from seven o'clock – all the way from junction of Balogun street to that flyover. (15-16)

This report settles the case of the time plan of the play *Beatification of Area Boy*. Again, this plan fits into the 12 hour time frame for unveiling the story of the play.

Concerning the evolving life of the cosmos of *The Road*, one can say that the average life span of the actions in the play is about sixty years. This is the true age of Professor, the oldest member of cast. Within this period, all his conflicts with the Church, and subsequent inauguration by him of an accident store, meant to stock and sell stolen motor parts from accidents caused by Professor, unveil. All of these, Professor does in aid of his pathological quest for the inviolate word which actually has the power to control being.

In *Beatification of Area Boy* the evolving life of the cosmos of the play can only be measured in relation to the age of judge. One is of this understanding because Judge seems to be the oldest of the characters in the play. According to Sanda, Judge has been 'debarred' a long time ago. Given such circumstances, a conservative guess of Judges age may be put at 56. It follows then that the evolving life of the cosmos of the play is within 60 years.

5. Ramifications of Transition as 'Unbroken Word': Between Essence and Manifestations.

It is interesting to note that even the over-bearing context of the 'unbroken word' is subjected to transition of sorts alongside manifestations between *The Road* and *Beatification of Area Boy*.

In the play, *The Road*, Professor's search for the 'unbroken word' continues endlessly to be redefined. Professor himself reveals the multifaceted nature of the 'unbroken word' by confessing that every discovery is a 'sign-post' of the word. However, three major dimensions of the itinerary of the search deserve mention here. They are as follows:

The Christian Church
The road
The drinking bar.

Each of the above bus-stops constitutes a phase of the search, and a distinction of the kind and context of the word. The salient point is that each of the above contexts of the search constitutes a transformation or change in the process of transition.

In *Beatification of Area Boy* the focus appears to be more concerned with manifestations of the word through souls, than with the search of the word in essential terms. This is understandable.

To be complete, the essential or spiritual context of the word needs to obey Hegel's theory of phenomenology, which insists on the complementary need of self-consciousness in consciousness. Ogun obeyed the same rule when he plunged into the infernal abyss on recognition of the 'loss of the eternal essence of his being. (*Myth Literature and African World View* 144-145). One is given to understand that the grief of such a recognition motivated Ogun to 'indulge in symbolic transactions to recover the totality of his being. Without reconciling himself with the alienated human complement, Ogun's being would be incomplete. The 'unbroken word' is similarly affected. Professor in *The Road* recognizes the necessary and complementary connection between the word and the soul. Without the reconciliation with the soul, the self-consciousness of the word in itself is impaired.

It is in the foregoing context that one submits that the manifestation of the word is a consequence of the experience of transition by the 'unbroken word'. This means that through the process of transition, the 'unbroken word' transforms into sentient, physical entities. Thus, it is possible in the light of the foregoing to conclude that most of the characters in *Beatification of Area Boy* are manifestations of the essential word.

Given the context of manifestations above, it is expedient to note that even Professor recognizes the need for souls to be free in *The Road*. He asks Kotonu: 'This millionaire – did he purchase your soul too?' (*Collected Plays* I 159). The same question finds irrepressible answers in most of the characters in *Beatification of Area Boy*. It is curious to note that Judge in *Beatification of Area Boy* puns on the notion of the soul to Trader's total discomfiture. Based on Trader's lack of understanding, Judge's retort – 'That's the way it must appear to the soulless' (*Beatification of Area Boy* 8) is intriguing. The statement credits Trader with anything but having a soul, and this is done indirectly. It implies among other imports that Trader is a 'dead soul', or that indeed, he had none at all. The point made here is that so early in the morning Judge begins to insist on the life of souls in *Beatification of Area Boy*. He recognizes that souls must be free, and not bound. No! Not even intimidated by the military which sacks Maroko and turns a million souls into vagrants and destitutes. Judge is not only advancing argumentation legally, he also confronts the military single-handedly. He is the nerve-cell of manifestation in *Beatification of Area Boy*.

6. Transition: Evolving Values In The Two Plays

Here a synchronic treatment demands the determination of the values in the two plays, and how they have evolved. Some of these values include the search for knowledge, the necessity of freedom, boldness and justice, sanity, politics as a power resource, and gainful employment.

The search for knowledge, which Professor inaugurates in *The Road*, resurfaces after several transformations in *Beatification of Area Boy*. Beyond Samson who takes evening lessons in *The Road*, Sanda and Miseyi are university graduates in *Beatification of Area Boy*. Sourced from Professor in *The Road*, this transformation is a welcome one. It is however instructive to note that these transformations notwithstanding, many souls in *Beatification of Area Boy* are still bound. They remain so for as long as substantial knowledge continues to elude them. However, commendable is the fact that the responses of souls in the play have suffered dramatically radical changes, as opposed to the gropping disposition in *The Road*. To oversight the noticeable trend in *Beatification of Area Boy* where educated people like Sanda abandon their degrees to do menial jobs, would be a total disservice to the idea of transition.

Closely related to the value of knowledge are those of boldness, justice, politics as a power resource, etc. It is encouraging to note the impact of Professor's daring – however negatively – on all the characters in *Beatification of Area Boy*. In this play, the fears of Kotonu, Say-Tokyo, and some of the layabouts at the drinking shack, in *The Road*, transform into dare-devil ramifications in characters like Boyko, Sanda, Judge, Mama-Put, etc. Sanda on his part seems to have mastered the politics of power enough to embrace Miseyi after the spirited volt-face against her proposed groom at the marriage in Sanda's favour.

Most significant is the transformation of virtues like modesty, contentment, etc. into greed and ostentation. This development is spectacularly glaring with the arrival of cyclist who rides his special 'white-horse' bicycle into the plaza. He is greeted with awe by people like Trader who cannot reconcile this piece of antiquity with the present day vanity of the neuveau-riche in Lagos. Equally noticeable now is the extortionist trend in Lagos and the increased wave of crime and ritual killings. All these are transformations, in the transition of values.

Conclusion

The avenues of the search for the essence of life in *The Road* is extensive. Ogunba compares the 'unbroken word' with the 'philosopher's stone' (*Movement of Transition* 125) of Renaissance Europe. Due to the metaphysical engagement of the search for the word by Professor, virtually every character in their various dispositions and transactions in *The Road* become not just sign-posts of the search, but are themselves involved in the search. Significant is the fact that as devotees of Ogun most of the hangers-on at the shack engage in the search not just in chants in Ogun worship, but also in their vocations and general attitudes to life. It is not surprising thus that Sampson believes in killing a dog for Ogun, Say Tokyo Kid believes that 'there is a hundred spirits in every guy of timber' (*The Road* 171), the thugs are believed to be 'sons of timber' and Professor himself indulges terrible methods in the search. Above all, most important in *The Road* is the engagement of the road as a spiritual thoroughfare through which 'whole communities' move 'relentlessly towards a new consciousness'. Little wonder that Professor contemplates of the road as a snake lying in wait, and this is motivation for the accidents on the road which provide further sign-posts to the search.

One has attempted thus far to establish the metaphysical preoccupation of *The Road*. If one concedes the primary domain of this play as spiritual, then there is the need to recognize 'sign-posts' of manifestation in *Beatification of Area Boy*. The doubts about the soul originating in *The Boy* assume sentient and dramatic proofs in the lives of most of the characters in *Beatification of Area Boy*. One has proven that hardly any character in this play is as dumb as Murano. Rather all the characters constitute a system of solidarity in a people oriented goal and mission. Further, they all work out the freedom of the collective soul of the community.

Concerning vision, it is easy to see the post-independence confusion of the Nigerian state in the conflicts between politics in the church on the one hand, squaring up against indigenous tradition and religion, on the other. The advent of colonialism upon the Nigerian state has, and continues to foster a hybrid personality and identity in the average Nigerian. This crisis has affected every facet of the lives and behaviours of Nigerians who are seeking primarily to understand the meaning of being. The consequences of this search in the literal sense, assume multiple dimensions with dramatically and dialectically opposed and conflicting ends in view.

More assuring of hope and direction are the manifestations of vision in *Beatification of Area Boy*. In this play, one glimpses a satirical re-enactment of the contemporary pervasive disposition of Nigerians to hold the political destiny of the nation in their hands, particularly since the aborted June 12, 1993 elections, which saw M. K. O. Abiola as the people's unconfirmed winner of the presidential election. Today, there is a sense of political commitment by the people to protect Nigeria, which has assumed group or nationalist shapes needing the attention of the nation state. Beyond collectively electing President Olusegun Obasanjo, all the restive groups of political interests in Nigeria, are more than ever engaged in the struggle for recognition and attention. It is instructive to note how Soyinka has represented the groups of interests in *Beatification of Area Boy* while establishing their organic commitment to popular interests and focus. In this, there is no doubt that *The Road* and *Beatification of Area Boy* individually and collectively articulate a flow of vision from the essence to manifestation. Soyinka hardly presents a bed of roses, particularly when one considers the controversial end of the latter play which points out the problems of the political future of Nigeria.

Works Cited

Ogunba, Oyin, *The Movement of Tradition – A Study of the Plays of Wole Soyinka.* (Ibadan: Ibadan University Press, 1975).

Soyinka, Wole, *Collected Play I.* (Oxford: Oxford University Press, 1973).

_____. *Myth Literature and the African World Views.* (Cambridge: Cambridge University Press, 1976).

_____. *Beatification of Area Boy – A Lagosian Kaleidoscope.* (Ibadan: Spectrum Books Ltd., 1995).

20

The Artist As A Humanist

Soyinka's *From Zia With Love*

MARCELINUS OKHAKHU

This paper sets out to examine the artistic and political ferment of Wole Soyinka since the Nobel Prize was award to him in 1986. In doing this, due cognizance is paid to his previous position on societal issues, which has been highly welfarist. An attempt is therefore made to see how this philosophy has been sustained or otherwise. *From Zia With Love*, one of Soyinka's dramatic works since after the Nobel, forms the pivot of this paper.

Wole Soyinka is easily one of the best known dramatists of the African continent. He is also a poet, an essayist and political activist. His works have been consumed in virtually every part of the world. And in Nigeria, they have formed the basis of an emerging critical culture. The high point of his career was, no doubt, in 1986 when he won the coveted Nobel Prize for literature. Since the Nobel however, rather than be drunk with the glory and celebration of the world prize, Soyinka has been more dogged and consistent in his preachment against societal evils. This is because, for him, man is infinitely and inherently the sources of change in society. He must not wait for God alone to do so for him. Soyinka's philosophy tends to suggest that in spite of God's infinite goodness, if men were to rely solely on Him, he might fail because men have tried for solutions yet. Man therefore, must turn away from pre-ordination, fate, destiny to environment and objective reality. To change society then, man must assign himself some tasks.

For the avid watcher and consumer of Soyinka's works, it would be discovered that this writer has not only effectively used traditional materials from his background, he but that he has also written from his own "external reality". From his very first creative work through his latest, we find this attribute and the fact that he is aware of goings-on around him. He is not severed from the society in which he lives and thrives. He is in fact an active participant in the society and makes very apt commentaries on contemporary issues. This has drawn him into a somewhat bold conflict with some of his friends and colleagues on what ideological position he toes. In this regard, Soyinka has been able to reply to his critics, even if some think that his reply is lame. But one thing is sure; that is that he has a clear social vision (*Myth, Literature and the African World,* 1979: 61). This social vision runs through all his works and even those thought to be feudalist-oriented. It is this vision that would guide us in our analysis of the text in question.

Soyinka, no doubt, has etched a very large and enviable image for himself, particularly in the area of playwriting and play performance. But his impact as a writer and vision for human progress has also been greatly felt in his usage of other media of expression. For instance, his filmographic and discographic efforts have paid off handsomely. Let us quickly dispense with these efforts in relation to the prosecution of his social vision before we return to the consideration of *From Zia With Love.*

Soyinka's first attempt in film, which he used to propagate his welfarist philosophy, was in 1963 when *Culture in Transition* was made. *Culture in Transition* abridges Soyinka's stage play; *The Strong Breed* with other art forms. The thematic and structural arrangement of the film reveals this. Soyinka is the author-narrator of this film and what is perhaps, even more important, is his ideational presence imposed on the film (Ekwuazi, 1984: 370). In this work, Soyinka explicates his theory of culture, vis-à-vis the dynamics of transition to other genres of art in the Nigerian cultural milieu. Each episode in the film, apart from having a valid local significance "yields a thematic globule which the author-narrator adeptly puts together" (1984: 371) to form a thread of cultures in transition.

The social vision that runs through the various episodes of *Culture in Transition* reveals the workings and machinations of Soyinka's mind. He is a humanist who attempts to create a congenial society for man to live in. From the *Watermaid,* the *Agbor Dancers,* through the *Palmwine Drinkard, Oba Koso* and *The Strong Breed,* we find this humanist streak. There exist few points of disagreement which can be argued in this regard—for instance, the harassment of Emman to be the "carrier," especially against his will. However, the central philosophy in the episodes remains that of locating a social vision for the society.

In *Kongi's Harvest* (filmscript)[1] which was released in 1970, he gives a broader sense of this vision. But for some technical reasons, this vision seemed to have been distorted, even though not entirely. The filmscript is different from the film itself. No wonder then that Soyinka dissociated himself from the film later.

In both the stage play and film script, Soyinka sets out to portray despotism and tyrannical rule as a common phenomenon in post-Independent African states. In fact, the two scripts provide insight into the Soyinkaresque world view which we seek to point out in this paper. In terms of thematic relevance, the film script and play are the same. We see for instance that all the forces in *Kongi's Harvest,* both as play and filmscript, weigh so heavily in favour of the Segi/ Daodu coalition and their allies in the character of Oba Danlola and his retinue. Kongi is presented as a man in a real mess. This, of course, is a clear manifestation of Soyinka's disgust for *Kongism* in Africa. And as he says himself, "there are a thousand and one forms of Kongism . . . yet to be dethroned in Black Africa". Soyinka's vision here is so unambiguous that it calls for no special effort to see through it.

Blues For a Prodigal and *Unlimited Liability Company* are no less apt celebrations of this social vision. *Blues . . .* takes a jibe at the decadent political culture which engulfed Nigeria during the Second Republic. Arson, murder and other forms of deprivation became the order of the day. It was not enough to disagree politically. Somebody had to speak out in disagreement and put his life on the line on behalf of society at large. Treasuries were wantonly looted, and of course, indiscipline spending reached an all-time height. The consequence was that the Nigerian economy got depressed – a depression we are yet to recover from. Soyinka's usage of this medium to put through his primary vision was not so much to explore the aesthetic points of film but to further the discourse of humanism and the political mis-behavior of that regime in what is left the free public space in the soci-ety. In a somewhat definite sense, this work becomes more like an agit-prop device – a device meticulously approached to reveal the far-cical degradation and deterioration of the human race in the hands of human beings.

In *Unlimited Liability Company* in which he collaborated with Tunji Oyelana, this is also the case. Soyinka, in this work, goes down memory lane in the history of Nigeria to examine the numerous social philosophies that have been bandied by successive govern-ments. From Ethical Revolution, Green Revolution, Operation Feed the Nation (OFN) to the near successful War Against Indiscipline (W.A.I), he reveals a systematic dismantling of the Nigerian psyche and dignity. Values and mores have become completely warped. The entire value system almost irretrievably broke down. Soyinka's pri-mary objective in this long playing record is not so much to render a sonorous song but to satirize and condemn the way of new *feudal lords* who are nothing but parasites and carnivores. Soyinka's critical barbs can be likened to a call to arms against oppression – be it from the military or political class.

From Zia With Love (published by Fountain Publications, Ibadan, 1992), furthers and distills an argument Soyinka already began in *A Play of Giants*. Like *A Play of Giants*, Soyinka's preoccupation in *From Zia...* is with life and living in Africa, especially in relation to the ten-dentious and obnoxious rule of military despots. From Emperor Bokasa of Central African Republic through Mobutu Sese Seko of Zaire, Idi Amin of Uganda, Paul Biya of Cameroun, Eyademma of Benin, Samuel Doe of Liberia to Ibrahim Babangida of Nigeria, we see the same drama unfolding by the minute. We are presented with the scenario of *sit-tight rulers* who are merely interested in their personal well-being at the expense of ordinary citizens. To achieve their positions fueled by political greed, they put in place structures which they remotely manipulate through idiotic sycophants. These miscreants are mere pawns in big hands and Soyinka uses them metaphorically to protest and portray the ever rotten situation in our society (Africa).

Soyinka's recourse to this kind of protest does not only show his degree of alertness to developments in his society, but also it is an outright rejection of a society full of depravities. His literature then is not just a mere celebration of the agit-prop tradition but more importantly a celebration of protest. Louis James (1974: 109) argues this position succinctly but in a different situation but with the same political context in which Soyinka wrote this play in contest:

> In a situation as explosive as that of Africa today, there can be no creative literature that is not in some way political, some way protest. Even the writer who opts out of the social struggle of his country and tries to create a private world of art is saying something controversial about the responsibility of the artist to society.

James' position is no less relevant today as it was two decades ago. And crucially important is the fact that writers and commentators alike have continued, even in the face of harassment and deprivations, to hold up to society mirror-image of depravities and decadence. This enables them to give a kind of epiphanic illumination to the somewhat dull moments of life and living.

In his exploration of the socio-political problems of Africa, definitely takes on the image of the *artist-messiah* and this runs through most of his works. His entire dramaturgy therefore bothers on protest. He believes in fundamental humanism and advances this belief in his fight against corruption, feudalism, inhumanity and social injustices.

From Zia With Love is a dramatic satire. The chief point of this work lies in the ability of the artist to blend critical attitude with humour and wit in such a way that human institutions or humanity as a whole may be improved. Like other renown satirists, in the words of Holmer's, Soyinka is conscious of the frailty of institutions of man's devise, and attempts through laughter not so much to tear them down as to inspire a remolding.

As a satire, *From Zia With Love* adopts the African cultural trait of exposing, either to ostracize or to reform, collective and or individual wrong doers in the Swiftian tradition of satire.

Soyinka himself asserts in an interview in Ghana in 1974 that:

> We haven't begun actually using words to punch holes inside people. But let us do our best to use words and style when we have the opportunity to arrest ears of normally complement people: we must make sure we explore something inside them which is a paralleled of the sordidness which they ignore outside (Agetua, 1975: 38).

Soyinka returns to this position in *From Zia With Love*. In this play, he demonstrates his hold on and knowledge of the political situation in Nigeria. Although the setting is behind a prison bar, a metaphor for explicating the imprisonment of everyone by the despotic military class, the message is nonetheless clearly defined. Soyinka subjects both the military and religious class to ridicule. He exposes corruption in high places, uncovers man's inhumanity to man and paints the judiciary, and rightly too, in the colors of the devil. From the promulgation of Draconian decrees to the obnoxious and unlawful detention of persons adjudged to be anti-government – all these seem to form the thread with which the drama is woven. Like Antoin Artaud, Soyinka believes that the writer must create from his heart's content and from his environment. This is aptly demonstrated in *From Zia With Love* where he draws from the knowledge of the atrocious and iniquitous rule o the Idiagbon – Buhari administration.

In the world of the play, the prison becomes a mirror for viewing the rest of our society. Various administrative structures like the local government system, state cabinets, Eternal Ruling Council are set up to reflect the society from which the play derives. In this world of the prison, we see an adept manipulation of characters and circumstances in such a way as to establish the eternal madness of our rulers and their cohorts. For instance, Miguel Domingo, Detiba and Emuke are sent to prison. Their cases are pending before the judiciary. But this notwithstanding, they are sandwiched among dare-devil criminals who give them their first lessons in prison. It is not only that they were put in the wrong cell and given rough initiations by the inmates, but that they are made to undergo sordid experiences with the prison officials who are no better than the prisoner's themselves. Of course, the climax comes when they are executed without interogation.

The military administration depicted in *From Zia With Love* is not only truly representative of the despotic rule of the Zia of Pakistan, but finds parallel in the *militocracy* in Nigeria and elsewhere in Africa. The Cabinet session does not differ from modern military Cabinets. The responsibility of the security director, for instance, is waved aside and he is told:

> Security means only one thing – counter subversion, counter subversive talks, counter rumour mongery, counter incitement to subversion . . . (*From Zia* 8).

This is a clear demonstration of the warped philosophy of the military. There is no respect for the rule of law or natural justice. This is of course without prejudice to the fact that those being crushed may not even have been given a fair hearing. This injustice is possible because the military class has found itself in power only on account of the barrel of the gun. They do not understand what their jobs and responsibilities should be. They insist on the observation of full military protocol:

> No matter what style we are operating, you must address . . .
> with due respect and full protocol (*From Zia* 16).

Of course, full protocol does not just mean military obedience. It goes beyond this. It encapsulates the whole process of human torture and degradation which the civil society is subjected to. This is the bane of postcolonial African states.

The experiences of this play relates to our immediate society and reveals that the military in search of acceptance from the people they purport to rule usually promulgate all kinds of decrees either to back

their actions or to establish white elephant projects. It is this haphaz-
ard and bogus thinking of the military that Soyinka lampoons here
when he writes that the military

> Simply launch a special campaign—it may even bring you
> extra aid from World Health Organization. Make it the next
> stage of the Battle Against Indiscipline. (*From Zia With Love*
> 76).

For the average Nigerian, this message is very clear, especially
against the background that most of these programmes have attracted severe criticism from the larger society. But what is perhaps not
clear is the philosophy that continues to inform the banding of ideas
by successive military administrations which are hardly thoroughly
thought through.

In furtherance of his condemnation of the military elite class,
Soyinka declares in *From Zia With Love* that the military is the most
pretentious and dishonest amongst the groups in our society. He
argues that officers in high places engage in all kinds of dirty and
dubious businesses and also seek dirty means of covering them up:

> You can always mount a coup . . . it is an accepted cover up
> practice. (*From Zia With Love* 71).

Soyinka contends further that even Presidential consignments
become avenue for presidential smuggling. His dislike for this pretentious class cannot be more graphically represented. Soyinka's condemnation is not restricted to the military class alone. He berates the
religious class too for its compromising and cowardly position, and
for being as pretentious and devilish as the military class arguing that
in contemporary Nigerian society, the role of the church and mosque
has been nothing but a sham. Religious leaders have been known to
have buried social the truth for a mere "pot of porridge". Telling the
truth became for them a vice rather than a virtue. Sycophancy
reigned supreme for as long as bank accounts were stuffed and posh
cars driven. In condemnation of all of this, Soyinka examines various
sects within the religious gamut and subjects them to a critical scruti-

ny. For instance, he argues in *From Zia With Love* that they all profess "God and truth, yet that last Alfa was hanged for ritual murder".

The question that arises is an obvious one: where is the morality and godliness in the priest of God who supposedly should lead the flock to paradise? If the shepherd is as guilty as he has been painted, then what would happen to the sheep?

In *From Zia With Love*, Soyinka uses various theatrical and literary devices to advance his message. For instance, the plot of *From Zia With Love* contributes immensely to the realization of the thematic aspiration. The plot is episodic and the actions are laced and interwoven in such a way as to enhance the success and overall understanding of the play. The methodical crafting of the plot helps this understanding too. For instance, one cannot but notice the changes in the scenes from cell "G" to "C" just as well as the goings on outside the bar. Even the stage directions, which may be argued to be ancillary to the development of the plot but which nonetheless advance it, give a vivid picture of the helplessness and despair of the characters. As a point of illustration, we notice from the excerpt below, the psychological and physical torture of the character of Miguel from the stage direction:

Miguel (Turns and walks across to the door and shakes it gently). (*From Zia With Love* 25).

If we contextualize the action preceding this direction, especially the indecent harassment in the hands of bread-stealing warders, then the meaning of this stage direction would not be lost on us.

Soyinka also uses music to give weight to his message in this play and to create an overall balance on the understanding of his message. He achieves this in both the lyrics and rhythm of the songs. Songs in the play are not only expressive and rhythmical. They are also invested with the traits lampoon to cast aspersion on decadent values of society. This is easily noticeable in the "Songs of state assignment", "Song of the time machine", etc. He uses those elements so dexterously that they become the building blocks on which the play sustains its theme and aesthetic quality.

One aspect we have definitely paid the least attention to in this study is language. And this is because, in my opinion, the usual accusation by critics of language inaccessibility and obscurantism is no longer an issue to dissipate our energy on. However, in this play, Soyinka's language is very simple and appropriate. He seems to have deliberately chosen a less flowering kind of language, seeking and experimenting with a milder register of the English language in order to reach out to a large number of people. There is evidence in the play that points this fact of the text. For instance, he creates characters whose language registers seem deliberately contrived to make them appealing. Examples include the warders, the C-and-C of the prison, and some of the ordinary in-mates. However, this creation does not rob the characters of the meanings of their roles in the criminal world-view of an African prison condition.

Besides, these characters are so appropriately endowed with the language skills of their social class that in spite of their literary creations, their registers and local flavours remain distinct. It is this adept usage of language that Adelugba referred to as "Yorubanglish" in his consideration of *Kongi's Harvest,* an earlier work of Soyinka. Although all the characters speak the English language, one notices the local flavours and idiosyncrasies in their speech patterns. The prisoner's song, for instance, reveals this:

Oga warder Oga warder
. . . craw-craw warder
Jedi-jedi warder
Oga warder O, Oga warder (1992: 21).

This song uncovers clearly both the class and level of operation of the character. The same can be said for Miguel, "the man of resources" whose language is set out on page 25. It is flowery enough to depict both his level of education and means in society. The point then is that Soyinka endows his characters with an appropriate language register and diction and this ultimately helps him to fully explore the world-view of the characters concerned. All of the characters find parallels in contemporary society. For instance, the in-mates of cell "C" paint the gory picture of Rafindadi's[2] detention camp in the Idiagbon-Buhari regime where innocent detainees were surreptitiously killed almost on a daily basis in the prison.

Notes

1. The filmscript of Kongi's Harvest has generated a lot of controversy, with Soyinka disowning it after it was, according to him, misinterpreted in the shooting process by the director of the film, the African-American Ossie Davies. The original script which Soyinka wrote is deposited at the Kenneth Dike Library, University of Ibadan, Nigeria.
2. Alhaji Rafindadi was the notorious boss of the secret police during the regime of Generals Muhammadu Buhari and Tunde Idiagbon.

Works Cited

Agetua, John. *And The Man Died.* Benin: Bendel Newspaper Corporation, 1975.

Ekwuazi, Hyginus. "The Film In Nigeria: The Context of Production". Ph.D Dissertation. University of Ibadan, 1984.

James, Louis. *Arts and Society.* London: Caltop Press, 1974.

Soyinka, Wole. *Myth, Literature and The African World.* Cambridge: Cambridge University Press, 1979.

_____. *From Zia With Love.* Ibadan: Fountain Publication, 199

21

Soyinka and the Interfaith Dialogue

A Stylistic Analysis of
The Credo of Being and Nothingness

LANRE BAMIDELE

I

Since winning the Nobel Prize for Literature in 1986, new approaches to studying Soyinka's works have begun to develop. There is beginning to be a move away from the analysis of his novels, poems and plays to the analysis of his public lectures, speeches and interviews even to the media. The recourse to this new approach is consequent upon (i) his image in world politics and his social role as recognized and sustained in Nigeria and the fact that whatever he says would become reference material on world affairs, (ii) the realization that the quantity of pure literary texts he has written since then are few and limited while he has made more public speeches than hitherto. Therefore, the speeches have provided new focus to scholars of discourse analysis and public speaking.

While a study of rhetorics of persuasion in his plays could be discussed in regard to how the plays appeal to, or confuse, an audience in the theatre, his public lectures and interviews have become less difficult, very fluid and lucid in style with piercing truth and sometimes inspiring admonitions. There is an integrated focused goal in all these. He is the social critic who is concerned with justice, freedom, fairplay, human dignity and peace. This paper on *The Credo of Being and Nothingness* is an attempt to analyze the style of his religious thoughts. The rhetorical impact of the lecture speaks in its piercing truth about religious extremism and fanaticism across the globe with specific reference to the Nigerian situation. I find this study of his idea and its delivery more challenging and quite engaging in the analysis of art of rhetorics.

II

The title of the text is very mystifying to many people for different reasons. To those who have traced its antecedent to Jean Paul Sartre's *Being and Nothingness,* the lecture would be a philosophical journey into the concept of *others* and *being-in-itself.* To those who have not heard of Jean Paul Sartre's title, Soyinka's topic might be one of those obsfucating and obscurantic uses of language in discussions and lectures. On both scores, the lecture is compelling to read. The lecture has been regarded as an epistemology of our social malaise (Oladipo: 1990),[1] but many would not have thought it to be the religious thoughts of a social critic who has often being charged with irreligiousity.

The speech event was at the first Olusosoye Lectures organized by the Department of Religious Studies of the University of Ibadan. The mystic aura of the topic must have affected the published text by Spectrum[2] which has for its cover design a spider web, an amazing symbol for the unravelability of the cosmos. The text has become one of those few public lectures and speeches that have been published[3] and it has enriched the current research on how a popular figure uses his words and language[4] to dissuade us from violence, religious intolerance and to persuade us on the need to understand and regard each other's faith.

The meaning of *nothingness* takes various connotations from a phenomenology to the Christian idea of the void to the Yoruba syntax of *aijamonkan kan* (to be nothing) and also to the oriental philosophers' state of emptying the souls to the point of perfect motionlessness. With a conscious regard of the art of the novel, the beginning of the speech does not start like that of a lecture but with a narrative structure of the story-teller. The experience of being and non-being has its origin in the 'thought' and imagination of Soyinka early enough from childhood. The text starts with "I do not claim …" to situate the experience in a world of a child's attempt to unravel the world. This style is an unusual one for public lectures. As he tell the story, he chooses the moment of experience from which to look back from which to look ahead for what it is to exist or be effaced out of existence. With this beginning, the technical ability of a professional writer is displayed. The style gradually integrates the reader into the story of the *self* before transporting you into the realm of philosophic abstractions that the title connotes.

The speech act of defining *nothingness* starts with a macabre joke or pranks as employed by the child to experience the state of being and non-being. In its limpid sentences and precisions of drawing on the imagery of void and *nothingness* is the child's imagination, an entertaining background serves as the opening to a befuddling topic before we are launched into the mysticism of *nothingness* in the Buddhists' spiritual stage of Nirvana. In simple terms, the experience of non-being is an exercise towards wilful peace as Buddhists are wont to practise:

> Let your body and mind be turned into an inanimate object of nature like a piece of stone or a piece of wood, when a state of perfect motionlessness and unawareness is obtained all the signs of life will depart and every trace of limitation will vanish. This is the experience of *nothingness*, the state of the void in Buddhism.[5] (emphasis mine)

From a child's prank to the mystics' experience and the Christian's meaning of the void we are brusquely informed of what nothingness would connote in the context of the lecture through Sheik Gumi's[6] pronouncement of "Christianity is nothing". The brusqueness with which this "negative expression" was broached could, suspectingly, have aroused laughter but it could also have started a war of words. This is how the idea of interfaith dialogue would develop to a sort of Soyinka's ecumenical challenge.

It is striking that in these connotations language furnishes us with the *nothingness* of things and the *nothingness* of being. It is possible for us then to assume that Soyinka's *nothingness* is based purely on the Yoruba term of *aijamonkan kan* from Gumi's concept of what does not exist. It is on this propositional interpretation that the style of delivery, and the structure of organizing the idea shall engage us.

III

The *nothingness* that Soyinka speaks about becomes clearer when he made a recourse into Omar Khayyam's poetry:

"to be free from belief and unbelief is my religion".

He wonders why in the attempt to uphold the "unprovable, the merely imbibed or intuitively experienced", a religion would tear the world apart. In the philosophy of language used, everything is reduced to nothing, even faith itself since it is non-concrete, unseen and unprovable.

The rhetoric of proving the non-existence, otherwise the *nothingness* of other religions, is relayed with a seeming sense of ridicule when each religion engages in reducing the other to nothing before it can justify its own existence.

Eraze that temple. Demolish that mosque. Obliterate that Cathedral. Flatten that Shrine. (*The Credo*, 12)

This is a credo every religion recites to sustain itself. But the satire becomes pungent when it is stressed that each of these religions professed to be apostles of peace while they revel in the attitude of violence. "Violence appears to be the one constant in the histories of all the major religions of the world". (14)

There is contempt for this language of violence and destruction as employed by these religions while there is a hidden ridicule of their displayed motto and tenets of either the Christian's "Seek ye the path of peace" or the Islamic motto of "Islam is Peace". When you say one thing and do another the artist may ridicule your pretensions.

The phenomenon of violence and riot consequent on the credo of the *nothingness* of the other faith as expressed by fanatics is riddled with sordid description of the savagery in man. As in news reporting, the lecture relays a gory sight:

> Passengers in a travelling bus were forced to disembark and separated into their religious persuasions. One group is machine-gunned on the spot-women and children are not spared. (*Credo of Being*)

This and very many other forms of torture and horror perpetrated for the sake of religion take the style of news reporting with a view to striking the conscience of the better part of the nation, and the world, to ask if religion is really anything worthy of butchering one another for.

IV

Is religion truly anything? This is a poser that may lead one to risk a guess about the reception of *The Credo of Being and Nothingness* as a lecture piece. There is a scathing condemnation of the two major religions in their invasions of the Nigerian psyche with a degree of violence that no indigenous religion has ever done. There would be those who would charge Soyinka with being irreligious in his attempt to persuade the reader about the African spiritual heritage. This language and style of persuasion, though it can be supported by reasoned argument, would lead some people to condemn his plea for the acceptance of African religion as unrealistic belief.

Soyinka's posture as a drum-major for the African spiritual heritage is constant and long established and this has led to the "unreasoned" charged of irreligiousity against him. Unreasoned because he defines in the lecture, for those who do not know, what religion is and what to be ungodly is. The speech in its idea and delivery catches our attention as the style of a salesman – reasoned and persuasive – and we have to write it in full here even for its plain truth and admonition.

> Let those who have to retain or elevate religion as a twenty-first century project feel free to do so but let it not be done as continuation of the game of denigration against African spiritual heritage. It is sufficient to call the world's attention to the fact that religions do exist, such as on this continent

that can boast of never having launched a war, any form of jihad or crusade, for the furtherance of their beliefs . . .

Is there or is there not a lesson for our universe in this? Is there not a lesson here for those dogmatic, over-scriptured and over-annotated monumentalities whose rhetoric and secular appropriations far exceed the inner verities of their spiritual claims? (*The Credo* 17).

And in the tone of praise for and pride in African religion, the drum-major says that this is a religion that has "rescued us as conscious race in diaspora, preserved our identity and what is more, infected even those claimants to superior knowledge of the supreme deity". But can any diehard fanatics of Christianity or Islam be persuaded: would this call not be regarded as unrealistic belief, even when there is some logic and reason in this oratory of Soyinka on African religion?

The invasion by the two religions – Islam and Christianity – of Africa is berated and described as a form of imperialism of a cultural and spiritual kind. The reactionaries of history amongst Africans with their sing-song of referring to one of these religions as indigenous and the other alien he upbraids without sparing their intellect. In parenthesis but relevant to a proper interpretation of this view we can here remind ourselves of such sayings as:

Laye l'a ba'fa—We met Ifa here on earth
Laye l'a bamale—We met Islam here on earth
Osan gangan ni'gbagbo wole—It was in the blazing
afternoon that Christianity crept in.

Recorded history is Soyinka's witness to debunk this view.

There were digressions here and there in the lecture but there is an observed coherence or a focused goal which we shall touch upon very soon. But about the digression, it is a style that is consequent on the "social role" recognized as typical of the speaker to touch. Such issues as the war between the cross and the crescent in a university campus; the search for truth and the knowledge of the "godhead"; the attitude of self-acclaimed seers and prophets; the cynical treatment of the duo-form policy and other social services in Nigeria. All this could be seen in the context of topicalization as a stylistic mechanism to enliven the speaker's technique of capturing the audience's attention and moving his listeners to a state of rapture. In an implicit way, Soyinka is asking us to define what secularism means to us in Nigeria as a policy of state that encourages one rule of conduct for the Moslems and another for the Christians, for a government that shares, presumably, in the knowledge that African religion does not exist.

The lecturer's speech act is exhortatory rather than belligerent since it is to be an interfaith dialogue or sine it is based on the rhetorics of tolerance, as someone has put it.[7] Since this is the central idea of the lecture, it is essential to define what 'interfaith' means and implies in the lecture. Interfaith could be the interactions of people of divergent religions that could culminate in action or behaviour centred around central goal or set of goals – here the central goal is world or national peace. Perhaps it could go further to mean persons of one religion understanding the tenets and practices of other religions. It could also mean people beginning to have a more comprehensive understanding of other people of divergent religious views.[8]

In these various definitions resides the religious thought of Soyinka. He advises that all religions should shed their ignorance of the other religions and re-examine their relationships with other religions in promoting world unity. Soyinka in the lecture advises these religions:

> It is not enough to examine their own courses in world history but to equally re-examine the very nature of other beliefs with which they have interacted in their passage through history, including those which they do not accept as religions. (*The Credo* 15)

Let us examine what Michael Stubbs says in relation to the speech event as it dictates the speech act and consequently determine the syntactic structure of text/dialogue as can be analyzed in *The Credo of Being and Nothingness*. The syntactic structure here bears a direct influence of philosophy, the Bible and the Koran and some other religions of the world as seen on pages 32-33 as in "I say to you go to orisa, learn from them and be wise" (Biblical influence); "You do not believe, therefore you are not". (Influence of Philosophy). We can find some of these features and influences running through the text. It is a matter of style and a demand on any public speaker to choose his syntax in accordance with the speech event. A reading of Soyinka's lecture on "Power and Creative Strategies"[10] would reveal a syntax and idiom that is filled with ideological outpouring as the occasion demands. When he humours the readers of *The Credo of Being and Nothingness* as he did in the case of the gathering at the occasion of its delivery, he humours them in their own tenets and their ostentatious piety, if they are Christians or Moslems (and presumably most of them are).

The end of the lecture fascinates us in its unusual style of ending the discourse. It begins with the narrative "I" of the story-teller or the form of the novel and ends with a poetic form – an ode to the Yoruba gods. The intention of the ode is not to impose Soyinka's views on the reader or the listener but to exhibit what inspiration the gods have provided for his (Soyinka's) development as a writer and an apologist of the African spiritual heritage. It is presented in a tone of admiration for the god's essence and not in a tone of threat and fear of the malevolence of these gods. Its romantic tone can be equated with that of any religious poet who sings the glory of his own object of belief in such rich symbols. But we are not forced to accept his prescriptions since he himself is aware of the fact that the issue of belief and unbelief is an individual's choice.

The coherence of the lecture is based on the need to understand one another's faith and tolerate each other on what we believe. The preface to the lecture as published is clear and this underscores the difference between Sartre's *Being and Nothingness* and Soyinka's *The Credo of Being and Nothingness*. To answer those who must have raised quasi-naïve questions on the difference between Soyinka's idea of nothingness and its antecedent Sartrean philosophy, we shall stress that Sartre's use of nothingness is metaphysical and full of existentialist abstractions while Soyinka's is focused on religious intolerance and its attendant social upheavals. Each of the two has its separate style for the discourse of nothingness as a thematic preoccupation quite different and somehow far apart. That preface should be read again to come to grips with Soyinka's style of writing, the idea of the Lecture and its delivery. It says that we must beware of religions that turn their backs on the progress of history and society – especially the fanatics and the fundamentalist forces that are hostile to secularism.

V

What we have done in this approach to the study of Wole Soyinka's style is to provide a paradigm for the analysis of his speeches and lectures and possibly of those of other people as well. The interesting point in the study of Soyinka's speech style is that in all his recent lectures we notice that the sum of his experiences, his thoughts, and his personality are expressed in language that is clear and that deftly touches on sensitive ideas.

Wole Soyinka has become a compelling figure to listen to and his artful use of language is not just an exhibition of a flowery attempt to throw the listeners into a state of rapture but has become a challenge to communication scholars on such issues as the organization of the ideas, the presentation of these ideas, the choice of proper words to fit proper occasions. Issues on style that will repay a further study of Soyinka's speeches and addresses are: invective and irony, order of words and sentence structure, digressions and coherence, the impressive use of detailed examples, etc. Some of these have been briefly broached here but these and many more aspects of the Nobel Laureate's style deserve careful study.

Notes

1. Olusegun Oladipo, "Wole Soyinka on religious tolerance: Epistemology of a social malaise", *Alminba Tribune*, No. 45, Nov. 1991. Pp. 4-6.
2. *The Credo of being and Nothingness*, Spectrum, Ibadan, Nigeria, 1991, 35 pages I express my indebtedness to Val Olayemi, the Consultant Publisher, whose support for me in "providing" a copy of the text as stimulated my interest to interpret the communication styles I have embarked on here. The speech event preceding the publication took place at the University of Ibadan Faculty of Science Lakeside Lecture Theatre, January 25, 1991.

3. A collection of Soyinka's speeches and lectures is being packaged by Emanco Prints Ltd., Lagos, 1991, to be published soon under the title, "Continuity Amnesia". I am grateful to Emanco Prints and Mr. I. O. Oladele for giving me privileged access to the galleys of this forthcoming book.

4. The inspiration for this study is derived from two relevant essays, Sunday D. martin's "King and Interfaith Dialogue" and Melbourne S. Cummings' "King as Persuader". Both essays are in *The Journal of Religious Thought*, vol. 48 No. 2, Winter-Spring 1991-1992, pp. 34-49 and 59-65 respectively.

5. D. T. Suzuki, *An Introduction to Zen Buddhism*, An Evergreen Press, Inc., New York, 1964, p. 47.

6. Sheik Gumi is a Nigerian Muslim Cleric and Scholar who died recently. He is remembered in South Christian Nigeria for his declaration that Christianity is *nothing*.

7. I. O. Oladele, "Rhetoric of Tolerance from *The Credo* through Soyinka", a paper presented in the Department of Communication and Language Arts in 1991 for a course on Situation Public Speaking at the University of Ibadan, Ibadan.

8. Sunday D. Martin, "King and Interfaith Dialogue", in *The Journal of Religious Thought*, Vol. 48 No. 2, Winter-Spring, 1992, pp. 34-39.

9. Michael Stubbs, *Discourse Analysis: The Socio-linguistic Analysis of Natural Language*, Basil Blackwell, Oxford, 1983.

10. Page 10 of *The Punch* of Wednesday, May 4, 1988 carried Wole Soyinka's address, "Power and Creative Strategies". This is the keynote address to the International Symposium on African Literature held in Lagos, Nigeria at the National Arts Theatre.

Works Cited

Martin, D. Sunday. "King and The Interfaith Dialogue". *The Journal of Religious Thought*. 43/2, 1992.

Oladele, I. O. "Rhetorics of Tolerance From *Credo* Through Soyinka". Unpublished. A paper Presented at the Department of Communication and Language Arts, University of Ibadan, Nigeria.

Oladipo, Olusegun. "Wole Soyinka on Religious Tolerance: Epistemology of a Social Malaise". *Alminba Tribune,* No. 45, 1991.

Soyinka, Wole. *Credo of Being and Nothingness.* Ibadan: Spectrum Books, 1992.

_____. "Power and Creative Strategies". *The Punch,* May 4, 1988.

Stubbs, Michael. *Discourse Analysis: The Socio-Linguistic Analysis of Natural Language.* Oxford: Basil Blackwell, 1983.

Suzuki, D. T. *An Introduction to Zen Buddhism.* New York: An Evergreen Press, 1964.

22

X-Raying A Nation's Soul

Soyinka's *The Beatification of Area Boy*

CHRIS EGHAREVBA

Forest Head:	Aroni, does Demoke know the mean-ing of his act?
Aroni:	Demoke, you hold a doomed thing in your hand. It is no light matter to reverse the deed that was begun many lives ago.
	(Soyinka, 1973:71).

The above conversation came after Half-child (the symbol of the Nigerian nation at independence) in *A Dance of the Forests*, lost the game of life to Eshuoro. Yet Demoke the artist, the man of conscience felt the need to rescue Half-child from the game of death.

So, in 1960, the image of an abnormality was presented to the nation at independence by Wole Soyinka as a warning to the newly elected leaders of the need for maturity and care in the handling of the new Nation State. Events that followed the nation's independence were clear indications that the ominous signals presented to the leaders in that independence play, *A Dance of the Forests,* were ignored: the nation was plunged into a macabre dance of death before the end of the 1960s.

It was indeed a dance of the forests as evil took centre stage in national politics. Coups and counter-coups, political immaturity, greed, pride and religio-ethnic preoccupations gave rise to a civil war. Death and destruction became part of the national psyche. The prediction of Half-child himself: "I'll be born dead," (Soyinka, 1973:64) was finding fulfillment within so short a time. In fact, from this point in our national history, the equally terrible prediction in "Hemlock" of the monster child in *Kongi's Harvest* became significant:

Ogbo Aweri: Observe, when the monster child
                        was born, opele taught us to
                        Abandon him beneath the buttress tree
                        But the mother said, oh no,
                        A child is still a child
                        The mother in us said, a child
                        Is still the handiwork of Olukori.

Sarumi: Soon the head swelled
                        Too big for pillow
                        And it swelled too big
                        For the mother's back
                        And soon the mother's head
                        Was nowhere to be seen
                        (Soyinka, 1973:68-69)

The nation had nursed and nurtured a monster child who became a terror to his mother. Kongi took political control and from that moment, the spiritual health of the nation symbolized by the yam was replaced by the decapitated head in a platter. Leadership lost its spiritual essence and developmental commitment, and became preoccupied with self-succession and destruction of the people. Psychophancy became professionalized and national policy decisions and implementations became the product of "a reformed Aweri", a group held hostage to the whims and caprices of leadership thus paving way for the entrenchment of dictatorship. In subsequent years, sycophancy metamorphosed into a monstrous killer squad that became the machine of intimidation of psychopathic dictators.

In an interview in 1985 (Wilkinson, 1992) Soyinka observed that the political situation in the nation was "very sad, very distracting." It created not just a wasted generation but a generation whose future was mortgaged by a senselessly vicious leadership. Similarly, it is obvious that the experiences of the nation since the publication of *Kongi's Harvest* certify that one cannot "erect a pulpit" against "the batteries and the microphones and the insistence of one indefatigable madman" (Soyinka, 1974:99). It would obviously amount to being a mere antithesis to a messiah of pain as observed by Daodu. Soyinka's actions and pronouncements since *Kongi's Harvest* show his rejection of Segi's solution to the problem of dictatorship. They also showed a departure from Ngugi's earlier observation that:

> Confronted with the impotence of the elite, the corruption of those steering the ship of State of those looking after its organs of justice, Wole Soyinka does not know which way to turn. (Bjornson, 1990: 15)

Today, Wole Soyinka is not just talking about the impotence of the elite, the failure and corruption of leadership or the betrayal of the people by mediocre in leadership positions. Soyinka is highlighting on a more fundamental problems of psychopathic tyrants and killers as leaders. The nation, like Kongi's Isma but in a much more horrible dimension, is a land where fear, confusion and terror have become acceptable instruments of state governance. Truth is denied and illegality takes over the national psyche.

Does a nation, plagued by illegality and criminal corruption, possess a soul? What is the nature of such a nation's soul? The search for a nation's soul becomes imperative in the struggle for solution to its problems. This is one of the major concerns in *The Beatification of Area Boy.* In 1965, 30 years before the publication of *The Beatification of Area Boy,* Soyinka in *The Road,* presented the Professor who was in search of the Word. Ultimately, the road became a true pathway to the Word—the final province of the souls lost from the bodies at death. In *The Beatification of Area Boy,* the lost souls become metaphoric for the living dead, the masses that have become marginalize and living in *the back of beyond,* in the fringes of existence. These people who forage in the dustbins for existence that Judge set out to restore through his practice of Yoga. The day's violence and anxieties are gathered, as it were, into one breath, thereby internalizing the natural and environmental predicaments, transforming and purifying them with this higher spiritual awareness.

However, towards the end of *The Beatification* it became obvious that Judge's "purification" of the dawn was an illusion created by the violence of the military against the inhabitants of a slum settlement that was destroyed by Government. Still, Judge embarks on the journey into the kingdom of lost souls:

JUDGE: ... Today I start on a different journey.
                 I begin the long journey to the kingdom
                 of lost souls *(The Beatification* 7).

Judge is prepared to relieve the lost souls of their torment armed with the prerogative of mercy, not with the majesty of the Law for the Law has no majesty in a military regime. In fact, his choice of the prerogative of mercy became irrelevant too in the end because the military had no room for either Mercy or the Law. Judge, the embodiment of the Law and the prerogative of mercy was beaten, tear-gassed and locked inside the booth of the car of the military officer.

Initially, the search seemed a personal one but it gradually becomes obvious that the playwright is concerned not with the lost souls of the individuals as in *The Road* but with the soul of the nation:

JUDGE: ... Yes my journey to the kingdom of
                 souls begins today. People say the
                 nation has lost its soul but that is non-
                 sense. It is all a matter of finding out
                 where it's hidden. Unless it never had
                 any ... (*The Beatification* 10).

318

Thus the stage is set for us to begin a search for what constitute the soul of the nation.

At this point, it is relevant to consider the nature of the soul of the nation right from independence. Soyinka in *A Dance of the Forests* presents the nation as a half-child tossed between two forces–Ogun and Eshuoro, a child who at birth lost out in the game for life. Forest Head's verdict was very distinct: A child doomed at birth. But Dumoke struggled to save the Half-child from the opposing forces contesting for its soul. Man's humanity is tested by his ability to save, to preserve and bequeath to posterity a society better than what is inherited.

The military in Nigeria, inherited a nation that was blessed economically in such a manner that the nation's leader proclaimed to the world that money was not the nation's problem but how to spend it. Thirty years after, we have a nation of vagrants, of people "foraging in the disposal sector" (*The Beatification* 10) in order to exist. Instead of improving the soul of the nation, we have a nation of lost souls, of unemployed youths who take to petty crimes to survive; youths whose future has been mortgaged and for no just reasons.

It is interesting that the issue of debate between Judge and Trader at the beginning of the play centers on the dawn. The dawn presents both beauty and filthiness. To Trader, the dawn exposes the penurious and squalid state of the city of Lagos. Its reality is essentially sordid. Yet Judge, aided by his spiritual exercises, sees beauty in the dawn. However, Mama Put rejects this sense of a false dawn that has been plaguing the nation and sees the soul of the nation in its dawn: it is a soul plagued by images of bloodshed, destruction, violence and dispossession of the masses.

To Mama Put, who in this circumstance is the voice of the playwright, the civil war has never ended in the nation. Governmental neglect and exploitation of the Niger Delta areas, the demolition of Maroko and the displacements of the people who formed a ragged procession remind one of the continuation of the civil war:

MAMA PUT: I hoped I had escaped such sights forever. While the civil war lasted, oh yes.

> It was like that for us most of the time.
> First the Biafrans who insisted we were
> part of them. We packed our belong-
> ings and drifted to the villages. Then
> the Federal Army came with their
> gospel of liberation. So we trooped
> back, just like that. Then the Biafran
> Army returned and back we went on
> the roads, along bush paths, knee-deep
> in swamps and foraging for food like
> beasts of the forests. (*The Beatification*,
> p.75).

Mama Put's bayonet becomes a reminder of the war and her loss on a personal level, and for the nation, it is symbolic of the never ending presence of violence and bloodshed in the soul of the nation: a legacy of the military that permeates the national psyche.

A far greater expose of the soul of the nation is portrayed in the confrontation between Miseyi and Sanda. The confrontation brings to limelight the pains of a dream turned nightmare, the dislocation of idealism by a harsh unbelievable reality. The playwright captures the confrontation in his stage direction:

> *Enter MISEYI, accompanied by her housemaid, heading for the store entrance. SANDA does not look up. Instead, he focuses on the high heels, then slowly raises his gaze as their owner climbs the steps, so that his eyes become level with her head as she reaches the entrance, by which time her back is turned towards him. Suddenly, he freezes. At the same moment, the woman stops, then turns around. Their eyes meet. (The Beatification 46)*

It was like the freezing of time, of reality and of idealism. The brilliant Sanda of the Student Union Government has for real become a security staff and indeed the leader of the Area Boys in his vicinity. It was a far cry from the idealism of the student days. This destruction of idealism sets Miseyi angry – a misplaced anger for she unleashes her venom on Sanda:

MISEYI: ...People grow. They develop. You ...
                  you ... Christ, it makes one weep
                  inside to look at you! Did you aban-
                  don your degree programme, one year
                  to graduation – for this? A *megadi* uni-
                  form ... (*The Beatification*, 47-48).

A *megadi* uniform is the reality that materialises from the idealism that was to be 'an academic gown.' From this point, it was Miseyi that needed growing up. She had to realise that in a nation where "hundreds of Ph.Ds are roaming the streets jobless" (*The Beatification* 48), a job as a '*megadi*' (which in effect is masking a more dangerous job of the Chief of the Area Boys) is providential. Still Miseyi sees Sanda as a failure:

MISEYI: Oh you're lost. You've become decadent
                  ... ... you're nothing but a sham, a
                  poseur, masquerading among a class to
                  which you don't belong. You're a cheat
                  even, you know that? ... failed. You
                  were whipped. (*The Beatification* 49.)

Sanda counters her anger with a sardonic smile that speaks of an awareness of reality to Miseyi's ignorance of a nature of a society that has lost its soul. To Miseyi, Sanda's failure arises from his fear to "stand a little dirt for Utopia" (*The Beatification*, P. 50) which in her assessment amounted to a betrayal of the revolution. But for Sanda, it was not a question of a little dirt: "The waters were too murky. I couldn't swim in them" (*The Beatification*, P. 50)

This is the hard lesson that the masses learn everyday in their daily living.

MAMA PUT: It's a hard school we go to, a hard
                  school in a heartless city.... (*The Beat-
                  ification* 60)

and Sanda puts it thus:

> We live in a cruel land. A cruel time in a cruel land. To
> breathe at all is... cruelty... (*The Beatification* 61)

It is no wonder then that in such a nation, the prerogative of
Mercy or the majesty of the Law becomes irrelevant. Judge, the
embodiment of the Law, is portrayed as partly demented, practicing
undigested mysticism of Eastern religions. The salvation of the people cannot be entrusted to such a one. In reality, the majesty of the
Law and the prerogative of Mercy constitute the hope of the people
but in a nation ruled by the military, Law itself is a casualty.

Hence for daring to touch the uniform of the Military Officer –
not even the man within the uniform – Judge is teargassed and
locked inside a car booth. This is indeed the fate of the Law in a
nation that has lost its soul. In such a nation, a "journey to soul's
kingdom" (*The Beatification* 62) becomes imperative as the starting
point to solving the nation's problem.

To accomplish this, "the judicial wig must undergo some aging
process" *(The Beatification* 63). Judge aptly said:

> What you have there (ashes) represent fire in absolute purity,
> purge of passion, divorced of its past. It is the pure element
> that is fire, but without the heat, its destructive career sub-
> sumed in serenity (*The Beatification* 63).

The maturity, the dignity, honesty and fearlessness that are associated with age are required to change the judiciary to stand forth for
the people against an unjust social order.

In his search, Judge comes to awareness that the colour of the
nation's soul is black. Trader reports to Sanda:

> 'E say 'e done make de journey wey e tell me about, and at
> last 'e discover the colour of the soul, and na pitch black 'e be.
> (*The Beautification* 89)

The soul of the nation is plagued with evil, wickedness, greed, religious and ethnic killings and ritualistic killings for materialism. The
nation's soul is plagued with lack of development, thereby creating

despair and unfulfilment in the lives of the populace. Thus, we have a nation that beatifies honours and venerate criminals in uniform; a nation whose soul for years has been held hostage by visionless leaders and subsequently subjected to a systematic plundering.

Soyinka's *The Beatification of Area Boy* is a painfully realistic commentary on a nation that venerates criminality, which is symbolized in her leadership. Soyinka presents the harrowing and traumatic consequences of a nation that is led by Area Boys – leaders that unleash a network of intimidation, violence on the people and property; leaders that master-mind sufferings and hardships on the people, leaders that displace the masses and dispossess them of their property while masquerading as agent of security, leaders that benefit from acts of violence against the populace, and enrich themselves through the suffering of the masses.

Soyinka demonstrates in the play that the Area Boy leadership caucus holds the soul of the nation in its death grip and instead of a collective will to flush out these criminal leaders they are venerated, they are beatified.

The nation, like Kongi's Isma, is a land where fear and terror are accepted as instruments of state policy. Truth is denied and illegality takes the centre stage. The Area Boy mentality had permeated the psyche of leadership of the nation, dominating and destroying the social and economic spheres of the nation.

Miseyi and Sanda, like Segi and Daodu in *Kongi's Harvest*

> represent the spirit of freedom, love and fruitfulness; at the crisis moment, they demonstrate courage; they demonstrate high degree of ingenuity, and they are the hope of the oppressed (Udoeyop, 1997:51)

It is from this understanding that one observes Soyinka's optimistic vision in *The Beatification of Area Boy*. The coming together of Miseyi and Sanda creates an opportunity to outwit the corrupt leadership. Instead of dissipating energies in quarrels, accusations and counter-accusations, self-anger and self-pity, Soyinka proposes the need for decisive steps to be taken against the inhuman and corrupt leadership of the nation.

Thus, any marriage between the corrupt, visionless leadership and the revolutionary forces is not feasible. What is required, Soyinka seems to emphasise in the play, is the coming together of all progressive forces for a purging of the nation's soul. This vision makes *The Beatification of Area Boy*, Soyinka's most revolutionary play to date. And this certainly is what it should be if Soyinka's confrontations with the late psychopathic dictator Gen. Sani Abacha's government were to have any lesson for posterity.

Finally, it is significant that Judge survived extinction, saved by the bullet proof vest he foraged from the booth of the military officer's car. Indeed, this is symbolic. The Judiciary, after its traumatic bastardization and humiliation by the military, survived by being toughened from its experiences with the military. Judge comes to a new awareness:

JUDGE: I close the book of the prerogative of mercy against them. And their kind who masquerade in sheep's clothing. For ever! *(The Beatification* 104)

This is reinforced by his realization, howbeit with a sore back that "none of you lacked soul, it was a matter of finding out where it was hidden" (*The Beatification* 106). Judge has emerged from his ordeal with a conviction to abandon mysticism and face reality, and that reality is keeping "those vandals from interfering and rivaling my prerogative with a bestial conflagration." (*The Beatification* 106).

Work Cited.

Crehen, Stewart. "The Spirit of Negation in the Works of Soyinka." *Research in African Literatures.* 21/4, 1990.

Soyinka, Wole. *Collected Plays 1*. Oxford: Oxford University Press, Oxford, 1973.

_____. *Collected Plays 2*. Oxford: Oxford University Press, Oxford, 1974.

_____. *Art, Dialogue and Outrage*. Ibadan: New Horn Press, Ibadan, 1988.

_____. *The Beatification of Area Boy.* Ibadan: Spectrum, Ibadan, 1999.

Udoeyop, Nyong. "Soyinka and the Messianic Theme." *Critical Essays and Research in African Literatures.* No.1, 1997.

Wilkinson, Jane. *Talk with African Writers,* London: Heinemann, 1992.

23

Who Authorizes The Discourse?

The Subject of Nation in Soyinka and Ngugi.

ONYAEMACHI UDUMUKWU

I

The attempts to understand the significance of literary production must begin by questioning the philosophical and ideological assumptions behind texts. This is because the recreation of social experience through literature is animated by that Kantian truth, namely, that "all thinking, all positioning, is an I-think". In this regard, literary creativity represents this truth in the light of possible worlds. Therefore, literary criticism must engage itself in the attempts to illuminate the specific order or gestalt at work in any given literary situation. It is too easy to see words such as "gestalt" and "order" as indices to what M.H. Abrams has identified as the constants of literary criticism. By this it is hoped that the goals of the critic can be achieved from the point of view of either the work, or the world, or the writer or even the reader. However, these constants are merely shades of the same order. Thus, "constants" can become what must be there at any given point. Is the critical endeavor then, condemned in an act of repetition?. Are there possible points of exit or even continuity? Continuity and repetition are not used simply in the sense of sameness. Repetition essentially leads us back to a fixed point while continuity manifests as a conscious attempt to explore possibilities. In other words, continuity privileges sensibilities tending towards change while repetition draws consciousness to a dead-end.

The real question of African literary scholarship in the new millennium is not the absence of an authentic "I-think", the problem is the absence of a genuine effort to interrogate this "I-think" in the light of a specific world understood in space and time. Interrogation opens the possibility to understand the patterns of change. This process of interrogation is essentially relevant to the question of the nation in the African novel. Even though it was widely ridiculed in the past as a fabric in a large situational narrative, the African novel is becoming increasingly important as proving ground for questioning and articulating new possibilities for the nation. The nation emerges not as a fixed point of genesis but as panoply of voices and ideological interests. This panoply of voices finds authentic articulation in the novel of Wole Soyinka and Ngugi wa Thiong'O particularly *Season of Anomy* and *Petals of Blood*.

Understanding the relationship between the works of Soyinka and Ngugi and the nation demands an articulation of forms of difference- ethnic, gender, urban, rural, power, and religious. This is very important because the works of these two writers are inscribed both in the economy of communication, discourse, domination and power. Although it is important to make a distinction between textual space and political space, these are ultimately interwoven in the process of subjectification. As Homi Bhabha has reiterated in his case for "otherness", the "epithets racial or sexual come to be seen as modes of differentiation..." (Bhabha, 1994:150).

The interrogative, "who authorizes the discourse?" is predicated on the assumption that producers of discourse are rational decision-makers who must take into account the reasoning of other decision-makers and manipulate the expressive power of the signifier in order to achieve their goals. It goes beyond the so-called transactional function of language which expresses definite content, to the interactive function which focuses more on the expression of social relations and personal attitudes. Besides, this interrogative implies that the drama of everyday life in the nation demands a rethinking of forms and forces of identification. This interactive format of language intensifies in the novels of Soyinka and Ngugi in order to represent the actions of subjects. What animates my understanding of discourse here is the central conception in deconstructive criticism that all texts are constructive modes of signification that war against each other. This can be interwoven with Mikhail Bakhtin's concept of the dialogic nature of literary texts particularly in the sense that they present a number of independent and often conflicting voices, consciousness, none of which unifies or is superior to the other. Bakhtin asserts, that:

> We are taking language not as a system of abstract grammatical categories, but rather language conceived as ideologically saturated, language as a world view... (Bakhtin, 1934:232).\

This is consistent, with the view that the hardest test that the study of the African novel faces in the post-colonial and post-apartheid era is how it can rethink its own strategies in the light of ideological and political commitment. *Petals of Blood* and *Season of Anomy* will serve as indices to the type of text which, as Deirdre Burton has explained, "have something to say that goes beyond the confines of the text" (Burton, cited in Birch, 1989:30).

This, then, brings me to the issue of the subject. The exact meaning of the term is lacking. According to Pile and Thrift (1995:11) the subject has became a primary element of being and the Cartesian notion of the subject as a unitary being which is universal, neutral and gender-free is in error" (Pile and Thrift, 1995: 19). One way of negotiating the subject is in Althusser's definition of the subject of ideological formations. In this regard the individual has the value either as a free subjectivity a centre of initiative, or as a subjected being who submits to a higher authority and is stripped of freedom. I will chart out the figuration of the subject of the nation in Soyinka's *Season of Anomy* and Ngugi's *Petals of Blood*. The motivations and actions of the characters of Soyinka and Ngugi function inexorably to draw the nation away from global paradigms, into concrete specificity of social conditions. Thus, the characters become paradigmatic of efforts to construct endless centres of meaning in the nation.

II. Season of Anomy

Within the context of understanding who is authorizing the discourse of the nation Soyinka's *Season of Anomy* poses the problem of understanding the nation born of active self-questioning and self-reflexive action. In this regard, the story Soyinka's novel tells is animated not by a concern for the mechanistic master plot of Nigerian history as its origin. Rather this story is marked by the sense of becoming and being. A central idea that emerges in the work is that the crisis of nationhood can be negotiated on the account of our involvement and generation of the nation as a continuous process rather than as a closed political system. It is this type of involvement that animates the actions of the main character, Ofeyi. I intend to explore how Ofeyi's anxiety and perception of origin can lead to an understanding of the operation of the subject in *Season of Anomy*.

The distinction between origin and continuity in this novel is indebted to the current attempts in theory to map the difference between a conception of language as a fixed point of genesis and the conception of language as the basis for contesting meaning. In other words, origin is nurtured by a belief that the text, the final form of language in literature, springs from a point in a historical dimension that is its origin. Also, it assumes, then, that the language is the means of possessing the world. Continuity, by contrast, is used here in the sense of the text as a rhetorical entity that acquires identity on the basis of an arbitrary movement of self-criticality whereby language becomes a means of constructing others and for constructing ourselves. What is at stake here is a dialectic between nature, as origin, and its potentiality in action. The destination of the signifier lies not in this origin, but in its synchronic becoming. Ofeyi functions as the metaphor of the signifier unfolding itself out.

The difference between origin and continuity in Soyinka's novel is not born out of a simple pattern of opposition. The difference will crystallize when one explores the paradigmatic potentials of the two words. Origin connotes genesis, birth, genealogy and nature. Repetition, connotes genesis, birth, genealogy and nature. Continuity, by contrast, by contrasts connotes the sense of rebirth, restoration, renewal and redemption. Also, repetition has a significatory potential as mimicry, representation, and parody. The common value in the considerations of repetition is a desire to be different, to start all over again and to regain what was lost. The difference between origin and continuity in Soyinka's text is meant to elaborate one of the significant values of narrative fiction in our world. As I have already noted, what is of value here is not the creation of a master plot for the nation. The difference lies in the fact that narrative fiction takes on significance as the representation of the immanent tension and fissures of our society. Its story begins because all forms of origin tend to expel freedom from reality. That is to say, that narrative fiction acquires its identity because life is constituted by contradiction. Life here is another way of expressing origin. As Harry Levin has cautioned, narrative does not necessarily make us happy "when the road is muddy". (Levin, 23). Narrative, then, enables man to solve the contradictions of his objective condition in order to gain redemption. For the purpose of interpretation, it is important to note that origin and continuity manifest in multiple directions. That is it to say, that neither origin nor continuity develop through one single thread. On the contrary, they are woven with diverse forms of thread.

Soyinka's perception of origin is animated by what Hegel has called the inwardness of spirit withdrawing into its own domain (Kahler, 1973 qted in Miles, 1979:24). In his preface to *Myth, Literature and the World,* this origin manifests as "self-apprehension". Origin in this sense manifests as genius, original, or eccentric. This means, that the subject is defined by his eccentricity or transcendence of the group. The literary text becomes the product of a mind regressing into itself away from communal centre. This inward turn in Soyinka's perception of origin animates his other works. In the poem, "Abiku", the persona celebrates his eccentricity and transcendence of the community. This inward withdrawal to self is represented through language. In the thirty two lines poem, the "I" and its variants are used eleven times. In the last two lines we are told that "... Abiku moans, shaping/mounds from the yolk." "Shaping mounds from the yolk" means that the Abiku as origin is already shaping graves from the womb. Also, in *Death and the King's Horseman* this inward turn crystallizes in the hubristic act of Elesin and the redemptive act of Olunde. Soyinka's story in *Season of Anomy* is animated by this opposition between origin and continuity. This opposition becomes the guiding thread to the conflict, message and characterization. In this reading of *Season of Anomy*, I will examine origin in terms of genealogy (i.e. origin in a moral sense).

This sense of origin manifests in the distinction between Aiyero and Ilosa which are the dominant settings in the novel. This distinction in the landscape of the narrative is established in the first section of the novel, "seminal". First we are led into Aiyero. Thus:

> A quaint anomaly, had long governed and policed itself, was so single-kit that it obtained a tax assessment for the whole populace and paid it before the departure of the pith-helmeted assessor...held all property in common,- such an anachronism. (2).

One can note the features that mark the identity of Aiyero. It is named as "a quaint anomaly" and "it long governed and policed itself"; it is "single-knit' and "held all property in common" (2). An important attribute in this declaration is that a voice is made present. The present, as Derrida says, is that from which "we are able to think time" (Derrida, 166). At the same time, presence here banishes the possibility of another because the voice that is present is subject and centre. Who is this presence that can declare the other as "quaint"? To what order of interest does this discourse appeal? Present here is a mark of origin. The account begins with the discourse of Ilosa presenting itself as the origin and the authentic.

However, a common denominator emerges in this naming process. This is the factor of identity imputed in the presence of voice. Identity is the quality of being different. Therefore, we are led to a difference between Aiyero and Ilosa. But as this difference crystallizes, language becomes a means of possession. That is to say, by naming the features of Aiyero, the narrator takes possession of the landscape. Thus, Aiyero is referred to as "such an anachronism" which supports the very first name given earlier when the landscape is described as "a quaint anomaly".

However, as in all forms of naming process, a paradox is revealed as we are told that:

A definitive guffaw from the radical centres of debates headed by Ilosa a, dismissed Aiyero as the prime, example of unscientific communalism, primitive, and embarrassingly sentimental (2).

Here another landscape is introduced, viz.: "Ilosa." It is ascribed the quality as the head of radical centres of debates". The interesting fact about Ilosa is manifest in the way language is used. The narrator introduces it with a declarative, thus: 'a definitive guffaw:...." As in all forms of declarative which is used to name, Aiyero is "dismissed". Note the use of indefinite article in "guffaw" to represent the persons engaged in these radical centres of debates. Besides, these personages see themselves as subjects who can name others in language. Nevertheless by naming the other, these subjects name themselves. This is because there is a hint that Ilosa is a profit-hungry" society. As it turns out, its quest for profit makes Ofeyi the promotion man to take his team down to Aiyero. Also, the "guffaw" which is both a voice and a presence brings into being the identity of a different dimension of discourse and human society. But that "guffaw' is a fractured signifier that discloses Ilosa in its contradiction. It is "profit hungry", an indication of a state of desire. Its cynicism is opposed to the communalism and sentiment of Aiyero.

Therefore, the distinction between Aiyero and Ilosa is predicated on the sense of origin as genealogy. This is because each of the centres is constituted by distinct value systems. The value system in Aiyero, that is its moral foundation is rooted in what is called "the religion of the grain"(10). But Pa Ahime is quick to point out that:

why give it a name? We don't give of one. We don't even think of it as a religion, only as a way of life. Call it a philosophy if you like.(10)

Aiyero's sense of identity is rooted in this "religion of the grain" which is also a "way of life". However, it bears the mark of what I have identified as the "inwardness of spirit". This is because it issues out as the self-manifesting itself. In other words it is a sense of self of the founder living out his own presence and voice. As Ahime tells Ofeyi:

> No son his [founder] concern was to found a way of life, a near-copy of what he grew up with a Aiyetomo, but without paying-service to dubious gods. (11)

There is a lot here that reminds one of biography and origin. In simple terms, it means that Aiyero's identity issues out of what its custodian has perceived as authentic. Authenticity here lies in an origin in Aiyetomo, the parent community. By being a "near-copy", Aiyero is generated on the basis of dispersal. But since it is a dispersal that is at once a trace of the inward turn of the self, origin becomes the germ of self-sublimating itself to a reason. I think that origin here does produce the relationship between Aiyero and Aiyetomo on the basis of ancestor-worship. References are made to the custodian as the dominant paternal subject: He is "our departed founder", and "the founding Elder". Also, the detail of the funeral ceremony portrays this sensibility for the worship of ancestor (11-13). What type of mental picture does this portray? What order at feeling and thought does the link between Aiyero and Aiyetomo project the reader? Aiyero and Aiyetomo are only mere signs in their own right. But they acquire meaning and operational sense in the light of this sense of meaning—intention. It is from this meaning that I will make three comments here in order to explain this meaning-intention. First, the later part of Ahime's account, viz.: "but without paying-service to dubious gods", does anticipate a situation in *Ake: The years of childhood* as we see the author with Ransom Kuti. In this instance, the latter reminds him thus, "You must take an interest! Don't just stick your nose in that dead book you are reading" (Soyinka, 1981:228). This is linked with the second comment I want to make. In this case the detail of the custodian's funeral reminds us of a main issue in the *Death and The King's Horseman*.

The identity of Aiyero unfolds as Ofeyi seeks to understand the philosophy of the community. Thus:

"Is it time to tell me the secrets of Aiyero?" he asked him finally. "What do you wish to know exactly? Our story is a long one. (80)

Ahime becomes the guide to the identity of Aiyero. Ahime, as we are told, played the role of Chief Minister to the Custodian of the Grain. In this capacity, then, he has the experience to narrate the basis of the identity of, Aiyero. Before Ahime takes his turn, the narrator comments that Aiyero is "the earliest theocracy on the coast"(p.9). there, Ahime leads us to a description of the origin of the commune:

We do not believe ... in the shackles of memory. We are here, we prosper and we know harmony. It surfaces. It is the first principle we teach our children, they grow up despising dead knowledge whose nature is the nature of what is gone , dead, rotted. We founded Aiyero to seek truth, a better life all the things which men run after (9).

This narration on the identity of Aiyero creates the room for Soyinka to comment on his view on memory and the relationship between post origin and the nation state. Memory, for him should not become a shackle. That frees action. The critical issue is not that we should forget. It is rather that of how to make our memory of the past to be of relevance to the present. The issue of memory intersects with the relationship between past origin and the nation. In this regard Soyinka is insistent that the nation should be perceived as a fusion of two horizons. We are told that Aiyero did not fall from the sky ready made. It is embedded in its origin in Aiyetomo. Although it has separated itself from its origin, there is an indication that one cannot understand Aiyero without a recourse to the origin. Nevertheless, the past does not become a final vocabulary for the present. In a sense, I think that the link between Aiyero and Aiyetomo is sympathetic of the homology that exists between the nation state and the African, past. In other words, Soyinka is insistent that the nation is embedded in the African world. Set the nation needs to make a new sense of the African world in the light of new realities and challenges. This is why Ahime insist "we founded Aiyero to seek truth, a better life all the things which men run after. (9) That is to say, the nation acquires its significance in the light of new forms of social responsibility in the African world I think that this recalls what Soyinka has affirmed in early 1960s about the role of the writer in the modern African state. It is, he says, "...important to underscore this theme of social responsibility because the configuration of the nation does not freeze it in a global and undifferentiated African past. Besides this understanding of the link between the past origin and the nation is hinged on Soyinka's attack on negritude. "Negritude is simply the sum total of civilized values of the black world", (Senghor 1965 qt. in Nkosi 1981: 28). But are these values fixed and immutable? Soyinka's attack stems from what he perceives as the narcissism of negritude, and its penchant to fix forms of totalization. Therefore, as Ahime asserts: "they [the children of Aiyero] grow up despairing dead knowledge whose nature is the nature of what is gone dead, rotted". In this regard Ahime's assertion re-echoes Soyinka's earlier experiment and aversion of the narcissism of negritude.

The identity of Aiyero, then, is articulated in the image of the "religion of the grain". This is less a religion as such than an ontological system of values. The image of the grain is significant. This image relates the grain to the fusion of the nation and origin. In other words, it is an ontological system that insists on seeking out truth now. This is because grain has relevance as it meets the need for today and not the past.

Moreover, when we place this ontological essence in the light of character and action it will be seen that often explains the identity in the light of the goat. The youth of Aiyero are conscious of their origin. As such they are presented as impervious to the corruption in the cities where they have travelled to. So despite their travels abroad, they always returned to their Aiyero roots. This confirms Ofeyi's worries:

> And this was the unusual feature which intrigued the cocoa promotions man. They all returned. The near cities could not lure them away. The umbilical cord no matter how far it stretched never did snap. (3)

Soyinka's confident fusion of narrative clarity and sunny lyricism reveal two levels of sense in this account. The story here is about long-ing, yearning to be different than actuality. Thus, there is the longing of the youths (Aiyero's restless generation) for the bright light of modernity—a longing that is at the same time suffused with a deeper sense of roots. There is also the longing of Ofeyi for another reality different from the brutal opportunism of the Cartel. Aiyero meets that desire. Hence he sees the need to align with the youths in order to actualize his desire: "The waters of Aiyero need to burst their banks. The grain must find new seminal grounds or it will atrophy and die" (p.6). This has a significance for the nation, viz.: that the nation needs to eschew all forms of ethnocentrism originating from distinct ances-tral roots. The people who belong to different ethnic settings need to open up to the new realities in the nation.

At this point, one sees two options left for Ofeyi. The first is to join the people of Aiyero and inject new blood into their commune as the new Custodian of the Grain. This is the desire of Ahime. But Ofeyi chooses an alternative line of action-mobilize the entire youth of Aiyero in order to undermine the inordinate and crass growth of the Cartel.

In all, Ofeyi arrives at his decision for action when he perceives ori-gin not as an amputee buzz word, but as a moral reality. He calls into question the value of the Cartel and then articulates on alternative value by critiquing all existent values.

Soyinka's presentation of Aiyero is quite significant. This is because the identity of Aiyero will mark the basis for apprehending Ofeyi's action. By understanding the identity of Aiyero, Ofeyi succeeds in placing the commune against the grain of the contradictions in the Cartel. Thus he arrives at a consciousness viz., the need for the ideals of Aiyero to burst beyond its boundary. In this Ofeyi is not a mere dreamer. This reminds one of the case made by Roger Poole, viz.:

> All knowledge which does not inwardly relate itself to exis-tence, in the reflection of inwardness, essentially indifferent ... knowledge has a relationship to the knower who is essen-tially any existing individual; and for this reason all essential knowledge as related to this existence. (Poole, 100)

In other words, Ofeyi relates his know-how (knowledge) of Aiyero to

337

his own reality as an essential part of the Cartel. His knowledge activates his action and decision.

Obey's first action manifests as an attempt to extend the community's values beyond its boundaries. How can the ideals of Aiyero, then, be extended to the entire nation? First, this brings us to the initial question of "who is authorizing the discourse": Ofeyi or Aiyero? Here Soyinka gives us a paradox. We are told that the Founder is searching for the new Custodian of the Grain".(4) Also, we are told that "Aiyero adopted you almost as soon as we set eyes on you. (5) The paradox unfolds as we try to understand whether the founder is searching for the new Custodian of the Grain. (4) Also we are told that "Aiyero adopted you almost as soon as we set eyes on you. (5) Does it mean that the custodian has no confidence on the youth? Also, is Ofeyi truly working or bring the ideas of Aiyero to the world or is it that Aiyero is using him to project itself? The solution to this paradox lies in the fact that Soyinka is rejecting the idea of an abstract subject and can impose itself at will on society.

Ofeyi envisions the possibility of adopting the Cartel's strategy of capitalist pattern of investment in the developing context such as Nigeria, in order to create a new generation with its base in Aiyero. He sees this as his "official scheme". The Cartel like all foreign monopolies invest huge capital in the extractive industry based on cocoa as the chief raw material. The first set of conflict in the novel is rooted in the type of relationship between cocoa and Ofeyi and the Cartel respectively. The Cartel's conception of cocoa is puddle economic in terms of its drive to expand its financial and profit base. The Cartel views Aiyero as a potential place of domination that will eventually increase its monopoly over the cocoa produce and market in a way, Ofeyi; as the Cartel's promotion man, has set out on this same pedestal. For we are told that his mission to Aiyero is part of the superstructure of the Cartel. Thus:

> Even the Corporation, intent and ever expanding cocoa drive took, note of a new market for cocoa-fit and cocoa-viz. Ofeyi the promotions man took his team down to Aiyero. (2)

Note that Ofeyi is the promotion man for the driving force of the cartel, its ever-expanding cocoa drive". But the conflict ensures because once Ofeyi comes into contact with a "pouch of Aiyero's soil"(p.19) we see a change in his perception of cocoa. Rather than working in consonance with the purely economic interest of the Cartel Ofeyi assumes a more symbolic and ideological perception. The cocoa acquires a meaning. Much deeper than the profit motive. It acquires a more spiritual essence. This essence crystallizes in his "scheme". (19) In short it means using the strategies of the Cartel to fight the Cartel. Thus, rather than his preoccupation with a shallow world of jungles and debasement we see him acquiring a new sense of value and attachment to the earth.

This brings us back to a phrase used earlier on viz.: "Ofeyi's worries". Indeed, what is the basis of his worries? Is he worried that the people of Aiyero are dominated by a monopoly? Or, is it that he is worried that the people are poor? It is better to see his worries as predicated on an awareness that people are degraded by a maniacal profit-hungry system that has colluded with the military superstructure (RSA). In this regard, his worry is less with Aiyero than with Ilosa and the monstrous Cartel. Ofeyi's is chagrined that Ilosa has lost its soul and now wallows in the "... superstructure of robbery, indignities and murder, new phase of slavery." (27) Within the hierarchy of the Cartel itself, we are told that:

> The Cartel marionettes had long silted beggared vision molding to the last into a sunset apotheosis. (p.48).

It is this lack of vision that is Ofeyi's disgust. Soyinka vivid tapestry of visual imagery and innuendos project the degradation occasioned by the Cartel. The Cartel marionettes, we are told, have sailed beyond vision, i.e. one lost, and lack a sense of direction. Its guiding principle of mamonism has produced in turn, a "sunset apotheosis" i.e., the Cartel has became a dead god. The effects of this, degradation is not only physical but mainly biological. This biological destruction is manifest in the Trouble-shooter who has come from the headquarters to investigate the activities of Ofeyi His attitude is down..... chemical in approach prior to his arrival the chairman has been reminded from headquarters thus . "... head of that headless corpse which should be inferred as quickly as decently practicable. Etc. Etc."(p.50). Accordingly the Trouble Shooter has come to perform autopsy on the 'headless corpse",. The Trouble-shooter himself is perceived as "a piece of effrontery "(p.50). and "his inane grin which failed to mask the arrogance of their Trouble-shooter"(p.51). when he speaks he "spoke like chapters from a book"(p.51). All these serve as indices to the extent the cartel has corrupted human nature.

Another example of such degradation is manifest in the character, the Dentist. There is an alarmist disposition sounded as the narrator introduces the Dentist: Through Ofeyi's extended flashback we are told that" The doors swung open and a stranger intruded flesh and blood. Ofeyi winged. He was black too (p.94). In other words the mere appearance of the Dentist produces a sense of revision, that type of feeling that causes one to recall. Soyinka's use of visual imagery is profound. The movement of the doors balances with the action of the "stranger" to reproduce the innate violent nature in the Dentist.

Chapter seven, the second sub-division under the section "Tentacles" is filled with scenes of physical violence. These panoply of violent execution and outright savagery as the climax of the degradation that is the product of the activities of His Cartel. We are told that:

> Twenty miles from Irelu a woman was dragged from her bed, sliced open at the belly ... A fax assessor, she had beggared many ruthlessly in slavish obedience to the Cartel (p.109).

This scene of murderers revenge, we are told is supervised by the Dentist. When we meet the Dentist he explains this butchery as predicated on an attempt to "take control of that violence and direct it with a constructive economy (p.111). But for him it seems, violence exists of a violence's sake. Here Soyinka's presents the Dentist's sense of violence action as opposed to the philosophy of violence that is present, say in the work of Frantz Fanon. For Fanon, violence in the final analysis is recuperative and restoration . this is because farm champion's a type of violence that will through revolutionary praxis lead to charge. But the Dentists act of physical violence envisages no change. It is essentially a morbid act of willful extermination. The lesson here can be understood when we see the Dentist as a by-product of the Cartel. The dentist ordinarily pulls out the teeth. By extension, the cartel has pored a horrific type of violence that removes the "tech" from the nation by shearing men of their souls. The Dentist asserts: Beyond the elimination of men I know to be destructively evil, I envisage nothing.'(p. 112). This is the type of scheme that worries Ofeyi. This insensate destruction of lives.

Opposed to this, however, he renders the basis for action which is:

recovery of whatever has been seized from society by

a handful, remolding society itself. (p.117)

In this project Ofeyi perceives that violence can become instrumental. He says: "I have not excluded the likelihood of violence".

I have dwelt extensively on the root and content of Ofeyi's worries. At the same time the character's worries and revulsion at the tapestry of internecine violence that gives his setting is symptomatic of the writer's repugnance and reaction against the state of crisis in the nation state in the post-colonial era. I share the view that Soyinka's narrative tell us something about our world which we can get from no other source. Therefore, what is that something that Soyinka is telling us by reproducing the worries and, of his main character? In order to understand this, let us recall that the representative of Ilosa as built on: "... superstructure of robbery, indignities and modern... new phase of slavery". Here Soyinka accentuates the crisis of the nation state in the post-independence era. This is because the nation is on a structure that privileges robbery ... and knew "phase of slavery". In other words the nation has come to a crisis because the political warlords represented as the "Cartel marionettes" have unleashed a new era of slavery on the nation.

III. Petals of Blood

The traditional reading of Ngugi's *Petals of Blood* tends to begin by securing a centre of consciousness on which the elements of action, plot, character and point of view revolve. Eustace Palmer argues accordingly, that:

Of all African novels [*Petals of Blood*] probably presents the most comprehensive analysis of the evils perpetrated in independent African Society by black imperialists (Palmer, 1979:153).

In other words, *Petals of Bloods* can be perceived as a typical mirror of the negation of political independence in Africa. Chidi Amuta re-echoes this focus of Ngugi's novel when he argues that:

It is perhaps the consciousness of the contradictions in the present day Kenyan society and its main agencies that constitutes the major focus of the novel (Amuta, 1986:171).

As we have emphasized understanding how the novel functions as instrument of social reconstruction of a national profit does not depend on this kind of apophantic identification with the contradictions of reality as such. In other words, narrative must not be secure in highlighting the "consciousness of contradictions" as Amuta would have argued which it is supposed the writer has put into the text. Rather it must reconstruct those contradictions in the light of our being as readers. It is important to stress that *Petals of Blood* was published in 1977. The crucial question therefore, is that of underscoring the implication of the novel in the light of increasing social problems in Africa twenty three years later. This implication crystallizes in the way the novel negotiates the crisis of nationhood. This can be done by reading the network of relation between the subjects of action.

Therefore, the novel reveals two levels of social discourse. On the one hand, we can see these levels in the actions and movements of two main characters, Munira and Karega. In this regard, the novel as a semiotic unit, narrates the relation between these subjects.

Furthermore, that relation crystallizes in the different discourse situations in the novel. The notion of discourse situation is rooted in the understanding that the internal structural properties of a text is implicit in the text's communicative intentions. Discourse Analysis, and other communicative oriented approaches recognize the text on the basis of its discuss situation which crystallize in the form of inter-action between participants. By focusing on the link between the participants in the discourse situation in relation to the different felicity conditions of the utterances, speech act theories go beyond a formalist account of text on the basis of literariness. As Maria Pratt has argued, in the speech acts deriving from the context of situation, the focus of literariness shifts complex relation to the nation. Thus it is important to note that Ngugi's novel constitutes a kind of complex or global speech act of narration that subsumes other local speech acts involving the narrators and the interaction of the characters. It is true that the discourse situation crystallizes in the interaction between Munira and Karega, but in addition we need to see that interaction in the light of the other levels of narration in the text.

Petals of Blood is a detective novel. The action moves in a circle. Nevertheless, it begins somewhere very close to the denouement. From the perspective of the discourse situations of the text we can redefine the detective story, following Donna Bennet, on the basis of the relations between author and reader. As in *Petal of Blood,* "the author provides the reader with the problematic piece of narrative early in the text.(. . .) Thus as the action unfolds we are intimated of a murder mystery:

> A man, believed to be a trade union agitator, has been held after a leading industrialist and two educationists . . . were last night burnt to death in Ilmorog (4-5).

As Bennet shows the detective story presents us with this kind of narrative with a topic. But this topic raises an implicit question: Who killed the men? Why? Who is the man under arrest? The answers are not provided by the topic. Therefore, since this text fails to provide the solution to the reader, the reader ten constructs the solution by reading the rest of the text for additional information (Bennet, 236). This reminds us of what Kupevelt has said about topicality and answers. If answers are unsatisfactory it gives room for further questioning (Kuppevelt, 814). As we reads the text, then, one encounters three main levels of discourse situations. Ngugi manipulates these levels to interact with the reader who in turn solves the problem for himself, and also to highlight the relationship between subjects. Munira's act of peech is shrouded in complexity due to an implicit intention to conceal the unspeakable act. The tension created between words and action crystallizes in a deliberate plan to mar his testament with a brush covered not with one coat but with a mix of tar. Therefore Munira uses the indirect speech act rather than direct illocutionary act. As Searle has noted indirect speech act is indicative that the same sentence may perform different acts in different circumstances. Indirect speech act enlarges our understanding of the possible functions of an utterance in an environment of use by moving beyond the primary concern to the secondary level. For instance the interrogative which is a sentence type can function both as an expressive and a declarative illocationary actions. Thus, as Munira receives his turn from inspector Godfrey, he goes into a lengthy preamble which is presented in the form of questions.

This can be better illustrated in terms of the relation between Munira and Karega. The bulk of the narrative is constituted as Munira's prison notes. As the action rises in chapter 3, Godfrey Munira receives his turn from the police officer, inspector Godfrey. That is to say, that at the instance of the police officer, Munira acquires a new role, not only as a character, but also as a narrator. As Maria Pratt would have described, this exchange of role can be said to have won Munira the "battle for the floor" . In other words, he conceives himself as a rational decision-maker contesting for a control on the narrative code with which he establishes relationship to the message and to social responsibility. Once his entrance to the floor is guaranteed, Munira takes us back twelve years before the beginning of the action. He begins thus: "How does one tell of murder in a New Town?... How recreate the past so that one can show the operation of God's law? The working out of God's will, the revelation of His will ..."(p.45. Is Munira sincere in the questions he asks? Even though Munira asks questions, he is at the sometimes performing the indirect illocutionary act of using the expressive. That means, he is expressing a particular psychological state of rationalizing the murder, as an act of God. Such indirect illocutionary act will serve the purpose of the reader as he constructs the mystery before him. In his action therefore, Munira unfolds his relation with the people of Ilmorog as a teacher, his relation with Wanja, Karega and Abdulla. Indeed, in the course of that narrative he goes even further back to the 1940s as he traces his growth from his family and school at Siriana. The important fact to note is that in the course of this narrative, Munira defines a distinct form of social responsibility. Karega, also in the course of the account, maps out a different set of social responsibility and level of discourse. Indeed it is in the difference between these characters that we can see Ngugi's vision for post colonial African. Despite their differences these two characters share something in common. The factor that binds them is the educational apparatus. First, they both attended Siriana High School from where they are dismissed on different occasions and for different reasons. Secondly, the educational apparatus brings them together in a teacher-pupil relationship with Munira teaching the other at this time. Then, thirdly, the educational apparatus again unites them as teachers in the Ilmorog Primary School. In this regard, education acquires a strong force in the narrative so that it enables us to see the difference of language games and social responsibility that bind and separate these characters.

Hilary Seymour has explored the dialectics of the educational theme in *Petals of Blood*. According to her this dialectic has revealed the basic contrast between the two main characters, Munira and Karega. She notes that Munira sees education, and, in fact teaching, as a means of escape, while Karega perceives education as a tool for action. (Seymour, 16-17) Indeed one agrees with this opinion on the underlying dialectics of the educational theme. But De am keen in discovering how it emerges as an essential fabric in the overall construction of the subject.

It is imperative then to explore the two theories of education enunciated by the characters. One needs to stress, also, that these two theories emerge from the perspective of Munira's narration. Towards the end of the ninth chapter one encounters a speech situation in the context of Abdulla's bar. In fact Munira narrates:

> . . . I invited all the teachers for a drink at Abdulla's place . . .
> I steered the conversation to the school and the teaching of
> certain subjects like history and civics (.245).

As the background is set, Munira as the addresser addresses Karega while pretending to be addressing all the teachers:

You see what they need to know are facts. Simple
facts. Information, just so that can pass their CPE.
Yes, information, not interpretation. Later when
they go to High School ... they can start learning the
more complicated stuff. By that time they will have
learnt how to think and can stark interpreting. I say
let's teach them facts, facts, and not propaganda
about blackness, African peoples, all that, because
that is politics ... (246).

This is representative of Munira's theory of education. It is anchored
in a basic distinction between fact and interpretation. When one
reads this in the context of Heideggers two "as" structures it can be
seen that for Murira education is constituted as an apophantic fact,
the description of things and facts as they are. It is this vision of life
that generates Munira's set of actions and interactions in the novel.
He insists that the educator should accept things as they are and also
the pupils should be willing to accept things on their face value.

Earlier in the narrative as Munira takes the children out in the
open to study nature, he learns to his consternation that the children's
imagination cannot be bracketed in his banking system of learning, a
type of learning that flourishes by rote and eschews interrogation.
Thus:

... he had never thought deeply about these things, and he
swore that he would never again take the children to the
fields (22)

The explanation for this is that:

enclosed in the four walls he was the master, dispensing
knowledge to a concentration of faces looking up to him.
There he would avoid being drawn in ... (22).

As he teaches he describes a flower as a "worm-eaten flower ... It cannot bear fruit" (22). In the course of his teaching Munira engages in a
speech situation with his pupils:

The boys cry: "There is a worm—a green worm with several hands or legs" (p.22)

Munira asserts:

right. This is worn-eaten flower . . .
It cannot bear fruit. That's why we must always kill worms ...
(p.22)

Here Munira is at his very best. it is said: "he was pleased with himself." His certitude cannot explain the craving of the boys for understanding the relationship between worms and flower. He describes the flower as "worm eater." The emphasis on the past participle highlights his penchant to present facts as they are and not to explain their inner dynamism or possibility. As a teacher Munira is adept at teaching ready-made stuff (p.23). But it is in this readiness that we see the irony in the interchange between him and his pupils. He is ironically, the worm that eats the flower. But even in this the ability to eat is finished. Thus on his readiness to teach ready-made-stuff he emerges as the "worm-eaten flower" which does not bear any intellectual fruit.

What kind of social responsibility and what type of discourse games can are deduce from Munira? First, one must put an alert finger on Munira's form of motivation. His is a begotted form of religious rationalism borne out of his attempts to rationalize his failures. At the hub of his actions, therefore, is a degenerate psychologism that, like the worm, destroys the life around it. We should take note of his penchant for inaction. Rather than acting to show himself socially responsible, Munira hides under invisible laws of destiny. He asserts over and over that: "No, there was a design, a law ..." (191). Social responsibility cannot be achieved in this way. This is because the man of action must break through the illusions of tradition, of destiny and like the athlete focus diligently into the mark of responsibility and victory.

But Munira is also a realistic creation. As a character he is a simulacrum of a certain type of subject positions which have emerged in post-colonial Africa. For one thing, this subject is secure, almost inebriated, in all forms of inherited structures. This is a subject that is fixated and stunted by the grips of common sense. In *Anthills of the Savannah,* Chinua Achebe represents this form of subjectivity in the light of the failure of political leadership to be fully objective. Thus, we are told, in that novel, that: "we have seen so much trouble in Kangan since the whiteman left because those who make plans for themselves only and their families" (Achebe, 212). More often than not such kind of subjectivity will rationalize its failures on abstract terms by inciting ethnocentric and religious sentiments. But social responsibility is vehemently opposed to this clandestine and fixated rationalism in the African World.

Karega, by contrast, perceives education as a crucial question in the understanding of reality in postcolonial and post-apartheid Africa. I will explore these challenges from Karega's perspectives in the light of three dimensions, viz.; *Education in the definition of self, education in the definition of being,* and *Education and social responsibility beyond the classroom.*

Karega unlike Munira realizes that education is not an act of repetition. As an aspect of the ideological state Apparatus, (ISA) (we recall Louis Althusser's distinction between Repressive Ideological Apparatus (RSA) and Ideological State Apparatus (ISA) education functions as a question by posing problems and initiating dialogue between teacher and pupil. But Karega realizes that for the man of action to function adequately in this dialogue as a rational decision-maker, then he must, first and foremost, redefine himself, and begin at his own *presencing.* That is to say, that the subject of action must come to terms with his own being. Literally, he must see himself as he is, in a state of ignorance. Thomas Fay interprets this condition of presencing as the subject's own primordial comprehension (*verstehen)"* (Fay, 23).

Thus, by assuming the position as a teacher Karega feels a release of a sort. He realises that release can only crystalize in "continuing with the dialogue he had started with himself at Siriana..." (p.109). Thus he confesses:

> to confront the expectant eyes of those who tomorrow would run away to the cities whose cruelty he had experienced and where they would face a future which held the hope of a thousand mirages, was at once to confront himself

in a way all are profound and painful because the problem and the questions raised went beyond mere personal safety and salvation ... (p.110).

In other words, even though the educator will necessarily begin with his experiences and comprehension, education does not become a tool for acquiring "personal safety and salvation . . ."
From the definition of self, then, Karega questions the relationship between education and being in post-colonial Africa. So, while Munira is secure within the walls of the classroom, Karega advocates for an education that breaks the barriers. First he questions:

What had education, history, and geography and nature study and maths, got to say to this drought [in Ilmorog]? (p. 110)

Drought here is essentially a fictional representation of the crisis of the nation state in post-colonial Africa. This can be compared with Achebe's use of 'drought' in relation to politics and leadership in *anthills of the Savannah*. Karega's interest is that of defining education's role of social problems.

In order to understand this role Karega sees through Munira's eyes the root of the contradiction in the educational system in Kenya. Thus:

after internal self-government, the colour bar in schools admissions and the allocation of teachers was removed. The result was that while the former African schools remained equally poorly equipped, they now also lost the best African teachers (p.107)

With this background, Karega articulates his own decisions. He affirms:

But whatever the decisions he would not be able to teach under these conditions where theory seemed a mockery of the reality (p.113)

How then does he proceed in his dialogue? First, he works to enlarge the consciousness of the pupils to see and understand themselves, their self-dignity and confidence. In addition, they should understand their peculiar relation with their world. So whereas Munira has hitherto caged them as animals in his classrooms, Karega insists that they recognize their own containment, and for them to see that containment in the context of their world. With Munira, the children "knew no world outside Ilmorog" (109). With Karega by contrast, the children begin to see Ilmorog and Kenya as constituted by a history, in relation with the global context.

This then leads us to Karega's theory of education. It is from this framework that we can understand the relationship between education and social responsibility. Thus, against Munira's banking system of education, he argues:

> I cannot accept that there is a stage in our growth as human beings when all we need are so-called facts and information. Man is a thinking being from the time he is born to the time he dies ... he sifts ... impressions in his mind to arrive at a certain outlook in his direct experience of life... Liberation: no child is ever too young to think about this: it is the only way he can truely experience himself as he collects, breaks, collects, rejects, assimilates and cries to discover himself. (246-7)

Education for Karega is man-centred. As such it must be alert to man's desire to understand himself and his world, and to understand the possibilities inherent in his actual conditions. Education for him must discover the nature of our differences, our relationships and our potentials. The functional education, in this regard, must begin at the hermeneutic stage of Heideggar's "as" structure.

Karega's social responsibility crystallizes in a recognition of the relationship between words and action. He recognizes that words are veritable instruments of action. Earlier the lawyer reminds him thus:

> You who will seek the truth about words emitted by a voice, look first for the body behind the voice. The voice merely

rationalizes the needs, "whims caprices" of its own, the master ... (200).

Through Karega words come to acquire a particular form of authority born out of a rational decision to chart a path out of inherited condition. Consequently, Karega's utterances are coded in a specific form of illocutionary act called the declarative. The declarative as an illocutionary act serve to bring about a state of affairs referred t. He declares for example:

"We can go to the city" (112) and 'I believe we can save the donkey and save the community'(113). Furthermore, "To understand the present ... you must understand the past ... (127). And then to Wanga he declares: "Wake up ... and see signs of dawn over Ilmorog"(230). In all these example what guides Karega's perception of words in the light of action is the peculiar relationship between the preparatory condition and the sincerity condition of his words. His preparatory conditions help us to see the contradiction in the context of his words. For example when he declares: 'To understand the present ... you must understand the past" we are led to the preparatory condition in the context of his speech situation with Wanja. Wanja sees no relevance of the past to the present. For her, and also for Munira, the present and the past are independent of each other. But Karega sees it differently. He recognizes two time frames. Therefore by declaring his utterance he also highlights a sincerity condition of the nature of his responsibility to the past and the present. His sincerity condition amounts to a responsibility to change the context identified at the preparatory condition. Infact at the sincerity condition Karega exercises his responsibility by bringing the presence of what was previously uncalled into a nearness. By doing this he leads us from the given to the unknown.

My reading of the subject of the nation so far has concentrated on two levels of discourse situations in *Petals of Blood* viz.: the communal narrator and the reader on the one hand, and the first person narrator ("I"- narrator and the reader, on the other hand. This then leaves out the second level of discourse situation in the novel. This is the level occupied by the third person omniscient narrator.

While the communal "we"-narrator places the entire action

against an abstract global context, the I-narrator presents the action as a testimony. The third person narrator mediates in the relationship between the first person narrators and the characters. He does this by weaving the essential fabric of the narration either by commenting on the actions and narration of other characters and narrators. By commenting on the actions and the narration of other characters, the third person gives added piquancy to the rhetorical purpose of the novel. This is because by creating the appropriate situation in Munira's account, for example, he allows the reader to discern the mystery behind the murder. We can cite a particular instance.

After we have gone through the mass of information originating in the mystery behind the murder of Ilmorog, we are invited to the solution by the third person narrator. Here he leads us to a discourse situation involving Munira and Inspector Godfrey: Godfrey asks: Mr. Munira ... what were you doing on Ilmorog Hill on the Sunday morning after the arson? (332) The third person narrator comments: "Munira looked at the officer. He read everything in his eyes." (332) We notice that in that commentary based on the interaction between Munira and the police officer, the third person narrator subtly reveals the clue: "He read everything in his eyes." What had seemed to Munira as a game of concealment, emerges into the light .But that disclosure is meant more for us as readers. The police already knows that Munira is the criminal they are looking for. But what remains is his self-confession. Thus, as the officer asks him: "why did you do it?" Munira responds: " I—I wanted to save Karega (332). From this point of discovery the third person rounds up the rest of the denouement.

Besides, the third person narrator's commentary unveils a very significant edge in the peculiar structural property of the novel, considered primarily as writing. This has to do with the fact that writing defers the true nature of self. The word defers have a peculiar significance in post-structuralist account of how texts mean. It means to put off, to delay, until a later date, or to postpone. To defer raises the important problem that meaning is never complete and never fully realized. This important attribute of meaning in the context of language games and social responsibility is signalled through Munira. By writing his account, he sets his statement as an assertion. But it is an assertion which is re-written as writing. We can appreciate this by recalling the peculiar characteristic of writing. As Terence Hawkes has explained, writing is committed to *space*. Therefore, by writing Munira makes himself visible within a physical presence in space. We can recall a specific sense in Heidegger's case for the relationship of dwelling to building. In that case man dwells by making himself present, *to preserve his presencing*. Also, by writing his account Munira is making himself present. He declares: "... I who was a privileged witness of the growth of Ilmorog ..." (45). But it is also in the presentation of his presence that we see the power of writing over the subject. This is because by writing his account as a witness he renders himself visible for signification. In other words, by writing his account, the otherwise *speakerly* Munira that one encounters in the opening section of the novel as the assured teacher and man of God is reconstructed as a criminal, arsonist, and murderer. The self-certitude of Munira is reconstructed through writing for us as readers to see him for whom he is. By making the subject present, the novel becomes an index for understanding the levels and patterns of action and interaction in the nation.

The acid test that the study of African narrative fiction must undergo in the post-colonial and post-apartheid era is how to rethink its own strategies. This can be achieved on the model of a post-structuralist account of peculiar structural properties of the narrative text. We have argued, therefore, that rather than conceiving the African novel as an attempt to speak for or to capture the African world, it should be understood in the light of the different attempts made in the post-colonial and post-apartheid condition to communicate the fundamental relationship between knowledge and experience. This overall objective is tested by reading the peculiar relationship between subjects in Ngugi's *Petals of Blood*.

Soyinka's Ofeyi and Ngugi's Karega share certain qualities in common. As subjects they go forth, refuse to be contained within the dominant structures of their contexts, and they are optimists. Ofeyi is a Nietzschean personality whose process of subjectification manifests in an interrogation of the structures of exclusion in the nation. Karega is essentially a Leninist. His going forth manifests in his fight against reification. Nevertheless, the difference between these two characters is indicative of the two authors' construction of the nation's people in the post-colonial context. Thus, Soyinka constructs Aiyero as an ideal that Ofeyi yearns for, an ideal that can become a model for an alternative. Ngugi, by contrast, uses Ilmorog in order to construct the people at the margin, i.e. people who are capable of subjectification. Their march to the city becomes the inauguration of change in Ilmorog. Although, ironically, the change pushes them more and more to the margin, Ngugi's ultimate theme is the people's figuration. This, then, reaffirms my case that the real problem of African literature is how to interrogate the identity of the nation. A study of Soyinka's Ofeyi and Ngugi's Karega has become an index for appreciating the process of subjectification in the nation.

Works Cited

Abrams, M.H. *A Glossary of Literary Terms*. New York, Holt, Rhinehart and Winston, 1993.

Achebe, Chinua. *Anthills of the Savannah*. Ibadan: Heinemann, 1987.

Althusser, Louis. "Ideology and Ideological State Apparatuses". In *Lenin, Philosophy and Other Essays*. New York: Monthly Review Press, 1971: 127-186.

Bakhtin, Mikhail M. "Discourse in the Novel" *The Dialogical Imagination* .Trans. M. Holquist and C. Emerson. Austin: University of Texas Press, 1981:269-305.

Bennet, Donn. "The Detective Story: Towards the Definition of Genre". *PTL*. 4 (1979):233-266.

Bhabha, Homi. *The Location of Culture*. London: Routledge, 1994.

Birch, David. *Language, Literature, and Critical Paractice: Ways of Analysing Texts*. London: Routledge, 1989.

Derrida, Jacques. *Of Grammatology.*Trans. Gayatri Chakravorty Spivak. Baltimore: The John Hopkins University Press, 1980

Fay, Thomas A. *Heidegger: The Critique of Logic*. The Hague Martinus Nijoff, 1977.

Kuppervelt, van Jan. "Main Structure and Side Structure in Discourse". *Linguistics,* 33 (1995): 809-833.

Levin, Harry. *The Gates of Horn: Five French Realists*. New York: Macmillan, 1967.

Miles, David H. "The Portrait of the Marxist a s Young Hegelian:Lukacs' Theory of the Novel". *PMLA,* 94:1(1979):22-35

Nkosi, Lewis. *Tasks and Masks:Themes and Style of African Literature*. London: Longman, 1981.

Ngugi wa Thiong'O. *Petals of Blood*. London: Heinemann, 1977.

Palmer, Eustace. *The Growth of the African Novel*. London:Heinemann, 1979.

Pile, Steve and Nigel Thrift. "Introduction". *Mpping the Subject: Geographies of Cultural Transformation*. London: Routledge, 1995: 1-51

Poole, Roger. *Towards Deep Subjectivity*. London: Allen Lane, 1972.

Pratt, Mary Louise. *Towards a Speech Act Theory of Literary Discourse*. Bloomington:Indin University Press, 1977.

Seymour, Hilary. "Pedagogical Politics in Ngugi's *Petals of Blood*". *Journal of the Literary Society of Nigeria*, No. 1 (1981):7-25.

Soyinka, Wole. *Ake, The Years of Childhood*. Ibadan: Spectrum Books, 1981.

_____. *Season of Anomy*. London: Rex Collins, 1972.

24

Life, Politics and Literature After May 29

The Meiningen Parley With Wole Soyinka

ONOOKOME OKOME

In the small former East German town, Meiningen, I met and talked with Prof. Wole Soyinka about my book project on his literary works and political activism since he won the coveted Nobel Prize for Literature in 1986. The book project came out of the proposed sixtieth birthday celebration, which was to have held at the National Theatre Complex, Iganmu, Lagos in June 1994, during the heydays of General Abacha's dictatorship. Against many odds, some of which I have already written about in the introduction to this volume of essays, the proposed celebration did not quite make the mark. At every turn, the convener, Odia Ofeimun, then the President of ANA, (Association of Nigerian Authors) was faced with very difficult choices.

· Outside the famous theatre, Meiningen Theatre Complex, where outstanding theatre technology in the art of dramatic performance took place in the early part of the 20th century, I had a wonderful time listening to Professor Wole Soyinka. He had come to attend the launch of the European edition of the World Encyclopedia on Contemporary Theatre, Volume III. The African edition of The World Encyclopaedia of

Contemporary Theatre was launched on July 6, 1997 in Yaounde, Cameroun. Soyinka could not attend because the political stakes were too high for his personal security. He had gone on exile to overcome the frightening rule of the dictator, General Sanni Abacha. Yaounde was far too close to the Nigerian soil. Soyinka may not have considered that enough security was provided for his personal safety.

The Meiningen meeting was quite a way for Soyinka to show that he is still in touch with his primary constituency. It was mostly his work in drama that gave him the Nobel Prize for Literature because it was in drama that, according to the Swedish Academy, he "fashioned the drama of existence".

Outside the Meiningen theatre complex, Soyinka and I talked about my book project on his post-Nobel literature as well as the prospects of the newly restored democracy in his (my) country, Nigeria. And when the meeting finally came to an end and Soyinka walked elegantly away from the street-side café in that small, well-laid out Meiningen Street, I could not help being marveled at the figure who has created such great awareness in the politics and literature of my country. This was shortly after the May 29, 1999 hand-over when the former General of the Nigerian Army, Olusegun Obasanjo, fondly called Uncle Sege, was inaugurated as the democratic president of the Nigerian Federation.

Onookome: How are things shaping out in Nigeria? I know you are aware of things happening at home.

Soyinka: Well . . . I think what one is going to see are tensions within the new government – that is in the running of the new government. These tensions will be between the newly elected persons who are not ordinarily used to operating in a democratically elected administration. We are also going to see tensions in the relationship between the new president and some powerful Nigerians, in and outside government. Tensions will also be replicated in the party structure and in the houses of assembly. As to how these tensions would translate in terms of positive development is better left to the imagination.

Onookome: Would there be more sacrifices demanded of the people who are generally more concerned for a genuine move towards true democracy?

Soyinka: Well . . . nothing can be certain at the moment. This is why I do not want to predict how these tensions will be resolved but they will definitely dictate how little or how much sacrifice that the people will have to make. So one cannot pretend to predict how they will translate in terms of how much will be needed of the people's sacrifice. It seems to me that we will be in the realm of psychological rather than purely political battle.

Onookome: I ask this question in connection with my reading of your dramatic texts. In your dramatic texts, your preoccupation seems to me to be focused on the crucial role that the redeeming personage must give to society at periodic intervals to ensure continuity. The redeeming factor, that is the human agency, is often imbued with the spirit of Ogun, your patron god. Are we likely then to see redeeming qualities of Ogun's children in the new political dispensation?

Soyinka: Well . . . my understanding of your question is that you have chosen to describe the agents of change, the makers of the creative impulse, in this manner. This is your interpretation, not mine. So whatever name you choose to give to them, I believe that what will eventually guarantee change is the triumph of the creative instinct in society. Creativity in literature is not just thinking. Nation builders are very creative people. The formulators of national psyche are creative people – people with vision who see clearly what they want to put across into the new being. I think this experience matters a great deal. And I think there is so much difficulty in a country like Nigeria. And this shows that the masses are still being repressed, brutalized, and marginalized. Suspicion is rife everywhere and people cannot make out what are their rights anymore, especially when it pertains to their own privileges. People are so sacred that everyone displays one form of timidity or the other. Everybody. The land becomes the home of timidity. Timidity becomes part of the psyche of a good proportion of the people. So what you refer to as Ogun's children will always be suppressed in this situation.

They will always be in problems, in trouble with the perpetrators of this darkness, this mayhem. They will always be trouble because the oppressors know that society would not always be the way it is. They know that society can be something else. . . can attain a level of organization different from what it is currently.

Onookome: What do you see as contribution towards this change you speak about in relation to the direction of the new democracy and the problems in the Niger Delta?

Soyinka: The Niger Delta . . . people do not seem to understand the problem in that section of the country in relation to the rest of the country. In the sixties, if you like, it was the problem of the MIDDLE BELT. It was the region in which self-determination and identity were played out. I happen to know a lot about this because of my politics and the people with whom I was associated. It was a very crucial battle. It was one in which divided the Nigerian army. It has been written about and mentioned by a number of officers in the forces. At that time, many Nigerians did not know what was going on in the Tiv region of the country. But the Commanding Officers who were sent there to go and suppress the natural aspirations of Tiv people who were sick and tired of oppression of certain hegemonic power at the centre saw at close quarters the pains and anguish of the Tiv people. This kind of feeling has been with us for a long time. What is happening in the Niger Delta is not surprising in the least. It has only come into the forefront of national matters because of the petroleum factor . . . because of the global interest which it generates. Petroleum is at the heart of the matter. Big multinationals are also involved. But the issue of nation identity is not a new one in Nigeria. It has been with us even before we obtained independence. With all the attempts to suppress it, I do not think it will go away just like that. And this is because of the long historical background of each contesting nationalities. The Niger Delta people are more conscious now of their role in the economy. In addition to the wealth that is being taken away from their soil, the people of the Niger Delta are worried that their heritage will be degraded forever. I have known this long before now, long before Ken Saro-Wiwa came to see me with his Ogoni Bill of Rights. I saw the stories which were published in the *Guardian* concerning the degradation of the area, the crude oil wells. I have flown in low airplane over that area. I have seen the permanent emission of gas into the atmosphere which has gone on for years. What do you think happens to the vegetation? What do you think happens to the air? What do you think happens to water? So there has been a persistent ecological disaster and degradation and as far as the oil wells are there, something was bound to happen. And so it was to the credit of the Guardian Newspaper, amongst others, this plight was highlighted.

As far back as 1985, when I won the Agip Prize, I went to the Niger Delta to check what was happening in that area before I agreed to accept it. I actually went to check the records of Agip in that area before I decided that I was going to accept that Prize. And I was pleased to find that, at least, Agip was one of the most progressive. I am not saying that they are perfect or anything of the sort, no! But it is certainly progressive. I discussed with the representative of Agip in Lagos about the complaints which I heard during my investigation. And I was satisfied with certain explanations which he gave me. Some of the problems of the Niger Delta came from the Chiefs who are acting as representatives and intermediaries for the people. I thought there was a plausible case there. May be I did not investigate enough. I don't know. But I am telling you all of this to make you understand that I have been personally involved in the affairs of the Niger Delta long before the bubble exploded. And the problem is going to continue. It is going to continue until the central government recognizes the fact that there has to be autonomy. It is not just a matter of democracy. There ought to be a level of autonomy and re-arrangement of the resource-sharing formula in the nation. You may elect anyone into parliament, but except this re-arrangement is done, the previous generation will prove to be far more violent than the other.

Onookome: What kind of autonomy will you recommend to end this kind of anarchy again?

Soyinka: Negotiations. Treatment of all nationalities as equal parts, not as marginalized servants contributing to the national purse and only being given the left-overs. In other words, any formula of resource-sharing must be equitable. What is important is the recognition of the fact that there are minor independent entities. These are entities that deserve a certain measure of autonomy and control over their resources, whether it is petroleum or even value added tax (VAT). Such display of inequality that we are talking about affects national productivity. Even in dialogue and negotiations, not everybody is going to be satisfied. But if everybody within the political totality recognizes the fact that we are all interested co-partners, then compromises will be made based on terms of a common ground. But as long as someone is sitting at the centre, even if he is an elected person, passing laws that are binding on the various regions, we will still be in the same mess.

Onookome: Let me turn your attention to Ken Saro-Wiwa. What do you consider his legacy as a writer and environmental activist?

Soyinka: I think his greatest contribution is his satirical wit, his humour, his deflation of sacred cows and his very conscious and highly successful manipulation of the art of writing. I can talk about his able involvement in the production of soap like *Bassey and Company* and so on. As far as I am concerned, *Bassey* is as good as any soap operas as you can find anywhere. Ken Saro-Wiwa has an impressive sense of humour and satire. And then as an activist . . . his sense of talent for organization. He moved people in a way which very few people can do. Of course, people must also learn from his mistakes. I do not see any leader who doesn't make mistakes.

Onookome: Would you agree that one of such mistakes was that he concentrated his fight too squarely on his ethnic Ogoni people?

Soyinka: No! I think he did attempt to reach out to others. If you read some of his columns . . .

Onookome: (Interrupting). Well . . . I have read all of that. He told me once to go back to my village in the Niger Delta and do what he was doing for his people. He didn't hear me out. He didn't listen to my explanation. I told him that I teach in the University and that I cannot do what he is doing because I am not economically independent as he was.

Soyinka: But I know that at some time, he had meetings with other people. I know he did. But may be he didn't do it in that direction. I cannot argue about that. But I know that there was a stage during which he started making contacts with the Andoni, the Okrika and even beyond. I know that there was at least one meeting of that kind but at what stage it was I cannot remember.

Onookome: I was flying to New York, on my way to Brazil on November 10, 1995 when I heard of the death of Ken Saro-Wiwa. I then called up a friend who was in Michigan at the time. I said to him, "Oh, it is so sad that they killed the man". He replied, "Oh . . . well, it is sad that they killed him but he deserved to die". A little later I fell into a conversation with another friend on the subject and he said to me, "You know they wouldn't have killed Ken Saro-Wiwa if he came from one of the major ethnic groups in Nigeria". Do you agree with this controversial position?

Soyinka: Very simply. If Abacha succeeded in killing me, he probably wouldn't have killed Ken Saro-Wiwa. Abacha and the military people around him wanted to prove a point. They wanted to send a shock to Nigerians, to the world. The point they wanted to make was that they can do whatever they want and that there is nothing anyone can do about it. Ken Saro-Wiwa was a sacrifice for that principle; to that policy. We were dealing with a mad man. This man was sick. He had a complex and anybody who was close to him knew this. Anybody he perceived as being superior was immediately marked for destruction. In any case, anyone who came from a group that was actually asserting itself was marked for destruction. Abiola was killed slowly in prison. Yar'Adua was murdered that way too. He was injected with lethal substance against his will. All the evidence are coming out now. Confessions are coming out now by the doctor who injected him . . . how they tied his hands behind his back and forcibly injected him. It is all coming out. So it was not simply because it was Ken Saro-Wiwa. Yar'Adua wasn't just a military man. He was a blue blood-prince of the Sokoto Caliphate. And Abacha killed him. No . . . it is not that Ken Saro-Wiwa came from the minority, no! Obasanjo was only lucky. Ah . . . look at the other people he killed . . . Rewane, Mrs. Abiola. We had a psychopath amongst us. People should understand that. I know that he was a psychopath.

Bibliography

Abram, M. H. *A Glossary of Literary Terms.* New York: Holt, Rheinhart and Winston, 1993.

Adedeji, J. A. "Aesthetics of Soyinka's Theatre." *Before Our Very Eyes.* Ibadan: Spectrum Books, 1987.

Achebe, Chinua. *Things Fall Apart.* London: Heinemann, 1958.

_____. *No Longer At Ease.* London: Heinemann, 1960.

_____. *A Man of The People.*London:Heinemann,1966.

_____. *Arrow of God.*London:Heinemann,1974.

_____. *Hopes And Implements: Selected Essays.* New York/London: Doubleday, 1989.

_____. *The Trouble With Nigeria.* Enugu: Fourth Dimension Publishers, 1983

_____. *Anthills of The Savannah.* Ibadan: Heinemann, 1987.

Agetua, John. *And The Man Died.* Benin: Bendel Corporation, 1975.

Althusser, Louis. "Ideology and State Apparatuses." In *Lenin, Philosophy and Other Essays.* New York: Monthly Review Press, 1971:127-186.

Anyaoku, Emeka. "Nigeria: Back In The Commonwealth, Looking To The Future". Kayode Soyinka (ed.). *Africa Today,* V5/11, 1999: 9-10

Asein, Sam. "Troubadours, Wanderers and Other Exiles". Sam Asein (ed.) *Comparative Approaches to Modern African Literature.* Ibadan: Department of English, 1982.

Arimalu, Alexander et al."Eagle On Iroko", Nsukka, Feb. 1990.

Bhabha, Homi. *The Location of Culture.*London: Routlegde, 1994.

Baktin, Mikhail M. "Discourse in The Novel." *The Dialogic Imagination.* Trans. M. Holquist and C. Emerson. Austin: University of Texas Press, 1981:269 305.

Barth, John. "The Literature of Replenishment: Post-modern Fiction: *The Atlantic.* January 1980

Bebey, Francis. *Concert pour un vieux masque.* Paris: L' Harmattan, 1980.

Bennet, Don. "The Detective Story: Toward Definition of a Genre." PTL. 4(1979) 233-266.

Biakolo, Emevwo. *Narrative Categories and Oral-to-Written Literary Transformations.* Unpublished Doctoral Dissertation. Department of English, University of Ibadan, 1988.

_____. "Transformation From Oral to Written Tradition: An Analysis of Soyinka's *Idanre*". *Gege* (March 1991) 163-177.

Birch, David. *Language, Literature, and Critical Practice: Ways of Analysing The Text.* London: Routledge, 1989.

Blake, Susan. "Travel and Literature: The Liberian Narratives of Esther Warner and Graham Green". *Research in African Literature.* 22.2 (1991): 191-203.

Bodkin, Maud. *Archetypal Pattern in Poetry: Psychological Studies of Imagination* London: Oxford University Press, 1948.

Bodunde, Charles. "Tributes, Censures and Transitions: Soyinka's *Mandela's Earth and Other Poems.*" *Wasafiri* (1991): 2-6.

Brown, P. and Levinson, S. "Universals in Language Usage: Politeness Phenomena" in Goody (ed) *Questions and Politeness: Strategies in Social Interaction.* Cambridge: Cambridge University Press,1978.

_____. *Politeness: Some Universals in Language Usage.* Cambridge: Cambridge University Press,1987.

Bryce, Jane. "Voyage of Recovery." *West Africa* (21-27 May, 1990): 26

Chilton, P. *Orwellian Language and the Media.* London: Pluto Press,1988.

Christopher, Butler. "Ambiguity and Self-contradiction." *Interpretation, Deconstruction and Ideology.* Oxford Clavendon Press, 1984. (rep. 1986).

Clark, J. P. *A Decade of Tongues: Selected Poems* 1958-1968 Harlow: Longman, 1980.

Crehen, Stewart. "The Spirit of Negation in The Works of

Soyinka". *Research In African Literatures*, 21/4, 1990.

de Saussure, F. *Course in General Linguistics*. New York: McGraw Hill, (1915); Rep. 1959.

Derrida, Jacques. On Grammalology. Trans. Gayatri Chakravorty Spivak. Balyimore: John Hopkins University Press, 1980.

Ekwuazi, Hyginus. "Film in Nigeria. The Context of Production". Ph.D Dissertation. University of Ibadan, Nigeria, 1984.

Eliade, Micrea. *Images and Symbols: Studies in Religious Symbolistic* New York: A Search Book Sheed and Ward, 1969.

Fagg, William, John Penberton and Bryce Holcombs. *Yoruba Sculpture of West-Africa*. London: Jonathan Cape) 1992

Falana, Femi. "The Struggle Has Just Started". *Tell Magazine*, September 13, 1993.

Fawehinmi, Gani. "We Have Ears". *Tell Magazine*, September 13,1993.

Fay, Thomas A. *Heidegger: The Critic of Logic*. The Hague Matinus Nijoff, 1977.

Fraser, B. "Warming and Threatening", Centrum 3, 1969-180,1975.

Frost, Robert. "The Road Not Taken". In L. Perrine, *Literature Structure: Sound and Sense* New York: Harcourt, Brace and World Inc., 1970. Poem was recorded by the author on L.P: Caedmon TC 1060.

Gboyega, Kolawole. "On The Making of Wole Soyinka's Poetry: A Literary Inquiry into His Sources". *Journal of Asian and African Studies* No. 44, 1992: 119-130.

Gengiss, P. "Indirect Threats". *Word*, Vol. 37, No. 3,1986.

Gibbs, James . Review of *Blues For A Prodigal. Wasafari* Autumn, 1985.

Goffman, E. "On Face-work": An Analysis of Ritual Elements in Social Interaction". *Psychiatry*, 18 (August),1955.

_____. *Interaction Ritual*. New York: Anchor,1967.

Habermans, J. *Theory of Communicative Action*, Vol. 1, Boston: Beacon Press,1984.

_____. *Theory of Communicative Action*, Vol. 2, Boston: Press,1987.

Hatlen, Theodore. *Orientation To Theatre.*. Englewood Cliffs: Prentice-Hall International, 1987.

Ho, D. V. "On the Concept of Face". *American Journal of Sociology*, Vol. 81, No. 4,1976.

Hu, H. C. "The Chinese Concept of Face" .*American Anthropologist*, 46, (January-March),1946.

Iyayi, Festus.*Heroes*.Harlow:Longnman,1986.

Izevbaye, Dan. "Assets And Liabilities: Unlimited Liability Company As An Artist's Investment In The Popular Cause". *Before Our Very Eyes*. Ibadan: Spectrum Books Limited, 1987

Jakobson, R."Closing Statement: Linguistics and Poetics". In T. A. Sebeok (ed) *Style in Language*. Mass: The M. I. T. Press; 350-377. Also in Allen, J. P. B. & Corder, S. P. (eds.) (1973) *The Edinburgh Course in Applied Linguistics*, Vol. 1, Reading for Applied Linguistics. London: OUP,1966.

James, Louis. *Arts and Society*. London: Caltop Press, 1974.

Jeyifo, Biodun. *The Truthful Lie: Essays in a Sociology of African Drama*. London: New Beacon,1985.

Jones, Eldred. *The Writing of Wole Soyinka*. London: Heinemann, 1988.

Jeyifo, Biodun. 'Editorial Note'. In Wole Soyinka *Art, Dialogue and Outrage: Essays on Literature and Culture*, Ibadan: New Horn Press, 1988.

Keen,S. *Faces of the Enemy: Reflections of the Hostile Imagination*. San Francisco: Harper & Row,1986

Kott, Jan. "The Eating of Government Inspector". *Theatre Quarterly*. 5/17, 1975. (Cited in Hatlen)

Kuppert, van Jan. " Main Structure and Side Structure in Discourse." Linguistics. 33, 1995: 809-833.

Kunene, Daniel. "Journey in the African Epic." *Research in African Literature*. 22.2 (1991): 205-223.

La Guma, Alex. *A Walk In The Night*. London: Heinemnann, 1962.

Levin, Harry. *The Gate of Horn: Five French Realists*. New York:

MacMillan, 1967.

Lim, T. & Bowers, J. W. "Facework: Solidarity, Approbation, and Tact" *Human Communication Research*, Vol. 17, No. 3,1991:415-450.

Martin, D. Sunday. "King and The Interfaith Dialogue." The Jpournal of Religious Thought. 43/2, 1992.

Maurice,Iji. *Understanding Brecht and Soyinka*. Lagos: Kraft Books Ltd,1991.

Maduakor, Obi. Wole Soyinka: *An Introduction to His Writing*. Ibadan: Heinemann, 1991. Orig. New York and London:Garland,1986.

Miles, David H. " The Portrait of Λ Marxist As A Young Hegelian: Lukacs' Theory of The Novel." *PMLA*. 94/1, 1979:22-35.

Mortimer, Mildred. "African Journeys." *Research in African Literatures*. 22.2 (1991): 169-175.

Nassidi, Yakubu. "Review of Wole Soyinka's A Play of Giants Saiwa: A Journal of Communication, Issue 3, 1985, p. 94.

Nkosi, Lewis. *Tasks and Masks: Themes and Style in African Literature*. London: Heinemann, 1977.

Nnolim, Charles. "Jungian Archetypes and the Main Characters in Oyono's *Une Vie de Bay*." *African Literature Today 7* (1975):117-122.

Nwoga, Donatus. "Poetry As Revelation: Wole Soyinka." In *Critical Perspectives On Wole Soyinka*. (ED)James Gibbs. London:Heinemann,1981.

_____. Obscurantism and Commitment in Modern African Poetry. *African Literature Today*. 6,1982.

Jeyifo, Biodun. *The Truthful Lie :Essays in a Sociology of African Drama*. London: New Beacon,1985.

Jeyifo, Biodun. 'Editorial Note'. In Wole Soyinka *Art, Dialogue and Outrage: Essays on Literature and Culture*, Ibadan: New Horn Press, 1988.

Obafemi, Olu. "Political Perspectives and Popular Theatre in Nigeria". Claude Schumacher (ed). *Theatre Research*

International, Vol. VIII, 3, 1982.

Oha, O. "Discourse Strategies in Isidore Okpewho's *The Last Duty*". A paper presented at a symposium in honour of Prof. Isidore Okpewho, Ibadan, 9 November 1991.

Ogunba, Oyin. *The Movement of Transition*. Ibadan: University of Ibadan Press, 1975.

_____. "Tiger on Stage". Theatre In Africa. Ibadan: Ibadan University Press, 1979.

_____. "Wole Soyinka and A Living Dramatist: A Playwrights Encounter With Soyinka's Drama". Wole Soyinka: An Appraisal. Oxford: Heinemann, 1994.

Ojaide, Tanure. "Ogun Widens His Haunt. Wole Soyinka's New Poems". *Callaloo*. 14/3 (1991): 737-751.

_____. *Poetic Imagination In Black Africa*. North Carolina: Carolina Academy Press, 1996.

_____. *Great Boys: An African Childhood*. New Jersey: Africa World Press,1984.

Ojo-Ade, Femi. *On Black Culture*. Ile-Ife: Obafemi Awolowo University Press, 1984.

Oladele, I.O. "Rhetoric of Tolerance From The Credo Through Soyinka." Unpublished. A paper presented at the department of Communication and Language Arts, University of Ibadan, Nigeria.

Oladipo, Olusegun. "Wole Soyinka on religious Tolerance: Epistemology of A Social Malaise." *Alminba Tribune*.No. 45, 1991.

Okigbo, Christopher. *Labyrinths*. London: Heinemann, 1971.

Okome, Onookome. "Cinema and Social Change in Nigeria". *IRIS* . 18, 1995. 71-20.

Okpewho, Isidore. African Oral Literature: Background, Character and Continuity. Bloomington: Indiana University Press, 1972.

Okri, Ben. *An African Elegy*. London: Jonathan Cape, 1992.

Osofisan, Femi. "Soyinka In A Forest of A Thousand Revellers." *Perspectives on Nigerian Literature: 1700 To The Present*. Vol. 1

(Lagos: Guardian Book Ltd., 1988).

Orwell, G. *Nineteen Eighty-Four*. London: Heinemann,1980.

Osundare, Niyi. *Village Voices*. Ibadan: Evan,1984.

_____.*The Eye of The Earth*. Ibadan: Heinemann Educational Books,1986.

_____. *Songs of The Market Place*. Ibadan: New Horn Press, 1987.

_____. *Waiting Laughters*.Lagos:Malthouse,1990.

Orwell, G. *Nineteen Eighty-Four*. London: Heinemann,1980.

Oyekunle, S. *Katakata for Sofahead*. London: Macmillan,1983.

Palmer, Eustace. *The Growth of The African Novel*. London: Heinemann, 1979.

Peters, Jonathan A. *A Dance of Masks*. Washington, D. C.: Three Continent Press, 1978

Pile, Steve and Nigel Thrift. "Introduction." *Mapping The Subject: Geographies of Cultural Transformation*. London: Routledge,, 1995: 1-51.

Poole, Roger. *Toward Deep Subjectivity*. London: Allen Lane, 1972.

Pratt, Mary Louise. *Towards a Speech Act Theory of Literary Discourse*. Bloomington: Indiana University Press, 1977.

Rutherford, Anna and Kirsten Holst Petersen. *The Enigma of Values: An Introduction*. Aarhus, Denmark: Dangaroo Press,1975.

Seymour, Hilary. "Pedagogical Politics in Ngugi's *Petals of Blood*." Journal of the Literary society of Nigeria. No. 1, 1981: 7-25.

Schermbrucker, B. "The Personal Fight for Freedom in Africa". Review of *Isara: A Voyage Around Essay. The Globe and Mail*, Saturday, January 6, 1990.

Senghor, Leopold Sedar. *Selected Poems*. Trans. Craig Williamson London: Rex Collins,1976.

Soyinka, Wole: "The Writer in an African State". *Transition* 31, Vol. 6, June/July 1967.

_____. *Before the Blackout*. Ibadan: Orisun Acting Edition, 1960.

_____. *After The Blackout*. Ibadan: Orisun Acting Edition, 1960.

_____. Season of Anomy. London: Rex Collins, 1972.

_____. *Myth, Literature and the African World*. Cambridge: Cambridge University Press, 1976.

_____. *A Dance of The Forest*. In *Collected Plays 2*. Oxford: Oxford University Press, 1993.

_____. *The Road*. London: Oxford University Press, 1965.

_____. *Camwood On The Leaves*. London: Mentuen, 1973.

_____. *Kongi's Harvest*. London: Oxford University Press, 1967.

_____. *Death and The King's Horseman*. London: Metheun, 1978.

_____. *The Strong Breed*. In *Collected Plays*. London: Oxford, 1973.

_____. *The Credo of Being and Nothingness*. Ibadan: Spectrum Books, 1991.

_____. Power and Creative Strategy. *The Punch*, May 4, 1988.

_____. *The Man Died: Prison Notes*. London: Rex Collins, 1972.

_____. *Art, Dialogue and Outrage*. Ibadan: New Horn Press, 1986.

_____. *Ogun Abibiman*. London: Rex Collins, 1976.

_____. "This Past Must Address The Present", 1986 Nobel Lecture. *Statements: Occasional Papers of the Phelps-Stockes* Fund, No. 3. March 1988.

_____. *Mandela's Earth and Other Poems*. Ibadan: Fountain Publications, 1989.

_____. *Isara: A Voyage Around Essay*. Ibadan: Fountain Publications, 1989.

_____. *From Zia With Love*. Ibadan: Fountain Publication, 1992.

_____. *Trials of Brother Jero* London: Oxford, 1964.

_____. *Jero's Metamorphosis*. London: Oxford, 1964.

_____. *Collected Plays 1*. Oxford: OUP, 1989.

_____. *Collected Plays 2*. Oxford: OUP, 1974.

_____. *Soyinka: Six Plays*. London: Methuen, 1984.

_____. *This Past Must Address Its Present*. The Occasional Paper Stokes _____. *Idanre and Other Poems*. London: Methuen, 1967

_____. *A Shuttle in the Crypt*. London: Rex Collings/Methuen, 1972.

_____. *Ogun Abibiman*. London and Ibadan: Collings and Opon Ifa, 1976.

_____. "Ideology and Social Vision". In *Myth, Literature and the African World*, London/New York: Cambridge University Press, 1976.

_____. *Ake: The Years of Childhood.* London: Rex Collins,1981.

_____. "Aesthetic Illusions" in *Art, Dialogue and Outrage.* Ibadan: New Horn, 1988.

_____. *The Blackman and The Veil: Beyond The Berlin Wall.* Accra: W.E.B Du Bois Center,1995.

_____. *The Burden of Memory, The Muse of Forgiveness.* Oxford: Oxford University Press, 1999

_____. *Beatification of Area Boy.* Ibadan: Spectrum Books, 1999.

Stubbs, Michael. *Discourse Analysis: The Socio-Linguistic Analysis of Natural Language.* Oxford: Basil, Blackwell, 1983.

Suzuki, D. T. *An Introduction To Zen Buddhism.* New York: An Evergreen Press, 1964.

Udoeyop, Nyong. "Soyinka and the Messianic Theme". *Critical Essays and Researches in African Literatures,* No. 1, 1997

Wells, Ronald Austin. "Wole Soyinka" in *Statements: Occasional Papers of the Phelps-Stokes Fund,* Number 3, March 1988.

Williams, Adebayo. "Matador In Abuja". Kayode Soyinka (ed.) *Africa Today.* Volume 5, No. 9: 1999: 6-9.

Wilkinson, Jane. *Talk With African Writers.* London: Heinemann, 1992.

Woodcock, George. *Anarchism: A History of Libertarian Ideas and Movement.* London: Penguin, 1975.

About the Contributors

Frank Uche Mowah
Dr. Mowah was the chair of English, Edo State University, Nigeria, until November 13, 1998, when he died. He was a teacher and student of postcolonial theory. He also published a novel, *Eaten by the Flesh*.

Kalu Uka
Prof. Uka is a professor of drama at the Department of Theatre Arts, University of Calabar, Nigeria. A scholar of drama, he has also written a number of novels. *Colonel Ben Brim* and *Consummation of Fire* are two of his novels.

Simon Obikpeko Umukoro
Dr. Umokoro is Professor of dramatic literature at the Delta State University, Nigeria and a scholar of the Wole Soyinka's dramas. In 1994, he published *Drama and Politics in Nigeria* (Ibadan: Kraft Books, 1994).

Tanimu Abubakar
Dr. Abubakar is the chair of English and Dean of the Faculty of Arts at the Ahmadu Bello University, Zaria. He has published extensively in the area of political drama.

Daniel Gover
Prof. Gover is an associate professor at Kean College, New Jersey, USA.

Onookome Okome
Dr. Okome teaches cinema and theatre studies at the Dept. of Theatre Arts, University of Calabar, Nigeria. He is currently a visiting Professor at Iwalewa Haus, Afrikazentrum, Universität Bayreuth, Germany. With Jonathan Haynes, he published *Cinema and Social Change in West Africa* (Jos: Nigerian Film Corporation, 1997).

Emevwo Biakolo
Until recently, Dr. Biakolo was of the Department of English, University of Ibadan. He has since moved to the National University of Botswana. A poet and scholar of oral literature, Dr. Biakolo teaches oral and written African literature in Botswana.

Chukwuma Okoye
Dr. Okoye is a costume and make-up designer. He teaches at the Dept. of Theatre Arts, University of Ibadan, Nigeria. His Ph.D. is on the art of Igbo masquerade performance.

Edde Maurice Iji
Dr. Iji teaches dramatic theory and criticism at the University of Calabar. He published two books on modern world dramatic artists - *Understanding Brecht and Soyinka* and *Three Radical Dramatists: Brecht, Artaud and Soyinka.* He is a leading scholar of Soyinka's drama in Nigeria.

Chris Dunton
Prof. Dunton is Professor and the chair of English at the National University of Lesotho, South-Africa. One of his influential scholarly publications is *Make Man Talk True: Nigerian Drama in English Since 1970* (London: Hans Zell, 1992)

Bernth Lindfors
Prof. Lindfors is the acknowledged scholar and authority on Nigerian (African) Literature. He is of the English Department at the University of Texas, Austin. His books on (Nigerian) African literature include *Popular Literature in Africa* (AWP 1991) *Long Drums and Canons: Teaching and Researching African Literature* (AWP 1995) and *The Blind Men and the Elephant and Other Essays in Biographic Criticism* (AWP 1999). He was formally the editor of *Research in African Literatures.*

Charles Bodunde

Dr. Bodunde teaches literature at the University of Ilorin, Nigeria. His area of interest is modern poetry. He is currently preparing a book on modern Nigerian poetry.

Harry Garuba

Harry Garuba teaches at the Institute of African Studies, University of Capetown, Capetown, South Africa.

Obododimma Oha

Dr. Oha teaches English language and stylistics at the Dept. of English, University of Ibadan, Nigeria. Among his recently published essays is "Culture and Gender Semantics in Flora Nwapa's Poetry" (in *Writing African Women: Gender, Popular Culture and Literature in West Africa* (ed).

Imo Ubokudom Ben Eshiet

Imo Ben Eshiet teaches Afro-American and African Drama at the Department of English, University of Calabar, Nigeria.

Paul Ugor

Ugor is of the Department of Theatre Arts, University of Calabar, Nigeria.

Asodionye Ejiofor

Ejiofor teaches dramatic literature at the Department of Creative Arts, Faculty of Arts, University of Port Harcourt.

Marcelinus Okhakhu

Dr. Okhakhu teaches media and theatre Studies, Department of Theatre Art, University of Benin, Benin City, Nigeria.

Lanre Bamidele

Dr. Bamidele teaches dramatic literature at the Department of Theatre Arts, University of Ibadan, Ibadan, Nigeria.

Chris Egbarevba
Egbarevba teaches at the Department of English, University of Uyo, Akwa Ibom State, Nigeria. He is currently preparing a Ph.D. dissertation of recent Nigerian dramatic tradition. He is a senior lecturer.

Onyemachi Udumukwu teaches literary theory at the University of Port Harcourt, Nigeria. He has published widely on African literature and is one of the leading experts on the novels of Chinua Achebe.